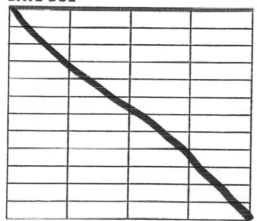

THE ENCYCLOPEDIA OF
SPORTS TALK

Edited by ZANDER HOLLANDER

An Associated Features Book

© CORWIN BOOKS   NEW YORK

THE ENCYCLOPEDIA OF
SPORTS TALK

Photo Credits

Baseball Hall of Fame	40
Lawrence Berman	73
Brunswick Corporation	93, 97, 100
Malcolm Emmons	52 (top), 139, 169
Kiekhaefer Mercury	259
Scotty Kilpatrick	196
The Harry Markson Collection	109
Miami Dolphins	150
New York Cosmos	217
The Ted Patterson Collection	68
Pittsburgh Steelers	149
Ken Regan—Camera 5	iii (right), 8, 69, 131
Robert Shaver	iii (left), 198
UPI	ii (left), ii (right), iii (middle), 1, 5, 11, 15, 17, 21, 24, 27, 28, 29, 31, 36, 38, 42, 44, 46, 52 (bottom), 56, 58, 65, 70, 79, 82, 84, 88, 90, 105, 111, 112, 118, 123, 128, 134, 143, 145, 152, 153, 155, 159, 176, 179, 184, 186, 189, 192, 201, 210, 215, 231, 234, 236, 242, 248, 251, 254, 261, 267, 269, 274

Copyright © 1976 by Associated Features, Inc.
Library of Congress Catalog Card No. 76-19253
ISBN 0-498-01998-5

Acknowledgments
Some of the material in the basketball chapter originally appeared in *Basketball Lingo*, published by Grosset & Dunlap, Inc. in 1971, and is reprinted with permission of the publisher.

Manufactured in the United States of America

Published by
CORWIN BOOKS
275 Madison Avenue
New York, N.Y. 10016

To Peter,
who has heard the language

THE CONTRIBUTORS

All those who can speak fifteen languages, speak up. Well, we concluded that it is a rare man or woman, indeed, who can be expert in so many tongues, and this explains why different linguists—professionals in their respective sporting fields—have written on the fifteen major sports covered in *The Encyclopedia of Sports Talk*.

We acknowledge the invaluable contributions of these linguists:

BOB FENDELL (Auto Competition)—Author of *The New Era Car Book and Auto Survival Guide* and coauthor of *The Encyclopedia of Auto Racing Greats*, Fendell is New York editor of *Automotive News*, and a contributor to the *Encyclopedia Britannica Yearbook*. His articles have appeared in a number of publications, including *The New York Times*. He was auto columnist for the *New York World-Telegram and Sun*.

PHIL PEPE (Baseball)—Sports writer and columnist for the *New York Daily News*, Pepe has written a dozen books, including *From Ghetto to Glory: The Bob Gibson Story*, *The Wit and Wisdom of Yogi Berra*, *No-Hitter*, and *Come Out Smokin': Joe Frazier*. He was a sports columnist on the *New York World-Telegram and Sun*, later the *World Journal Tribune*.

SANDY PADWE (Basketball)—Currently sports news editor of Long Island's *Newsday*, Padwe has long written about basketball—when he was an undergradu-ate at Penn State, then at UPI, Newspaper Enterprise Association, and the *Philadelphia Inquirer*, where he was a sports columnist. Padwe wrote *Basketball's Hall of Fame*, and his series, "Basketball's Underground Railroad," was included in the anthology *Best Sports Stories of 1967*.

PAT McDONOUGH (Bowling) McDonough has covered the bowling scene for more than thirty years as bowling editor of the *New York World-Telegram and Sun*, as editor of a weekly bowling newspaper, and as a tournament director. Before World War II he traveled briefly with the Brooklyn Dodgers, an assignment that, he says, prepared him for anything that might ever happen in sports.

BOB WATERS (Boxing)—A veteran newspaperman who has worked in upstate New York, Chicago, and, for the past sixteen years, at Long Island's *Newsday*, Waters has covered twenty-seven of Muhammad Ali's fights on five continents, a claim no other sportswriter can make. He has written hundreds of boxing stories for magazines, many under the name of Max Carroll.

BILL CHRISTINE (Football)—At one time or another Christine has been a sportswriter, sports editor, or columnist on newspapers in East St. Louis, Ill., St. Louis, Baltimore, Louisville, Pittsburgh, and Chicago. He started out in journalism writing movie reviews for his college newspaper at Southern Illinois University. In

Baltimore he covered the Colts, in Chicago the Bears, in Pittsburgh the Steelers, and his assignments have taken him to the Super Bowl.

JOE SCHWENDEMAN (Golf)—In more than twenty years as a golf writer for Philadelphia newspapers (*Inquirer* and *Bulletin*), Schwendeman got to cover all the big tournaments and leading pros. He has written magazine articles and booklets on his favorite sport and is currently public information director of the Tournament Players Division of the PGA (Professional Golfers' Association of America).

TIM MORIARTY (Hockey)—For more than a quarter of a century, Moriarty has covered the National Hockey League, first for UPI, and now for Long Island's *Newsday*. His book credits include *The Brothers Esposito*, *They Call me Gump*, Emile Francis's *Secrets of Winning Hockey*, *Vic Hadfield's Hockey Diary*, and *The Incredible Islanders*.

MORT LUND (Skiing)— A former staff writer for skiing on *Sports Illustrated*, Lund is a general editor of *Ski* magazine and a major authority on the graduated-length method of skiing. He has written *Skiers' Paradise*, *The Skier's Bible*, *Ski GLM*, *The Pleasures of Cross-Country Skiing*, and *Skiers' World*.

PAUL GARDNER (Soccer)—Gardner is United States correspondent for the London magazine *World Soccer*. He has lived and freelanced in the United States since 1959 and has written articles on soccer for *The New York Times*, *The Sporting News*, *The National Observer*, and other publications. He wrote the award-winning film *Pele: The Master and His Method* and *Nice Guys Finish Last*, a study of the place of sport in American life. His next book will provide an intimate look at the world of soccer.

BUD COLLINS (Tennis)—Television commentator, newspaper columnist, and author, Collins was covering tennis long before it became the booming sport of the seventies. In fact, he has played a significant role in the "net explosion" through his writings and telecasts (he is now chief tennis commentator for NBC and was the tennis voice of the National Educational Television Network). Collins's first tennis assignment was as a young reporter on the *Boston Herald*. He later did a general sports column, then switched to the *Boston Globe*, where, between global tennis assignments, he does a weekly column. Collins wrote, with Rod Laver, *A Thinking Man's Guide to Tennis*, and, with Evonne Goolagong, *Evonne! On The Move.*

PHYLLIS HOLLANDER (Water Sports)—An avid sportswoman who has taught swimming and boating, Hollander wrote *American Women in Sports* and *100 Greatest Women Athletes*, and coedited *The Complete Book of Cheerleading*, *They Dared to Lead*, and *It's the Final Score That Counts*. Her writing credits also include chapters in several sports books produced by Associated Features, packagers of sports books, for whom Hollander is senior editor.

The editor further wishes to express his appreciation for contributions along the way to Bill Roeder of *Newsweek;* Dan Daniel, baseball historian; Herman Masin of *Scholastic Coach*, and Joe Stetz, AAU swimming official.

About the Editor

As a sportswriter on the *New York World-Telegram and Sun*, where he covered a variety of sports over a twenty-year period, Zander Hollander wrote his first book, *Yankee Batboy*. Since then he has authored and-or edited more than one hundred books and magazines, including *The Modern Encyclopedia of Basketball* and *The Complete Encyclopedia of Ice Hockey*. Hollander is president of Associated Features, specialists in sports and recreation publishing.

CONTENTS

PREFACE

PREFACE

It started out as a game of sorts among friends who prided themselves on their knowledge of sport. Anyone can play it. It went like this: See how many terms you can come up with in a particular sport.

No ground rules. For expanding your source material, watch a game on television, listen to radio, study the sports pages, talk to an athlete. Make up the list as you go along, whether you understand every expression or not.

It was every man for himself. The winner? That's where the fun began. The one with the longest list didn't understand 40 percent of his expressions. Another, with a shorter total, knew most of his. And there was debate over the proper translation. Whose is the last word?

We hope we are.

The goal of the editor and writers of *The Encyclopedia of Sports Talk* was to translate the slang of the athlete; the idiom of the dugout, the playing field and the clubhouse; the prose of the writers, and the jargon of the television and radio sportscasters. Also, to record some of the rules, history, and traditions of sports that have increasing meaning to the millions of Americans who play and watch them.

The intent was to produce a reference work that would be at once informative and entertaining. It would provide definitions and anecdotes for thousands of terms (over 3,500), from the commonplace but essential to the obscure.

There are fifteen sports covered in this edition, chosen for their popularity and special appeal: Auto Competition, Baseball, Basketball, Boating, Bowling, Boxing, Football, Golf, Hockey, Skiing, Soccer, Surfing, Swimming, Tennis, and Water Skiing.

It's the Whole Ball of Wax, and here's a chance to meet the Kangaroo Kids and Daffiness Boys without Going Around the Horn or so much as doing a Double Dribble or a Wedel. As Casey Stengel used to say, "You can look it up."

ZANDER HOLLANDER

AUTO COMPETITION

A. J. Foyt, three-time winner of the Indy, races down the back stretch on the way to victory in the 1961 running of the Memorial Day classic.

AUTO COMPETITION

"A" or A-BONE: Model "A" Ford, once very popular in drag racing for certain classes of competition.

ACCELERATION: Rate of gaining speed.

AFTERBURNER: Second fuel-firing compartment on a jet engine; it gives added power.

AHA: American Hot Rod Association.

AIRFOIL: A wing-shaped piece placed in the front of a race car to help hold the wheels down at high speed. Sometimes airfoils also are located in the rear.

ALKY: Alcohol used as a racing fuel, frequently mixed with nitromethane.

ALTERED CLASS: A class of cars greatly changed from the original form, usually just recognizable as a type once built for public use.

ANCHORS: Brakes.

ANTIROLL (British): See Roll Bars.

APPLIQUÉ: Decorative material that is applied to basic interior or exterior panel. May be metal, plastic, or combination, with bright, textured, or painted finish.

ARCA: Auto Racing Club of America, a midwestern U.S. stock-car-racing organization.

ARCING: Drag racing. Full speed; all out.

BACK OFF: Reduce speed.

BALDIES: Worn tires. Also, drag-racing slicks.

BANZAI: In drag racing, an all-out run; bringing engine to absolute peak performance.

BEND: Damage a racing car. Also, in rallying or road racing, a turn that may be safely taken at rally speed.

BENT: Racing car that has been damaged.

BENT STOVEBOLT: Chevrolet V-8 engine.

BIG BANGER: Car with engine of large volume displacement.

BINDERS: Brakes.

BLACK FLAG: A signal used to call in a driver, whether to eliminate him from a race, inspect his car, or even to delay him (as a penalty) for improper conduct.

BLACKY CARBON: Gasoline; term used by those who use exotic fuel mixtures.

BLEND: Racing fuel mixture. Also, flowing together of two or more surfaces.

BLOW: Engine failure. "His engine blew on the second lap."

BLOWER: Supercharger.

BLOWN CAR: A supercharged car.

BLOWN DRAGSTER: A supercharged car.

BLOWN ENGINE: Supercharged engine. Also, an engine that has become inoperative, usually in rather spectacular fashion.

BOONDOCKS: Off the course.

BORED ENGINE: An engine that has had its cylinder walls ground out to increase the air-fuel capacity.

BOSS: Drag or stock-car term for ultimate in perfection.

BOTTOMING: Making contact with the track or some part of the track with the underside of a race car.

BRAKES: Means of stopping car. Most common current types are drum or disc, or a combination of both.

BREAK LOOSE: When the car loses traction and its wheels spin.

BRICKYARD: Indianapolis Motor Speedway. See Indy.

BROADSLIDING: Coming through a turn sideways

so as to reach a straightaway with the car pointed straight. Essential on dirt-track racing around an oval.

BROKE: Out of competition due to mechanical failure.

BUCKET SEAT: Individual seat, often contoured so as to provide lateral support.

BUG CATCHER: Scoop that catches air and forces it into the carburetor.

BUMPING: Aside from making contact with another car, this term applies to a car that is surpassed by another with a lower elapsed time during qualification or time trials. For instance, after thirty-three cars have qualified for the Indianapolis "500," the slower of those are in danger of being bumped if any cars then qualify faster.

BUSTED LUNG: One spark plug not firing.

CAM: Camshaft.

CAN: Nitromethane racing fuel; when heavy percentages of nitro are used for an all-out final run.

CANCER: Metal rot in car body; rust.

CAROLINA STOCKER: Stock car running with illegal equipment or engine size.

CHAMPIONSHIP CAR or **INDY CAR:** Open-cockpit racing car conforming to regulations set up for Indy and USAC championship series.

CHARGER: A very aggressive driver who holds the lead as long as he can. Also, a kind of Dodge automobile.

CHAUFFEUR: Race driver; reference bears connotation of paid or professional driver.

CHEAT: Exaggerate an element in a drawing or rendering. Also, violate rules under which competition is organized.

CHEATER SLICKS: Special tires made of racing rubber compounds, but with tread design to simulate street tires.

CHOP: Cut off another car in a corner. Also, to alter an automobile chassis (hot rodding) by cutting out metal.

CHRISTMAS TREE: Electronic drag-racing starting system with yellow warning lights followed by a green go or a red foul light.

CHRONDEKS: Electronic timing system built by Chrondek Corporation. Used in pairs by drag-racing courses.

CHUTE: Safety drag parachute used to stop high-speed racing cars. Also, straightaway on racing circuits.

CIRCUIT: Road course either simulated or of actual public road, used for conducting automobile races.

CLASSIFICATION: Putting cars into groups according to body style, engine size, or some other standard.

CLOSE THE GATE: When a driver, by maneuvering, makes it impossible for a competitor to get ahead of him.

CLUB RACE: Automobile competition organized by a club for its members and guests, almost always an amateur event.

CONTROL: A checkpoint or timing station in a rally located at a place on the course unknown to the contestants in advance.

CRAFTY: Wise and seasoned driver or mechanic.

CRASH BOX: Nonsynchronized manual transmission.

CSI: Commission Internationale Sportive. Racing rules-making body within FIA (International Auto Federation).

CURB HEIGHT: Height of vehicle without passengers or trunk load.

CURB WEIGHT: Weight of vehicle in full touring trim with oil, water, spare wheel and tire (usually five gallons of fuel), but otherwise unladen.

CUT: To eliminate another drag-racing car.

DEMOLITION DERBY: An auto event in which cars are crashed into each other until only one, the winner, is left.

DEUCE: 1932 Ford.

DICE: A battle between two or more cars for position, not necessarily for the lead.

DIRT CAR: A race car designed for dirt tracks, such as a sprint car.

DISC(S): Brake disc; disclike steel surface onto which brake pads clamp when brakes are applied. Also, covers designed to cover road wheel lugs. Disc brakes.

DISPLACEMENT: The size of an engine, expressed in cubic centimeters, cubic inches, or liters.

DRAFTING: Using a car in front as an air buffer by closely following it and getting into its slipstream. A racer may draft as close as a few inches behind the man in front. Since the front car has literally pushed the air aside, the car directly behind can run as fast with less engine effort.

DRAG or **DRAG RACE:** Usually quarter-mile acceleration race between two cars. Major drag-racing associations include National Hot Rod Association, American Hot Rod Association, United Drag Racers Association, and International Hot Rod Association.

DRAGSTER: Specially designed car for straight-line acceleration events.

DROP THE HAMMER: Rapid engagement of clutch.

DRUM: Brake drum; circular steel housing onto which brake liners seat on application of brakes.

DUMPING THE CLUTCH: Removing foot from

The drag racers *are on the starting line in the national championships at Indianapolis.*

clutch pedal and allowing engine and wheels to turn together.

DYNO: Short for dynamometer; a machine to measure engine power.

ELAPSED TIME or **E.T.:** The time in seconds and fractions it takes a car to cover the quarter-mile drag-racing distance. Also used for time in oval- or road-course racing for a specific distance, usually one lap.

ELIMINATED: Beaten in a drag race.

ELIMINATIONS: Two cars racing to determine eventual class winners.

ENTRY BLANK: *See* Registration.

EQUIPMENT: The race car, all parts included.

ESSES: Winding **S** turns in road-racing circuit.

E.T.: *See* Elapsed Time.

EYE: Light beam that starts and stops electronic timer.

E-Z: Pit signal for "Take it easy, your position is secure."

F1, F2...: Formula 1, Formula 2, etc. Kinds of race cars made to fit respective sets of rules.

FACE MASK: A fireproof mask that must be worn in certain classes of car.

FIA: International Auto Federation.

FIRE SUIT: Aluminized, fireproof, completely body-covering driver's suit.

FIRE UP: Start up an engine.

FIRE-UP LANE or **FIRE-UP ROAD:** A road where cars are pushed to start engines.

FIREWALL: A fireproof metal wall between engine and driver compartment.

FLAG: International racing flag as used in road racing for signal to drivers.

FLAGMAN: Marshal responsible for manning flags at control station on race circuit.

FLAME SUIT: *See* Fire Suit.

FLAT FOUR: Horizontally opposed four-cylinder engine.

FLATHEAD: Engine with valves located in block.

FLAT SIX: Horizontally opposed six-cylinder engine.

FLAT SPOT: A certain place in the range of engine revolutions where the engine will run below par.

FLYING START: Racing start wherein competing cars take starting flag approaching racing speed.

FORMULA: A detailed set of specifications that categorize racing cars, thus creating an equalized class for a championship series in which cars compete.

FORMULA LIBRE: Free or open racing organized without reference or conforming to any FIA formula or CIS category.

FOUL: An act that disqualifies a driver, such as leaving the starting line before the green light.

FOUR-ON-THE-FLOOR: Four-speed manual transmission.

FUEL: Generally, the liquid used to power an engine. In drag racing, anything used to power an engine except gasoline, i.e., alky or nitro-based mixtures.

FUELER: Car using special racing fuels in drag racing.

FUEL SHUTOFF VALVE: A safety arrangement that shuts off flow of fuel in case of engine failure or accident.

FULL BORE: Full speed.

GASOLINE ALLEY: The garage area at a race track.

GASSER: In drag racing, a car competing in either Gas Coupe/Sedan or Supercharged Gas Coupe/Sedan class.

GET OUT OF SHAPE: Lose it; lose control of a car.

GETTING A TOW: *See* Slipstreaming.

G.P. or GRAND PRIX: Strictly used, a championship race for Formula cars. Loosely, any single-seater race, and occasionally other forms of racing as well.

GRID: Alignment for cars at start of race. Also, the start markings on the circuit at the starting line.

GRID START: Racing start where competing cars are positioned on grid lines according to qualifying times or by draw.

GROOVE: The route around a race course one driver or many drivers take that seems the best one, usually the fastest way around.

GROUP: As in Group 2, 5, 7, etc., a detailed set of specifications that categorizes racing cars, as the Formula does for single-seaters, and thus sets up equalized classes for its championships. Often Group cars from several categories race together, unlike Formula racing, where such joint racing is fairly rare.

GRUDGE RACE: Like it sounds, a race for revenge or a challenge race.

G.T. or GRAND TOURING: A category of sedans in racing.

GYMKHANA: Automobile competition where the cars execute prescribed driving maneuvers, not one against the other, but against the clock. Most gymkhana courses are set up with traffic pylons.

HAIRPIN: Acute corner on road-racing circuit. In rallying, a hairpin turn has to be approximately 180 degrees.

HAIRY: Hair-raising, unusual, or extraordinary.

HANDLER: Driver.

HARNESS: Straps used to keep driver in place in case of accident. Harness straps usually go over shoulders and through legs. They are generally equipped with a quick-release buckle to allow driver to get out in case of fire. They are, in fact, a version of seat belt.

HAULER: An exceptionally fast car.

HEADERS: Short exhaust pipes shaped to get exhaust gases out and away from engine rapidly.

HEAVY METAL: Racing cars with large displacement engine.

HEMI: Engine with hemispherical combustion chambers.

HILL CLIMB: Speed competition between cars of one or more classes over a closed hill circuit. Cars compete one at a time against the clock.

HOBBY: NASCAR stock-car racing division for moderate-performance cars and amateur or semipro drivers.

HOG or PIG: A slow race car.

HOLD: Racing instruction from pit crew to driver meaning, "Hold position—maintain speed."

HOMOLOGATED: Procedure in which a car manufacturer guarantees that a particular model is produced in numbers conforming to FIA rules for a given category.

HONKER: Exceptionally fast car.

HONKING: Full speed.

HOP-UP: In styling, upward change of direction of a surface or line. Also, to supertune engine.

HOT CAR: General class of car in faster drag-racing speed groups. Also, any fast car.

HOT DOG: A wild driver.

HOT ROD: Car that is greatly modified, either in body style or engine.

HUFFER: Supercharger.

IHRA: International Hot Rod Association.

INDEPENDENT TRACK: A drag-racing strip or racing oval that sets its own rules of operation and does not belong to any racing association.

INDY: Nickname for both the Indianapolis Motor

Speedway and the Indianapolis "500" Sweepstakes. Indianapolis Speedway, on the outskirts of the Indiana city of the same name, is a 2½-mile elliptical track with turns slightly banked. It is the site for the oldest and richest single auto race in the world, the Indianapolis "500," where a driver can literally become a millionaire for a few hours' work.

The Indy began in 1911. Held around Memorial Day, now with a 33-car field, the "500" has been the grail of American and some foreign drivers. To even make the starting field is a great honor; to win means lifetime respect in U.S. racing. To win twice or three times means a place among the greats: Men like Wilbur Shaw, Lon Meyer, Mauri Rose, and A. J. Foyt won thrice; Tommy Milton, Bill Vukovich, Rodger Ward, and Bobby Unser were among the repeat winners.

The "500," the only race held at the track each year, may attract 300,000 fans or more. The management has not given attendance figures since industrialist Tony Hulman took control.

INJECTED- or **CARBURETED-GAS DRAGSTER:** A drag racer using gasoline and injectors or carburetors, but *not* "fuel" or a supercharger.

INSPECTOR or **INSPECTION TEAM:** Person who checks cars for safety features and adherence to the rules of the racing association as to engine type, body style; sometimes done by several persons, an inspection team.

IN THE CHUTE: When a drag-racing car is positioned in a staging area that is a special area just before the starting line.

INVERTED START: When the fastest qualifiers start at the back of the field. This is popular in sprint and midget-car oval racing.

JET DRAGSTER: Drag racer powered by jet engine.

JUICE: Racing-fuel blend. Also, electrical current.

JUMP: To leave the starting line before the green light or before starter's flag signal.

KICKS RACE: A race between two cars, just for fun and not as part of the regular racing.

KNERFING: One racing car deliberately tapping another from behind.

KNOCK-OFFS: Large wing nuts used to retain wheels for rapid attachment or removal of racing wheels; sometimes ornamental.

LAP: One full turn around a course.

LEADFOOT: A charger.

LE MANS START: Racing start where drivers run across the course to their cars, jump in, start their engines, and depart. It has largely been abandoned because of the danger involved.

LICENSING: Tracks and associations issue a racing permit to a driver after he has shown himself to be a skillful and safe driver. This license may be just for one track or for tracks belonging to certain associations.

LUNCH AN ENGINE: In drag racing, destroy an engine.

MAGS: Wheels cast in magnesium, then machined for attachment to hubs, etc. Used primarily for racing because of extremely light weight, but sometimes used or simulated to add a racy appearance.

MATCH RACES: Races scheduled in advance between two cars, usually two out of three races to determine the winner.

MICKEY MOUSE CIRCUIT: Small, winding race circuit. Also, any easily mastered course.

MIDGET CAR: A single-seat car that looks like an old championship car but is much smaller. Designed for indoor or very small track oval racing.

MILL: Engine.

MISS THE SHOW: Fail to qualify for a race, depending on the predetermined size of the starting field.

MODIFIED: Class of cars changed in design.

MONOPOSTO: Single-seat racing car, a term used in road-course racing.

MO PAR: Chrysler Corporation automobile. Also, official Chrysler Corporation replacement part.

NASCAR: National Association for Stock Car Auto Racing, the premier organization for this type of auto competition, originally based in the Southeast but now spread to all sections.

NHRA: National Hot Rod Association.

NITRO: Nitromethane, a racing-fuel additive.

NONSPEED EVENT: Includes rallies, concours d'elegance, gymkhanas, etc. Events not requiring special competition licenses.

NURSING A CAR: "Babying" it or driving it carefully.

OUT TO LUNCH: In drag racing, an inconsequential person.

OVAL: Oval-shaped race track.

PACE CAR: Vehicle used to pace race cars.

PACED START: Flying start led by pace car.

PACER: Driver who races at predetermined speed.

PAD(S): Part of disc-brake assembly. *See also* Discs.

PARACHUTE: The large, umbrella-shaped cloth used to slow down cars at end of race. It is made in ribbonlike sections so that it does not pull too hard. *See also* Chute.

PIG: *See* Hog.

PILOT CHUTE: A small parachute with springs to open it; when released, it pulls out the main parachute. Used in drag racing to slow the vehicle.

In the Le Mans start, *this one at Sebring, Fla., the drivers must run across the course to their cars.*

PIT(S):   The areas set aside for working on cars. Also, where cars line up for racing.

PIT LANE: Lane in front of pits for entrance and exit of racing cars.

PIT STOP: Stop made at pit by competing car.

POLE: The lead position at the start of the race, i.e., next to the fence on the inside; theoretically an advantage, though not necessarily so. Capturing the pole (by turning the fastest qualifying lap) usually means extra money.

POPPING THE CHUTE: Releasing the parachute.

PROTOTYPE: Test model of new car. Also, any sports racing car that does not conform to standards or minimum production requirements for homologated sports car.

PUMP FUEL: Racing fuel of no higher octane rating than that available for sale at gasoline-station pumps.

PUSH CAR: Car used to give the engine a starting push when car is not equipped with starter.

PUT YOUR FOOT IN IT: *See* Stand on It.

RAIL or **RAIL JOB:**   Dragster.

RALLY: Organized automobile run conducted in compliance with applicable motor vehicle laws, designed to test the driving and navigational skills of the contestants. The contestants start from given points at fixed intervals, with the object of following a prescribed course at specified legal and safe speeds without deviating from schedule times of arrival at predetermined points unknown to the contestants.

RAM-CHARGED ENGINE: Similar to injected

engine, except that carefully shaped tubes force air into it.

RAM TUBES: Tubes or pipes shaped to help force air into the carburetors.

RAUNCHY: Undisciplined or sloppy behavior. Also, rough, poorly constructed or badly painted car.

RED-LIGHTING: Leaving the starting line too soon and getting the red or foul light that means disqualification.

REVS: Engine revolutions.

RIDING THE RAILS: Taking the outside line in flat tracks or riding high on banked speedways.

ROLL BARS: Sturdy tubing welded to the car's chassis and arched over the driver's head, to protect him in case of an accident, especially a roll-over.

SCATTER SHIELDS: Heavy metal or plastic plates or covers placed around gears, shafts, or other rapidly rotating parts; protection in case something breaks and scatters hunks of metal.

SCRUTINEERING: Detailed technical inspection to assess race-worthiness or conformity of competing cars.

SHIM: Thin metal packing piece, much used for accurate spacing.

SHOCKS: Shock absorbers.

SHOES: Tires.

SHOW CAR: Display car having features or shapes not offered in production cars. Also, a good-looking race car that is noncompetitive.

SHUNT: Accident.

SHUTDOWN AREA: The part of a drag track after the finish line where cars slow down, coast to a stop, and turn off the track.

SHUTOFF: When a car moves right in front of another that must then slow down sharply or change direction to avoid hitting it.

SHUT THE GATE: *See* Close the Gate.

SKINS: Tires.

SLICKS: Wide, flat tires of soft rubber used on the rear of drag-racing vehicles for increased traction.

SLINGSHOT: Dragster design where driver sits behind rear wheels.

SLINGSHOTTING: To pull out of a slipstream of a car one is drafting and shoot past.

SLIPSTREAMING: When a car at high speed tucks in close to the bumper of the car ahead in order to gain the benefit of the other car's airstream. Its engine does not have to work as hard to go as fast as the one ahead, which, in effect, is pulling it along. This is known as getting a tow.

SLUSH BOX: Automatic hydraulic transmission.

SOLO: In drag racing, a single run.

SOUPING: Increasing engine output by modification.

SPOILER: An air deflector or airfoil mounted on a car, front or back, to aid in road holding by controlling lift tendencies.

SPORTSMAN: In NASCAR, term defining stock classification of cars using light bodies and modified passenger-car engines. Fuel-system modifications are limited, switching of engines and bodies not allowed. Fuel restricted to pump grade.

SPORTY CAR: Automobile designed to give the impression that it is a sports car though it is not.

SPRINT CAR: A car about two-thirds the size of an Indy or championship car.

STACKS: Exhaust pipes. Also, throats or long choke tubes sometimes fitted to carburetors.

STAGING LIGHTS: Lights at the starting line that show a driver when his front wheels are on the starting line.

STAND ON IT or **PUT YOUR FOOT IN IT:** To accelerate as fast as possible.

STOCK: Basically unmodified car conforming to certain specifications; opposite of modified cars.

STOCKER: Stock automobile.

STOVEBOLT: Chevrolet.

STRAIGHT PIPE: Straight-through (unmuffled) exhaust pipe.

STREET CLASSES: Cars that meet requirements of the law to run on public streets.

STROKE: Distance piston travels in cylinder bore. Also, driving to plan, slower than maximum speed.

STROKER: Stroked engine. An engine in which the piston travel has been lengthened to increase amount and compression of air-fuel mix.

STROKING IT: Driving well below potential.

STUFFER: *See* Supercharger.

SUPERCHARGER: Blower. A pump like mechanism placed on engines to force the air-fuel mix into the cylinders.

SWALLOW-A-VALVE: When a valve breaks off at the stem and drops down into the cylinder.

SYNCH: Synchromesh. Device for synchronizing gears to eliminate clash or grinding when gear-ratio changes are made.

TACH: Tachometer. Instrument that measures engine speed in revolutions per minute.

T.E. or **TOP ELIMINATOR:** In drag racing, the fastest car of the meet.

TECH INSPECTION: *See* Scrutineering.

THIRTEEN TWENTY: The quarter mile; 1,320 feet.

TIME TRIALS: Speed competition on closed course

with each car running against the clock for fastest time. Also, timed practice laps to determine starting position.

TIMING TOWER: Tower from which racing is timed and directed.

TIRED IRON: Out-of-date racing car.

TOP SPEED: The average speed of a racer as measured 33 feet before and after the finish line.

TOP TIME: Terminal speed attained by vehicle on a drag-racing run.

TOUGH: Especially pleasing or durable.

TOW: *See* Slipstreaming.

TRAILERED: Being eliminated from further racing, since the car is then placed on its trailer, ready to be returned to the garage.

TRAP(S):   Three-light system at finish line of course that measures vehicle's top speed. Also, speed-measurement trap set up on fastest straightaway of a race circuit.

UDRA: United Drag Racers Association.

UNSANITARY: Dirty, carelessly prepared, or unsafe race car.

USAC: United States Auto Club.

WHEELIE or **WHEEL STAND:**   In drag racing, phenomenon of front wheels lifting off pavement when throttle is opened at starting line.

WINDOUT: Letting an engine increase in speed to maximum.

YELLOW TAIL: Rookie driver who must show yellow bumper to indicate inexperience.

ZOOMIES: Upswept exhaust headers.

Babe Ruth and Lou Gehrig, flanking promoter-ghost writer Christy Walsh, drew vast audiences wherever they went barnstorming.

ABOARD: On base. When a team has a base runner, it is said to have a man aboard. Therefore, a team may have nobody aboard (bases empty) or it may have one, two, or the maximum three runners aboard.

ACE: The top pitcher on any team; the ace of the staff. Often called ace by teammates as a sign of acknowledgment. For years, Whitey Ford was the ace of the New York Yankee pitching staff; catcher Elston Howard gave him the highest tribute by calling him "the Chairman of the Board."

AGENT: The advent of television and big bonuses introduced the agent to baseball. Later, arbitration and contentions against baseball's reserve clause expanded the role of the agent. Now players use agents to negotiate salary with club owners.

The role of the sports agent is not unlike that of the theatrical or the literary agent, who is paid a fee for negotiating contracts. In the case of bonus players, the agent (often a lawyer) serves as the bargainer between the ball club and the player, and his fee is a percentage (usually from 10 to 20 percent) of the bonus.

Among established stars, the agent may negotiate a contract or he may serve as a representative in obtaining commercial endorsements for the player, the agent's payment being a percentage of the player's fee. The first of the successful sports agents was Frank Scott, but today there are dozens of skilled and successful agents negotiating contracts and obtaining commercial endorsements for players in football, hockey, tennis, golf, and basketball as well as baseball.

So when you see Catfish Hunter on television extolling the virtues of a certain make of pickup truck or Pete Rose telling you why he uses a certain aftershave lotion, be assured that the athlete is getting well paid for his advice and that an agent is getting his share of the fee.

ALL-STAR GAME: In 1933 Arch Ward, sports editor of the *Chicago Tribune*, seeking to add a baseball flavor to Chicago's centennial celebration, had the idea that fans would be interested in seeing a game between the best players of the National League and the best from the American League. So, on July 6, 1933, the first All-Star game was played at Chicago's Comiskey Park. The American League won the game on a two-run home run by Babe Ruth. Lefty Gomez of the New York Yankees was the winning pitcher.

The All-Star game became an annual attraction and has been played every year since its inception, with the exception of 1945, when the game was called off because of World War II. In 1959 the players of both leagues voted to play two All-Star games and did so until 1963, when, realizing they were destroying the impact of the attraction, they returned to one game a year.

Part of the proceeds from the All-Star game goes to the players' pension fund, which is one reason players have no objection to playing on what would otherwise be a day of rest. Another reason is the honor that accompanies selection. Stan Musial, Willie Mays, and Henry Aaron hold the record of having participated in 24 All-Star games.

The American League dominated the All-Star game

in the beginning, winning the first 3 and 12 of the first 16. However, the National League won 24 of the next 31 (there was one tie) for a 28-18-1 margin through 1976.

The most memorable All-Star feat occurred in the 1934 game at New York's Polo Grounds. Pitching in his home park, Carl Hubbell, New York Giant left-hander, struck out in succession the mighty Babe Ruth, Lou Gehrig, Jimmy Foxx, Al Simmons, and Joe Cronin.

AMERICAN LEAGUE: This is the younger of baseball's two major leagues, the other being the National League. Sometimes called the junior circuit. The American League was conceived in 1892, although it did not become a reality until nine years later.

In 1892 Charles Albert Comiskey, player-manager for the Cincinnati club, and Byron Bancroft "Ban" Johnson, baseball columnist for the *Cincinnati Gazette*, began to grow disenchanted with the antiquated and unwieldy twelve-team National League and started thinking of opening their own store across the street.

Comiskey talked up the idea of restoring the old Western Association with a new name to operate in competition with the National League. Interest was great among owners, and Comiskey recommended Johnson as president of the new league.

Even with the imaginative and energetic Johnson at the head, the new league moved slowly until 1899, when four teams were dropped by the National League, and the new league was in business. Johnson added the four teams to his league, changed the name from the Western Association to the American League, and on April 24, 1901, the American League began operations with a gala inaugural in which Cleveland played Chicago in Chicago.

Charter members of the American League in 1901 were Chicago (first American League champion), Boston, Detroit, Philadelphia, Baltimore, Washington, Cleveland, and Milwaukee.

The next year Milwaukee was replaced by St. Louis, and in 1903 John McGraw sold out his Baltimore holdings and jumped back to the National League to head the New York Giants. Johnson's reply was one of defiance. He dared to move the Baltimore franchise to New York in direct competition with the Giants of the National League, despite politicians' threats to run city streets through his ball park.

In 1903 the American League had an eight-team alignment, which was to remain intact until the 1954 season, when the St. Louis Browns asked for and received permission to move to Baltimore. The following year the Philadelphia Athletics moved to Kansas City.

In 1961 the American League voted to expand to ten teams. To achieve this, the Washington Senators moved to the twin cities of Minneapolis-St. Paul and were called the Minnesota Twins, and new franchises were awarded to Los Angeles and Washington. Players for the two new teams were taken from a pool contributed by the eight established teams. Each team submitted a list of available players, from which the Los Angeles Angels and Washington Senators could purchase players to stock their teams. The season schedule was increased from 154 games to 162.

In 1965 the Angels moved out of Los Angeles in a dispute with that city's National League entry, the Dodgers. The Angels had been tenants in Dodger Stadium and considered the rental exorbitant. They began construction of a new stadium in nearby Anaheim (site of Disneyland) and opened the 1966 season in their new home. To create broader appeal, the Angels changed their name from the Los Angeles Angels to the California Angels.

In 1968 the Kansas City club moved to Oakland, and a year later, the American League expanded to 12 teams with a new franchise in Kansas City and one in Seattle, and division play began.

The Eastern Division had New York, Boston, Baltimore, Detroit, Cleveland, and Washington. The Western Division included Minnesota, California, Oakland, Kansas City, Chicago, and Seattle.

The following year the Seattle franchise was shifted to Milwaukee, which went into the Eastern Division, Washington moving from East to West. Eventually the Washington franchise moved to Texas.

With expansion and division play, a new method of determining the league champion was devised, the winner in the East meeting the winner in the West to determine the league champion and the league's representative in the World Series.

Under the guidance of Ban Johnson, the American League thrived once it got off the ground, but Johnson's failure to get along with Baseball Commissioner Kenesaw Mountain Landis caused him to resign his position in 1927. He was succeeded by Ernest S. Barnard, who reigned until his untimely death in 1931 (the same year Ban Johnson died). Upon Barnard's death Will Harridge was elevated from American League secretary to the league's presidency. Harridge resigned after the 1958 season, and in 1959 Joe Cronin became the American League president. In 1973 Cronin became Chairman of the Board of the American League and was succeeded as president by Leland (Lee) MacPhail.

ANNIE OAKLEY: The real Annie was a crack rifle shot who toured with Buffalo Bill before the turn of the century. One of her tricks was to shoot a card full of holes. In sports, it is a practice to punch complimentary

Connie Mack (left), American League, and John McGraw, National League, were the opposing managers in the first All-Star game in 1933.

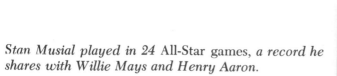

Stan Musial played in 24 All-Star games, a record he shares with Willie Mays and Henry Aaron.

tickets full of holes to distinguish them from the paid tickets, thus the name Annie Oakley. Eventually it came to mean anything received free, so a base on balls is a free ticket to first base.

APPEAL: The act of a member of the defensive team in claiming a violation of the rules by the offensive team when such a violation is not automatically penalized. Example: If a batter bats out of turn or a runner fails to touch a base, the umpire cannot call the batter or runner out unless the defensive team appeals to the umpire.

AROUND THE HORN: A double play completed from the third baseman to the second baseman to the first baseman. The expression originated from the fact it is the longest way to make a double play, just as the route around Cape Horn, at the tip of South America, was the longest one from the Atlantic Ocean to the Pacific Ocean, until the construction of the Panama Canal.

ASPIRIN TABLET: A slang expression hitters use to explain what a ball thrown by Nolan Ryan (at 107 miles per hour) looks like when it comes up to the plate. It's not difficult to swallow, but it sure is tough to hit.

ASSIST: Official credit awarded in the scoring of a game to a player who throws or deflects a batted or thrown ball in such a way that a put-out results or would have resulted except for a subsequent error. In the case of a deflection, the player must slow the ball down or change its direction to rate an assist. Assists by infielders are common; they are relatively uncommon by outfielders, since it requires throwing a runner out while he is attempting to take an extra base or throwing a man out to complete a double play after an outfield catch. The record for most outfield assists in one season is 44, held by Chuck Klein of the Philadelphia Phillies, in 1930. The record for most outfield assists in one game is 4 and is held by many players. The record for most outfield assists in one inning is 2 and is also held by many players.

AT BAT: An official hitting turn charged to a player except when he receives a base on balls, is hit by a pitched ball, makes a sacrifice hit, or is interfered with by the catcher.

AUTOMATIC STRIKE: This is a pitch delivered with a count of three balls and no strikes. Usually it is a called strike, as the pitcher simply tries to get it over, and the batter is usually under orders to let it go on the chance that either it will be a ball or that the pitcher is unlikely to throw two more strikes in succession. It is considered automatic because the pitcher is deliberately aiming for the strike zone without using his most effective pitch. The pitcher does this because he knows that the batter will probably not swing. Also called the cripple.

BACKSTOP: The catcher. Also, a screened structure behind home plate to stop foul balls from going into the stands.

BAD BODY: A ballplayer's description of a paunchy fellow. Use of the adjective *bad* is common and is coupled with many different nouns. For example: "bad wheels" (legs), "bad head" (not very intelligent), "bad fuel" (food), and "bad hands," which describes a poor fielder, as in "He's got the bad hands."

BAG OF BONES: Any player who is extremely thin. The opposition will refer to him as a bag of bones to tease him. Also, a blade.

BAIL OUT: When a pitch comes too close for comfort and the batter pulls away hurriedly to escape being hit, it is called bailing out. Sometimes it is used as an uncomplimentary appraisal of a batter. If a batter bails out unnecessarily too often, it indicates he is fearful of being hit, and pitchers will work on that weakness to keep him away from the plate.

BALK: This is a time-honored accusation that comes ringing from the stands whenever the pitcher makes a false move, or what looks like one. But the umpire hardly evers calls it a balk. How come?

The answer usually lies in the pitcher's relationship to the pitching plate or rubber. As long as he is not standing on the rubber, the pitcher can make almost any move he pleases, including the business of wheeling toward a base and bluffing a throw or even charging toward the runner, and these are the procedures that so many fans think are balks. Almost always the pitcher remembers to step off the rubber before indulging in such tactics.

A balk can be committed in thirteen different ways, most of which are subject to variation, but in actual practice only three types of balks are common: the pitcher checks himself illegally, breaking his delivery when he is already committed to the pitch; he fails to come to a dead stop while bringing his hands down from the stretch; or the ball slips out of his hand while his foot is on the rubber.

The late Tommy Holmes, a baseball writer, used to say that every fan should be presented with a copy of the balk rule on entering the park. That would help, although the rule itself is no model of clarity. Umpires, in calling balks, tend to rely more on custom and experience than on the fine print.

BALL: Called by many other names, including horsehide, apple, onion, pill, pea, sphere, and agate. The rules specify that the ball shall be a sphere formed by yarn wound around a small core of cork and rubber that is then covered with two strips of white horsehide tightly stitched together. It shall weigh not less than 5 nor more than 5¼ ounces avoirdupois and measure not less than 9 nor more than 9¼ inches in circumference.

Suspicions regarding a lively, or rabbit, ball have

Nolan Ryan throws his aspirin tablet.

been prevalent since 1919, when a marked increase in distance hitting was first noticed. In the next four years almost three times as many home runs were hit in the major leagues as in the four previous years. The rate kept going up until it leveled off in the 1950s, but baseball officials have never admitted to any change in the composition of the ball.

A core of cork mixed with rubber is encased in a layer of black rubber and a layer of red rubber and wound with yarn—121 yards of rough gray wool, 48 yards of white wool, 53 yards of fine gray wool, and 150 yards of fine white cotton. After a coating of rubber cement is applied, the cover is sewn by hand—two figure-eight-shaped pieces of white horsehide joined by 108 double stitches of red thread.

Balls used in the two leagues are identical except that each has the signature of its own league president stamped on the cover. A. G. Spalding & Brothers was the exclusive manufacturer of major-league baseballs from the time the leagues began until 1976, when the contract was awarded to the Rawlings Company.

Production costs have risen so sharply in recent years that most of the baseballs used in the major leagues have been manufactured in Haiti.

In 1965 it was alleged that the Chicago White Sox stored a number of balls in a cold spot before using them in a game. The purpose of the "frozen" baseballs was to give them a deadening effect that would keep them from being hit for long distances. This was presumed to be beneficial to the White Sox, a team with little hitting ability and an abundance of pitching. The charge was denied by Chicago and never proved by the accusers, but if the White Sox did, indeed, attempt such shenanigans, it was to no avail. They still failed to win the American League pennant.

BALL HAWK: Outfielder, particularly one who is exceptionally fast and adept at chasing down fly balls—and catching them. Terry Moore of the St. Louis

Cardinals, Willie Mays of the New York and San Francisco Giants, and Paul Blair of the Baltimore Orioles are examples of outfielders who may be termed all-time ball hawks.

BALLS AND STRIKES: A pitch outside a prescribed zone is called a ball, four of which entitle the batter to first base. A pitch that passes through the zone without being hit is a strike, as is any pitch swung at and missed or a pitch fouled with less than two strikes or bunted foul no matter what the count. Three strikes are an out. The umpire behind the plate is the unquestioned (in theory, not in practice) judge of whether a pitch is a ball or a strike. He keeps track of how many balls and strikes are on a batter by means of an indicator, a piece of equipment small enough for the umpire to hold in the palm of his hand. In announcing the count (number of balls and strikes on a batter), it is proper to give the balls first, strikes second. Therefore, a count of three and two means three balls and two strikes; one and two means one ball and two strikes; "oh and one" means no balls and one strike, etc.

BALTIMORE CHOP: A batted ball that takes an extremely high bounce soon after it leaves the bat, bringing a disgusted glare from the infielder, who must wait helplessly for the ball to come down. Often by the time it does come down, it is too late to throw out the batter. It's called Baltimore chop because it was in Baltimore that Wee Willie Keeler played, and he frequently cooked up this kind of chop.

In the unique jargon of Casey Stengel, venerable ex-manager of the Brooklyn Dodgers, Boston Braves, New York Yankees, and New York Mets, a Baltimore chop is a butcher boy, its derivation being that the batter chops at the ball like a butcher cutting meat. Stengel is a strong advocate of the intentional Baltimore chop or butcher boy, because it is a difficult play for the defense to make.

BAND BOX: A sneering reference to a ball park that is so small that home runs are easy to hit there. During the 1950s the term was used most often to describe Ebbets Field, home of the Brooklyn Dodgers, because the dimensions in left centerfield and right centerfield (where the majority of home runs are hit) were considerably shorter than in most parks. Construction of modern parks, with measurements almost standard, has made the term practically obsolete, although it is still sometimes used to describe left field in Boston's Fenway Park, which measures a mere 315 feet from home plate to the wall.

BANJO HITTER: A weak hitter who seems to strum the ball as one would a banjo. It is a term of disparagement, but any player will say that even a banjo hit is music to his ears.

BANNER DAY: A recent innovation among baseball's many promotions designed to create spectator participation and increase attendance. Banner Day (Camera Day, Old-timers' Day, Senior Citizens' Day, and Ladies' Day are other promotions of longer standing) had its origin with the New York Mets in the old Polo Grounds and came about purely by accident. Fans began carrying signs, placards, and banners to the ball park to hail their personal heroes, to make known their grievances, to support their favorite team, or simply to show off their cleverness.

They used bed sheets and cardboard and rolled-up pieces of paper and, at first, the slogans were simple statements in crayon, pen, or pencil. Soon the banners evolved into works of art, and the slogans rivaled Madison Avenue advertising campaigns.

Finally the Mets' promotion department decided to conduct a competition for creator of the best banner, and among the winners were the following banners:

Who Says a Good Baseball Team Has to Win?
World Series Reservations on Sale . . . for 1999.
We're in the Cellar But We're Not in the Dumps.
To Error Is Human, to Forgive Is a Mets Fan.

BARNSTORMING: Taken from the political and theatrical colloquialism that originally meant to appear in small country towns, where barns served as gathering places. Baseball teams barnstorm in the spring, playing exhibitions on their way home from training camp, and star players often assemble into barnstorming units in the fall, playing not only in the United States but occasionally on foreign soil as well. The first foreign tour dates back to 1874, when members of the Boston and Athletic teams of the National Association went to Ireland and England to play 14 baseball games and 7 cricket matches.

Five years later Frank Bancroft took a barnstorming team to Havana. In 1888 A. G. Spalding gathered a group of twenty players, mostly from the Chicago National League team, and made the first around-the-world baseball tour, playing in such faraway places as New Zealand, Australia, Ceylon, Egypt, Italy, France, England, and Ireland.

In 1908 the Reach All-America Team made the first tour of Japan, and later there were additional tours to Japan. In 1931 many of the top stars of the day played four games in Japan and drew the staggering total of 250,000 admissions. Soon after this tour the Japanese developed professional teams for the first time. One of the players on the 1931 trip was Lefty O'Doul, who made five more trips to Japan and became the second greatest sports idol in that country, the first being Babe

Ruth, who played on the 18-game Japanese tour headed by Connie Mack in 1934. In 1955 the New York Yankees went to Japan as a unit to play exhibitions, and since then many teams have been invited to play there.

Still, it was mainly through the appearance of Babe Ruth and Lefty O'Doul that the Japanese took to the game of baseball to such a degree that today they are as fanatical about the game as we are in the United States.

BASE: Also called bag, sack, cushion, hassock, etc. Any of the four objects to be touched or occupied by the runners. Home base is usually called the plate or the dish and is the starting and finishing point of a trip around the bases, which, when made successfully, results in the scoring of a run. First, second, and third bases are white canvas bags 15 inches square, not less than 3 nor more than 5 inches in thickness, filled with soft material, and securely attached to the ground. They differ from home base, which is a five-sided slab of whitened rubber. It is 12 inches square with two of the corners filled in so that one edge is 17 inches long, two are 8½ inches and two are 12 inches. It is set in the ground so that the 17-inch edge faces the pitcher. All bases, including home base, are in fair territory, and the bases are 90 feet apart in the counterclockwise order in which they are to be negotiated.

BASEBALL: A game between two teams of nine players each, with adequate substitutes, under the direction of a manager, played in accordance with official rules under the jurisdiction of an umpire or umpires on an enclosed field of regulation size. The object of the game is to win by scoring more runs than the opponent. The winner of the game is the team that shall have scored, in accordance with the rules, the greater number of runs at the conclusion of a regulation game.

As far as organized baseball is concerned, Abner Doubleday is the father of the game. It may well be, however, that one Alexander J. Cartwright conceived the sport as we know it and that baseball is perpetuating a myth in crediting Doubleday.

During the depression of the 1930s the major leagues, in an effort to stimulate interest in the lagging game, came upon a thirty-year-old report by A. G. Mills, who had been commissioned to look into the origin of baseball. Mills stated, without a particle of substantiation, that it had been devised in 1839 in Cooperstown, N.Y., by Doubleday, a West Point cadet who later became a Union general as well as a close friend of Mills. The major leagues seized on the report, set up a centennial celebration for 1939, and made Cooperstown the site of an official baseball museum and Hall of Fame.

Most baseball historians consider the Mills report a work of fiction, preferring to believe that the sport evolved from old English games, notably rounders, and that Cartwright should have been given credit for formalizing it. Cartwright, a surveyor, laid out the field with the bases 90 feet apart and drew up rules (including three strikes and three outs) for the first game played between organized teams, in Hoboken, N. J. in 1846.

BASELINE: The boundary line within which a base runner must keep when running between the bases. The baseline is not the foul line and is, in fact, extended to three feet on either side of the foul line. Whether or not a runner has stayed within the boundary of the baseline is a source of many heated disputes between players and umpires because, since the action is so fast, the decision is up to the umpire, who has the last word in any case.

BASE ON BALLS: An award of first base granted to a batter who during his time at bat receives four pitches outside the strike zone. Also called a walk. This is the play that defensive managers detest more than any other in baseball because there is no defense against a base on balls—the batter is given a free ticket to a base. Give enough free tickets and they will soon prove to be very damaging.

Frank Frisch was a player and manager turned radio broadcaster for the New York Giants, and not a day would pass when he would not deplore the base on balls. "Oh, those bases on balls" became a Frank Frisch trademark.

The record for receiving most bases on balls in a single season is 170 by Babe Ruth in 1923. The National League record is 148 by Eddie Stanky of the Brooklyn Dodgers in 1945 and Jim Wynn of the Houston Astros in 1969. Ruth's record was based on the pitchers' fear of his great ability as a hitter, while Stanky's is a tribute to his ability to distract pitchers into throwing balls. He did this by constantly fouling pitches that would have been strikes and by moving around and crouching in the batter's box so that he was a difficult target.

At the time when Stanky was the unchallenged king of the base on balls, Andrei Gromyko was the Russian ambassador to the United Nations, and he occasionally walked out of UN meetings to display his displeasure over the proceedings. This caused one sports writer to tag Stanky with the nickname Gromyko, and the name stuck.

BASE RUNNER: A player of the team at bat who has finished his turn at bat, reached base, and has not yet been put out.

BASES LOADED: When first, second, and third bases are all occupied by runners, which is the maximum. Also called bases full, bags bulging, and the ducks are on the pond.

BAT: A smooth, rounded stick not more than 2¾ inches in diameter at the thickest part and not more than 42 inches long. The rules state that it shall be one piece of solid wood or formed from a block of wood consisting of two or more pieces of wood bonded together with an adhesive in such a way that the grain direction of all pieces is essentially parallel to the length of the bat. Any such laminated bat shall contain only wood or adhesive, except for a clear finish.

Bat nicknames have survived long usage, some of the more enduring being lumber, wood, wand, willow, war club, stick, shillelagh. A bat is still called the hickory because it used to be made of that hardwood, although white ash has long since proved more satisfactory. The wagon tongue as a synonym dates to the 1880s when A.G. Spalding advertised for 100,000 wagon tongues to be turned into bats.

Thanks to Babe Ruth, bats are much lighter than they were in the days when Babe himself swung a 54-ounce club. Other hitters, going for distance to keep up with Ruth, found they couldn't get the bat around fast enough. Today's bats are seldom heavier than 36 ounces, and most are in the 30- to 33-ounce range.

Most professional bats are made by Hillerich & Bradsby. Their Louisville Slugger, in production since 1894, is still the favorite big-league bat. It comes in any number of models, and most players have bats manufactured to their own specifications, so that each player has his own specific bat model almost from the time he first joins a major-league team. The most popular bat at the moment features a rather bulbous barrel and a very thin handle.

There is a legend that if a player hits the ball on the trademark of the bat, the bat will break, but that story was born on the sandlots and is not true. During the 1958 World Series, Henry Aaron of the Milwaukee Braves came to bat, and the New York Yankee catcher Yogi Berra, noticed that the trademark was down.

"Henry," Yogi said, "you'd better turn the trademark around so you can read it, otherwise you'll break your bat."

"Yogi," Aaron replied, "I came up here to hit, not to read."

BAT AROUND: When all nine batters of one team come to bat in the same inning before three outs are recorded.

BATBOY: A young man, usually a teen-ager, who assists a team by handing the player his bat, picking up the bat after the player has hit, and generally helping a team by caring for equipment and keeping equipment neat and tidy during a game. It is a job that boys want because they get to rub shoulders with their heroes, the players, and are usually on a first-name basis with them. Batboys are paid a nominal fee by the team and depend on tips from the players for additional income. Another attraction is the opportunity to make a road trip with the team. Teams also employ ballboys, who gather up foul balls and supply the umpire with the game's baseballs. A ballboy does not get to make a trip and does not work in close association with the players, but he can work his way up from ballboy to batboy.

BATTER: An offensive player who takes his position in the batter's box for purposes of hitting the ball. Traditionally, play is in progress when the home-plate umpire shouts, "Batter up."

BATTER'S BOX: The area within which the batter stands during his time at bat. It is a rectangle six feet long and four feet wide, and the batter must keep both feet in the box at all times when he is hitting.

BATTERY: The pitcher and the catcher. The name has a military origin and dates back to Civil War days, when a battery was a group of cannons. Just as the cannons did, the pitcher and catcher start all of the fireworks in a baseball game.

BATTING AVERAGE: A method of evaluating a player's batting ability. Determined by the number of hits he has made divided by his official times at bat and carried to three decimal places. The batting average is an outgrowth of the box score, first kept by Henry Chadwick, the pioneer of all baseball writers, in 1853. Currently, the standard of excellence is for a batter to bat .300 (three hits for every ten times at bat).

If a .300 batting average is the standard of excellence, a .400 average is the epitome of excellence, and in modern times (since 1900) there have been just eight different players who batted .400 or higher for a full season, including Ty Cobb of the Detroit Tigers and Rogers Hornsby of the St. Louis Cardinals, who each did it three times, and George Sisler of the St. Louis Cardinals, who did it twice. The last player in the major leagues to hit .400 was Ted Williams of the Boston Red Sox, who batted .406 in 1941. The last player in the National League to hit .400 was Bill Terry of the New York Giants, who batted .401 in 1930.

The highest batting average in modern times for a single season is .424 by Hornsby in 1924 (536 at-bats, 227 hits). The highest batting average for an entire career is by Cobb, who batted a remarkable .367 for twenty-four years covering 3,033 games and including 4,191 hits in 11,429 at-bats, the number of games, at-bats, and hits each being records.

BATTING CAGE: A metal device on wheels used during batting practice, but not during the game, that serves both as a backstop and to keep foul balls from going into the stands, where they would, undoubtedly, remain. Primarily, the batting cage is used to prevent the loss of too many baseballs during practice.

BATTING ORDER: The order in which a team must

Ted Williams' batting average in 1941 was .406, and no major leaguer has hit .400 since then.

come to bat. Also called the lineup. If a player bats out of turn, deliberately or otherwise, he is out, provided the team in the field realizes the error and appeals to the umpire before the illegal batter is disposed of. The only way the batting order can be changed is by the use of a substitute batter (one not already in the game). If a player is substituted for, he is no longer permitted to remain in the game.

The batting order is made out in triplicate by the manager on a form provided by the league. The manager keeps one copy for his use, gives one copy to the opposing manager and another to the umpire just prior to the start of the game.

Many years ago a team would start nine men and almost always finish with the same nine men. In recent years, baseball has evolved as a game of specialization, and use of substitutes has become so widespread that it is a rarity when a team finishes a game with the same nine men that started it.

BATTING PRACTICE: The players' favorite pastime. A given amount of time, usually an hour, is set aside before each game so that hitters can hone their skills and sharpen their hitting eyes by taking batting practice. The poor hitters need it the most, but get it the least, because most of the time is taken up by the regulars, who are protective of their allotted time.

BEANBALL: A pitch suspected of having been aimed at the batter's head. Pitchers, according to pitchers, never throw beanballs. Quote: "It slipped" or "I was just brushing him back" (throwing close to keep the batter from taking a toehold). At times such explanations are regarded with a certain amount of cynicism, especially by batters. In recent years, umpires have been empowered to censure a pitcher thought to be deliberately throwing a beanball (whether he connects or not). With the censure comes an automatic fifty-dollar fine, and repeated violations can lead to a larger fine and/or banishment from the game.

In 1920 Carl Mays, a pitcher with the New York Yankees hit Ray Chapman, a shortstop for the Cleveland Indians, in the head with a pitch. Chapman was rushed to New York's Knickerbocker Hospital, where he died from the blow the following morning. Because it was fatal, this has been regarded as the most famous, or infamous, of all the beanings. But there is no evidence that it was intentional.

In the early 1950s Branch Rickey, then president of the Pittsburgh Pirates, instructed all of his players to wear a specially constructed plastic helmet to protect the head when batting. The practice soon became widespread, and it is now mandatory for a batter to go to the plate with a protective helmet on.

BEAT OUT: To hit safely by beating an infielder's throw to first base. Most commonly used in connection with a bunt. A player beats out a bunt.

BENCH: Applies not only to the seating facilities reserved for players, substitutes, and other team members in uniform in the dugout, but also to a team's substitutes as a group. Thus the saying, "A team is only as strong as its bench." To bench a player means to remove him from the starting lineup for substandard play. A player who does not play frequently is said to be riding the bench or a bench warmer. He is a substitute or utility player, sometimes called a scrub or, in modern jargon, scrubeenie. Frank Torre, when he played for the Milwaukee Braves, used the expression "Vitalis" for a scrub. "Because," as he put it, "he would get only a sixty-second workout." This was inspired by a popular television hair-tonic commercial of the day.

In bygone days a bench warmer or scrub was a much maligned and sneered-at player who rarely got into a game because he was not considered good enough to play. In recent years, with the age of the specialist, the bench has become a very vital part of any team. Casey Stengel, when he managed the Yankees, made popular the use of the bench. He would literally have almost two offensive teams, one right-handed team to bat against left-handed pitchers and one left-handed hitting team to bat against right-handed pitchers, although certain players, such as Joe DiMaggio, were exempt from the manipulations. Stengel also made use of defensive specialists, who made their appearance late in games in which the Yankees had a lead. Many of Stengel's theories are in practice now, at least to some degree, by each of the major-league managers.

In 1954 Dusty Rhodes of the New York Giants gave the bench warmer added stature. Rhodes rarely started a game, but, used mostly as a pinch-hitter, he batted .341 for the season. In the World Series, against Cleveland, Rhodes came off the bench in each of the first three games to deliver important hits and help the Giants sweep the Series four games to none. Rhodes's three-run, pinch-hit home run in the tenth inning won the first game, 5-2.

BETWEEN THE LINES: The field, foul line to foul line. Players often say, "It's what happens between the lines that counts," meaning that what a player does in the game is the yardstick by which he should be judged, not his off-field activities.

BIG BILL: Infielders' pet term for the last long hop taken by some ground balls, making them easy to field. Sometimes called a charity hop.

BLADE: *See* Bag of Bones.

BLEACHERS: Stands that got their names because they were uncovered, leaving the occupants to bleach in the sun.

BLEEDER: A lucky one-base hit, sometimes called a

scratch hit. Usually it is a grounder that is softly hit and trickles through the infield, takes a bad hop, or rolls dead in front of a charging infielder.

BLOWOUT: A leg injury; a bad wheel.

BLOW UP: To lose effectiveness suddenly. Used almost exclusively for a pitcher.

BLUE DARTER: A ball sharply hit through the infield, usually a low line drive.

BONER: A foolish blunder, known also as a bone-head play, a skull or skuller, a rock, or a John Anderson (specifically attempting to steal a base already occupied). The classic example of a baseball boner was Fred Merkle's failure to touch second base when a teammate drove in the winning run for the New York Giants in 1908. Johnny Evers of the Chicago Cubs called for the ball, touched second base, and had Merkle declared out, nullifying the run and eventually costing the Giants the pennant. Another classic boner was when three Brooklyn Dodgers in the 1920s wound up at third base simultaneously after a pop fly dropped safely in right field. One player thought the ball would be caught, the other two did not, thus the mix-up.

BONUS PLAYER: Modern term for a raw prospect who receives a substantial sum of money for signing. Robin Roberts ($25,000), Al Kaline ($60,000), and Tony Conigliaro ($35,000) are among the minority of bonus players who made good. A celebrated failure was Paul Pettit, who won one game in his brief career with the Pittsburgh Pirates after he had been peddled to them for $100,000 by a Hollywood agent, who kept 10 percent.

The largest bonuses ever paid are reputed to be the $175,000 the Pirates gave Bob Bailey and the $200,000 the Los Angeles Angels handed to Rick Reichardt in 1964, which may never be topped. To put an end to the bartering that threatened to drive bonuses to ridiculous heights, the major leagues, in 1965, adopted a program of drafting free-agent players. The first player drafted was Rick Monday, an outfielder from Arizona State University, who was selected by the Kansas City Athletics. He got $100,000 for signing, but might have received more than twice that amount under the free-agent rule.

With all the money being spent on talent, with the bonuses, vast scouting system, and free-agent draft, a club still doesn't know where its next star is coming from. Mickey Mantle, after all, was discovered by Yankee scout Tom Greenwade, who showed up on the Oklahoma sandlots to sign another player and took Mantle for a mere $1,100.

BOOT: To miss a ground ball. Also a bobble, kick, fumble, etc.

BOTTOM: The second, or home team's, half of an inning.

BOX SCORE: A standardized digest showing at a glance how many hits each player made, what position he played, and where he batted in the lineup. Individual fielding totals were carried until 1958, when the press associations, over some objections, dropped the put-out and assist columns. A subtable reveals who made the errors and offers a capsule listing of other major credits and debits. The first box score appeared in the *New York Clipper* in 1853. Now almost every newspaper in the United States publishes daily box scores of local games, major-league games, or both. In recent years a pitching table has been added to the box score, showing at a glance a pitcher's performance, including runs allowed, earned runs allowed, hits allowed, walks, strikeouts, and whether he won or lost the game.

Seventh Game, 1975 World Series

CINCINNATI	ab	r	h	rbi	BOSTON	ab	r	h	rbi
Rose 3b	4	0	2	1	Carbo lf	3	1	1	0
Morgan 2b	4	0	2	1	Miller lf	0	0	0	0
Bench c	4	1	0	0	Beniquez ph	1	0	0	0
Perez 1b	5	1	1	2	Doyle 2b	4	1	1	0
Foster lf	4	0	1	0	Montgomery ph	1	0	0	0
Concepcion ss	4	0	1	0	Yastrzemski 1b	5	1	1	1
Griffey rf	2	2	1	0	Fisk c	3	0	0	0
Geronimo cf	3	0	0	0	Lynn cf	2	0	0	0
Gullett p	1	0	1	0	Petrocelli 3b	3	0	1	1
Rettenmund ph	1	0	0	0	Evans rf	2	0	0	1
Billingham p	0	0	0	0	Burleson ss	3	0	0	0
Armbrister ph	0	0	0	0	Lee p	3	0	1	0
Carroll p	0	0	0	0	Moret p	0	0	0	0
Driessen ph	1	0	0	0	Willoughby p	0	0	0	0
McEnaney p	0	0	0	0	Cooper ph	1	0	0	0
					Burton p	0	0	0	0
					Cleveland p	0	0	0	0
Total	33	4	9	4	Total	31	3	5	3

Cincinnati .... 000 002 101—4
Boston .... 003 000 000—3

E—Doyle 2. DP—Cincinnati 1, Boston 2. LOB—Cincinnati 9, Boston 9. 2B—Carbo. HR—Perez (3). SB—Morgan, Griffey. S—Geronimo.

	IP	H	R	ER	BB	SO
Gullett	4	4	3	3	5	5
Billingham	2	1	0	0	2	1
Carroll (W, 1-0)	2	0	0	0	1	1
McEnaney	1	0	0	0	0	0
Lee	6 1/3	7	3	3	1	2
Moret	1/3	1	0	0	2	0
Willoughby	1 1/3	0	0	0	0	0
Burton (L, 0-1)	2/3	1	1	1	2	0
Cleveland	1/3	0	0	0	1	0

Save—McEnaney (1). WP—Gullett. T—2:52. A—35,205.

BREAK HIS DISHES: To break the hitter's bat, as in "He (the pitcher) got in his kitchen and broke his dishes." Term has been refined, as in "He got in his refrigerator and broke his eggs." It probably originates from the idea of taking bread out of a hitter's mouth.

BRING IT: To throw swiftly, as in "Nolan Ryan can really bring it."

BROADWAY: An obsolete nickname for an elegant dresser. Charlie Wagner, a pitcher with the Red Sox around the time of World War II, was the last player widely known as Broadway.

BRUSHBACK: *See* Duster.

BULLPEN: An area adjoining the playing field, usually alongside the foul lines, where relief pitchers and other substitutes warm up. The word *bullpen*, which is also prison slang for a place of temporary confinement, is of uncertain origin in baseball. Some think it can be traced to the Bull Durham tobacco signs that were posted on the fences of many ball parks in 1909. Featured on the sign was a picture of a gigantic bull, and in many parks relief pitchers warmed up directly in front of it. As far back as 1877, though, bullpen was the name used for a roped-off section of the outfield that served as standing room. It is known that the term was used in Civil War days to describe the stockade.

BUNT: A ball that is not swung at but intentionally hit with the bat and tapped slowly within the infield, a maneuver perfected, usually, by speedy runners, because a well-placed bunt is almost always a safe hit. Among those more proficient at the art of bunting for a base hit were Jackie Robinson with the Brooklyn Dodgers, Phil Rizzuto with the New York Yankees, and, more recently, Maury Wills with the Los Angeles Dodgers.

BUSH: Any league below the majors, but especially a

Jackie Robinson of the Brooklyn Dodgers knew how to lay down the perfect bunt.

league of very low classification, may be referred to as a bush league. Bush is also the ballplayers' scornful adjective for any person, thing, or action not meeting with their approval, whether or not it has anything to do with baseball. A player whose conduct or ability is considered not befitting major-league status is called bush, bush league, or a busher. Playing in the minor leagues is also called playing in the bushes.

BUTCHER: A player who is very poor defensively. He is also said to have a bad glove or bad hands. Such a player was Dick Stuart, a hard hitter for the Pittsburgh Pirates, Boston Red Sox, and Philadelphia Phillies, but one who would never dazzle you with his defensive work at first base. A Boston sports writer dubbed him Dr. Strangeglove. Another who had a reputation for being a poor fielder, perhaps without justification, was Chuck Hiller, a second baseman with the San Francisco Giants and New York Mets. His nicknames were Iron Hands, No Hands, and Dr. No.

BUTCHER BOY: *See* Baltimore Chop.

CALLED GAME: A game in which, for any reason, the umpire-in-chief terminates play. The most common reason is rain, but games have been called because of snow, fog, and wind. If a game is called before the team trailing has been to bat five times, it is replayed from the beginning. If a game is called after the team trailing has been to bat five times, it is an official game and goes into the records as a shortened game.

CAN OF CORN: A high fly within easy reach of a fielder.

CASEY: The well-known nickname of the late Charles Dillon Stengel, famed manager of the Brooklyn Dodgers, Boston Braves, New York Yankees, and New York Mets until past his seventy-fifth birthday. He holds the record of having won ten American League pennants and seven world championships in twelve years, and was the only manager to have won five consecutive world championships (1949 to 1953 with the Yankees). Along with Babe Ruth, Casey was regarded as baseball's greatest ambassador, and he had spent more than fifty years in the game until his retirement in 1965. His nickname stems from the fact he came from Kansas City (KC), Mo.

CASEY AT THE BAT: The foremost ballad of baseball, written in 1888 by Ernest L. Thayer and made popular by the recitations of De Wolfe Hopper:

The outlook wasn't brilliant for the Mudville nine that day;
The score stood four to two with but one inning more to play.
And then when Cooney died at first, and Barrows did the same,
A sickly silence fell upon the patrons of the game.

A straggling few got up to go in deep despair. The rest
Clung to that hope which springs eternal in the human breast.
They thought if only Casey could but get a whack at that—
We'd put up even money now with Casey at the bat.

But Flynn preceded Casey, as did also Jimmy Blake,
And the former was a lulu and the latter was a cake;
So upon the strucken multitude grim melancholy sat,
For there seemed but little chance of Casey's getting to the bat.

But Flynn let drive a single, to the wonderment of all,
And Blake, the much despised, tore the cover off the ball;
And when the dust had lifted and the men saw what had occurred,
There was Johnny safe at second and Flynn a-hugging third.

Then from five-thousand throats and more there rose a lusty yell;
It rambled through the valley, it rattled in the dell;
It knocked upon the mountain and recoiled upon the flat,
For Casey, mighty Casey, was advancing to the bat.

There was ease in Casey's manner as he stepped into his place;
There was pride in Casey's bearing and a smile on Casey's face.
And when, responding to the cheers, he lightly doffed his hat,
No stranger in the crowd could doubt 'twas Casey at the bat.

Ten thousand eyes were on him as he rubbed his hands with dirt;
Five thousand tongues applauded when he wiped them on his shirt.
Then while the writhing pitcher ground the ball into his hip,
Defiance gleamed in Casey's eye, a sneer curled Casey's lip.

And now the leather-covered sphere came hurtling through the air,
And Casey stood a-watching it in haughty grandeur there.
Close by the sturdy batsman the ball unheeded sped—
"That ain't my style," said Casey. "Strike one," the umpire said.

From the benches, black with people, there went up
a muffled roar,
Like the beating of the storm waves on a stern and
distant shore.
"Kill him! Kill the umpire!" shouted someone in the
stand,
And it's likely they'd have killed him had not Casey
raised his hand.

With a smile of Christian charity great Casey's visage
shone;
He stilled the rising tumult, he bade the game go on;
He signaled to the pitcher, and once more the
spheroid flew;
But Casey still ignored it, and the umpire said, "Strike
two."

"Fraud!" cried the maddened thousands, and the
echo answered, "Fraud!"
But one scornful look from Casey and the audience
was awed.
They saw his face grow stern and cold, they saw his
muscles strain,
And they knew that Casey wouldn't let that ball go by
again.

The sneer is gone from Casey's lip, his teeth are
clenched in hate;
He pounds with cruel violence his bat upon the plate.
And now the pitcher holds the ball, and now he lets it
go,
And now the air is shattered by the force of Casey's
blow.

Oh! somewhere in this favored land the sun is shining
bright;
The band is playing somewhere, and somewhere
hearts are light.
And somewhere men are laughing, and somewhere
children shout;
But there is no joy in Mudville—mighty Casey has
struck out.

CASTOFF: A discarded player, often one who makes
a resounding comeback with another team. Among
outstanding examples of castoffs are Dixie Walker,
Lew Burdette, and John Mayberry. Walker could not
succeed with the Yankees, White Sox, and Tigers, but
when he was picked up by the Brooklyn Dodgers, for
whom he played nine seasons, he won the National
League batting title with a .357 average in 1944 and
finished with a lifetime batting average of .306. He
became such a great favorite with Brooklyn fans that he
got to be known as The Peepuls' Cherce.

Burdette was a minor-leaguer in the Yankee farm
system when they traded him to the Braves, then in
Boston. Burdette went on to win 173 games in 11
seasons with the Braves, and in the 1957 World Series he
beat the Yankees three times, including two shutouts.

Mayberry was traded by the Houston Astros to the
Kansas City Royals when he was just twenty, and he
became a star in the American League, once given the
chance to play. In his first four seasons he drove in 100
or more runs three times.

CATBALL: Sometimes called One Old Cat. A
forerunner of the American game of baseball, played in
an organized fashion for the first time by the
Knickerbocker Club of New York in 1845.

CATCH: The act of a fielder in getting secure
possession in his hand or glove of a ball in flight and
firmly holding it, provided he does not use any part of
his uniform in getting possession. It is not a catch,
however, if simultaneously or immediately following
his contact with the ball he collides with a player or with
a wall or if he falls down and, as a result, drops the ball.
If a fielder has made the catch and drops the ball while
in the act of throwing, the ball shall be adjudged to have
been caught. In establishing the validity of the catch,
the fielder shall hold the ball long enough to prove that
he has complete control of it and that his release of the
ball is voluntary and intentional.

CATCHER: The fielder who squats behind the plate
to receive the pitch. Included among the catcher's
special equipment are a mask made of metal, shin
guards, and a padded chest protector. Until 1966 the
rules permitted the catcher to be the only man on the
team who could wear a glove of unlimited size, shape,
or weight, the only restriction being that it be made of
leather. However, some teams abused the privilege,
using oversized gloves, usually for the purpose of
catching the unpredictable knuckle ball, so the rule was
changed. In 1966 the size of the catcher's glove was
restricted to no more than 38 inches in circumference
and no more than 15½ inches from top to bottom.

CATCHER'S BOX: That area within which the
catcher stands until the pitcher delivers the ball. He
may stay anywhere in the area, which is 8 feet long and
43 inches wide, provided he does not interfere with the
batter.

CATCHER'S INTERFERENCE: Interference by
the catcher with the batsman, for which the batsman is
awarded first base and is not charged with a time at bat
and the catcher is charged with an error. Sometimes
called a catcher's balk. If a base runner should be

All the world knew Charles Dillon Stengel simply as Casey.

attempting to steal at the time the catcher interferes with the batter, the runner is awarded the stolen base (even if he is tagged out), and the batter is still awarded first base.

CENTER FIELD: The outfield territory beyond second base and between that usually covered by the right and left fielders. The outfielder who covers center field is called the center fielder. He is usually the fastest and best of the three outfielders. Among the outstanding center fielders have been Tris Speaker of the Cleveland Indians, Terry Moore of the St. Louis Cardinals, Joe DiMaggio of the New York Yankees, Duke Snider of the Brooklyn Dodgers, Willie Mays of the San Francisco Giants, Mickey Mantle of the Yankees, and Paul Blair of the Baltimore Orioles.

CHANCE: Any opportunity to field a ball with the possibility of making or helping to make a put-out. Traditionally, the first baseman accepts the most chances, since all infield outs culminate with him, and the record for most chances accepted in a season was set by a first baseman, John Donohue of the Chicago White Sox, who had 1,986 chances in 1907; the record for most chances in a game is 22, shared by many first basemen.

CHANGE OF PACE: Also called change-up, change, letup, or pulling the string. A slow ball usually thrown after a fast ball, with the same motion as the fast ball, the purpose being to catch the batter off stride. Some speed can also be taken off a curve ball and used as a change of pace. The fork ball, palm ball, and slip pitch are all examples of pitches used as changes of pace.

CHARITY HOP: *See* Big Bill.

CHINESE HOMER: An expression used widely in the 1950s to describe a cheap home run. The term is a carry-over from the days long past when Chinese labor was vastly underpaid, and it was most commonly used in connection with New York's Polo Grounds (since demolished to make room for a housing development), where the distances along the foul lines were 257 feet in right field and 279 in left field.

CHIN MUSIC: A knockdown pitch.

CHOKE: To grip a bat several inches up from the end. It is done deliberately when a batter wants to bunt the ball. Also to fail in a critical situation, the person in question being said to have let his emotions get the better of him. So, under pressure, the player may choke, choke up, get the apple, get the lump, get the olive, get tight.

CIRCUIT: A home run (a circuit clout) or a league (senior circuit for National League, junior circuit for American League).

CIRCUS CATCH: A spectacular catch of a fly ball, usually by an outfielder.

CLANK: The supposed sound of a bad fielder (iron hands) catching a ball. Clank is synonymous with "bad hands." There is no known cure.

CLEAN-UP BATTER: The fourth position in the batting order, so called because it is usually manned by a slugger, who consistently drives in any runners who may have reached base ahead of him, thus cleaning the bases. It used to be customary for a manager to bat his best hitter in the clean-up position, but in recent years the trend has been to bat the best hitter third because of the possibility that the third batter will get more times at bat than the clean-up hitter.

CLOWN: There are many in baseball, described as such not so much for their sense of humor as for their ability. Most commonly, however, it is used to describe an entertainer who is part of a baseball sideshow before games, between games of a doubleheader, etc. He is there to help entertain the fans. The most famous baseball clown, Al Schacht, a pitcher of limited skill but great humor with the Washington Senators in the 1920s, became a successful New York restaurateur. Schacht's antics at major- and minor-league ball parks brought him the title Clown Prince of Baseball. Another successful baseball clown is Max Patkin, who works primarily in the minor leagues. Like Schacht, Patkin also is a former pitcher, but one who never made the major leagues.

Center field *was home for such illustrious players as Mickey Mantle (left), Willie Mays (center), and Duke Snider.*

Al Schacht, the clown prince (left), did his tightrope-walking act with partner Nick Altrock.

CLUBHOUSE LAWYER: Any player given to airing his opinions, particularly if they are radical opinions by baseball standards.

CLUTCH: A tight spot in a game. A player who consistently comes through in such spots is known as a clutch hitter or pitcher, or a money player. Such a player was Tommy Henrich of the New York Yankees. During the late 1940s Henrich was such a successful clutch hitter that he was dubbed Old Reliable. Another was Henry Aaron of the Milwaukee (Atlanta) Braves and the Milwaukee Brewers, called Money in the Bank or Mr. Chips by his teammates because he usually delivered in important situations.

COACH: One of the manager's assistants, almost always a former player. Coaches serve as hitting, pitching, and fielding instructors, and when a team is at bat, one coach is stationed near first base and one near third base to direct traffic, if any.

COLLAR: Going through an entire game without getting a hit. If a player fails to hit, he is said to have gotten the collar.

COMMISSIONER: Baseball's top-ranking administrator. Internal strife among major-league owners, capped by the revelation that several members of the Chicago White Sox conspired with gamblers to deliberately lose the 1919 World Series to the Cincinnati Reds, prompted the appointment of a commissioner. The White Sox lost the series, but the conspiracy wasn't uncovered for a full year, and it was the blackest day in baseball history, forever to be known as the Black Sox scandal.

In an attempt to restore public confidence in the

game, baseball appointed the respected Judge Kenesaw Mountain Landis as its first commissioner. He served from 1921 to his death in 1944, when he was succeeded by Albert B. ("Happy") Chandler, former governor of Kentucky. Chandler reigned until 1950, when the owners voted him out of office and gave the job to the National League president, Ford C. Frick, who retired after the 1965 season.

As Frick's successor the baseball owners selected William D. Eckert, a retired lieutenant-general of the U.S. Air Force. Eckert assumed his duties beginning with the 1966 season. The new commissioner accepted a seven-year contract at $65,000 a year plus unlimited expenses. In 1969 Eckert was fired, and Bowie K. Kuhn, former counsel to the National League, became baseball's fifth commissioner. A palace revolt to oust Kuhn in 1975 failed and, instead, he was elected to a new seven-year term.

The commissioner's major duties include settling grievances of players, clubs, or leagues in organized baseball, including the minor leagues; investigating and punishing acts that he may deem detrimental to baseball; and running the World Series. In addition to the commissioner each league has its own president— Lee MacPhail in the American League and Charles ("Chub") Feeney in the National League are the current presidents—whose functions are to act in the manner of a commissioner on situations pertaining to their leagues.

CONTRACT: All major- and minor-league teams employ players on a contract basis. In the winter the clubs enjoy a great amount of publicity by announcing day after day that this player or that one has signed his contract, come to terms, inked his pact.

CORK: Slang for a man considered a team's most effective relief pitcher. The expression became popular with Ted Wilks, who choked off many rallies as a relief pitcher for the St. Louis Cardinals in the 1940s.

COUNT: The number of balls and strikes on a batter, the highest count being three and two—three balls and two strikes—which is known as a full count.

COUSIN: The name given to a pitcher by a certain batter or even a certain team that finds him easy to hit.

CRIPPLE: *See* Automatic Strike.

CROOKED ARM: An uncomplimentary reference to a pitcher who throws with a peculiar motion. It is usually applied to left-handers, because they have unorthodox deliveries.

CURVE: One of the two standard pitches of baseball, the other being the fast ball. The orthodox curve ball is thrown with a decided snap and twist of the wrist. A right-hander's curve breaks from right to left as he faces the plate, a left-hander's curve breaks from left to right.

The sinker or drop is a curve that breaks down as well as out. Most curve balls sink, some more sharply than others. A slider is a fast curve with small break, sometimes denounced as a nickel curve. It is probably the most widely used pitch, since it gets its effectiveness from breaking late, is easier to control, and causes less strain on the pitcher's arm. By the time it breaks, the hitter may be swinging in the wrong place or he may let it go only to see it slip into the strike zone. A curve ball is also known as a jug (for jug handle), rainbow, dipsy-do, hook, and snake. Among the more proficient curve-ball pitchers have been Sal Maglie, Johnny Sain, Camilo Pascual, and Bert Blyleven.

The curve ball was first used in 1867 by W. A. Cummings. There have been many claims by scientists that a curve ball is nothing more than an optical illusion. To dispute such claims, Freddie Fitzsimmons of the Brooklyn Dodgers staged a demonstration that silenced the doubters for good. On December 1, 1941, he set up three posts in a straight line between himself and the pitcher's distance of 60 feet 6 inches. He released the ball to the right of the first post and made it go to the left of the second post and to the right of the third post.

Whitlow Wyatt, also a Dodger pitcher of that time, offered to perform a more spectacular demonstration. Anyone who did not believe that a curve ball curves could stand behind a tree, Wyatt proposed, "and I'll whomp him to death with an optical illusion." There were no takers.

CUTDOWN DATE: That time of year when a team must cut its roster to the maximum number of players allowed, by trading, selling, or sending to the minor leagues all surplus players. The player limit is now twenty-five, and the cutdown date is opening day.

CUTOFF: An interception of a thrown ball, usually from the outfield for the purpose of trapping a runner off base or attempting to keep a runner or runners from advancing. If performed properly, it is one of the most exciting and important plays in the game. An example of its importance was evident in the final game of the 1962 World Series.

The Yankees led the Giants, 1-0, with two out in the last of the ninth, a man on first, and Willie Mays at bat. Mays hit a line drive down the right-field line, a ball that normally would score a man from first. But Roger Maris raced over, picked up the ball on the run, and threw quickly to the cutoff, second baseman Bobby Richardson, who had gone into short right field for the throw. Richardson turned and threw quickly, strongly, and accurately to home plate, preventing the tying run from scoring. The next batter lined out, and the Yankees had won the game and the World Series, largely because Maris and Richardson had performed the cutoff play to perfection.

CYCLE: When a batter hits a single, double, triple,

and home run, not necessarily in that order but all in the same game, it is called hitting for the cycle. It is so rare a feat that a couple of years may go by without its happening in the major leagues.

DAFFINESS BOYS: A name to describe the famous Dean brothers of the 1930s, Jerome Hanna ("Dizzy") Dean and Paul Dee ("Daffy") Dean, who came out of Arkansas with little education and captivated the public with their eccentricities on and off the field. Dizzy, the older, more successful, and zanier of the two, became a successful broadcaster and telecaster whose trademark was telling stories in his country jargon and singing country songs on the air.

Once the mother of a young boy berated Dizzy for his horrible grammar on the air, which, she said, was a bad example for her son. "You don't even know the king's English," the woman said.

"Old Diz knows the king's English," Dean protested, "and not only that, I also know the queen is English."

Despite their reputations as characters, the Dean brothers were among the best pitchers of their day. Dizzy won twenty or more games four straight years for the St. Louis Cardinals, is the last pitcher to win 30 games (30-7 in 1934), and amassed 150 victories before his career was shortened by a foot injury. Brother Paul twice won 19 games for the Cardinals, and in 1934 the brothers won 49 games between them, pitching the Cardinals to the pennant, then won all 4 games as the Cardinals defeated the Detroit Tigers in the World Series.

As the Daffiness Boys, *Dizzy (left) and Paul Dean were a colorful combination who pitched the St. Louis Cardinals to the world championship in 1934.*

DEAD BALL: A ball legally out of play that results in a suspension of play. Examples are a fair ball that hits a base runner, or a foul ball.

DEADHEAD: Management slang for a person admitted on a complimentary ticket. Baseball got the expression from the theater.

DEAD RED: An extraordinary fast ball. A pitcher throwing dead red is throwing "small baseballs" or "aspirin tablets."

DEATH VALLEY: The most spacious part of any ball park, so called because to hit a ball there is almost certain death (a sure out). The best known Death Valley is left centerfield in Yankee Stadium, which measures 430 feet to the fence. When the St. Louis Cardinals arrived at Yankee Stadium for the third game of the 1964 World Series, Lou Brock took one look at Death Valley and said, "There's a lot of room out there."

"That's no room," said Curt Flood, "that's a penthouse."

DEEKED: Short for the word *decoy* or *decoyed*, usually used by a batter who expects a fast ball and gets a curve.

DESIGNATED HITTER: A rule adopted by the American League in 1973 in which each team may designate a hitter for the pitcher. That hitter need not play in the field, but he may take a regular turn at bat in place of the pitcher, in any position in the batting order the manager chooses to insert him.

DEUCE: Players' name for the curve ball. The term is a carry-over from sandlot days, when the catcher's signals to the pitcher were simply one finger for the fast ball, two for the curve.

DIAMOND: Originally the infield, which is shaped like a diamond, but now expanded to include the entire field.

DIED: A man who had a bad day is said to have died. If he's on a bad streak, he is dying. Also, a player who has been traded, released, or sent to the minor leagues is said to have died and is spoken of in hushed whispers, out of respect for the dead.

DINGER: Modern expression for a home run, as in "...and then Johnny Bench hit a dinger."

"DON'T LOSE THE GLOVE": A friendly insult tossed at a good fielder who isn't much of a hitter. Sometimes, as an ironic barb, it is directed at a notoriously weak fielder.

DOUBLE: A two-base hit. Also called a two-bagger. Tris Speaker, whose career spanned twenty-two years and four American League teams, hit a record 793 doubles in his career. Stan Musial of the St. Louis Cardinals holds the National League record of 725 lifetime doubles. The record for most doubles in a single season is by Earl Webb—67 for the Boston Red Sox in 1931. Joe Medwick of the Cardinals holds the National League record—64 in 1936. The record for the most doubles in a game is 4, held by many players.

DOUBLEHEADER: Two games for the price of one. Also known as a bargain bill or twin bill. It has been an occasional feature of the baseball schedule since 1882. The second game of a doubleheader has long been known as the nightcap or afterpiece. In recent years, some teams introduced what is called the day-night doubleheader, which isn't a doubleheader at all. It is two games for the price of two games that just happen to be played on the same day.

DOUBLE PLAY: The act of retiring two men on a single play, in a continuous sequence. It is also known as a twin killing and, among players, as getting two. The Philadelphia Athletics made a record 217 double plays during the 1949 season, and the New York Yankees made a record 7 double plays in one game on August 14, 1942. While it is desirable to make many double plays, it is not always a sign of strength, because for a team to make a double play it must have an unusual number of opposition players on base during the season.

The most famous of all double-play combinations was the one known as Tinker to Evers to Chance. Joe Tinker, shortstop, Johnny Evers, second baseman, and Frank Chance, first baseman, played together with the Chicago Cubs from 1902 to 1912 and helped the Cubs win three straight pennants, in 1906, 1907, and 1908. Although this double-play combination was not the greatest of all time, it was the most feared of its day and inspired Franklin P. Adams (the famed FPA) of the *New York Evening Mail* to immortalize them with this poem:

> These are the saddest of possible words:
> "Tinker to Evers to Chance."
> Trio of bear Cubs and fleeter than birds,
> "Tinker to Evers to Chance."
> Ruthlessly pricking our gonfalon bubble,
> Making a Giant hit into a double—
> Words that are heavy with nothing but trouble:
> "Tinker to Evers to Chance."

DOUBLE STEAL: Two base runners successfully stealing bases on the same play.

DOWN THE ALLEY: Pitch thrown through the middle of the strike zone, frequently the automatic strike.

DRAFT: There are two. One is the free-agent draft, an annual auction during which clubs get to choose, in reverse order of how they finished the previous season, the eligible high school and college players who are free to be selected. The other permits a team to select players from other teams when they have spent a certain number of years in the minor leagues without promotion.

DRAG BUNT: A bunt pulled down the first-base line by a left-handed hitter. A bunt in the same direction by a right-handed hitter is a push bunt. A bunt toward the third-base line by either type of batter is dropped or dumped, while "laying one down" is an expression that applies to bunting in general. A drag bunt is the favorite device of many fast runners because it is a virtual certainty that they will make first base safely if the bunt is well placed. Among the more effective drag bunters have been Mickey Mantle of the Yankees and Maury Wills of the Dodgers.

DUGOUT: The area that houses seating facilities for players, substitutes, and other team members not in the game. It gets its name from the fact it is dug into the ground so that part of the dugout is below the playing field.

DUST BOWL: A field that has not been watered enough so that, at times, players feel like they are actors in the film *Lawrence of Arabia*.

DUSTER: A pitch thrown close to the batter's head, its intention being to keep the batter from taking a toehold at the plate. Unlike the beanball, a duster does not usually hit a batter, but accidents can happen, and some dusters become beanballs, intentionally or otherwise. Also called a brushback pitch. When a player has been dusted or brushed back so that he has to fall to the ground to avoid being hit, he says he was decked or flipped. If he is hit, he has been beaned (in the head) or plugged (elsewhere).

EARNED RUN: A run for which the pitcher is held accountable, as opposed to an unearned run, which scores as the direct or indirect result of an error, passed ball, interference, or obstruction.

EARNED-RUN AVERAGE: A method of evaluating the efficiency of a pitcher, determined by dividing the total number of earned runs off his pitching by the total number of innings he has pitched, then multiplying by nine. This gives you the pitcher's earned-run average, or ERA, for a 9-inning game—that is, the number of earned runs he has allowed for every 9 innings. Anything under three earned runs per game is considered particularly efficient. The lowest ERA on record for 300 innings or more is 1.12 by Bob Gibson of the St. Louis Cardinals in 1968.

EMERY BALL: A ball that has been illegally roughed up by rubbing a piece of emery paper over its surface, causing it, when thrown, to soar, dip, or fade

suddenly and unexpectedly. This was a common practice in the 1920s, but it was declared illegal. Pitchers no longer throw emery balls—unless they can avoid being caught.

ERROR: Fielding mistake charged for each fumble, muff, or wild throw that prolongs the time at bat of a batter or the stay of a runner on base or that permits a runner to advance or a batter to reach base safely. Kicking one or booting one is the players' usual parlance for making an error. Errors have become less frequent through the years as players' skills and their gloves improve.

EXHIBITION GAME: A baseball game that has no bearing on the official records of either the players or teams, such as spring-training games and barnstorming games. Teams play a full schedule of from 20 to 30 exhibition games in spring training in order to (1) help defray spring-training expenses by charging admission, (2) gain advance publicity, and (3) enable the manager to evaluate the strengths and weaknesses of both his team and the opposition. An annual exhibition game is played each year at the Baseball Hall of Fame in Cooperstown, N.Y., as part of a ceremony during which members are inducted into the Hall of Fame. In recent years exhibition games have also been scheduled during the season, usually for the benefit of charity.

EXPLODES: What Nolan Ryan's fast ball does. Recently the word has taken on a new meaning, and it is the result of the nimble brain of Bill Veeck, baseball's master promoter. When he was president of the Cleveland Indians (having gone there following a similar job with the St. Louis Browns), Veeck introduced all kinds of promotional stunts, the most famous of which was the construction of a huge scoreboard that set off fireworks, rockets, blaring trumpets, and other noise each time a member of the home team hit a home run. It became known as Bill Veeck's exploding scoreboard and is still in use in Cleveland, although Veeck has long since departed. He went to Chicago and introduced his exploding scoreboard there too, and it also still remains, though Veeck himself was absent from Chicago for more than a decade, until 1976.

EXTRA-BASE HIT: A hit that is good for more than one base—i.e., a two-base hit (double), three-base hit (triple), or four-base hit (home run). Also called long hits. Babe Ruth holds the record for having made 119 extra-base hits in one season ((44 doubles, 16 triples, and 59 home runs in 1921), and five players have made 5 extra-base hits in one game; the last to do so were Joe Adcock of the Milwaukee Braves, who hit 4 home runs and 1 double on July 31, 1954; Lou Boudreau, who hit 4 doubles and 1 home run for Cleveland on July 14, 1946;

and Willie Stargell, who hit 2 home runs and 3 doubles for Pittsburgh on August 1, 1970.

EXTRA INNINGS: When a game is tied after 9 innings, play continues until one team has scored more runs than the other in an equal number of completed innings, or until the team batting last takes the lead. On May 1, 1920, the Boston Braves and the Brooklyn Dodgers struggled through a 1-1, 26-inning game, the longest ever played in the major leagues. Both starting pitchers, Joe Oeschger and Leon Cadore, went all the way.

On May 31, 1964, the New York Mets and San Francisco Giants played 23 innings, the Giants winning, 8-6, in the second game of a doubleheader. It was the longest game ever played in the major leagues, the game ending at 11:18 P.M., exactly 7 hours and 32 minutes after it started. The longest night game started on September 11, 1974, and ended 25 innings (7 hours and 4 minutes) later, the following morning at Shea Stadium, Flushing, N.Y. The antagonists were the New York Mets and the St. Louis Cardinals.

FADEAWAY: Obsolete term for what is now known as the screwball, or reverse curve. Used with great success by Christy Mathewson, a New York Giant great from 1900 to 1916, when Matty's fadeaway was the scourge of batters.

FAIR BALL: A legally batted ball that is hit within the foul lines.

FAN: To strike out swinging; to fan the breeze. The term is also applied to a rooter or a supporter of a team or of baseball in general, and is a short form of the word *fanatic*.

FARM SYSTEM: Branch Rickey introduced chain-store baseball when he was running the St. Louis Cardinals in the 1920s. Big-league players had been optioned to the minors as far back as 1887, but Rickey was the first to build a network of farm teams controlled by the parent club either through ownership or through exclusive agreements. Other teams borrowed the idea after it began producing pennants for the Cardinals.

There is, of course, more to the farm system than acquiring teams. The secret of success is to keep the farms (or minor leagues) stocked with good players and to know which players to advance and which to sell, and when. In addition to scouts who can dig up the right players, the operation requires someone at the top like Rickey, who knew what scouts to hire and what countermoves to make against the antifarm legislation that is constantly cooked up by the have-not organizations.

FAST BALL: Also fireball, high hard one. A ball pitched at the top speed of a particular pitcher. The most frequently used pitch in the game.

FAT ONE: A ball pitched right down the middle, easy to hit.

FENCE: Outfield fences have two major effects on the game. Their height and distance from the plate help govern the number of home runs and they also affect fielding, as outfielders must learn how far and at what angle a ball is likely to bounce off a given fence. Most major-league parks were built before distance hitting, or fence-busting, came into vogue, and for many years the fences were beyond the range of the hitters. To keep up with the home-run craze, stands have been built in order to shorten some parks, while inner fences have been strung across the outfields of others. The following shows distances to the left-, center- (farthest point), and right-field fences in each park.

AMERICAN LEAGUE

	L	C	R
Baltimore	309	410	309
Boston	315	420	302
California	333	404	333
Chicago	352	400	352
Cleveland	320	400	320
Detroit	340	440	325
Kansas City	330	410	330
Milwaukee	320	402	362
Minnesota	330	430	373
New York	313	419	310
Oakland	330	400	330
Texas	330	400	330

NATIONAL LEAGUE

	L	C	R
Atlanta	330	400	330
Chicago	355	400	353
Cincinnati	330	404	330
Houston	340	406	340
Los Angeles	330	395	330
Montreal	340	420	340
New York	341	410	341
Philadelphia	330	408	330
Pittsburgh	335	400	335
St. Louis	330	404	330
San Diego	330	410	330
San Francisco	335	410	335

FIELD: To handle a batted or thrown ball while on the defense. Also, the area in which opponents do battle.

FIELDER'S CHOICE: The act of a fielder who handles a ground ball and throws to some base other than first, attempting to retire a runner already on base rather than the batter. There is the assumption that the fielder could have retired the batter, but chose to make a play on the preceding runner. Whether or not the fielder completes the play successfully, the batter is scored as having hit into a fielder's choice and is charged with an official time at bat and no hit.

FINE: An assessment against a player made by his manager, owner, league president, or the commissioner for any action deemed detrimental to his team, league, or all of baseball, or for violating any rule set down by his team, league, or baseball. In 1925 the largest fine ever levied on a player was slapped on Babe Ruth. His manager, Miller Huggins, had had his fill of the Babe's consistent violation of training regulations, so he fined Ruth $5,000 and made it stick.

However, there is a story that when Joe McCarthy succeeded Huggins as Yankee manager, he got Babe's $5,000 back, in an effort to win the big guy over. Babe also suffered the second largest fine, this one from Commissioner Landis in 1921. The Babe hit 59 home runs that year, and after the season he lined up an exhibition tour, which was against league rules. When Landis found out about it, he fined Babe his entire check from the 1921 World Series ($3,362.26) and suspended him until May 20, so that Ruth also lost a month's pay.

The largest fine in National League history came in 1965 and was assessed against pitcher Juan Marichal of the San Francisco Giants. Marichal, afraid of being hit by John Roseboro, catcher for the Los Angeles Dodgers, hit Roseboro on the head several times with a baseball bat. Marichal was censured by league president Warren Giles, suspended nine days in the midst of a close pennant race, and fined $1,750.

FIREMAN: *See* Relief Pitcher.

FIRST BALL: A pregame ceremony most commonly associated with opening day of the season and the President of the United States. It all began in 1910 when President William Howard Taft attended the year's inaugural between the Washington Senators and the Philadelphia Athletics. As an added touch, Taft tossed out the first ball from his box seat and began what has become a ritual practiced by every President since then with the exception of Gerald Ford. Over the years the first-ball happening has been extended to cover other significant games, such as the playoffs and World Series, and assorted dignitaries are usually tapped for the tossing.

FIRST BASE: The base to which the batter runs first, a 15-inch-square bag located diagonally to the right and 90 feet from home plate. The defensive player whose duty it is to cover the area around first base is the first baseman.

FLAKEY: A term, usually of endearment, to describe a player who is slightly eccentric, offbeat, kooky. Tops among the baseball flakes is Phil Linz, formerly with the New York Yankees, who earned the distinction because of stories like this:

During the 1963 spring-training season, Linz experimented with contact lenses, but abandoned them after a run-in with Fort Lauderdale police.

"I was driving to the ball park when I was stopped by a motorcycle cop," Linz explained. "He said I was exceeding the speed limit and asked to see my driver's license."

"This license says you're supposed to wear glasses when you drive," the policeman said.

"That's all right," replied Linz. "I've got contacts."

"I don't care who you know," said the cop, "you're still getting the ticket."

See? Flakey.

FLY BALL: A batted ball that goes high in the air.

FLY-OUT: A fairly hit ball that is caught before it touches the ground by a fielder—usually, but not necessarily, an outfielder.

FOOT IN THE BUCKET: A batting stance in which the front foot is withdrawn toward the foul line (toward the old water bucket in the dugout) instead of pointing toward the pitcher. Often such a stance is a sign of timidity, the foot being planted that way to give the batter a head start in getting out of the way of a close pitch. But the foot-in-the-bucket stance has been used by a number of outstanding hitters, among them Al Simmons, who had a lifetime batting average of .334 for twenty big-league seasons; Roy Campanella; and Arky Vaughn.

FORCED OUT: A fielder retiring a base runner by touching the base to which the runner is forced to advance. The only time a force play arises is when there is a runner on first base, runners on first and second, or runners on first, second, and third, and a batted ball hits the ground, either in the infield or the outfield.

FORFEIT: Any one of several rules violations, most of them concerned with the failure to appear or refusal to continue playing, may cause the umpire to declare the game forfeited. The forfeit score in baseball is 9-0 in favor of the offended team.

FORK BALL: A ball that is pitched by holding it at the top with the index and middle fingers wide apart (as a fork) and at the bottom by the thumb, and that, in its delivery, breaks down as does the knuckle ball. The leading exponent of the fork ball was Elroy Face, who popularized it by using it to win 18 games and lose 1 for the Pittsburgh Pirates in 1959.

FOUL BALL: Any legally batted ball that lands in foul territory, whether it be a fly ball or a ground ball, a ball tipped by the batter or one hit out of the park. A

President William Howard Taft threw out the first ball
in 1910.

foul ball is a strike, unless it is caught on the fly by a fielder, in which case the batter is out. If a ball is tipped by the batter, it is a strike; if there are already two strikes on the batter, the batter is out, the pitcher being credited with a strikeout. A foul ball is not an automatic third strike if the batter already has two strikes on him. However, if the batter has two strikes and he attempts to bunt, and it goes foul, he is automatically out.

FRANCHISE: The right granted by a governing body to operate a business in a particular location. In baseball it is the right granted by the commissioner for a person or persons to operate a team in a particular city. The Cincinnati Red Stockings, formed in 1869, were the first professional team, thereby establishing the Cincinnati franchise. In recent years franchises have been shifted (Brooklyn to Los Angeles, Milwaukee to Atlanta, etc.), but only after permission had been secured from the league and the commissioner.

FREE AGENT: Any player who is not under contract to a team and is, therefore, free to sign a contract. He may be a young player who has never been under contract or an older one who has secured a release from his contract, such as Catfish Hunter, who was declared a free agent by a judge in 1974 because his Oakland contract had been breached. He signed with the New York Yankees for $2.8 million for five years.

FUNGO: A ball hit to the infield or outfield during a practice session. Fungoes are hit with a specially constructed thin, light bat, called a fungo stick. The fungo hitter tosses the ball a few feet in the air, resumes his grip, and swings, directing fly balls at the outfielders or ground balls at the infielders. The practice is usually directed by a coach, and coaches such as Leo Durocher and Johnny Keane took pride in their precision with a fungo stick. A dying art, however, is the trick of fungoing a high pop-up straight overhead for the catcher. The word *fungible* means something that can be substituted for another, and it is thought that in baseball the thin fungo stick got its name because it replaces the conventional bat.

GAME: The game consists of nine full innings, each team having nine turns at bat, except when the home team is ahead after eight and a half innings at which point the game would be automatically completed. A game is also completed if play is suspended (by rain, snow, city ordinance, etc.) after the team that is trailing has been to bat at least five times.

GASHOUSE GANG: A nickname given to the St. Louis Cardinals of the 1930s because they were a collection of rowdy, fiery, daring, hell-for-leather players headed by manager Frank Frisch, Pepper Martin, Ducky Medwick, Leo Durocher, and Dizzy Dean. Frank Graham, then with the *New York Sun*, suggested to Durocher that the Cardinals were so good they could win in any league, including the vaunted American League. "They wouldn't let us play in the American League," Durocher corrected. "They'd say we were just a lot of gashouse players." Graham picked up the expression, started calling the Cardinals the Gashouse Gang, and the name stuck.

GATE: The paid attendance at a given game. The largest attendance for a regular-season game was 84,587, the New York Yankees vs. the Cleveland Indians at Cleveland, September 12, 1954. The all-time record attendance at a baseball game was 92,706, at the fifth game of the 1959 World Series, between the Los Angeles Dodgers and the Chicago White Sox, at the Los Angeles Coliseum. The Dodgers set a major-league attendance record for one season in 1962, when they attracted 2,755,184.

GATE CRASHER: One who gains entry to any event without buying a ticket. Not so common in baseball, because bleacher seats are priced so cheaply. When baseball first started charging admission to games, bleacher seats cost twenty-five cents, and after the fourth inning one could enter the bleachers for ten cents. The price of bleacher seats remained within anyone's budget even after inflation set in. The only evidence of gate crashing in baseball has occurred in the World Series, and even then not by the general public, because the gates are always well guarded. For years a newspaper in Fargo, N.D., would request and receive credentials to the World Series for that paper's sports editor. The editor would, in turn, give the ticket to his dentist, butcher, or grocer. This continued until one year the culprit was discovered, and the sports editor's request for World Series credentials was denied thereafter.

GETAWAY DAY: The last day of a series of games between two teams. The expression refers to the fact that after the game the visiting team leaves for another city, either by airplane or train, to begin another series.

GLOVE: Originally intended for protection of the hand, but now designed as a fielding aid as well. The early gloves were formfitting. As late as 1920 George Sisler's first-baseman's mitt was scarcely larger than his hand. Today's gloves, particularly first-baseman's trapper models, are enormous, wide-webbed affairs that have led to a general improvement in fielding.

GLOVE MAN: An outstanding fielder, also called a leather man. Among the best glove men are Mark Belanger and Brooks Robinson of the Baltimore Orioles. The term is usually, but not necessarily, applied to infielders. Billy Cox of the Brooklyn Dodgers and Marty Marion of the St. Louis Cardinals were great glove men of the recent past.

Baltimore's Brooks Robinson shows what makes a
glove man *in the 1970 World Series against Cincinnati.*

GOAT: Traditional label for a player whose poor performance or mental lapse is felt to have cost his team the game.

GOOD FIELD, NO HIT: Applied to any player who fits the description, i.e., any player who is a good fielder and poor hitter. Mike Gonzalez, a Cuban famed as a judge of players, was with the Brooklyn Dodgers in spring training of 1924 when they sent rookie Moe Berg to Minneapolis. Receiving a request from the Minneapolis club for his appraisal of Berg, Gonzalez wired back, "Good field, no hit."

GOPHER: A pitch hit for a home run. First used when Lefty Gomez pitched for the Yankees. Writers joked about his gopher ball, which would "go fer the stands" or "go fer four bases." The all-time gopher champion is Robin Roberts, who threw 46 gopher balls when he was with the Philadelphia Phillies in 1956. Ironically, Roberts still won 19 games that year.

GRAND SLAM: Home run with the bases full, occasionally called a jackpot. Lou Gehrig hit 23 career grand slams, the major-league record. Henry Aaron holds the National League record, with 16 for the Milwaukee and Atlanta Braves. Ernie Banks of the Chicago Cubs set the record for grand slams in a season, with 5 in 1955, and it was tied by Jim Gentile in 1961, when he was with the Baltimore Orioles. In that year Gentile tied Tony Lazzeri of the New York Yankees, Jim Tabor of the Boston Red Sox, and Rudy York of the Red Sox by hitting 2 grand slams in one game. Since then, Jim Northrup, Frank Robinson, Tony Cloninger have done the same.

GRANDSTAND PLAY: A comparatively easy fielding play made to look more difficult by a player who wants to attract the spectators' attention.

GRAPEFRUIT LEAGUE: General term for spring training, technically referring to exhibition games played in Florida and differing from Cactus League in Arizona. Ostensibly, the idea of spring training is to get the athletes into playing condition, aided by a warm climate, but it has equal if not greater value as an extended publicity stunt that keeps baseball in the headlines for two months before the season opens. Even southern minor-league teams pitch camp away from home on the theory that distance lends enchantment to their doings.

The Chicago White Stockings originated the custom when they trained in New Orleans in 1870. By the 1890s the practice had become general, although the teams were still treated like outcasts. Connie Mack, recalling a trip to Jacksonville with the Washington club in 1888, said, "The hotel clerk made the strict stipulation that the ballplayers would not mingle with the other guests or eat in the same dining room."

Eventually the clubs were welcomed as a tourist attraction. Thanks to a Florida booster named Al Lang, who began going after teams in 1914, the Tampa Bay area has long been the focal point of big-league training activity. As a tribute to Al Lang's foresight, the field in St. Petersburg on which the St. Louis Cardinals and New York Mets play their spring-training games is called Al Lang Field.

GROUNDER: Also ground ball, roller, bouncer, hopper, grass cutter. A batted ball that rolls or bounces on the ground to an infielder or through the infield for a hit.

GROUND OUT: To hit a ground ball to an infielder and be thrown out at first base.

GROUND RULES: Special rules covering conditions in a given park. Most ground rules have to do with whether or not a batted ball or thrown ball is in play if it strikes designated obstacles on the sidelines or on the walls. A humorous incident concerning ground rules occurred during the 1965 World Series. A guest at the first game was Vice President Hubert Humphrey, who sat next to the Minnesota Twins' dugout on the first-base side. It became part of the ground rules for the game that any ball was still in play if it hit the secret-service man sitting on the field guarding the vice president.

HALF SWING: The action of a batter trying to hold up his swing, but failing to do so. Even a half swing counts as a whole strike.

HALL OF FAME: Baseball maintains a Hall of Fame honoring outstanding players, managers, umpires, and others connected with the game. Proposed by Ford Frick in 1935 soon after he became National League president, it was instituted the next year with the election of Ty Cobb, Walter Johnson, Christy Mathewson, Babe Ruth, and Honus Wagner. There are now more than 150 members.

The method of selection has varied from time to time, but under present regulations members are chosen each year from two categories by two independent groups. Qualified members of the Baseball Writers Association pass on players who have been retired at least five years and not more than twenty years, while a committee on veterans considers players of the more distant past and others who had distinguished themselves in various branches of the game.

Each year a baseball game between two major-league teams is played in conjunction with the induction of new members into the Hall of Fame. The actual Hall of Fame, containing bronze likenesses of those elected, is a room in the Baseball Museum in Cooperstown, N.Y., a site chosen in the now-disputed belief that baseball was invented there by Abner

Babe Ruth's plaque hangs with the other immortals in
the Baseball Hall of Fame in Cooperstown, N.Y.

Doubleday. Ironically, Doubleday is not in the Hall of Fame.

In addition to the bronze likenesses of the members, there are other mementos in the Hall of Fame that help make it a favorite tourist attraction. Among them are the bench Connie Mack sat on in the Philadelphia Athletic dugout for many years; a ball used in 1866; Stan Musial's spikes; the baseball with which Cy Young won his five-hundredth game; the lockers of Honus Wagner, Babe Ruth, Lou Gehrig, and Joe DiMaggio; and the sliding pads used by Ty Cobb when he stole 96 bases in 1915.

Besides the players, managers, and umpires elected to the Hall of Fame, the following persons have also been honored: Morgan Bulkeley, first president of the National League; Henry Chadwick, early baseball writer credited with inventing the box score; Kenesaw Mountain Landis, first commissioner; and Alexander Cartwright, whom many historians recognize as the true founder of baseball rather than Doubleday.

HANDCUFFED: Applicable to a fielder if he cannot handle a hard-hit ball or a hitter if he is unable to make a hit during a game.

HANDLE HIT: Disparaging term for a hit that falls safe though the batter fails to get solid wood on the ball.

HEADS UP: Said of a player who is constantly on the alert, always ready to take advantage of the slightest lapse by the opposition.

HEAT: A fast ball. Also, hard stuff or heater.

HIT: A hit, safety, safe blow, bingle, or base knock is a batted ball on which the batter reaches base without benefit of an error, fielder's choice, interference, or the retirement of a preceding runner. A one-base hit is a single, a two-base hit a double, a three-base hit a triple, and a four-base hit a home run.

The official scorer decides whether or not a hit shall be credited. Most hits are obvious and some are automatic, such as when a batted ball strikes an umpire or runner before touching a fielder, but there are close decisions in almost every game.

To the casual fan many a hit looks like an error. But the scorer must allow for such things as freak hops or drives that are smashed too hard for the fielder to handle smoothly. Often when a slow ground ball is fumbled, it will still be scored as a hit. Usually this brings a hoot from the stands, but the scorer may well have been justified in deciding that the batter would have beaten it out even if the ball had been fielded cleanly.

Ty Cobb is baseball's all-time hit producer, having smacked out 4,191 in his twenty-four-year major-league career. Stan Musial's 3,630 for twenty-two years is tops in the National League. George Sisler made the most

hits in one season, 257 for the St. Louis Browns in 1920 and 3 more than Lefty O'Doul made for the Philadelphia Phillies in 1929 and Bill Terry for the New York Giants a year later. O'Doul and Terry share the National League record.

Many players have had 6 hits in one game, but Rennie Stenett of Pittsburgh made 7 hits in a 9-inning game in 1975 and John Burnett of the Cleveland Indians made 9 hits in an 18-inning game in 1932.

The standard of excellence is 200 hits in a season, and Cobb did it nine times, a record. He is only one of eight to make more than 3,000 hits in a career, and the only one to make more than 4,000.

The team record for hits in a season is 1,783 by the Philadelphia Phillies in 1930. The New York Giants made 31 hits in a game in 1901, and the Boston Red Sox made 14 hits in one inning in 1953.

HIT AND RUN: Prearranged play in which the runner on first starts for second as the ball is pitched and the batter swings. Ideally, the batter pokes a hit through the spot vacated by an infielder who was drawn away to cover the base runner. This is a rare happening and used to be practiced with particular success by Maury Wills and Jim Gilliam of the Los Angeles Dodgers, but the hit and run can still be an effective weapon in avoiding double plays even if the batter does not achieve the desired result. The run and hit differs slightly from the hit and run in that the batter is not committed to hit at the ball in the run and hit unless the pitch is to his liking.

HIT BATTER or **HIT BY PITCH:** A batter hit by a pitched ball is entitled to first base, a rule that traces to 1884, when a minor-league pitcher named Will White made a fetish of hitting batters in order to keep them at a respectable distance from the plate.

HITCH: A flaw in a batter's swing, considered undesirable because it is contrary to the theory that a batter must have a smooth swing to be effective. Many hitters have been successful even with a hitch, the most notable being Walker Cooper, a catcher with the St. Louis Cardinals and New York Giants in the 1940s and 1950s, who dropped his bat before every pitch but had such powerful wrists that he always got the bat back into hitting position in time.

HIT THE DIRT: Ballplayers' slang meaning "to slide." Also, to fall hurriedly to the ground to avoid being hit by a pitched ball.

HOLDOUT: Player who delays signing his contract to bargain for more money. The most celebrated baseball holdout was Edd Roush, the old Cincinnati Red and New York Giant outfielder. In 1929 Roush hit .324 for the Giants in the last year of a three-year contract calling for $21,500 a year. Roush expected a

Nobody produced more hits than Ty Cobb, whose 4,191 safeties are not likely to be surpassed.

raise, but when the Giants sent him his 1930 contract, it called for a cut. Roush and the Giants entered into a bitter dispute, with neither backing down on their original demand. As a result, Roush sat out the entire 1930 season as a matter of principle.

In 1919 Zack Wheat, the great Brooklyn Dodger outfielder, was unhappy with his contract. A war of nerves resulted between Wheat and Dodger owner Charley Ebbets. It was settled when Abe Yaeger, sports editor of the *Brooklyn Eagle*, sent the following wire to Wheat from the Dodgers' spring-training headquarters: "Report immediately." It was signed "Charley Ebbets." When Wheat reported he had a good laugh with Ebbets over the joke and then signed his contract.

Babe Ruth frequently held out. He once insisted on a raise over his previous year's salary of $50,000. Yankee owner Col. Jake Ruppert thought $50,000 was ample. The Babe settled for $50,001.

Thanks to Babe's insistence on value for value, ballplayers' salaries in general were raised. In 1965 Willie Mays of the San Francisco Giants signed for the then highest salary of all time, $105,000, joining Joe DiMaggio, Stan Musial, Ted Williams, and Mickey Mantle in the $100,000 bracket. Since then, player salaries have soared over the $250,000 mark.

HOME RUN: A four-base hit, also known as a homer; round tripper; four-bagger; four-ply swat, blow, or wallop; circuit blow; four master; or circuit clout. It is usually a ball driven out of the playing field, but a ball hit within the park that allows the batter to circle the bases also counts as a home run.

Babe Ruth set the big-league standard of 60 home runs in one season (1927) and 714 for a career, records that lasted for years and were presumed unbreakable.

But in 1961 Roger Maris of the New York Yankees hit 61 home runs and set up a storm of controversy. First, it was said that Maris hit his home runs during an era of the lively ball. Second, it was pointed out that he hit his home runs during a 162-game schedule, while Ruth hit his during a 154-game schedule (Maris had 59 after 154 games). Commissioner Ford Frick decreed that Maris's record would stand, but with an asterisk denoting the 162-game schedule, and that there would be *two* records—Ruth's for 154 games and Maris's for 162 games.

Ruth's career mark of 714 home runs lasted until April 8, 1974, when Henry Aaron hit number 715 for the Atlanta Braves against Al Downing and the Los Angeles Dodgers. Again, defenders of Ruth as the game's greatest slugger came forward to point out that Babe's 714 home runs came in 8,399 at-bats, while Aaron had been to bat over 11,000 times.

In addition to the expressions for a home run listed above, ballplayers have their own slang. They say a batter "hit one downtown" or he "went for the pump." Casey Stengel said that a batter "hit one over a building."

Sportscasters, too, have chipped in with their own expressions for baseball's most satisfying play. Many broadcasters use their home-run call as a trademark. Russ Hodges, who did the games for the San Francisco Giants, greeted each blast with "It's bye bye baby." Others use "it's gone" or "it's out of here."

Whatever they use, you know when it's a home run, a homer, a circuit smash, or a four-ply swat.

HOME TEAM: The team on whose grounds the game is played. By tradition, the home team bats last, which is considered to be an advantage.

HOOK: Another name for a curve ball. Also used to describe what a manager does to a pitcher in trouble: he comes out and gives him the hook.

HOP: A sudden rise taken by a pitch, usually a fast ball. Also, the bounce of the ball. A grounder takes a bad hop when the infielder doesn't catch it or a good one when he does.

HOSE: Also, gun and whip. Slang for a player's arm. A player who has a good hose or gun has a strong arm, while a bad hose means a bad arm, one that is either weak or sore.

HOT CORNER: Third base, so called because of the hot shots hit at the third baseman. Third base is also called the far turn or far corner.

HOT DOG: Not only the kind you put mustard on, but also a player who, the opposition believes, is showing off for the fans or the television camera. A leading hot dog is Reggie Jackson, and going back a few years there was none like Vic Power, a fancy-dan first baseman who had the habit of catching every ball with one hand. Because Power was a Spanish-speaking native of Puerto Rico, hot dog was translated into *perro caliente* for his and his followers' benefit.

HOT-STOVE LEAGUE: Fan-to-fan baseball conversation, discussion, or argument during the winter, so called because of the custom of a group of men sitting around a pot-bellied stove in the local general store to talk baseball.

HUMMER: Ballplayers' slang for a pitcher's fast ball because if thrown fast enough, the ball will whistle, buzz, or hum. "Throw the hummer" and "hum that pill" are two often heard cries of encouragement to a pitcher.

HUSTLE: The desirable quality of trying hard at all times, regardless of the score of the game or the standing of the team. The most well-known hustling

When Henry Aaron hit his 715th home run, *it was a blow
heard 'round the baseball world.*

ballplayer is the Cincinnati Reds' Pete Rose, called Charlie Hustle by teammates and opponents because he runs, does not walk, at all times.

INFIELD: The territory including the four bases and that area within it, although there is no strict ruling on where the infield ends and the outfield begins. Sometimes called the diamond because the infield is shaped like a diamond with the distance from home to second being greater than from home to first, home to third, or first to third. The infield is also the all-inclusive term for the four infielders—the first baseman, second baseman, third baseman, and shortstop.

INFIELDER: One who mans a defensive position in the infield. The first baseman, second baseman, third baseman, and shortstop are generally thought of as a team's infielders, although, technically, the pitcher and catcher are also members of the infield.

INFIELD FLY: A fair fly ball (not a line drive or bunt) that can be caught by an infielder with ordinary effort, when first and second or first, second, and third bases are occupied before two are out. The umpire simply declares "infield fly" and the batter is automatically out whether the ball is caught or not. This is for the protection of the runners, who may advance at their own risk.

INFIELD HIT: A base hit, usually a grounder, which is made from a ball that is not hit beyond the infield. Often called a bleeder or scratch hit.

INNING: That portion of a game within which the teams alternate on offense and defense and in which there are three put-outs for each team. Each team's time at bat is a half inning, and a regulation game consists of nine full innings, although a game can go longer if the score is tied after regulation time.

INTENTIONAL WALK: Deliberate, strategic base on balls. The pitcher throws so wide that the batter has little chance of reaching the pitch. Unpopular with fans, the intentional walk is standard practice in certain situations, most commonly in the late innings of a close game. If second base is occupied and first is not, a dangerous batter may be walked in hope of setting up a double play or a force play. An intentional walk is usually a sign of respect for the batter. In 1969 Willie McCovey of the San Francisco Giants received 45 intentional walks, and Roger Maris of the New York Yankees received 4 intentional walks in one 12-inning game in 1962.

INTERFERENCE: The act of obstructing, impeding, or hindering a play. Interference may be caused by the offense (obstructing a fielder attempting to make a play), defense (preventing a batter from hitting at a pitched ball), umpire (hindering a catcher's throw or being hit with a batted ball), or a spectator (reaching out of the stands to touch a live ball). On any interference the ball is dead, and all runners must return to the last base that was, in the judgment of the umpire, legally touched at the time of interference unless otherwise provided by the rules.

IN THE HOLE: A pitcher is in the hole when he is behind by at least two pitches—two balls and no strikes, three and nothing, three and one. Another meaning applies to the territory to the shortstop's right and the second baseman's left or any other normally unguarded territory. If the shortstop or second baseman goes into the hole to throw a man out, it's an exceptionally good play.

IRON MAN: A player who rarely leaves a game, playing despite minor injuries. Some examples are Iron Man Joe McGinnity, a New York Giant pitcher soon after the turn of the century who often pitched two games in one day; Lou Gehrig of the New York Yankees, who played in a record 2,130 consecutive games. Billy Williams holds the National League Iron Man record, having played in 1,117 consecutive games when he was with the Chicago Cubs.

IRON MIKE: Automatic pitching device. Such machines have been experimented with since 1896, but they did not come into practical use until Branch Rickey, as president of the Brooklyn Dodgers, popularized them for batting practice in training camps after World War II. Now Iron Mike has been perfected to such a point that he can deliver just about every kind of pitch except a spitball. He is the coolest pitcher of them all, he does not need three days' rest between starts, and he never complains about a sore arm or breaks training.

JAKER: A player who habitually begs out of the lineup by claiming an injury.

JAMMED: A batter says he was jammed when he's been pitched close (the intention being to restrict his swing, not hit him).

JOCKEY: Player who rides the opposition with taunts. He is often called a bench jockey because the heckling comes chiefly from the dugout. It is an art and a vital part of the tradition of the game. The taunts are designed to disturb, upset, and break the concentration of a rival player and usually they are given and taken in good spirit, but occasionally they precipitate eruptions and ill feelings. It is legend that in the 1932 World Series the Chicago Cubs so annoyed Babe Ruth with their bench jockeying that in the fifth inning of the third game Ruth deliberately took two strikes from pitcher Charley Root, then pointed to the most distant part of Wrigley Field and hit the next pitch right where he had pointed.

JUNK MAN: Term applied, not necessarily with disparagement, to a pitcher who relies on off-speed

Although Iron Mike *occasionally needs some oil, he is one pitcher whose arm never gets tired.*

pitches and guile instead of a fast ball. It was first applied to Ed Lopat of the Yankees and then to Stu Miller of the Baltimore Orioles.

Garry Schumacher, public relations director of the San Francisco Giants, once described Miller's fast ball as the Wells Fargo pitch—"It comes to you in easy stages."

Dusty Rhodes of the Giants said of Miller: "He's the only pitcher I ever saw that changes speeds on his change-up."

The most famous remark concerning Stu Miller, the junk man, is that he has three speeds—slow, slower, and slowest.

KEYSTONE: Second base, so called because it is often the scene of the most important action in the infield. The shortstop and second baseman make up the keystone combination.

KITCHEN: The high inside portion of a hitter's strike zone. As in "He got in my kitchen with his good heat and broke my dishes." Obviously, it is tough to hit a good fast ball that is high and inside in the strike zone.

KNUCKLE BALL: A pitch thrown by gripping the ball with the fingernails, fingertips, or knuckles and thrown with little effort and no rotation. It is used as an off-speed pitch and is usually acted upon by air currents or wind, which make the ball react in a strange manner. The pitcher rarely knows how the ball will break, and it is a difficult ball to catch and, therefore, a difficult ball to hit. It is also difficult to throw effectively. The leading exponent of the knuckleball, butterfly, or flutterball was Hoyt Wilhelm of the New York Giants, Baltimore Orioles, St. Louis Cardinals, and Chicago White Sox, who had a great deal more success with the knuckle ball than any other pitcher. Other successful knuckle-ball pitchers: Dutch Leonard, Wilbur Wood, and Phil Niekro.

LADIES' DAY: A day set aside when women are admitted free or on payment of a service charge and tax. The St. Louis Browns established the custom in 1912. A provision requiring that the ladies have escorts who must purchase a ticket was abandoned when the Browns found themselves running an impromptu date bureau as girls congregated outside the gates shopping for escorts.

LAUGHER: Ballplayers' description of a game in which they have such a commanding lead they can stop worrying. In their first four years the New York Mets had one laugher—when they had a 19-1 lead over the Cubs with two out in the ninth inning. After that game the sports department of a Connecticut newspaper received a call from a fan:

"Is it true the Mets scored nineteen runs today?" asked the fan.

"Yes," said the newspaperman, "it's true."

"Did they win?" asked the fan.

LAY ONE DOWN: To bunt.

LEAD-OFF MAN: Also known as the leading lady. The first batter in the lineup or in any inning. The lead-off man in the lineup is a very important player because he comes to bat more often than anyone else on the team, and consequently certain attributes are desirable in a lead-off man. He should be an exceptional judge of a pitch and therefore get many bases on balls (Eddie Stanky and Eddie Yost were tops in this category) or he should be an exceptional hitter with excellent speed and one who rarely strikes out (Richie Ashburn and Maury Wills, for example).

LEFT FIELD: The outfield territory beyond third base and extending down that line in fair territory, bordered by the area covered by the center fielder. The outfielder who covers left field is the left fielder.

LEFT-HANDER: Left-handers are known as southpaws, portsiders, and, traditionally and affectionately, eccentrics. This applies only to left-handed throwers, particularly pitchers. There is nothing crazy about left-handed batting. In fact, it is something to be desired, even cultivated.

Left-handed hitters have two advantages. Swinging from the first-base side, they get a head start toward the base and thus have a better chance of beating out ground balls or double-play relays. Second, the average batter is more effective against a pitcher who throws from his opposite side, giving left-handed swingers another edge, since most pitchers are right-handed.

Many batters, naturally right-handed but bothered by right-handed curve balls, turn left-handed in their youth. This accounts for the fact that while fewer than a fifth of the players who reach the majors are left-handed throwers (and the majority of these are pitchers), almost a third are left-handed batters.

LEFT ON BASE: Those runners who are left on base when the third out is recorded.

LEG HITTER: A fast batter who frequently beats out infield hits. Lloyd Waner of the Pittsburgh Pirates was considered the leg hitter supreme. Thanks greatly to his ability to beat 'em out, he set the modern record of 198 singles in a season.

LETUP: *See* Change of Pace.

LINE DRIVE: A hard-hit ball that travels a straight, relatively low course and carries as far as the infielders or farther before bouncing or being caught. Also a blue dart, screamer, rope, or clothesline. A player who hits a line drive is said to have hung out the clothes.

LINEUP: *See* Batting Order.

LITTLE LEAGUE: In 1939 in the city of Williamsport, Pa., Carl E. Stotz started the first Little League, comprised of three teams of neighborhood youngsters, its purpose being to provide summer activity. The following year there were four teams in the league, and soon the idea of Little League began to spread and grow by leaps and bounds.

By 1975 there were nearly three million boys in eight thousand leagues in thirty-one countries in the Little League program. And, indicative of how times have changed, thanks in large measure to a court order, girls are now in the Little League too. There were, in 1975, one thousand girls' softball leagues.

The boys' program culminates with the annual Little League World Series in Williamsport, which is official Little League headquarters. Little League has its own rules and regulations, the most basic of which is that no boy shall be eligible to compete if he will be thirteen years old before August 1 of that year.

LIVELY BALL: *See* Ball.

LOLLIPOP: Slang for a pitch that is ridiculously easy to hit. Sometimes called a cookie. Late in the 1964 season the Cincinnati Reds were involved in a scoreless tie with the Pittsburgh Pirates in the thirteenth inning. The Reds' Leo Cardenas came to bat against Al McBean of the Pirates. With two strikes on him, Cardenas called out to McBean, "You're not going anywhere, throw me a lollipop." McBean promptly struck out Cardenas with his best fast ball.

LONG BALL: A ball that is batted deep to the outfield or out of the playing area. A home-run hitter is a long-ball hitter.

LONG MAN: A relief pitcher who normally comes in early in the game and is expected to pitch five or six innings.

LONG STRIKE: Television commentators' vernacular for a batted ball that travels a long distance but is foul.

LOOSEY-GOOSEY: A player who is calm and loose under extreme pressure.

LOSING PITCHER: The pitcher charged by the official scorer as being the loser of the game. Often referred to as simply the loser. A pitcher is adjudged the loser if he leaves the game with his team trailing and if his team never ties the score.

LOWER HALF: The last half of an inning.

MAGIC NUMBER: Near the end of the season newspapers begin printing the magic number, which indicates the pennant-winning combination in terms of the leading team's required victories and any contender's required defeats. Growing smaller as the victories and defeats accumulate, the magic number dramatizes the approaching end of the race.

To determine a magic number, start with the team that has lost the fewest games (Team A). Add Team B's games won and games remaining and, from this total, subtract Team A's games won. The difference plus one is the magic number, the number that will eliminate Team B.

For example, assume the Minnesota Twins have won 93 and lost 59. The Chicago White Sox have won 89 and lost 63. The schedule consists of 162 games, leaving both teams with 10 games to play. Add the number of White Sox victories (89) to their games remaining (10). Subtract the number of Minnesota victories (93), then add 1. The result is 7, the magic number. Thus, any combination of seven Twin victories and White Sox defeats eliminates the White Sox.

Stated more simply, the idea is to see how many victories the trailing team would have if it won all its remaining games, and how many victories the leading team would need to top that. In the above, the White Sox could win 99 games at most. The Twins, having won 93, would need seven victories to top 99.

MAJOR LEAGUES: The term applied to the American and National leagues combined. Often called the big leagues or simply the bigs or majors.

MANAGER: The field director of a team, usually a noncombatant, although player-managers have not been uncommon, particularly in the minor leagues. Players traditionally call the manager Skipper or Skip to his face and The Old Man or worse behind his back. In print the manager may be the pilot; boss; boss man; or the fearless, peerless, or cheerless leader.

MEAL TICKET: A club's best or most reliable pitcher and one who wins the big games. The name is most closely associated with Carl Hubbell, who won 115 games for the New York Giants from 1933 to 1937.

MEAT HAND: The opposite of glove hand—the hand unprotected by the glove. If a player throws right-handed, this is his meat hand, while his left is his glove hand. Meat hand has no connection with meathead, another expression heard around the ball park.

MINOR LEAGUES: Leagues that are of secondary importance to the majors, yet still considered part of the overall structure of the sport. There have been minor-league teams for almost as long as there have been major-league teams, but it wasn't until Branch Rickey conceived the idea that minor-league teams became aligned with the majors as part of the farm system.

Previously, minor-league teams operated independently. They signed their own players and sold them to the highest bidder when they became in demand. Now every minor-league team is either owned directly by a major-league team or has a working agreement with a major, and more than 90 percent of the minor-league players are owned by the major leagues.

At their peak in 1948 there were 448 teams in 59 minor leagues, but they diminished to 137 clubs in 18 leagues by 1974. Minor-league teams are distributed among graded classifications, namely, AAA leagues, AA leagues, A leagues, and rookie leagues. Previously, there were B, C, and D leagues. The higher the classification, the larger the cities it represents and the more skilled are the players in that league.

MONEY BAGS: Sarcastic term applied to bonus player by envious veterans.

MONEY PLAYER: A player who performs particularly well in important games and/or when money is on the line.

MONKEY SUIT: Player's uniform.

MOP-UP MAN: A pitcher used late in the game when the outcome of the game is no longer in doubt.

MOTORMOUTH: A player who talks all the time. Paul Blair of the Baltimore Orioles is called Motormouth by teammates.

MOUND: Also called the hill. The raised portion of the infield, 15 inches high at its crest. The pitcher takes his position on a rectangular plate, known as the slab or rubber, set into the top of the mound.

MULLION: An ugly person, male or female. The most common putdown of one player to another is to call him a mullion, or to ask, "Who was that mullion I saw you out with last night?"

MURDERER'S ROW: Name given to the 1927 Yankees, considered to be the greatest hitting team ever assembled. There was no weak hitter on the team, which won 110 games led by Babe Ruth's 60 home runs and Lou Gehrig's 47 at a time when home runs were relatively rare.

MVP: Short for Most Valuable Player, chosen annually in each major league by a committee of baseball writers. The practice of honoring outstanding players began in 1911, when the manufacturers of the Chalmers automobile presented a car to the leading player in each league.

The Chalmers Award was eventually replaced by the league awards, sponsored by the two major leagues but with the provision in the American League that there be no repeaters. Thus Babe Ruth, when he hit 60 homers in 1927, was ineligible because he had won it before. Lou Gehrig was named instead.

The league awards were abandoned after 1929, and the MVP award, sponsored by the Baseball Writers Association, has been voted annually since 1931. There is no rule against winning it more than once. In fact, several players have won it three times.

Other important honors include the Cy Young Award for the outstanding pitcher in the major leagues, established in 1956, and the Rookie of the Year awards, one in each league, established in 1949.

NATIONAL LEAGUE: The older of baseball's two major leagues, the other being the American League. Sometimes called the senior circuit. The National League began in 1876 and represented a rebellion against the establishment of the day, namely the National Association.

Early in the 1875 season owners of the Chicago franchise, weary of constant failure, offered the team's presidency to William A. Hulbert, a successful businessman and rabid fan of the Chicago White Stockings. Hulbert asked for a few weeks to consider the offer.

When the champion Boston club came to Chicago, Hulbert met with A. G. Spalding, the league's outstanding pitcher. Hulbert begged Spalding to join him in Chicago. He told Spalding how Chicagoans were anxious to get a powerful team but were unable to do so because of the piracy of the eastern clubs. He listed other evils of the game, including gambling, and when Hulbert promised Spalding a huge contract for the 1876 season, Spalding agreed to come to Chicago the following year. What's more, Spalding helped Hulbert sign his teammates Ross Barnes, Cal McVey, and Deacon Jim White, three of the outstanding players in the National Association.

The deal was not supposed to be announced until after the 1875 season, but it leaked out before the season ended, to the embarrassment of Spalding and his friends.

Now there were rumors that Spalding and the other club jumpers might be expelled from the National Association following the 1875 season, making it impossible for them to fulfill their contracts with Hulbert and the White Stockings. Spalding told Hulbert

of his fears, and it gave Hulbert an idea. He decided to form a new league. He even had a name. Instead of the National Association of Base Ball Players, he would call his new league the National League of Professional Base Ball Clubs.

Hulbert had a formal constitution drawn up, and then he called in officials of the St. Louis, Cincinnati, and Louisville clubs to a secret meeting. He told them of his plan and got a strong vote of confidence. Now he had four teams in his new league, and the next step was to get some eastern teams represented. Hulbert invited the remaining National Association teams to a conference "on matters of interest to the game at large, with special reference to reformation of existing abuses." His summons was answered by all four eastern teams— Philadelphia, Boston, Hartford, and the New York Mutuals.

Hulbert spoke to officials of these teams for an hour behind locked doors. He outlined the evils that were demoralizing the players and fans and charged that the National Association was either unable or unwilling to correct the abuses. He called for a new league and produced the constitution of his National League. He won their complete support, and on April 22, 1876, the National League began play with Boston defeating Philadelphia, 6-5, at Philadelphia, one of eight charter members in the National League.

The National League grew to twelve teams and flourished until 1899, when four teams were dropped. They promptly linked up with an outlaw league and formed the eight-team American League. In 1901, when the American League formally opened play as an eight-team league, teams in the National League included Pittsburgh, Philadelphia, Brooklyn, St. Louis, Boston, Chicago, New York, and Cincinnati.

The National League stayed with that alignment until 1953, when the Boston Braves asked for, and received, permission to move to Milwaukee. In 1958 the Brooklyn Dodgers moved to Los Angeles and the New York Giants to San Francisco.

In 1962 the National League expanded to ten teams, one franchise being awarded to New York and nicknamed the Mets, the other going to Houston and called the Colt 45s, later Astros. Players for the two new teams were taken from a pool provided by the eight established teams, and the schedule was expanded from 154 games to 162.

In 1966 the Braves became the first club to move twice, shifting from Milwaukee to Atlanta after much legal action. Expansion came again in 1969, Montreal and San Diego being admitted to the National League.

With the league expanded to twelve teams, division

play was conceived. The Eastern Division of the National League consisted of New York, Philadelphia, Pittsburgh, St. Louis, Chicago, and Montreal. The Western Division included Los Angeles, San Francisco, Houston, San Diego, Cincinnati, and Atlanta.

As in the American League, the winners of each division meet in a best-of-five playoff series to determine which team will represent the National League in the World Series.

NEW BREED: Name first used by baseball writer Dick Young of the *New York Daily News* to describe unusually rabid Met fans. The term was inspired by the television series of the same name.

NEXT STOP PEORIA: Peoria was a St. Louis Cardinal minor-league team under Branch Rickey, and it became the source of many jokes. In fact, at the annual New York Baseball Writers' show, a song was dedicated to Peoria. Written and sung by baseball writer Arthur Mann, it went, in part, like this:

They promised me glory and gold
Before I was hoary and old.
  I was too young to know that I blundered when
  I signed up for life, batted .400 then
Rickey said, "That boy will do,
Rush him right down to St. Lou."
  He said, "I wish we had more o' ya."
  Yet I wind up that fall in Peoria.

NICKNAMES: Five players named Rhodes or Rhoades have appeared in the big leagues, and all but one were nicknamed Dusty. This is cited to illustrate two points about baseball nicknames: They're almost inevitable in certain cases (a Rhodes will be Dusty and a Watters will be Muddy), and they're not noted for their originality.

Some obvious physical characteristic or personality trait is the most common basis for a nickname. Examples include players named Red, Whitey, or Lefty, as well as Dizzy Dean, Bugs Raymond, Sad Sam Jones, Slim Sallee, Fats Fothergill, Stubby Overmire, King Kong Keller, Moose Skowron, Ducky Medwick for his waddling gait, and Hawk for any large-nosed player (or Schnozz, as Ernie Lombardi was dubbed).

Harry Brecheen was The Cat because he resembled a cat in the way he charged off the mound to field, and Harvey Haddix was The Kitten because he resembled Harry Brecheen. Marty Marion was The Octopus because he appeared to be all arms as he fielded a ball at shortstop, and Emil Verban became The Antelope mostly because he was Marion's second-base partner with the St. Louis Cardinals and it seemed proper that The Octopus should have The Antelope for a partner.

Harold Reese became PeeWee, not because he was small but because he was once a marble champion, and Jim Bouton was dubbed Bulldog because of his tenacity. Cap Peterson got his nickname because his real name is Charles Andrew Peterson and his initials are C.A.P.

Nervous habits lead to nicknames: Jittery Joe Berry, Fidgety Phil Collins, Shuffling Phil Douglas. One of the best of these, coined by columnist Jimmy Cannon, was Hot Potato Hamlin for Luke Hamlin, a pitcher who juggled the ball in the palm of his hand before winding up.

Babe and Rube are baseball nicknames of long standing. Others on this general order, but which have not had such longevity, are Kid and Doc. Bobo, made famous by Bobo Newsom, is now used less as a nickname than as a derogatory label for any player who is thought of as the manager's pet ("He's the old man's bobo").

Many nicknames become famous although their origins are never discovered. Pumpsie Green, whose real name is Elijah, said, "Some day I'll write a book and call it *How I Got the Nickname Pumpsie* and sell it for a dollar, and if everybody who ever asked me that question buys the book, I'll be a millionaire."

Nationalities have produced nicknames like Frenchy Bordagaray, Germany Schaefer, Lou ("The Mad Russian") Novikoff, Shanty Hogan. Years ago almost any Indian or part-Indian player was known as Chief. Almost half of the Spanish-speaking players are certain to wind up being called Chico. There have been Chico Carrasquel, Chico Fernandez, Chico Salmon, Chico Cardenas, and Chico Ruiz.

Charles Dillon Stengel became Casey because he came from Kansas City (KC), but most nicknames of that variety spring from quaint-sounding home towns: Wahoo Sam Crawford from Wahoo, Nebr.; Pea Ridge Day from a town of that name in Arkansas, and Vinegar Bend Mizell from the thriving metropolis of Vinegar Bend, Ala.

Another popular source is a player's skill or his record, whether favorable or not. Denton Young threw so hard he became known as Cyclone, later shortened to Cy. Joe Wood, another fireballer, was to win fame as Smokey Joe Wood. Odell Hale was Bad News to the pitchers he clobbered, and then there were Home Run Baker, Sliding Billy Hamilton, and Swish Nicholson (for his repeated practice swings, which fascinated the fans).

Not very flattering, although the recipients didn't seem to mind, were names like Boom Boom Beck, Line Drive Nelson, and Losing Pitcher Mulcahy for pitchers who continually took their lumps, and Rocky for anybody with a reputation as a rockhead. Of course, if Rocky's given name happened to be Rocco, you could give him the benefit of the doubt.

There were certain inflammatory nicknames that would be saved for the time and place when their use might have the most apoplectic effect. John McGraw liked Mugsy about as much as he liked an extra-inning defeat, while a player who wanted the rest of the day off might have said to umpire Bill Klem, "Where was that last pitch, Catfish?"

But Klem is gone, and the connotation of the nickname Catfish has changed since it's become the name by which the millionaire Yankee pitcher James Augustus Hunter is known.

It has been said that Catfish Hunter got his nickname when he was a boy of six. One day his parents frantically searched for him for hours. When they finally found him that evening, he was at his favorite fishing hole, and he had hauled in a mess of catfish. From that day to this, he has been called Catfish, a story that may simply be the figment of the imagination of Charles O. Finley, Hunter's colorful and controversial former employer at Kansas City and Oakland.

NIGHT BALL: Baseball was first played under lights in 1880 at Nantasket Beach near Boston. A half century later, night ball was introduced to organized baseball at Independence, Kans., and Larry MacPhail brought it to the big leagues by way of Cincinnati in 1935.

Since then, with one lingering exception, every big-league club installed lights and has been playing an increasing share of its schedule after dark. The Chicago Cubs are the exception. Their owner, Phil Wrigley, clings to the notion that baseball was meant to be played under the sun.

At first major-league clubs were limited to seven home night games a season, but the rate kept stepping up until it has reached a point where an afternoon game, except on a Saturday, Sunday, or holiday, is all but passé in most big-league ball parks.

When, in 1971, the Baltimore Orioles and Pittsburgh Pirates played the first World Series game at night in Pittsburgh, baseball was firmly established as a nighttime spectacle.

NINE: A baseball team, so called because there are nine players on a side.

NINE MILES: Dugout term applied to an exceptionally long drive, proving that even baseball lingo is a victim of inflation. The batter used to hit the ball a country mile; now he hits it nine miles.

NO-HITTER: A no-hit, no-run game. A game in which the pitcher permits the opposing team no base hits and no runs for the entire game. No-hitters are rare enough to be a special event, but plentiful enough so as not to be freakish. As a typical ten-year period, take the years 1948-57. In that time there was at least 1 no-hitter in every year except 1949. In all, there were 17 no-hitters during the ten-year span, or almost 2 per year. In 1951 there were 4. In 1965 Sandy Koufax of the Los Angeles Dodgers became the first pitcher to pitch 4 no-hitters, a feat matched by Nolan Ryan of the California Angels in 1975.

A perfect game is a no-hitter in which not one batter reaches base safely, either by hit, walk, or error. In a perfect game the pitcher faces the minimum of 27 opposing batters. Obviously, perfect games are rarer than no-hitters. From 1904 to 1975 there were only 8 perfect games, or 1 for every ten years.

The most famous perfect game came in 1956, and it was the only perfect game ever pitched in a World Series. Don Larsen, a journeyman pitcher who had won 30 and lost 40 in four big-league seasons, pitched it for the New York Yankees against the Brooklyn Dodgers in the fifth game.

After the game, in the madhouse around Larsen's locker, a rookie reporter asked Don, "Is that the best game you ever pitched?"

NO SWEAT: Players say this when they mean there is nothing to be concerned about during a particular situation. However, in 1965 this took on a new and more humorous meaning. During the previous winter Whitey Ford, the great New York Yankee pitcher, underwent surgery to relieve a circulatory problem in his left shoulder. In order to free the circulation, doctors were forced to remove sweat glands on the left side, which did nothing harmful to Ford except make him a curiosity.

It became a gag to see Whitey, after pitching a game, perspiring freely from the right side but not from his left. Therefore, the right side of his uniform was wet and the left side was dry, and if he removed his cap, only the right side was damp.

Because he is such a quick-witted fellow, Ford seized upon the situation as a source of humor.

"I'm the only guy," he would say, "who can get ten days out of a five-day deodorant pad."

OLD FOLKS: Young player's pet name for the oldest member of his team. The Old Folks of them all is LeRoy ("Satchel") Paige, legendary pitcher of the Negro leagues. Paige, who pitched briefly in the American League with Cleveland, St. Louis, and Kansas City, has managed to keep his right age a well-guarded, much-publicized secret. However, it is known he was a contemporary of Babe Ruth. The best guess on Satch's age is "he's fifty-five going on seventy."

ON DECK: The player waiting to follow the current batter is said to be on deck. According to the rules, he

Dodger Sandy Koufax threw four no-hitters.

Don Larsen of the Yankees is moments away from the first perfect no-hitter *in a World Series.*

must wait in the on-deck circle, a chalk-marked area placed halfway between home plate and the dugout. The purpose of the on-deck circle is to speed up the game.

ONE O'CLOCK HITTER: This changes with the times. It used to be a two o'clock hitter when games were played at 3:00 P.M., and sometimes it is a seven o'clock hitter for night games, which start at 8:00 P.M. It means a batter who is the greatest hitter in the game in batting practice (which usually comes an hour before game time), but is a bust during a game. The greatest two o'clock hitter of all time was Tommy Brown, a young wartime infielder for the Brooklyn Dodgers. Brown, who played his first major-league game when he was sixteen, used to keep complete records of his home runs during batting practice. Each year he would break Babe Ruth's home-run record by June at the latest, in batting practice of course. However, in 1953, his last year in the major leagues, he hit only two home runs in 65 games for the Chicago Cubs during working hours.

OUT: The game is never over until the last man is. Each team gets three outs an inning. Failure to reach first base means you're out. *Also see* Forced Out and Fielder's Choice.

OUTFIELD: All the area in fair territory beyond the infield and usually bounded by fences or stands. There is no strict dividing mark between the infield and the outfield. The player who habitually covers any one of the three outfield positions—left field, center field, right field—is called an outfielder. More specifically, he is called the left fielder, center fielder, or right fielder, depending upon the field he covers. Colloquially an outfielder is called a gardener; flychaser; member of the outer garden, outer pasture, or picket patrol; and the entire outfield is often called the picket line.

OUT IN ORDER: A team is out in order, or a pitcher is said to have retired the side in order, if the first three batters in any inning are retired with none reaching base safely.

OUT MAN: Exceptionally weak hitter, sometimes called a lamb, flea hitter, ping hitter, or weak sister. Traditionally, the weakest hitter on a team bats eighth. Often he would bat ninth, except that it is considered humiliating to have him bat after the pitcher, usually the poorest hitter on any team. However, there are exceptions, and it was no disgrace to bat after Don Drysdale of the Los Angeles Dodgers in 1965. An exceptional hitter for a pitcher, Drysdale's season's batting average was higher than any regular on the team.

OUTSIDE: A pitched ball that is away from the batter and out of the strike zone.

OWNERS: That curious band of monopolists who not only own the baseball teams but run the game, for all practical purposes. They are called moguls, magnates, and lords of baseball and, in most cases, the references are more than just figuratively true. It is the owners who make policy for the game and who approve or disapprove expansion and franchise shifts and things of that nature. A typical example of the hypocrisy of baseball is that the owners decide who shall be baseball's ranking authority, the commissioner. Therefore, this sets up a situation in which a man is expected to guide, represent, and reprimand, when necessary, the very men who put him in power.

It used to be that baseball teams were owned by individual citizens whose only interest and only income was the baseball team. That is no longer true. Baseball is now big business, and that is reflected in the ownership of the teams.

For instance, the St. Louis Cardinals are owned by Gussie Busch (Budweiser Beer), the Chicago Cubs by Philip K. Wrigley (Wrigley Gum). And the owner of the Oakland Athletics is Charles O. Finley, a somewhat eccentric business tycoon who made his money in insurance. Nobody is sure what O. stands for, but some believe it was put there by Finley himself, who wants the world to know that he is an Owner and proud of it.

PASSED BALL: The catcher's failure to control a pitched ball that should have been controlled with ordinary effort and that results in a base runner advancing. It is charged as an error to the catcher if the batter reaches first base because of a dropped third strike. There can be no passed ball charged unless there is an advance by a base runner.

PAYOFF PITCH: Pitch following a three-ball, two-strike count on the batter. It is so called because, except for a foul ball, this pitch disposes of the batter. A batter who has reached a count of three and two is said to have "run out the string."

PEG: A throw. For example, an outfielder pegs the ball to third base. Also called whip, chuck, fire.

PENNANT: Materially, a pennant is the commemorative flag awarded to the team that wins a championship. However, the term is more commonly used symbolically for a league championship. Therefore, when it is said the Yankees won the pennant, it means they won the league championship. It is only incidental that for winning the pennant the Yankees receive an actual flag or pennant.

The raising of the championship flag at the beginning of each season is a traditional ceremony in the park of the previous year's league champion. It is a ceremony the Yankees have enjoyed most frequently. Through 1964 the Yankees had won 29 pennants, almost twice as many as any other team. The pennant winners in the American and National leagues meet each fall in the World Series, the winner of which is considered the champion of all baseball.

PEPPER: Traditional warm-up game played on the sidelines. One batter and one or more throwers take positions at rather close range, the batter rapping or peppering sharp ground balls to each of the throwers in turn.

PHANTOM INFIELD: Stunt drill, occasionally put on before exhibition games, in which a team goes through the motions of infield practice—fungo hitter and all—without a ball.

PHEENOM: Modern lingo for a highly touted rookie. Derived from the word *phenomenon* and coined by Garry Schumacher, public relations director of the New York (now San Francisco) Giants, and first applied to Clint Hartung, a player of questionable ability, with the Giants just after World War II.

Hartung, nicknamed the Hondo Hurricane because he hailed from Hondo, Tex., came to the Giants with such a reputation for versatility and great deeds that the major concern was whether to make him a .400-hitting outfielder or a 30-game-winning pitcher. Hartung lasted six years with the Giants, during which time he won 29 games and lost the same number and had a lifetime batting average of .212. Since then, the term *pheenom* has had a connotation of skepticism.

PICK IT: A term of praise used to describe a good fielder, especially an infielder, as in "Mark Belanger can really pick it."

PICK-OFF: To catch a runner off base as the result of a sudden throw from the pitcher or catcher. A good pick-off motion is essential to the success of a pitcher, and therefore many work hard at perfecting their move to first. It comes naturally to a left-hander, but it is rare that a right-hander has a good pick-off move. An exception is Mike Marshall.

PICK-UP: To catch a ball immediately after it hits the ground. Sometimes called trapping a ball or getting it on the short hop.

PINCH HITTER: One batter substituted for another, so called because he is usually used in a pinch, i.e., when there are runners on base late in the game and a hit is needed. Men used as pinch hitters are often players who are not noted for their defensive ability or those who are veteran players unable to perform at peak efficiency if played daily.

Pinch hitting is a valued art, and there have been many successful pinch hitters. Johnny Frederick, for example, hit 6 pinch-hit home runs for the Brooklyn Dodgers in 1932. Dave Philley had 9 consecutive pinch hits (a record) for the Philadelphia Phillies in 1958 and

1959, and two years later he had 24 pinch hits in a season (another record) for the Baltimore Orioles. In the 1965 season Smokey Burgess, playing with the Chicago White Sox, broke a thirty-year-old record when he got the 108th pinch hit of his career, making him the all-time pinch-hit king.

PINCH RUNNER: A substitute runner for a teammate who has reached a base; the original runner is out of the game from that time on.

PITCH: A ball delivered to the batter by the pitcher.

PITCHER: The hurler, twirler, flinger, slinger, flipper, chucker, tosser, moundsman. By any name, he's the man who does the pitching.

PITCHERS' DUEL: A close, low-scoring game that is dominated by the pitchers. Acclaimed by old-time baseball fans as those good old pitchers' duels; discredited by modern fans as those boring pitchers' duels.

PITCHER'S PLATE: A rectangular slab of whitened rubber 24 inches long by 6 inches wide set in the ground on the pitcher's mound. The pitcher's plate is the key to whether a pitcher is making a proper or improper delivery.

PITCHOUT: Pitch delivered wide of the plate on signal when the catcher suspects that a runner intends to steal. It is thrown wide so the batter cannot reach it and so the catcher will have a clear path for his throw. The penalty for the privilege of throwing a pitchout is that the pitch counts as a ball.

PIVOT: The pitcher's pivot foot is that foot that is in contact with the pitcher's plate as he delivers the pitch.

PLATOON: The practice of using two different men for one position, common in football and frequently used in baseball. The greatest exponent of platoon baseball was Casey Stengel, who often had one team to play against right-handed pitchers, another against left-handed pitchers. While the law of averages supports the idea that a left-handed hitter fares better against a right-handed pitcher and a right-handed hitter fares better against a left-handed pitcher, players like Babe Ruth, Joe DiMaggio, Henry Aaron, Stan Musial, and Willie Mays never had to be platooned.

PLAYER REPRESENTATIVE: Baseball has its own union, the Major League Players Association, and each team selects a player representative as a union leader or liaison between the players and owners. It is the player representative's duty to discuss problems with his teammates and to carry all grievances to the owners through the director of the MLPA.

The greatest achievement the players have enjoyed during this arrangement is the formation of a pension plan. Money is contributed to this fund by both the players and owners, and a player who has played four seasons or more in the major leagues can now look forward to a pension in his old age. Monthly pensions range from $200 to $1,000, depending on length of service and age at retirement. The pension plan was started in 1947 after members of the Pittsburgh Pirates threatened to strike. The plan also provides for life-insurance policies and hospitalization for players and their families.

PLAY-OFF: Since 1969, under divisional play in the major leagues, this has taken on a new meaning. It refers to that series of games between champions of the eastern and western divisions in both leagues, the winner of which is declared the pennant winner and is its league representative in the World Series.

While baseball officially chooses to refer to this best-of-five series as the National (or American) League Championship Series, it is more popularly known as the National (or American) League Play-off.

Originally, the reference was to an unscheduled series of games that were required when two (or more) teams finished tied at the conclusion of the regular season. The play-off was necessary to determine the pennant winner.

For the first forty-five years of baseball history there was not one play-off in the major leagues, but there were five in the next twenty years.

In 1946 the Brooklyn Dodgers and St. Louis Cardinals finished the season tied for first place in the National League. It was decided they would play a series of three games, the winner of the best two out of three to be crowned champion. The Cardinals defeated the Dodgers in the first two games, making a third game unnecessary.

The American League got into the act two years later when the Boston Red Sox tied the Cleveland Indians. They decided to play just one game to decide the winner. Cleveland defeated Boston and earned the right to represent the American League in the World Series.

All the National League's first four play-offs involved the Dodgers. In Brooklyn they lost to St. Louis in 1946 and to the New York Giants in 1951. In Los Angeles they beat the Milwaukee Braves in 1959 and lost to the San Francisco Giants in 1962.

The most memorable of all play-offs, however, was the one involving the Brooklyn Dodgers and New York Giants in 1951. Behind by 13½ games as late as August, the Giants stormed back to tie the Dodgers in the last days of the season. The Giants won the first play-off game and the Dodgers the second, setting up the third game as "sudden death."

Going into the last of the ninth inning, the Dodgers led by 4-1. The Giants began hitting Don Newcombe,

the starting Dodger pitcher. A series of hits made the score 4-2, and the Giants had two runners on base with just one out. Dodger manager Charlie Dressen replaced Newcombe with Ralph Branca, and Giant Bobby Thomson hit Branca's second pitch for the most dramatic home run in baseball history. The Giants won the game, 5-4, and the play-off and went right into the World Series, climaxing what has been romantically described as The Little Miracle of Coogan's Bluff. (Coogan's Bluff overlooked the Polo Grounds, where the game was played.)

POP FLY: A ball hit on a high fly to the infield, which is usually easily caught. Also called a pop-up and, when in foul territory, a foul pop.

PRESS BOX: The quarters assigned to reporters at the game, usually equipped with communication facilities. It is the place from which reporters view the game and write the stories that appear in the next day's newspapers. Press boxes have evolved from the old wooden boxes (still used in some minor-league parks) to modern, plush quarters.

In most cases, the ball club does everything possible to make life comfortable for baseball's Boswells, who are a vital part of the history, tradition, and success of the game. In some parks, such as the Astrodome in Houston, the baseball writer sits in a soft, upholstered swivel chair. However, the jurisdiction of the press box rests not with the home team, but with the Baseball Writers Association of America, a powerful national group with a chapter in each major-league city. The local BBWAA in any particular city is responsible for policing the press box and keeping it free of interlopers by enforcing a most rigid rule stating that only BBWAA members and others whose work requires it be allowed in the press box.

This is not to imply that the denizens of the press box perform their daily chores without benefit of levity. On the contrary, baseball writers are renowned for being a fun-loving, sharp-quipping crew.

The most famous press-box story involves Bill Roeder, a former baseball writer who covered the Brooklyn Dodgers for the *New York World-Telegram*. One day in Ebbets Field late in a season in which the Dodgers were involved in one of their typical torrid pennant races with the St. Louis Cardinals, Roeder answered the telephone in the press box. The caller was Tex Rickard, the venerable and colorful public-address announcer at Ebbets Field.

Rickard sat next to the Dodger bench, and on this particular day the scoreboard prominently showed that in the Midwest the Chicago Cubs were leading the Cardinals in the sixth inning. The Dodger players, interested in the game and hoping to protect their financial investment in the race, asked Rickard to telephone the press box and find out who was pitching that game for Chicago.

"Just a minute, Tex," Roeder replied. "I'll check the Western Union ticker and call you back."

Roeder checked the ticker and discovered the pitcher to be Bob Rush, a strong and able right-hander. Seconds later, he called Rickard, who answered the phone with a cheery "Hellooo."

"Hello, Tex," Roeder said. "It's Bob Rush."

"Oh," said Rickard. "Hello, Bob. How are you?"

PROMOTER: Baseball became spoiled because for years it received such a great amount of free publicity that all the owners had to do was to open the gates and the people would come. However, when other professional sports and television began to compete for the entertainment dollar, many club owners realized they had to promote their product, although a number clung to the old notion that baseball did not need promoting.

The most flamboyant and most successful promoter in the game was Bill Veeck, who owned, at different times, the St. Louis Browns, Cleveland Indians, and Chicago White Sox and, not accidentally, set attendance records with each of them. Veeck employed Barnum and Bailey promotional stunts with unprecedented success. He gave away orchids to ladies and established a baby-sitting room so that young parents could go to the ball park and not have to worry about what to do with the kiddies. His stunts were endless. His most famous one was using a midget, Eddie Gaedel, as pinch hitter in a regulation ball game.

Baseball's sideshows, as promoted by Veeck and others like him, are most common in the minor leagues and may feature anything from golf exhibitions to weddings at home plate. They may include fireworks, songfests, clown acts, foot races, beauty parades, giveaway shows, and participation by the players in such events as hitting baseballs into the stands, throwing a ball into a barrel, heaving eggs at each other, and milking a cow.

Veeck was scorned by his competitors, but many of his innovations are still used. Today most major-league clubs have sideshows such as Old Timers' Day, Bat Day, Banner Day, Camera Day, and others, which are nothing more than promotional gimmicks.

Three-foot, seven-inch Eddie Gaedel pinch hit for the St. Louis Browns against the Detroit Tigers in 1951—a stunt conceived by promoter Bill Veeck.

PSYCHED: When a player feels he has attained a psychological and intangible edge on another player, he says he has psyched him. It is a sign of these times that people are conscious of one another's psyche. It is a device used most effectively in boxing by Muhammad Ali, and it has been carried over to baseball.

PULL A ROCK: To make a boner or a mental error, sometimes called a rock.

PULL HITTER: One who consistently and effectively hits a ball down or close to the foul line—left field for a right-handed hitter, right field for a left-handed hitter. It is so called because the action of a right-handed hitter leaves him pointing in the direction of left field when he has followed through. If a right-handed hitter hits to right field or a left-handed hitter to left field, it is called hitting to the opposite field or pushing the ball, a very useful device if done successfully. One who can hit the ball effectively to all fields is called a spray hitter.

PULLING THE STRING: *See* Change of Pace.

PUNCH AND JUDY: Description of a batter who does not swing full force but slaps at the ball, punching it to the opposite field, trying to drop it over the infielders' heads. The derivation of the term is unknown, although it is assumed to have some connection with the original Punch and Judy, a pair of English puppets.

PUNCHED OUT: What a pitcher says, boastfully, when he has struck out a hitter. "I punched him out."

PUT-OUT: The retiring of an opponent by a defensive player.

QUICK PITCH: Also, a quick return. A pitch thrown hurriedly with the obvious intention of catching the batter unaware. If it is detected by the umpire—which often it is not—a quick pitch is called a balk, entitling all runners to advance one base, or, if bases are unoccupied, it is called a ball.

RABBIT EARS: Said of players or umpires who are quick to take offense to needling or jockeying.

RAG ARM: Disparagement of a pitcher who has nothing on the ball.

RAINCHECK: Ticket stub good for future admission if less than four and a half innings have been played before the game is called. Rainchecks were first used in New Orleans in 1888. The word has been taken into general slang, and thus to take a raincheck means to decline an invitation while expressing the hope that it will be good at a later date.

REGULATION GAME: A game that has come to a decision after the prescribed nine innings or more. Also, a game that has been called off, for whatever reason, after the losing team has been to bat five times. If it is called off before that time or if it is tied when it is called off, it is not a regulation game and must be replayed.

RELIEF PITCHER: A substitute pitcher who replaces the starting pitcher or another relief pitcher. Relief pitchers fall into three basic categories—the long man, the short man, and the mop-up man. The mop-up man is usually the man considered to be the weakest or least experienced pitcher on the team. He comes in when the outcome of the game is no longer in doubt. The long man is usually an alternate starter who gets the call when the starting pitcher gets in trouble early in the game, within the first four innings. The long man is expected to pitch anywhere from five to seven good innings.

The short man is the famed fireman, the relief specialist whom no good team can do without. He comes in late in the game when the score is close and the situation is serious but not hopeless. He is the fireman because he is called in to put out the fire (an opposing team's rally).

The fireman is a vital member of the team, and he has gained great prominence in recent years, although his importance was acknowledged as far back as the mid-1920s, when Wilcy Moore and Firpo Marberry were the first of the great firemen. Marberry appeared in 64 games for the Washington Senators in 1926 and was so important to the team that they would push the starting time back so that when Firpo was ready to go to work, late in the game, shadows would have begun to descend and his fast ball would be more effective.

Johnny Murphy was the number-one fireman in the 1930s, but it wasn't until the early 1940s that Hugh Casey of the Brooklyn Dodgers and Joe Page of the New York Yankees put the fireman on the baseball map. Ace Adams appeared in 70 games for the New York Giants in 1943, and Jim Konstanty topped that for the Philadelphia Phillies in 1950, appearing in 74 games and winning the National League Most Valuable Player Award, a first for a relief pitcher. Konstanty's record was broken, and the current mark is 106 games, by Mike Marshall of the Los Angeles Dodgers in 1974.

Today just about every team has a crackerjack fireman as the relief pitcher has become more and more crucial to the outcome of a game. Some teams, in fact, have two outstanding relief pitchers, a right-hander and a left-hander.

RESERVE CLAUSE: The controversial clause binding a player to his team that had been an integral part of baseball for more than 50 years until it was buried by agreement in the summer of 1976. The standard players' contract had stipulated that a player signing for one year also agreed to an option year, at the

Relief pitcher *Hugh Casey saved many a Dodger starter as a fireman in the late 1940s.*

club's discretion. Since players always signed contracts each year before being permitted to play, the reserve clause was, in effect, a contract for life.

Under the historic new agreement, unsigned players in the 1976 season had the right to become free agents at the end of that season; signed players could become free agents after playing out the renewal year in their current contracts; and in future contracts a player with six years' major league service may become a free agent by notifying his club in writing after the season that he wants to be a free agent. Further, a player with five years' major league service has the right to ask to be traded at the end of a season, and he may list a maximum of six clubs to which he doesn't want to be traded. If he isn't traded by the following March 15, he becomes a free agent.

RESIN BAG: A bag that is placed in back of the pitcher's mound and from which he may apply resin, a sticky substance, to his hands in order to dry them, though he may not apply resin to the ball. Resin is the only foreign substance permitted to be applied to the pitcher's hand, but that does not stop pitchers from trying (and succeeding in some cases) to apply some other substance. The purpose of resin is to keep the ball from slipping. It is also used at certain times by a batter when his hands become so moist that gripping the bat is difficult. In recent years batters have switched from resin to a rag saturated with pine tar, another sticky substance.

RHUBARB: A baseball controversy or argument, particularly an explosive one, on the field. Red Barber, the distinguished, longtime baseball broadcaster with the Cincinnati Reds, Brooklyn Dodgers, and New York Yankees, began using the expression on the air in 1939 after picking it up from Garry Schumacher and Tom Meany, baseball writers, who in turn heard the word used by a Brooklyn bartender to describe a barroom rumpus. A synonym, also used by Barber, is, "They're tearing up the pea patch."

RIBBY: Players' slang for Runs Batted In, derived from trying to pronounce the initials by which the term is commonly known, RBI.

RIGHT FIELD: The outfield territory beyond first base and extending down that line in fair territory, bordered by the area covered by the center fielder. The outfielder who covers right field is called the right fielder.

ROCK PILE: An infield that has an unusual amount of pebbles, causing a baseball to take those funny bounces so often talked about. Nowadays infields are attended to very carefully, and most of the pebbles are removed; however, the term is still applied to an infield that is particularly hard and on which a baseball still takes a funny hop.

ROLLER: Slow ground ball that trickles toward the infielder.

ROOKIE: Also, a rook. A first-year player; the term is derived from military jargon. Traditionally, rookies are supposed to be naive, and veteran players often take advantage of this by making them the butt of their inevitable gags. The most famous gag is to give the rookie a message to call a Mrs. Lyons. Upon calling the number given him, the rookie finds he has reached the zoo.

RUBBER: The pitcher's plate.

RUBBER ARM: A pitcher who can work day after day and maintain effectiveness. Such a pitcher is Mike Marshall, a relief pitcher for the Los Angeles Dodgers, who set a major-league record by appearing in 106 of his team's 162 games in 1974.

In baseball history, there have been 39 pitchers who have pitched and won two complete games in one day, the last being Emil Levsen of the Cleveland Indians in 1926. Four men performed the rubber-arm stunt twice, and another, Joe McGinnity of the New York Giants, did it three times, earning him the nickname Iron Man.

RUBBER GAME: The deciding or odd game of a series that will break a tie in that series is called the rubber game.

RUN: The score made by an offensive player who advances from batter to runner and touches first, second, third, and home base in that order. "Let's get some runs" is probably the most widely used and oft-repeated phrase in ball-field history. In 1950 the Boston Red Sox scored 29 runs to the St. Louis Browns's 4, a record tied five years later by the Chicago White Sox, who defeated the Kansas City Athletics, 29-6. In 1953 the Boston Red Sox set a modern record by scoring 17 runs in a single inning.

RUNDOWN: The defensive act that attempts to put out a runner caught between bases.

RUNS BATTED IN: Also known as RBI, or ribbies by the players attempting to pronounce *RBIs*. Credit given to a batter for each run that scores when he makes a safe hit, is retired by an infield or outfield put-out, or when a run is forced in because he becomes a base runner. This is the lifeblood of the offense and the most coveted statistic by hitters, even more than hits, homers, and batting average.

Babe Ruth shares with Lou Gehrig and Jimmy Foxx the record for having thirteen years of 100 or more RBIs, although Hack Wilson of the Chicago Cubs holds the record for the most RBIs in a single season, 190 in 1930.

The following year Lou Gehrig set the American League record of 184. Jim Bottomley of the St. Louis Cardinals had 12 RBIs in one game, and seven players in modern times have knocked in 6 runs in an inning, including Sam Mele, manager of the 1965 American League champion Minnesota Twins, and, most recently, Jim Ray Hart of the San Francisco Giants in 1970.

SACRIFICE: A play in which the batter is out but is not charged with an official time at bat because he has succeeded in moving a teammate along on the bases at the expense of his turn at bat, whether intentionally or not. There are two types of sacrifices, the sacrifice bunt (sometimes called sacrifice hit) and the sacrifice fly.

The sacrifice bunt is laid down, usually under orders, to advance another runner. The batter willfully surrenders his time at bat for the purpose of improving his team's chances of scoring. The sacrifice fly is rarely done intentionally. It occurs only when a batter has hit a ball far enough so that a runner may score from third base after the catch. The batter gets an RBI and is credited with a sacrifice (no official time at bat) only if the runner scores.

SAFE: A declaration by the umpire that a runner is entitled to the base for which he was trying. The umpire signals a runner safe by putting his hands down, palms parallel to the ground.

SAILER: A pitched ball that takes off or sails.

SANDLOT: Informal field, such as a vacant lot, meadow, or yard, on which youngsters play baseball. The sandlots were made practically obsolete by the Little League, but before Little League just about every youngster in America played sandlot baseball. They were largely disorganized teams that rarely had uniforms and played on makeshift diamonds. In some places there were organized teams, after a fashion, but most often a sandlot game would get started just as soon as a handful of boys had gathered.

SAVE: Credit given to a relief pitcher who enters a game and protects a lead for another pitcher, who is credited with the victory. Because the save is a relatively new statistic and because qualifications for a save have varied so frequently, it makes no sense to repeat the record for saves. The latest rules grant a save to a pitcher who meets one of two qualifications: (1) he pitches at least three innings and protects a lead and is the last pitcher in the game; (2) he enters the game with his team ahead and faces one man less than the tying run and finishes the game.

SCORECARD: A printed card that helps spectators identify the players, giving their numbers and positions, and upon which an account of the game can be recorded. Scorecards are sold by vendors in the stands, and the familiar cry of the scorecard huckster is, "You can't tell the players without a scorecard."

Scorecards date back to the 1880s, when a young man named Harry Stevens and another named Ed Barrow sold scorecards in the ball park at Wheeling, W. Va., in the Tri-State League. Barrow went on to great success as general manager of the New York Yankees, and in 1890 Stevens went to New York to sell his scorecards and parlayed them into a multimillion-dollar concessions operation. To this day the Stevens family is the dominant concessionaire at baseball parks, football stadiums, and racetracks throughout the United States.

SCORING: The official scorer, usually a baseball writer, is appointed by the league president. With the job goes a welcome fee from the league and some unwelcome abuse from disgruntled athletes, up to and including an occasional punch in the nose. Apart from the official scorer, who is responsible for deciding on hits and errors and other rulings associated with the statistics of the game, all baseball writers and broadcasters and many fans keep score in books or on scorecards.

Scorekeeping methods vary, but there are a number of fairly uniform basics, including the system of assigning a number for each position. The standard numbering code is as follows: pitcher (1), catcher (2) first baseman (3), second baseman (4), third baseman (5), shortstop (6), left fielder (7), center fielder (8), and right fielder (9).

Fielding plays are recorded by number, with X often denoting a force play. Walks are B or W, strikeouts traditionally are K, or a reversed K (K) for a called third strike. Base-path advances are noted in counterclockwise fashion with home plate in the lower left corner or in the lower center. A hit is usually a horizontal line (two lines for a double, three lines for a triple) intersected by a vertical or diagonal line to indicate the direction of the hit.

The accompanying score sheet is taken from the final game of the 1975 World Series, showing how the Reds beat the Red Sox in the seventh game, 4-3.

Notice that in the first inning Pete Rose started the game by flying out to the right fielder. Joe Morgan struck out swinging, and Johnny Bench grounded out, shortstop to first base.

In the third inning the Red Sox scored first, three runs, to take a 3-0 lead. After Bill Lee struck out swinging, Bernie Carbo walked. Denny Doyle and Carl Yastrzemski singled, Carbo scoring, and when the throw went home, Doyle went to third and Yastrzemski to second.

With first base open, Carlton Fisk was intentionally walked (IW). Fred Lynn struck out looking, but Rico Petrocelli walked to force in one run, and Dwight Evans walked to force in the third run before Rick Burleson struck out.

The Reds retaliated with two runs in the sixth on Rose's single and a home run by Tony Perez. They tied it in the seventh on a walk to Ken Griffey with one out, another walk to pinch hitter Ed Armbrister with two out, and a single by Rose.

The final, and winning, run was scored in the top of the ninth. Griffey again walked and was sacrificed to second by Cesar Geronimo. Dan Driessen grounded out as a pinch hitter, but Rose walked and Morgan singled to center to score Griffey with what proved to be the winning run.

In their final chance in the last of the ninth, the Red Sox went out in order. With Will McEnaney pitching for the Reds, Juan Beniquez batted for Rick Miller and flied to right. Bob Montgomery batted for Doyle and grounded to shortstop. Yastrzemski flied to center for the final out of the game, and the Cincinnati Reds were World Champions!

SCOUT: Expert assigned to gather information on rival teams or, if he is a talent scout, to recruit players. A bird dog is a paid tipster.

SCRATCH HIT: A batted ball that results in a base hit, although it was not solidly hit, usually just eluding an infielder as it dribbles past him.

SCREWBALL: The pitch, not the person, is a ball rolling in a reverse spin off the outer side of the middle finger. Its action is the opposite of a curve ball, breaking away from a left-handed hitter and into a right-handed hitter when thrown by a right-hander and breaking away from a right-handed hitter and into a left-handed hitter when thrown by a left-hander. Sometimes called a reverse curve, it was popularized by Carl Hubbell, the great Giant left-hander, who used it when he struck out

Scoring *the seventh game of the 1975 World Series.*

Cincinnati		1	2	3	4	5	6	7	8	9	Boston		1	2	3	4	5	6	7	8	9
Rose	5	9		14			+	+		W	Carbo	7	+		W	43		34			
Morgan	4	K			+		9	W		+	Miller ⑦	7									
Bench	2	63			8		64	F2		W	Beniquez										9
Perez	3		53		9		∓		5	9	Doyle	4	9		+	53		7			
Foster	7		74		F2		9		63		Montgomery										63
Concepcion	6		63			+		63	53		Yastrzemski	3	43		+	F4		43			8
Griffey	9			+		E4		W		W	Fisk	2	K		14		K		K		
Geronimo	8			DP 463			↗	6		SS4	Lynn	8		W	↗		W		31		
Gullett	1			14 +							Petrocelli	5		K	W		+		63		
Rettenmund						DP 643					Evans	9		FS	W		8				W
Billingham ⑤ 1											Burleson	6		9	K		W			DP 543	
Armbrister								W			Lee	1			K	+	8				
Carroll ⑦ 1											Moret ⑦ 1										
Driessen										43	Willoughby ⑦ 1										
McEnaney ⑨ 1											Cooper										FS
											Burton ⑨ 1										
											Cleveland ⑨ 1										
Totals		0/0	0/1	0/2	0/2	0/1	2/1	1/2	0/1	1/1	Totals		0/1	0/0	3/2	0/1	0/1	0/0	0/0	0/0	0/0

Babe Ruth, Lou Gehrig, Jimmy Foxx, Al Simmons, and Joe Cronin in succession in the 1934 All-Star game. Players call it the Scroogie.

SECOND BASE: The middle stop on the way around all four bases; the base a runner goes to after having reached first base. Second base, colloquially called the keystone, is in the middle of the diamond. The second baseman is responsible for the territory around and to the first-base side of second base.

SECOND-GUESSER: Grandstand manager or would-be strategist. The guy who says, "Alston shoulda had Johnson bunting" after Johnson hits into a double play, but says nothing if Johnson hits a home run in the same situation. Baseball writers are the most notorious second-guessers, but often with justification since it is part of their job.

SEMIPRO: One who receives money for playing, but does it outside of organized baseball and not as his sole source of income.

SENT TO THE SHOWERS: An expression meaning a pitcher was ineffective and had to be replaced. Often he is said to have gone for an early shower. During the summer of 1965 New York City experienced a drought, and city officials appealed to citizens to conserve water. One young citizen at Shea Stadium had his own idea on how New York could help fight the water shortage and made his suggestion in the form of a banner that read: "Save Water—Don't Send Met Pitchers to the Showers."

SEVENTH-INNING STRETCH: The period during a game when fans customarily stand up and stretch and physically announce support for their favorite team by standing just before their team comes to bat in the seventh inning. Nobody knows how the tradition got started, not even veteran baseball writer Dan Daniel, the game's foremost historian. "It just grew, like Topsy," Dan says. "It probably originated as an expression of fatigue and tedium, which seems to explain why the stretch comes late in the game instead of at the halfway point.

SHAKE OFF: When a pitcher disagrees with the catcher's suggestion on which pitch should be thrown, he shakes off the catcher's signal with a prearranged signal of his own, most commonly by shaking his head in the negative or by flapping his glove back and forth.

SHOESTRING CATCH: To catch a line drive. This is usually done by an outfielder, who grabs the ball just as it is about to fall—or off his shoe tops, so to speak. It is one of the most difficult and, consequently, one of the most spectacular catches in the game.

SHORT PORCH: Attractive home-run target, descriptive of overhanging upper deck in some ball parks.

SHORTSTOP: The infield position between second base and third base (sometimes called the short field); the infielder who covers this position.

SHOWBOAT: Derogatory term describing one who plays for the crowd, i.e., shows off. *See also* Hot Dog.

SHUTOUT: When one team fails to score in the course of a game. Also called whitewash, kalsomine, blank. The term *Chicagoed*, now obsolete, was once a favorite. It was so named when, on June 23, 1870, the Mutuals team defeated the Chicagos, 9-0. Thus it was reported that the Mutuals Chicagoed the Chicagos.

The record for shutouts in a career is 113, by Walter Johnson of the Washington Senators from 1907 to 1927. Grover Cleveland Alexander of the Philadelphia Phillies set the record for one season, 16 in 1916. And Don Drysdale pitched 58 consecutive shutout innings in 1968—a record, of course.

SIGNALS: When you see a third-base coach go through all kinds of gyrations, it does not necessarily mean he has ants in his pants. If he scratches his left ear, it may not be because he is itching; rather, he wants the man on first to try to steal second base on the next pitch. These are baseball signals used by the coach to tell the batters and runners what the manager wants him to do in a given situation, and by the catcher to suggest to the pitcher what pitch should be thrown.

Signals are usually very intricate so that the opposing team can't interpret them and thereby anticipate a play. Sometimes they are so intricate that they are missed by the one for whom they are intended, which usually results in the reduction of the guilty player's bankroll. There is, however, no pattern to signals, and sometimes they are so simple as to be difficult to detect.

Charlie Dressen was reputed to be the best at stealing the opposition's signals, and there is a story about a particular All-Star game during which Charlie was sent to coach at third base.

"What signals are we using?" asked one player at a pregame meeting.

"Just use the signals you use with your regular team all season long," Charlie said. "I know them all."

The catcher signals on every pitch, and it is something of a baseball legend that the catcher's signals are one finger for a fast ball and two for a curve. That is an oversimplification. The catcher may be using one finger for a fast ball and two for a curve, but he is actually working in a series. For example, he prearranges with the pitcher that the real signal shall be the second number he flashes. Then, he will put down a series of numbers, for instance, four fingers, followed by two, two, three, one. Since the second signal is the one that counts, the pitcher knows the catcher wants a curve ball because the second signal was two fingers.

The catcher can change the code every inning if he

chooses; however, he usually keeps the same code and becomes more cautious and his signals become more complex only when there is a runner on second base, from where it is easy to see the catcher's signals.

SINGLE: A base hit on which only first base is legally and safely reached. In 1927 Lloyd Waner got the incredible total of 198 one-base hits for the Pittsburgh Pirates, a modern-day record.

SINKER: Either a pitched or a batted ball that breaks downward.

SKIN: That portion of the diamond in the infield that is, by intent, devoid of grass.

SLICE: To hit a ball to the opposite field by accident. That is, a right-handed hitter hitting to right field and a left-handed hitter hitting to left field. While a slice on the golf course can cost you three strokes, on the ball field it can get you three bases.

SLIDE: In order to make a smaller target for the fielder and to make sure not to overrun the base, a runner going into a base will often slide or "hit the dirt." Without breaking stride, he drops to the ground a few feet from his objective. Some players slide on their bellies and go in head first, but the most common slide is feet first, with the player sliding on his side. One of the prettiest and most exciting plays in baseball is the hook slide, in which the runner slides with his body flung away from the bag and hooks the bag with his trailing foot. This is done when the fielder has already received the ball and is waiting for the runner and a conventional slide is useless.

SLUGGER: A heavy or long-ball hitter. Usually the third, fourth, or fifth batters in the lineup.

SLUGGING PERCENTAGE: A method of determining a batter's effectiveness in making extra-base hits, the percentage being obtained by dividing the batter's times at bat into his total bases. For example, if a batter hits a home run (four bases) in four at-bats, his slugging percentage would be 1.000. A maximum slugging percentage would be 4.000, a home run every time at bat. In 1920 Babe Ruth had a remarkable slugging percentage of .847 on 388 total bases in 458 at-bats. For his career, Ruth had a slugging percentage of .692 on 5,762 total bases for 8,324 at-bats.

SLUMP: A long period of ineffectiveness, usually by a batter, but also by a team, a pitcher, or a fielder. Lee Maye once described his batting slump: "I'm nothing for August."

SNAKE BIT: Having extremely bad luck, like a pitcher losing 1-0 and 2-1 games quite often. Origin is unknown, but since baseball was a game played by country boys who know of such things as snakes, that probably was the derivation. Being bitten by a snake is about as bad luck as one can have.

SONGS: Baseball is indeed America's favorite pastime. Even songs have been written about it. The most popular is "Take Me Out to the Ball Game," which has become baseball's theme song. It was written at the turn of the century by Jack Norworth and Albert Von Tilzer and did as much for baseball as it did for its authors. Songs have been written about individual players, the most famous of which was "Joltin' Joe DiMaggio," which was a hit record just before World War II. Other songs have glorifed Jackie Robinson, Willie Mays, and Mickey Mantle.

SPIES: Every so often there is a rash of stories in the newspapers telling of teams being accused of planting spies in scoreboards or buildings in center field for the purpose of stealing the signals of the opposition catcher and passing them on to the batter by various prearranged signals. Usually the accusations are laughed at and vehemently denied and then forgotten. However, the Chicago White Sox were exposed for spying not by the opposition but by one of their own players, Al Worthington, a pitcher of high principles who threatened to quit the team if the Sox did not stop spying. They stopped.

SPITBALL: A ball moistened on a small spot, either with saliva or perspiration, that sails or sinks in an unpredictable manner. For this reason, the spitball (or spitter) is an illegal pitch. The spitball used to be a great weapon for the pitcher, but in 1920 baseball legislated against the spitball as well as the emery ball (roughing one side of the ball with emery paper), the talcum-powder ball (one side of the ball was made slick by the application of talcum powder), and the resin ball.

However, all those who were recognized spitball pitchers then in the major leagues were permitted to continue to use the pitch without penalty for the remainder of their major-league careers. The last of the legal spitball pitchers was Burleigh Grimes, who pitched until 1934. Although the spitball has been illegal for half a century, it is generally believed that at least 25 percent of the pitchers in the major leagues make occasional use of the illegal delivery.

When Don Drysdale of the Los Angeles Dodgers was accused of throwing a spitball, his only defense was, "My mother told me never to put my dirty fingers in my mouth."

Among the common expressions ballplayers use to say a pitcher threw a spitball are: "The bottom dropped out of that one," "That was a wet one," "He loaded that one up," or they shout to the umpire in charge, "Give him a bucket."

SQUEEZE PLAY: A bunt with a man on third and less than two out. If the runner breaks with the pitch, it is called the suicide squeeze. If he breaks for the plate after the ball has been bunted, it is a safety squeeze. In either case, it is a difficult play, but a very effective weapon if properly executed.

STARTING PITCHER: The pitcher nominated to start the game. He is officially in the game once his name has been presented to the umpire-in-chief, and he must complete pitching to at least one batter unless he has suffered an injury that, in the judgment of the umpire, has incapacitated him.

STARTING ROTATION: The order in which a manager uses his starting pitchers, subject to change if one member of the rotation is unsuccessful for an extended period. Ideally, most teams use a four-man rotation (each pitcher working every fourth game), but sometimes it becomes necessary to utilize a five-man rotation.

STATISTICIAN: A fellow who keeps statistics on the game. There are many amateur statisticians, including newspapermen and fans, but each team and both leagues employ official statisticians. The Elias Sports Bureau in New York is the official statistician for the National League; the Howe Bureau in Chicago was the official statistician for the American League until replaced by a computer.

Allan Roth revolutionized the use of statistics for ball clubs when he worked for the Dodgers in Brooklyn and Los Angeles. He recorded every pitch to every batter and kept voluminous records that were invaluable to the team. Should the manager want to know how Joe Blow batted for a season with a count of no balls and two strikes against left-handed pitchers, for example, Roth could produce the answer almost immediately.

STEAL: A stolen base. It is credited to a runner who advances without benefit of batting support or fielding developments. Speed is important, but good base stealers are also adept at taking a lead, getting a jump on the pitch, and sliding. In 1915 Ty Cobb of the Detroit Tigers stole 96 bases, which stood as a modern record until Maury Wills of the Los Angeles Dodgers stole 104 in 1962. Then Lou Brock of the St. Louis Cardinals stole 118 bases in 1974. However, Cobb made his record in 156 games, Wills made his in 165 games, and Brock in 162 games.

STENGELESE: A foreign language not taught at Berlitz. It was the unique double-talk of Casey Stengel. An example of Stengelese follows:

"No manager is ever gonna run a tail-end club and be popular because there is no strikeout king that he's gonna go up and shake hands with and they're gonna love ya because who's gonna kiss a player when he strikes out and I got a shortstop which I don't think a coulda been a success without him if ya mix up the infield ya can't have teamwork and it's a strange thing if ya look it up that the Milwaukee club in the morning paper lost a doubleheader and they got three of my players on their team and you can think it over.... Now ya ask what's wrong with Drysdale and he's pitched too much and I didn't make a success with my pitching staff because they had a bad year all along with myself and..."

Is that clear?

STICK IT IN HIS EAR: Shouted from the dugout to unnerve the opposing batter, urging the pitcher to throw at his head.

STOLEN BASE: *See* Steal.

STRAWBERRY: Splotchy red bruise, usually the result of a slide.

STREAK: A batter is on a streak when he has hit safely in a number of consecutive games. A team is on a winning (or losing) streak when it has won (or lost) a number of games consecutively. A hitter is said to be a streak hitter or streaky if he does most of his hitting in clusters. The most famous hitting streak was by Joe DiMaggio, who batted safely in 56 consecutive games in 1941, a record many observers feel will never be equaled. The longest winning streak by any team was made by the New York Giants, who won 26 straight games in 1916. The longest losing streak is the 23 consecutive defeats suffered by the Philadelphia Phillies in 1961.

STRIKE: A legal pitch when so called by the umpire. A strike can be achieved in the following ways:

1. A pitch is struck at by the batter and missed.
2. A pitch enters the strike zone and is not struck at.
3. A pitch is fouled by the batter when he has less than two strikes.
4. A pitch is bunted foul.
5. A pitch touches the batter as he strikes at it.
6. A pitch touches the batter when he is leaning into the strike zone. It doesn't matter that he hasn't struck at the ball.
7. A pitch is tipped foul by the batter.

STRIKEOUT: Retirement of the batter due to his being charged with three strikes. Sometimes called whiffing or fanning a batter. The ultimate in effectiveness for a pitcher. Nolan Ryan of the California Angels holds the record for having struck out the most batters in one season (383) and shares with Tom Seaver of the New York Mets and Steve Carlton of the St. Louis Cardinals the record for having struck out the most batters in one game (19).

STRIKE ZONE: That space over home plate that is between the batter's armpits and the top of his knees when he assumes his natural stance. A pitch must be

The classic, formful Joe DiMaggio swing produced a hitting streak of 56 games in 1941.

thrown in that zone to be called a strike if it isn't hit by the batter.

SUBMARINE: An underhand delivery. A difficult pitch, since the pitcher throws from an elevation. Submarine pitchers are a vanishing breed. The most recent one to use that delivery with any effectiveness was Ted Abernathy of the Cubs, Braves, and Reds. Ballplayers, in describing his motion, used to say, "He comes from out of the ground."

SUN FIELD: That part of the field where the sun shines most, making the position more difficult to play. The most notorious sun field in baseball is left field at Yankee Stadium during the time of a World Series, and many games have been lost there by fly balls lost in the sun. A new twist was added during the 1952 World Series when Billy Loes, a somewhat eccentric pitcher for the Brooklyn Dodgers, insisted he lost a ground ball in the sun.

SUPERSTITION: Baseball has bred many superstitions, including the belief that finding a hairpin would bring a base hit, spotting a wagonload of barrels or hay would insure good luck, a pitcher who struck out the first batter would be sure to lose, the man who led off an inning with a triple would die at third base, and the player who makes a sensational fielding play would be the first to come to bat the following inning.

Most superstitions are out of date, but ballplayers and managers still wear the same shirt or tie throughout a winning streak, shun number 13 or else make a point of wearing it, and insist on touching or not touching a certain base going on and off the field.

Leo Durocher, when he coached at third base, always made certain to erase with his spikes the chalk markings that designated the coaching box. An almost universal superstition among players is their avoidance of any reference to a no-hit game if a pitcher is in the process of pitching one, although many pitchers who are not superstitious will take pressure off by mentioning their own no-hitter.

Somebody once asked Babe Ruth if he had any superstitions. "Just one," the Babe said. "Whenever I hit a home run, I make certain I touch all four bases."

SUSPENDED GAME: A called game that at a later date is to be resumed from the very point at which it was suspended.

SWINGING BUNT: A topped ball by the batter that dribbles slowly. It's not meant to be a bunt, but the ball travels no farther than a bunt after a full swing.

SWITCH-HITTER: Batter who swings from either side of the plate, hitting left-handed against right-handed pitchers and right-handed against left-handed pitchers. At one time switch-hitters were rare, and for years the only truly successful ones were Frank Frisch and Red Schoendienst. Then, along came Mickey Mantle to switch-hit with such amazing success that switch-hitting became the vogue. During the 1965 World Series the Los Angeles Dodgers presented an infield in which all four members—Wes Parker, Jim Lefebvre, Maury Wills, and Jim Gilliam—were switch-hitters.

TAG: The action of a fielder in touching a runner with the ball or with his hand or glove holding the ball in order to register an out.

TAG UP: To maintain contact with the base the runner is entitled to with the intention of advancing after a ball is caught.

TAKE: To let a pitched ball go by without swinging. When a coach wants a batter to let a pitch go, he gives the take sign. Small boys often use "taking a pitch" to mean swinging at it, but in grown-up baseball the meaning is just the opposite.

TAKE-CHARGE GUY: A player who assumes the leadership of a team, particularly during a situation of stress.

TATER: Ballplayers' current slang for a home run, arrived at by a long process. Originally, 'tater, slang for potato, was a synonym for *baseball*, just as *pill*, *apple*, and *seed* are. Later, a home run was a *long 'tater*. Then it was shortened to just *tater*.

TEE OFF: To hit a ball hard. The term is taken from golf, which is not surprising, because since the days of Babe Ruth baseball players have been avid golfers. Each year, in fact, during spring training there is a baseball players golf tournament. Among the more adept golfing baseball players in recent years have been Alvin Dark, Peanuts Lowery, Albie Pearson, Ken Harrelson, and Wayne Granger.

TEXAS LEAGUER: A looping fly ball that drops safely just beyond the infield and just in front of an outfielder. So called because before the turn of the century the parks in the Texas League were particularly small. Puny hits of this and other varieties are also known as sea gulls, dying swans, bloopers, bleeders, banjo hits, and scratch hits.

THIRD BASE: The base to which the runner hopefully heads after having reached second base safely. It is located diagonally to the left of home plate and is 90 feet away from home and 90 feet away from second base. The player who covers third base is the third baseman.

THREADS: Clothes. Also called vines.

THUMBED OUT: To be banished from a game by an umpire for any number of reasons, most common of which is disputing a call. A ballplayer thrown out of a game is said to have been thumbed, given the thumb, chased, ejected. Joe Garagiola tells a story about disputing an umpire's call and growing so incensed that he threw his catcher's mask 20 feet into the air. "If that mask comes down," said the umpire, "you're out of this game."

TIME OUT: Play temporarily suspended by order of the umpire, often at the request of a player.

TOEHOLD: Batter's stance at the plate when he digs in to swing.

TOE PLATE: A piece of leather (previously metal was used) sewn to the pivot shoe of a pitcher to protect the shoe. It is necessary because of the pitcher's need to drag his pivot foot after making his pitch.

TOOLS OF IGNORANCE: Catching equipment; mask, chest protector, and shin guards. They are so called because a catcher is so prone to injury that it is legend that only the ignorant would select such a position.

TOP: The first half of an inning, e.g., the top of the ninth. Also used in newspaper headlines to denote one team defeating another. For example, "Dodgers Top Cardinals, 4-3."

TOTAL BASES: The total number of bases credited to a batter on his base hits—a single giving him one base; a double, two bases; a triple, three bases; and a home run, four bases. Babe Ruth's 457 total bases (85 singles, 44 doubles, 16 triples, and 59 home runs) made in 1921 are a record for one season. In 1954 Joe Adcock of the Milwaukee Braves made 18 total bases in one game on 4 home runs and a double.

TRADING DEADLINE: That time of year after which it is no longer permissible for two teams to trade players, although players may be sold through waivers after that date. June 15 has been the trading deadline in recent years.

TRIPLE: A three-base hit. Also a three-bagger. The triple is the rarest of base hits, combining as it does power and speed on the part of the hitter. It is not surprising, therefore, that the record for three-base hits for a career is 312, less than half the record for home runs. The records for three-base hits in each league, coincidentally, were set in the same year, 1912. J. Owen Wilson smacked 36 triples for the Pittsburgh Pirates that year to establish the National League record, and Joe Jackson of the Cleveland Indians set the American League record (tied two years later by Sam Crawford of the Detroit Tigers) with 26.

TRIPLE PLAY: The act of retiring three men in one sequence, rare in any form but especially if it is an unassisted triple play, only seven of which have been made in big-league history. It was last achieved in 1927, when, oddly enough, two were made on successive days by Jimmy Cooney of the Chicago Cubs and Johnny Neun of the Detroit Tigers.

TRIPLE STEAL: All three base runners stealing a base on the same play.

TV AND RADIO: Baseball broadcasters not only picked up and popularized a number of obscure dugout idioms (such as "swung on" instead of "swung at"), but they have added their own pet expressions to the lingo of the game.

Red Barber contributed "sittin' in the catbird seat" to describe a team or player in position of advantage, and "squeaker" for a close game. Exclamations like Mel Allen's "How about that?" and Harry Caray's "Holy cow!" are frequently mimicked when something odd or sensational occurs.

Barber and Allen were the first of the well-known baseball broadcasters. In recent years ex-ballplayers moved into the field with extraordinary results. When Frankie Frisch did the New York Giant games, he used to repeat his favorite expression, "Oh, those bases on balls!" Dizzy Dean rambled delightfully along about outfielders who "throwed" the ball and runners who "slud" into third.

Following the lead of Frisch and Dean and Waite Hoyt in Cincinnati, ex-players took radio by storm. Phil Rizzuto, Jerry Coleman, Ralph Kiner, Bill White, Don Drysdale, Bob Uecker, Buddy Blattner, Richie Ashburn, and Johnny Pesky became regulars behind the microphone.

Baseball went on the air in 1921, when Graham McNamee broadcast the World Series between the Giants and Yankees. The Chicago Cubs instituted regular season broadcasts in 1924, with Hal Totten at the microphone.

Television entered the field in 1939, with Barber doing the commentary in a game between the Dodgers and the Reds in Brooklyn. Today television is big business for ball clubs, and every team in the major leagues and some in the minors broadcast and telecast at least a portion of their games.

TWEENER: A ball hit between two outfielders (up the alley), usually going for a double or triple, sometimes an inside-the-park home run.

TWI-NIGHT: A one-admission doubleheader consisting of a twilight game (starting at approximately 6:00 P.M.) and a night game immediately following the twilight game.

UMPIRE: One of the officials who administers the rules. Umpires have been called arbiters, men in blue, Blind Toms, and worse. Usually there are four umpires for a game, one at home plate (he is the umpire in charge of the game, calling balls and strikes as well as any play at home) and one each at first base, second base, and third base. For a World Series two umpires are added, one down each foul line. Umpires are chosen by the league president to work in the World Series, and it is considered a reward, because there is extra money to be made from the assignment, not to mention the prestige.

Pioneer baseball radio *broadcaster Graham McNamee interviews Babe Ruth.*

The umpire is a much maligned individual, yet any player will admit the game would be a travesty without strong and courageous umpires. That was exactly the case until the 1920s, when along came a stern individual named Bill Klem to give the umpire new stature and respect. Klem is most famous for his comment: "I never made a wrong call in my life."

Like a player, an umpire starts out in the minor leagues and is scouted by the major leagues. The good ones make it to the big leagues.

An umpire's life is a lonely one. He travels ten months of the year, and while a player spends half of his season at home, the umpire is almost always on the road. He must stay at hotels other than the ones the players stay at, and he must never be seen associating with players. An umpire earns between $15,000 and $30,000 per year plus traveling expenses. He must purchase his own uniforms and equipment, at a cost of about $1,000 every three years.

UNCLE CHARLEY: A curve ball.

UNIFORM: The players' whites, grays, flannels, or monkey suit. The New York Knickerbockers wore the first uniforms in 1849. For years the uniforms were standard, white designating the home team and gray for the visiting team, and all uniforms were made of flannel. With the advent of night baseball, the Cincinnati Reds and the Brooklyn Dodgers experimented with a satin uniform for night games. Now uniforms come in sundry pastel shades of various textures, and some teams even use a sleeveless uniform shirt, such as the Oakland A's, who vary their three-piece uniforms in three colors, Kelly green, Fort Knox gold, and wedding-gown white.

UP: The team at bat or the player at bat. Traditionally, the game begins when the home-plate umpire cries, "Batter up!"

VEST-POCKET CATCH: To catch a high fly ball at the waist. Also called the basket catch, which was made famous by Willie Mays.

VICTORY PARTY: It is traditional that the team that wins the pennant or World Series celebrates with a victory party in the clubhouse after the winning game. The highlight of the party is the uncorking of champagne, most of which is poured on players' heads in celebration instead of in their mouths. Often the players continue the victory party long after they leave the clubhouse, sometimes with disastrous results.

After one pennant clinching the Yankees continued their celebration on the train returning to New York. Pitcher Ryne Duren got in a playful mood and smashed a cigar in the face of Ralph Houk, then a Yankee coach. Houk became manager some years later, and after his first season, Duren was traded.

The Pittsburgh Pirates clinched the 1960 pennant and kept their party going on the bus back to the hotel from the ball park. Another playful chap was innocently tugging at the foot of Vern Law, the Pirates's ace pitcher, and accidentally sprained Law's ankle. The ankle was still sore when Law pitched in the World Series and, favoring the ankle, he thereby put added strain on his pitching arm with the result that he developed a sore arm that almost ended his career.

WAIT OUT: To wait for a type of pitch the batter wants to hit. In waiting out a pitcher, the hitter will often try to foul off strikes until he receives his favorite pitch, or force the pitcher to walk him. Eddie Stanky of the Boston Braves, Brooklyn Dodgers, and New York Giants, and Eddie Yost of the Washington Senators were masters at fouling off pitches while waiting out the pitcher for a walk.

WAIVER: The means by which a team can sell a player or send him to the minor leagues after the cutdown date. The team places the player's name on a waiver list. He must then be passed on by all the other teams in the big leagues, who select in reverse order of their standing. If he is passed on (waived), he may then be disposed of. However, if a team puts in a claim for that player, his team must either remove his name from the list and retain him or sell him to the claiming team for the waiver price of $20,000. After the trading deadline a player cannot be sent from one team to another without first being cleared through waivers.

WALLY PIPP: To mention this name to a player is a reminder that if he sits out a game, he may never get his job back. It derives from Wally Pipp, a Yankee of the 1920s. Pipp, the regular first baseman, became ill on

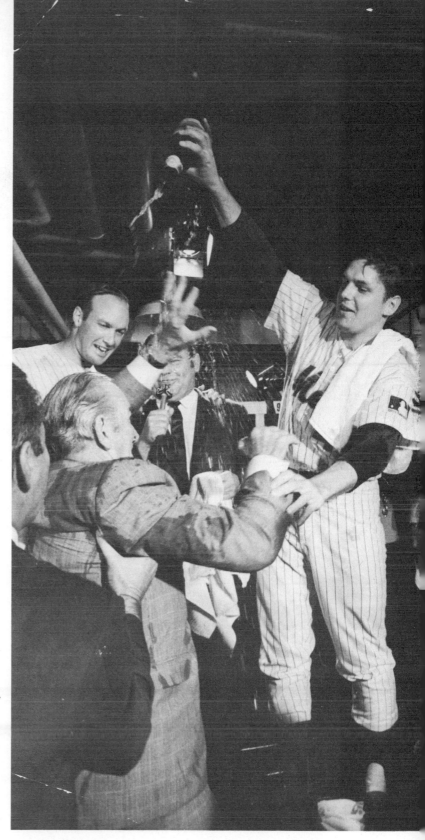

The pitcher, Tom Seaver, appropriately pours the champagne as the New York Mets have their victory party following their World Series triumph over the Baltimore Orioles in 1969.

Pete Rose (14) and his Cincinnati Reds teammates whoop it up after their 1975 World Series *triumph over the Boston Red Sox.*

June 1, 1925. His place was taken by a young man named Lou Gehrig, who did not miss a game thereafter until May 2, 1939. Gehrig played in a record 2,130 consecutive games, and, of course, Wally Pipp never got his job back.

WARM UP: Practice before getting into a game, vital for professional athletes because it is often harmful for a player to use muscles before they are sufficiently loose. One of the traditions of baseball, but one that is more a physical necessity than just a tradition, has the starting pitcher warming up his arm anywhere from ten to twenty minutes before he is scheduled to pitch. This leads to idiosyncrasies.

Pitchers have been known to warm up with a baseball that is heavier than the regulation ball so that the regulation ball will feel lighter and the pitcher can throw it harder and faster. This is similar to a batter swinging a leaded bat before getting up to hit so that the regulation bat will seem lighter and easier to control.

Joe Black, a pitcher for the Brooklyn Dodgers in the 1950s, warmed up from about 15 feet behind the regulation distance of 60 feet 6 inches, which served the same purpose as the heavy baseball. Jim Bouton of the New York Yankees used to experience difficulties in the early innings and, concluding that the reason was lack of sufficient warm-up, he would begin his pregame activity as early as forty-five minutes before the umpire's "Play ball!"

WASTE ONE: When the count on the batter is strongly in the pitcher's favor, the pitcher might waste one (throw one deliberately out of the strike zone) with the hope of getting the batter to swing at a bad ball or to set up his next delivery.

WHEELS: Legs. If a player says another player has bad wheels, it means that the player cannot run, either as the result of an injury or as the result of nature's gifts.

WHIZ KIDS: The name given to the Philadelphia Phillies of 1950, who surprised everybody by winning the National League pennant. Not one of the starting players had yet reached his thirtieth birthday, thus the name Whiz Kids, a variation of "Quiz Kids," a popular radio show of the time that featured a panel of child prodigies.

WHOLE BALL OF WAX: Slang for the pennant or championship.

WILD PITCH: A legally delivered ball thrown so high and so wide of the plate that it cannot be handled by the catcher and results in a base runner moving up one or more bases. It is charged against the pitcher as simply a wild pitch, not an error. There can be no wild pitch if there is no runner on base or if a runner does not advance. It is interesting to note that the most wild pitches made in an inning was four, by Walter Johnson, one of baseball's greatest pitchers, which gives rise to the thought that a little wildness is a good weapon because it may cause batters to be afraid to dig in at the plate.

WILD THROW: A fielder's erratic throw that enables a runner or runners to advance one or more bases. Unlike the wild pitch, a wild throw is scored as an error even if it is by the pitcher.

WINDUP: One of the two legal pitching positions, the other being the stretch position. A pitcher winds up when there are no runners on base or runners are on third or second and third or first, second, and third. He stretches at all other times. The stretch is a short windup and insures against a potential base stealer taking too big a lead.

WINNING PITCHER: The pitcher credited by the official scorer, according to the rules, as the winner of the game. It is what all pitchers strive for. In the case of a starting pitcher, he must pitch at least five complete innings to receive credit for a victory. A relief pitcher may pitch to only one batter and still be the winning pitcher if he happens to be the pitcher of record when his team goes ahead and stays ahead.

WORLD SERIES: Fall classic and the culmination of seven months of work commencing with spring training, in which the champions of the two major leagues meet in a best-of-seven series, the winner being acclaimed the world champion. It has been held annually since 1903, except for 1904, when John McGraw, manager of the lordly New York Giants, refused to let his team play the upstart Boston Red Sox of the new American League.

The World Series operates on an alternating schedule, opening in the American League city one year and in the National the next. After two games the Series shifts to the other team's park for the third, fourth, and, if necessary, the fifth game. If more than five games are needed to determine a winner, the Series reverts to the first park.

Among the most memorable Series incidents were: Babe Ruth's pointing finger, which may or may not have presaged the home run that followed against the Chicago Cubs, in 1932; Ol' Pete Alexander's dramatic march from the bullpen to strike out Tony Lazzeri with the bases full, in 1926; Mickey Owen dropping the disastrous third strike in 1941, opening the gates for a New York Yankee ninth-inning uprising and ultimate victory over the Brooklyn Dodgers; Cookie Lavagetto's game-winning two-out double in the ninth inning for the Dodgers, spoiling Bill Bevens's no-hitter for the Yankees in 1947; and two unbelievable catches—by Al Gionfriddo of the Brooklyn Dodgers against Joe DiMaggio of the New York Yankees in 1947 and by Willie Mays of the New York Giants against Vic Wertz of the Cleveland Indians in 1954.

Two of baseball's rarest rarities popped up in the World Series—an unassisted triple play by Bill Wambsganss of Cleveland in 1920 and Don Larsen's perfect game for the Yankees against the Dodgers in 1956.

BASKETBALL

The most exciting modern player in basketball is Dr. J, otherwise known as Julius Erving of the New York Nets.

BASKETBALL

ABA: American Basketball Association. Founded in February 1967, with franchises in Pittsburgh, New Orleans, Dallas, Denver, Indianapolis, Louisville, Houston, Oakland, Minneapolis, Anaheim, Calif. and Teaneck, N.J. As the league grew, franchises shifted. Others collapsed under financial duress. The survivors—the New York Nets, Denver Nuggets, Indiana Pacers, San Antonio Spurs—joined the National Basketball Association in 1976.

ABL: American Basketball League. A name used by several professional groups, the last time in 1961 when Harlem Globetrotters' owner Abe Saperstein started a league with teams in Cleveland, Pittsburgh, Chicago, Washington, Kansas City, Mo., Los Angeles, San Francisco, and Honolulu. The league lasted a year and a half, folding December 31, 1963. An earlier ABL was founded in 1926 by Washingtonian George Preston Marshall and included teams like the Original Celtics, the Washington Palace Fives, and the Cleveland Rosenblums. The league collapsed after about four years, to be revived in 1933 with such teams as the Philadelphia Sphas and the New York Jewels. The league gradually declined in status as franchises shifted to places like Scranton and Wilkes-Barre, Pa., Bridgeport and Hartford, Conn., and Elmira and Saratoga, N.Y. In 1946, the ABL lost its recognition as a major league.

AIR BALL: Television and broadcasting term, popularized in the last decade. It refers to a shot that misses everything: the backboard, the rim, and, of course, the net.

ASSIST: A pass, or feed, that leads directly to a field goal.

BAA: Basketball Association of America, forerunner of the National Basketball Association. Founded June 6, 1946, with teams in Boston, New York, Philadelphia, Providence, Toronto, Washington, Chicago, St. Louis, Cleveland, Detroit, and Pittsburgh. In 1949, the BAA absorbed the National Basketball League to form the National Basketball Association.

BACKBOARD: The glass, metal, or wood frame to which the basket is attached. It can be a 6- by 4-foot rectangle or a 35- by 54-inch fan shape and must be painted white if not transparent.

BACKCOURT: The two guards are referred to as the backcourt, such as Boston's backcourt combination of Bob Cousy and Bill Sharman, and the New York Knickerbockers' combination of Earl Monroe and Walt Frazier. Backcourt also refers to the defensive half of the court—from the defending goal to midcourt.

BACKCOURT FOUL: In professional basketball any personal foul in the backcourt is an automatic two-shot foul.

BACKCOURT VIOLATION: Occurs when a player on the offensive team touches the ball or carries it behind the midcourt line after it has been advanced into the forecourt and was last touched by the offensive team.

BACK-DOOR PLAY: When an offensive man cuts behind the defender, surprising him totally and moving in quickly for a clear shot—usually in close—at the basket. Many times the player using this device decoys by running along the baselines and then surprising his opponent with the quick move to the basket.

BALL CONTROL: Slow, patterned play by the offensive team that is used either to establish position for a good shot or a set play, or, especially near the end of a game, to consume time.

BALL HOG: Not a very popular guy for the simple reason that he doesn't like to pass the ball to his teammates.

BANKBOARD: Another term for backboard, so called because many players use the backboard to "bank" their shots toward the basket.

BANK SHOT: A shot that is thrown against the backboard rather than directly at the basket.

BASEBALL PASS: A long pass, thrown as though the player had a baseball in his hand.

BASE LINE: The line at either end of the court.

BASKET: What a player gets when he puts the ball into it. A field goal. If Dr. Naismith hadn't put up a basket in 1891, there wouldn't have been any game. He started by nailing a couple of peach baskets to the running track at the armory in Springfield, Mass., the object being to throw the ball into the baskets. There were different types of baskets, some made of leather, wood, or iron, until finally the 18-inch iron ring with a net was arrived at.

BASKET HANGING: Staying in the offensive area of the court when the rest of the players have moved to the other end. The basket hanger hopes to receive a long pass and take an uncontested shot. Also called cherry picking.

BIDDY BASKETBALL: A scaled-down version of the sport, developed in 1951 by Jay Archer, a physical-education instructor from Scranton, Pa. This was achieved by reducing the circumference of the ball from 30 to 28 inches, lowering the height of the basket from 10 to 8½ feet, and shortening the length of the court by putting snap-on extension units over regulation backboards. The game is played by children no taller than 5'6", boys twelve years of age and under, girls thirteen and under. A player is allowed six fouls. The first World Biddy Basketball championship was held in Scranton in 1967 with teams from Peru, Spain, Trinidad, Puerto Rico, Canada, Mexico, Ecuador, El Salvador, the Virgin Islands, and the United States.

BLOCKING: Has two meanings. Legally interfering with the flight of the ball after it has been shot and before it starts its downward arc toward the basket (after which it is called goaltending). Blocking is also obstructing the progress of an opponent who does not have the ball.

BOARDS: Slang for backboards, usually used in reference to rebounding as in "going to the boards."

Also refers to the court itself, which is made of wooden boards.

BONUS SITUATION: When a college team commits its seventh personal foul of a half, the opponent fouled is awarded a "one-and-one" shooting situation at the free-throw line. If the first shot is made, a second or "bonus" is awarded. This bonus situation goes into effect in high school ball at the fifth foul of any half of play. In pro ball, after a team commits its fourth foul of a regulation period, the next foul called leads to an extra free throw for the shooter.

BOUNCE PASS: A pass executed by bouncing the ball off the floor, rather than throwing it on a fly to another player.

BOX AND ONE: A defensive strategy where four men play zone defense and the fifth plays man-to-man.

BOXING OUT: Positioning by a rebounder to keep himself between an opponent and the backboard, screening or "boxing out" his foe.

BOX SCORE: The statistical table that recounts aspects of a game for individual players and the team totals, such as minutes played (Min.), field goals made (FGM), field goals attempted (FGA), free throws made (FTM), free throws attempted (FTA), assists (Ast.), personal fouls (PF), and points scored (Pts.). It also includes the score by periods, the total points, the names of referees, and the attendance. The box score on the facing page for the championship game of the National Basketball Association in 1975 is an example.

BREAKAWAY: A defensive player who executes a steal and moves quickly downcourt ahead of the other players and makes an easy shot is said to have scored on a breakaway.

CAGE: In the early days of basketball games were played with a cloth or wire netting around the floor to prevent the ball from going into the crowd. It also served to prevent unruly spectators from harming players and officials. The players were therefore in a cage, thus the nickname cagers.

CARRYING: *See* Palming.

CATCH-UP: A team that falls behind by a wide margin early must play catch-up ball, which usually means taking greater risks in order to score more points faster.

CENTER: Usually the tallest man on the team is the center, or pivotman. The game starts with a jump ball between the opposing centers. During the game he is a key man on offense, with many plays being worked around him. On defense the center usually plays immediately in front of the basket.

CENTER JUMP: A jump ball between opposing centers at midcourt. In high school games, there is a center jump at the start of each of the four periods. In

1975 NBA PLAY-OFF SERIES

Game No. 4

At Washington, May 25, 1975

GOLDEN STATE	Pos.	Min.	FGM	FGA	FTM	FTA	REBOUNDS Off.	Def.	Tot.	Ast.	PF	Stls.	Pts.
Rick Barry	F	43	10	24	0	0	2	1	3	5	4	3	20
Keith Wilkes	F	32	5	13	2	3	3	5	8	0	3	2	12
Clifford Ray	C	26	6	8	0	2	4	7	11	2	1	2	12
Butch Beard	G	25	6	12	4	7	0	5	5	2	4	3	16
Charles Johnson	G	23	2	5	0	0	1	3	4	2	2	0	4
Phil Smith		21	2	6	2	4	0	3	3	1	1	1	6
Jeff Mullins		21	4	7	0	2	2	2	4	3	3	1	8
Derrek Dickey		18	4	7	0	0	1	1	2	1	2	1	8
George Johnson		22	4	6	0	0	6	5	11	2	3	1	8
Charles Dudley		6	0	1	0	0	0	0	0	2	1	1	0
Bill Bridges		3	1	1	0	0	1	0	1	0	1	0	2
Totals		240	44	90	8	18	20	32	52	20	25	15	96

FG Pct.: .489   FT Pct.: .444   Turnovers: 31   Team Rebounds: 8

WASHINGTON	Pos.	Min.	FGM	FGA	FTM	FTA	REBOUNDS Off.	Def.	Tot.	Ast.	PF	Stls.	Pts.
Elvin Hayes	F	41	7	13	1	2	2	6	8	1	6	1	15
Mike Riordan	F	21	3	11	2	2	1	0	1	3	3	1	8
Wes Unseld	C	44	9	14	1	1	3	13	16	2	3	1	19
Phil Chenier	G	46	8	17	10	10	2	3	5	11	3	5	26
Kevin Porter	G	48	9	16	1	6	1	0	1	8	5	2	19
Len Robinson		10	0	2	0	0	0	1	1	3	2	2	0
Nick Weatherspoon		15	1	5	2	2	2	2	4	0	1	1	4
Tom Kozelko		9	2	2	0	0	0	0	0	0	1	0	4
Clem Haskins		2	0	0	0	0	0	0	0	0	0	0	0
Dick Gibbs		4	0	3	0	0	0	1	1	0	0	0	0
Totals		240	39	83	17	23	11	26	37	28	24	13	95

FG Pct.: .470   FT Pct.: .739   Turnovers: 29   Team Rebounds: 9

Score by Periods:	1st	2nd	3rd	4th	Totals
Golden State	20	28	22	26	96
Washington	30	22	21	22	95

Blocked Shots: G. Johnson 4, Hayes 3, Wilkes 2, Smith, Unseld, Chenier
Officials: Richie Powers and Manny Sokol
Attendance: 19,035

college, the jump is at the beginning of each half. The National Basketball Association has the center jump at the beginning of the first and fourth periods. The center jump is also called the tap-off or tip-off.

CHARGING: A foul committed by an offensive player who runs into a defender. Also called player-control foul.

CHASER: Normally the man nearest midcourt in a zone defense. His job is to harass or chase the man with the ball.

CHERRY PICKING: *See* Basket Hanging.

CHEST PASS: A two-handed pass that starts with the ball held in front of the player's chest.

CHUCK SHOT: A poor, oftentimes desperation shot from a long distance. It also can refer to the shots thrown up by a gunner, or player who likes to shoot from any part of the court.

CINDERELLA TEAM: A team with little hope at the beginning of a season or tournament that goes on to unexpected success. Among the most notable Cinderella teams were Utah's 1944 NCAA champions, CCNY's 1950 NCAA and NIT champions, and Texas Western's 1965 NCAA champions.

CLEARING THE BOARDS: Grabbing rebounds.

CLEAR OUT: To leave open, or clear out, a section of the offensive court to give a player a chance to operate alone.

CLOCK: The electronic device that keeps time—elapsed time—in a basketball game. Also, a special timing device that marks the 24-second (NBA) or 30-second (International) span in which an offensive player has to shoot the ball.

COLD HAND: A player who has trouble making shots is said to have a cold hand.

COMBINATION DEFENSE: A tactic that combines elements of a zone defense and a man-to-man defense, such as box-and-one.

CORDS: A basket net.

CORNER: Refers to a section of the court near the out-of-bounds lines. It is where forwards roam, leading to the term *corner man* for players who have good long shots and are effective on these deep shots.

CORNER MAN: A forward, so called because he generally plays in the corner area of the court.

COURT: The playing floor or surface, most frequently made of wood but also of composition, plastic, stone, or dirt. Courts for high school-age players may be 50 by 84 feet; for college age and older, 50 by 94 feet.

CRADLE THE BALL: When a player takes the ball off the offensive or defensive backboard, holding it close to his chest and protecting it with both arms. The player also can resort to this tactic if he feels he is in danger of being tied up for a jump ball.

CRASHING THE BOARDS: Aggressive rebounding, when players go crashing into the backboards.

CROSS-COURT PASS: In modern basketball this is a "no-no." It is a pass that travels the width of the court and may easily be intercepted.

"D": Slang for defense. A coach might exhort his team to "play the big 'D'," meaning to get tough on defense.

DEAD BALL: The ball becomes dead—may not be played—when a foul is called, when there is a held ball, when a floor violation is called, when time expires (except for shots that are already in flight), when the first throw of a two-shot foul has been taken, or any time the official's whistle is blown.

DEFENSE: The method used to stop an attacking team from scoring points. The two basic defenses are the man-to-man, where each player is responsible for an individual opponent, and zone, where each player is responsible for a certain area of the court. Some popular zone formations are the 3-2, with three men closer to midcourt and two in back; the 2-1-2, with two men in front, one in the middle, and two closer to the basket; the 1-3-1, with one man out front, three deployed across the middle and a deep man; and the 2-3, with two men out front and three behind. A tight defense is one well played; a leaky defense is one that allows many points.

DELIBERATE FOUL: An intentional infraction of the rules, with the offended player automatically getting two free throws.

DISQUALIFICATION: Reaching the maximum number of personal fouls results in disqualification. In the pros this is six fouls; for colleges and other amateurs it is five fouls. Also known as fouling out.

DOUBLE DRIBBLE: Results in loss of the ball when a player dribbles a second time after having held the ball or touched it with both hands simultaneously.

DOUBLE FOUL: Occurs when two players foul each other at the same time. Each is awarded a free throw, and then there is a center jump. Double fouls are a rarity.

DOUBLEHEADER: Playing two games in one arena on the same afternoon or evening. Almost always involves four different teams. The idea started as a promotional gimmick in New York's Madison Square Garden in the 1930s and proved an immediate hit with college basketball fans. It was later adopted by the pros.

DOUBLE-TEAM: To use two defenders against one opponent, usually an exceptional scorer.

DOWNTOWN: Popularized by television and radio announcers in the defunct American Basketball Association. It referred to a three-point basket (more than 25 feet); also known as a home run.

Defense *was the trademark of Celtic Bill Russell,*
harassing Wilt Chamberlain.

DRAFT: A system of obtaining players for the professional teams. Its legality has been challenged. Professional leagues select any number of players. They choose in reverse order of their finish in the league standings. Top draft choices can command million-dollar contracts in some instances. During the late 1960s and the 1970s, when the NBA and ABA fought for talent, some contracts for first choices went higher than a million dollars.

DRAW A FOUL: Covers several situations. Either an offensive or defensive man can cause the opposition to foul him, thus drawing the foul. Some defensive players are adept at getting into a position where the offensive man cannot help but run into him. Some of these players could qualify for an Academy Award.

DRIBBLE: Has nothing to do with sloppy eating but rather is the main method of moving a basketball around the court. The only other method is the pass. The dribble is accomplished by bouncing the ball off the floor with the palm of the hand. Some players—like Marques Haynes when he was a Harlem Globetrotter—become so proficient at dribbling that they can move through an entire defense with ease or can stall for several minutes.

DRIVE: One of the most exciting plays in basketball, when a player heads straight for the basket and challenges the defense to stop his drive. There are different types of drives, such as the baseline drive, where a player dribbles along the end line, looking for an opening to pass or shoot.

DROPPING OFF: Defensive teams troubled by a particularly effective forward or center will send another player back to help guard this person. The act of doing so is "dropping off" one player to help cover another.

DUMPING: Basketball people would rather forget this term, but it is a part of the game's history. It means to "throw" a game, or lose it on purpose. *See also* Point Shaving and Point Spread.

DUNK: A crowd-pleasing shot made popular by big men who could hold the ball in one hand and leap high enough to stuff it into the ten-foot-high basket. Big men like Kareem Abdul-Jabbar perfected this art, and in 1968 the dunk was banned in colleges in an effort to take a weapon away from the big man. But in 1976 the rules makers made the dunk legal again.

EBL: Eastern Basketball League, formed in 1946 with teams in Binghamton, N.Y., and Hazelton, Reading, Wilkes-Barre, Lancaster, and Allentown, Pa. It later expanded to include cities throughout the Northeast. It serves as a farm system for the National Basketball Association.

END LINE: The baseline.

EXTRA PERIOD: A five-minute period of play that is added when the score is tied at the end of regulation time. Also called overtime. In 1954, Niagara and Siena played six extra periods before Niagara won, 88-81. The professional record for extra periods is six: Indianapolis beat Rochester in the NBA, 75-73, in six overtimes on January 6, 1951.

FADEAWAY SHOT: Popularized by jump shooters. They usually shoot the ball as they are fading away from the defensive man. Wali Jones and Dick Barnett, two longtime National Basketball Association players, had effective fadeaway shots. A good fadeaway shooter is hard to defense.

FAKING: Exactly what you think. A sneaky, crafty move enabling an offensive man to lose his defensive shadow and break loose for a basket. Many different fakes can be employed, e.g., the head fake, the body fake, and the eye fake.

FALLAWAY: A jump shot taken while the shooter is falling backward, away from the basket. Also called a fadeaway.

FAST BREAK: Essentially, moving or breaking downcourt in a hurry. The object is to break downcourt ahead of the defenders, receive a quick pass, and make an easy shot. The Boston Celtics of the late 1950s and 1960s were noted for their fast break, which was started by Bill Russell, who was able to take a rebound and pass the ball with precision to his teammates breaking downcourt.

FEED: A pass that starts an offensive play. If it leads directly to a basket, it is an assist.

FIELD GOAL: A shot, other than a free throw, which goes into the basket. It counts two points and is the main means of scoring. The ABA had a three-point play, awarded for a shot from 25 feet or beyond.

FIGURE EIGHT: An offensive pattern where the passer cuts behind the man to whom he has just passed the ball. Its purpose is to create enough movement to confuse the defense and break a man free. Also called a weave.

FIVE: The number of players on a team, hence the newspaper stories and headlines referring to fives when they mean basketball teams.

FIVE-SECOND VIOLATION: When the offensive team is inbounding the ball, it has five seconds to put the ball in play. If it does not, the official blows his whistle, a turnover ensues, and the defensive team gets the ball at the point of the infraction.

FIX: Not a very popular term. It has meant a lot of trouble to a lot of people who have conspired to control or "fix" the outcome of a game either by "dumping" or "shaving"—i.e., reducing the final point spread between teams.

FLOOR VIOLATION: Any of a number of errors for which the offensive team loses possession of the ball, such as double-dribbling, walking, or violating the three-second rule.

FORCE: To attempt a shot or pass when the defense has sufficiently limited the opportunity to make the shot or complete the pass.

FORCE-OUT: Occurs when the player with the ball is forced out of bounds with minimal body contact by a defensive player.

FORWARD: The two men who usually play in the forecourt area on either side of the basket are called forwards.

FOUL: A violation usually involving body contact between players. In most cases it results in a free throw for the offended, or fouled, player. There are many fouls—such as charging, holding, blocking, tripping, pushing, and elbowing. *See also* Technical Foul.

FOUL LANE: The area at each end of the court enclosed by the end line, the free-throw line, and two parallel lines 16 feet apart for the pros and 12 feet apart for amateurs.

FOUL LINE: A line 15 feet from the basket where a player shoots free throws.

FOUL OUT: Disqualification from a game by committing five personal fouls in high school, college, and amateur games or six in the pros. A disqualified player is one who "fouls out."

FOUL SHOT: *See* Free Throw.

FREE LANCE: Originated on the playgrounds. It means that each of the five players has an individual style rather than a team game with a one-for-all attitude.

FREE THROW: Awarded after a foul. So called because it is taken uncontested from the foul line. Each free throw if successful is worth one point. Also called a foul shot.

FREE-THROW CIRCLE: Each half of the basketball court has a circle in which the foul line is enclosed. Its radius is six feet, split by the two-inch-wide foul line, which is also known as the free-throw line.

FREEWHEELING OFFENSE: A high-scoring, diverse offensive team capable of scoring a lot and of using numerous devices to upset the defense. Devices can vary from set patterns to one-on-one play to a good fast break. A mixture of these with consistent success will confuse any defense.

FREEZE: Has nothing to do with the temperature outside. It means stalling for time by controlling the ball by dribbling, passing or a combination of both. Prevented in the pros and international competition—by the 24- and 30-second clocks—the freeze is still a strategic weapon in high school and college games.

Usually used by a team in the late stages of a game to protect a lead but also used against a superior opponent in an effort to reduce the margin of victory or perhaps even win.

FRONT COURT or FORECOURT: That part of the playing area where most of the offensive action takes place.

FULL-COURT PRESS: A man-to-man defense where the defenders play their opponents for the entire length of the court.

GAMBLE: To take a risk on a certain play or defense at an opportune time during a game. It has other meanings, too, since basketball is a game that seems to attract a number of people who bet on the point spread of the game.

GAMBLE ON DEFENSE: To take a chance, mostly hoping for a steal or hoping to break up the offensive flow. The defensive player usually goes for the ball or he may try to cut off a passing lane, thus confusing the offense for a moment.

GARBAGE TIME: Does not refer to the time after the game when the cleaning crew puts the arena back in shape. It describes the last few minutes of a game whose outcome has been decided, when the players play individual basketball rather than a team game and try to fatten their scoring averages.

GET INSIDE: When the offensive team moves a player (or players) close to the basket, breaking or cracking the defense and opening up the game underneath.

GIVE AND GO: An offensive play where one man passes the ball to another, who is usually standing near the free-throw line, and cuts past him toward the basket in hopes of breaking clear and getting the ball back for an easy shot.

GOAL: A field goal; a basket.

GOALTENDING: Defensively, interfering with a shot that has begun its downward flight toward the basket. On offense, goaltending is touching the ball while it is still on the rim of the basket.

GOON: When giant players began dominating the game, they were often disparagingly referred to as goons.

GUARD(S): The two players—usually the smallest men on the team—who bring the ball up the court and control the game from the backcourt. The guards are agile and adept at ball handling. Guard also means to play a person defensively.

GUNNER: Has its roots in the Old West and refers to a player who has a tendency to shoot very often. Pete Maravich of the New Orleans Jazz was a classic example of a gunner with talent. Not many players who like to shoot the ball that often can match his ability.

HACK: Hitting a player across the hands or arms as he tries to dribble or pass the ball.

HALF-COURT: Refers to either of the two halves that constitute a basketball court. In playground or choose-up games, it means a game played entirely at one basket with teams of two or three men each.

HALL OF FAME: *See* Naismith.

HANDS: An expression used by coaches to remind players to get their hands up on defense so they can be ready to break up a pass or interfere with a shooter.

HARLEM GLOBETROTTERS: The clown princes of basketball, organized in 1926 by Abe Saperstein. Even though they were originally from Chicago, the name Harlem was adopted to denote that all the players were black. They have toured the world, playing before the biggest crowds any team has ever drawn. Originally a serious, barnstorming team, they are now as much entertainers as athletes.

HATCHET MEN: Those friendly gentlemen whose task is to foul somebody or perhaps rough up the opposing team's star. Frequently in college and high school it is a football player in shorts who rarely gets into the game and has fouls to spare. In the pros it is usually a player who sees little action. Alex Hannum was one of the great hatchet men in the early days of the NBA.

HEIGHT ADVANTAGE: Through the years the average height of a basketball team has increased steadily. It is not uncommon to find guards in the professional league who are 6′5″ and 6′6″. In the early days of the game the center often wasn't more than 6′1″ or 6′2″. The objective of the team with the height advantage over its opponent is to match up a taller player with someone a bit smaller.

HELD BALL: Occurs when two opposing players share control of the ball and possession is hard to

Marques Haynes, a great dribbler, was one of the most famous of the Harlem Globetrotters.

determine. It also occurs when a closely guarded player holds the ball in his own front court without moving for five seconds. Decided by a jump ball.

HELPING OUT: Can refer to any defensive man who tries to aid one of his teammates in containing a particularly good offensive player. The player helping out leaves his defensive assignment and helps cover the troublesome person on any part of the floor.

HIGH-LOW: *See* High Post.

HIGH POST: The center or pivot man is also known as the post man, and when he plays in the area near the foul line, he is playing a high post. Some teams play with one man "high" and another "low," or in close to the basket. This is called high-low.

HOLDING: Personal contact with an opponent that interferes with his freedom of movement.

HOME-COURT ADVANTAGE: Coaches say it is usually worth six to ten points a game. It refers to a game being played by the home team on its own floor before its own fans. The supportive fans and the familiarity with the floor itself, the backboards and the rims, often gives the home team a decided advantage. It is also a term used in describing professional teams trying to get the odd-game advantage for a play-off series. These play-offs are usually best of three, five, or seven. The team with home-court advantage would play the deciding game on familiar territory.

HOMER: Not the Greek poet. A subtle reference to an official who favors the home team because the crowd, by its boisterousness, intimidates him. Also, the officials are usually paid by the home team, and a referee concerned about his next assignment may favor the home team—hence homer.

HOME RUN: In the American Basketball Association or the Eastern Basketball Association, any shot made from outside the three-point circle (25 feet) was called a home run; also known as downtown.

HOOK PASS: *See* Palming.

HOOK SHOT: An over-the-head shot, usually made close to the basket, taken while pivoting toward the basket.

HOOP: One of the terms used to describe the basket.

HOT HAND: The player who is having a good night with his shooting and "can't miss" from the field.

IN AND OUT: A term used to describe a shot that appears to be ready to drop through the rim but is just a fraction off line and bounces or spins out.

INBOUND: After a basket or after a ball is knocked out of bounds, an offensive player takes the ball from the official and throws it in play to a teammate. He is inbounding the ball.

INTENTIONAL FOUL: Deliberate foul.

INTERMISSION: The 15-minute period between halves.

INTERSECTIONAL GAME: College game between schools from different parts of the country.

IN THE ACT: When an offensive player is in the process of taking a shot and is fouled by a defensive player, he is considered to be in the act of shooting and is awarded a two-shot foul.

INTIMIDATE: To so harass and confuse—thus intimidate—an opponent, either offensively or defensively, that his game becomes useless. The term usually refers to big men like Kareem Abdul-Jabbar and Bill Walton, whose very presence alters the usual game and thinking of their opponents.

JAM THE MIDDLE: Clogging the area of the foul lane by a defensive team to prevent getting the ball into the center or to prevent driving to the basket.

JUMP BALL: Putting the ball in play by tossing it between two players facing each other at center court or in either of the two free-throw circles. Also called tip-off or tap.

JUMP SHOT: Probably the most popular shot in basketball—since the early 1950s. Made by releasing the ball, usually with one hand, at the top of a jump in an effort to offset any height advantage a defender might have.

KEY or KEYHOLE: That area of the court enclosed by the foul lane and free-throw circle. So called because it resembles a keyhole. It is the area where many of the offensive patterns are established.

KILLING THE CLOCK: Another way of saying "freezing the ball."

LANE: Foul lane.

LAUGHER: An easy victory—so easy that the winning team has fun. One big laugh.

LAY-UP: A basic shot executed by throwing the ball from in close against the backboard and into the basket. Usually taken on fast breaks and drives. All teams warm up before a game by first going through a lay-up drill. It is considered the easiest shot in basketball. Taller men frequently dunk rather than shoot a lay-up.

LINE-DRIVE SHOT: Some players favor hard, low trajectory shots at the basket. But often this is a hard shot to make unless the player is extremely proficient. The shot also has a lot of velocity.

LOB: A high, arching pass thrown softly from one player to another, frequently to a tall player who has a distinct height advantage over the man guarding him.

LOOSE-BALL FOUL: In the pros, a foul committed when no one has possession—usually in a rebounding situation. The offended team gets the ball out of bounds instead of a free throw. The rule was instituted in an effort to speed up the game.

LOW POST: Position near the basket where the pivot man or another player sets himself to work offensive patterns.

Kareem Abdul-Jabbar's hook shot *is so singular and* lofty it is often referred to as a sky hook.

MADISON SQUARE GARDEN: Considered the indoor mecca of sports in America and a historical building for basketball—pro, college, and high school. The first basketball game at the Garden (then on Eighth Avenue between Forty-ninth and Fiftieth streets in Manhattan) was on December 6, 1925, between the Original Celtics and the Washington Palace Five. Since that time numerous championships were played there and in the current building between Thirty-first and Thirty-third streets and Seventh and Eighth avenues in New York City.

MAN-TO-MAN: A system of defense where each of the five players is responsible for a specific opponent and guards him wherever he goes.

MATCH-UP(S): Most often heard in reference to pros since it refers to the individual pairings when both teams play man-to-man defense—the only kind allowed in the pros. Mismatches occur when, during the course of play, the defenders switch men and a smaller man winds up guarding a tall opponent.

MIDCOURT LINE: The solid two-inch line painted across the middle of the court, dividing it into two equal parts. If the offensive team advances the ball across the line within the allotted ten seconds, the ball cannot go into the backcourt. If it does and the defensive team has not touched it, it is a backcourt violation and the ball changes hands.

MISSES EVERYTHING: A shot that doesn't come close. It doesn't find the rim, the net, or the backboard. Also known as an air ball.

MONEY PLAYER: A player who comes through in key situations, when money is at stake, such as in the play-offs and championship games. Also used to describe big-salaried rookies like Bill Walton and David Thompson who signed pro contracts for financial packages estimated at more than two million dollars.

MOVING SCREEN: A violation occurring when a player, after assuming a screening position, moves in a direction other than the same direction and path as his opponent.

MOVING WITHOUT THE BALL: To keep an offense fluid and dangerous to the defense, the players without the ball must try to cause as much motion for the defense as possible. Players who do not stand still on the court but move around instead even when they do not have the ball increase the team's chances of breaking into the clear for a basket, or they open up a spot for another player to drive or shoot.

MVP: Most Valuable Player. An award in all-star games, tournaments, and leagues that goes to the player who has contributed the most to the success of his team.

NAIA: The National Association of Intercollegiate Athletics. Another governing body for college sports in America. It represents mostly small colleges and has championship play-offs in basketball and other sports.

NAISMITH: Dr. James Naismith, the founder of basketball. As a physical-education instructor looking for an indoor winter sport, he invented the game in Springfield, Mass., in 1891. The first game was played at the Springfield Armory with nine men on a side. Two peach baskets had been nailed to the bottom of the running track at the armory, ten feet above the ground. Dr. Naismith, a quiet, scholarly man, later taught and coached at the University of Kansas. He died in 1939. A memorial to him, the Naismith Basketball Hall of Fame, has been erected on the campus of Springfield College.

NBA: The name National Basketball Association was adopted for the 1949-50 season after the BAA (Basketball Association of America) and NBL (National Basketball League) merged. Started as a seventeen-team league with three divisions, in five years it was reduced to eight teams in two divisions after franchises disbanded. The number of teams increased in the 1960s with expansion drafts and in 1976 when it added four teams from the ABA (American Basketball Association).

NCAA: The National Collegiate Athletic Association, the major governing body of American intercollegiate sports. It represents nearly seven hundred colleges and universities and is responsible for game as well as administrative rules. It also has different classifications for the larger colleges (Division I schools) and the smaller ones (Divisions II and III). Its offices are in Shawnee Mission, Kans. It holds annual championships for basketball teams in all three divisions.

NET: The twine cords attached to the basket rim.

NICKNAMES: Much of the game's color comes from the nicknames of its individuals such as Forest ("Phog") Allen, Wallace ("Wah Wah") Jones, Easy Ed Macauley, Horace, ("Bones") McKinney, Hot Rod Hundley, Bob ("Foothills") Kurland, Oscar ("The Big O") Robertson, Harry ("The Horse") Gallatin, Nat ("Sweetwater") Clifton, Dick ("Trick Dick") McGuire, Billy ("The Hill") McGill, Earl ("The Pearl") Monroe, Clarence ("Bevo") Francis, Walt ("Clyde") Frazier, and Julius ("Dr. J") Erving.

NIT: The National Invitation Tournament. Started by New York's Metropolitan Basketball Writers Association at the end of the 1937-38 season, the NIT was the first of the major postseason tournaments for college teams. Six teams competed in the first NIT, which has always been held in Madison Square Garden in New York, with Temple defeating Colorado for the championship. In the final game, Byron ("Whizzer")

White, who nearly two decades later would be named to the Supreme Court of the United States, scored ten points. The number of teams in the tournament increased from eight to twelve to sixteen, and then in 1976 it was cut back to twelve.

NUMBER: Each man in uniform must be identified, and so he carries a number on the front and back of his jersey. Many of the numbers have become as notable as their wearers' names, such as George Mikan's 99, Wilt Chamberlain's 13, Jerry West's 44, Kareem Abdul-Jabbar's 33, and Julius Erving's 32.

OFFENSE: The part of the game when one team is on the attack, trying to score points. There are many types of offenses ranging from the patterned or set-play sequences to the free lance.

OFFICIAL(S): The two men who control the game and make sure it is played by the rules.

ONE-AND-ONE: The free-throw opportunity during the bonus situation in high school or college ball in which a player has the chance to shoot an extra foul shot if he successfully makes the first.

ONE-HANDER: A shot taken with one hand. It was popularized in the 1930s by Stanford's Hank Luisetti, who revolutionized basketball with a running one-hander.

ONE-ON-ONE: This connotes the type of game played in most schoolyards and backyards, where one player guards another while the offensive player tries to score. In a five-man game one-on-one usually means that a player is challenging the defensive player without the defensive player getting any help from teammates. Earl Monroe and Rick Barry are considered superior one-on-one players, and more often than not they score when the defensive man lets up in this situation.

ONE-THREE-ONE: A zone defense with a man stationed out front, three men across the court about 15 feet from the end line, and a fifth man playing close to the basket. It is used to stop a team that is known to have an excellent driving offense.

OPENING TAP: At the beginning of each game an official steps to center court, throws the ball into the air, and play begins. In the National Basketball Association there is an opening tap at the start of the first and fourth periods. In college ball there is an opening tap at the beginning of each half, and in high school there is an opening tap at the start of each of the four periods.

OPEN MAN: Any offensive player who breaks free of his defender and is in a clear position for an uncontested shot at the basket. Good basketball players always will look to this man before taking a shot.

OPEN SHOT: A coach's dream. When an offensive player breaks into the clear relatively close to the basket for an uncontested shot.

ORIGINAL CELTICS: The first of basketball's great professional teams. They achieved prominence in the 1920s and 1930s by averaging more than 100 victories a season. The Celtics, founded in New York, featured such players as Nat Holman, Joe Lapchick, Dutch Dehnert, and Pete Barry. The Celtics are one of four teams enshrined in the Hall of Fame.

OUTLET PASS: The pass that starts a fast break. It goes from the rebounder to a man positioned near the midcourt line, usually toward one side or the other of the court. The faster the rebounder can clear the outlet pass, the better chance the fast break has of working.

OUT OF BOUNDS: Any area outside the court. When a ball goes out of bounds, play stops and the ball is awarded to the team that did not last touch it.

OUTREBOUND: The team that dominates the boards on offense and defense outrebounds its opponents. A rebound is possession of a ball (shot) that does not go in the basket. The team that gets the most of these has the advantage in rebounding.

OUTSIDE SHOT: Twenty-five years ago the term would have referred to a set-shot artist. But the game has changed, and there are few of those shooters around today. So an outside shot usually refers to a long jump shot from more than 25 or 30 feet.

OVERLOAD THE ZONE: When the defensive team resorts to a zone defense (where each of the players is responsible for an area of the court), the offensive team tries to get a player free for a shot by flooding the zone with as many players as possible. The more offensive players to contend with, the tougher the defense's job.

OVER THE LIMIT: A team that has exceeded the number of team fouls allowed in a period is said to be over the limit. When a team is over the limit, the opponents are awarded a bonus free throw after each foul. *See also* Penalty Shot.

OVERTIME: The extra period needed to decide a game when the score has been tied at the end of regulation play. There can be as many of these five-minute periods as needed to determine a winner.

PALMING: Losing control of a dribble and—for a split second—carrying the ball in the palm of the hand. If a referee spots it, the other team gets the ball. Also called carrying.

PASS: Moving the ball from one point to another by throwing from one player to another. Some types of passes are the chest pass, the bounce pass, the hook pass, and the baseball pass.

PATTERNED OFFENSE: A set offense relying on preplanned plays. It is a very deliberate offense, one that hopes to capitalize on the percentage shot.

PENALTY SHOT: An extra free-throw attempt awarded in pro ball when a team has picked up its fifth personal foul during any quarter, not counting offensive fouls. This offers three chances to convert a two-shot foul, or two chances to convert a one-shot foul. Although similar to the "bonus" situation in college, it is strictly differentiated by the pros, for the penalty shot offers an additional chance at a free throw while in the bonus situation, the player must make his first shot to have a chance at a second.

PENETRATE: The objective is to send a guard, and in some cases a forward, through the defense, thus opening an opportunity for himself or drawing the defense toward him and giving another player on his team a scoring chance. Good penetration keeps the defense moving and often forces it off balance.

PERCENTAGE SHOT: What every coach loves. This is the shot that a patterned, deliberate team works for. It is one taken from an excellent position and stands a good chance of being made.

PERIMETER SHOOTING: Imagine a circle around the court from the top of the key to the end lines. The radius would be about 20 feet. Any shot from that imaginary area would be a perimeter shot.

PERIOD: Playing time, be it a quarter, half, or overtime. Colleges play two 20-minute halves, high schools play four 8-minute quarters, and the pros play four 12-minute quarters. All overtimes are 5 minutes.

PERSONAL FOUL: The penalty assessed against a player who hits, restricts, impedes, trips, or illegally blocks an opponent. Each player is allowed five personal fouls in high school and college and six in the pros before being disqualified.

PICK: To assume a position at the side or in front of an opponent and by so doing remove him from the play for a split second.

PICK AND ROLL: An offensive play where one man sets a pick, then moves or rolls around the defender and heads toward the basket to receive a pass.

PICKING UP: Assuming defense, e.g., defensive guards picking up their men at half court.

PIVOT: Another term for the position played by the center.

PIVOT MAN: The man who plays in the middle and around whom plays are run.

PLAYER-CONTROL FOUL: *See* Charging.

PLAYING THE BALL: Concentrating the defense on the path of the ball rather than on individual opponents in an effort to deflect or intercept a pass or steal the ball.

PLAYMAKER: The brainy, slick ball-handling guard who specializes in setting up plays for the team. Oscar Robertson was a rare type who, in addition to being a great scorer, was an exceptional playmaker. Bob Cousy was also an exceptional playmaker. Some of the top moderns in this category include Kevin Porter of Detroit, Brian Taylor of the New York Nets, Mike

Newlin of Houston, and Walt Frazier of the New York Knicks.

PLAY-OFF: A system in any classification of basketball for determining a champion. There are numerous variations of the system, ranging from a one-game play-off to the best of three, best of five, or best of seven. Colleges and high schools normally use one-game play-offs, while professional leagues use the best of three, five, and seven.

POINT: The method by which the score in basketball is computed. Free throws count for one point, field goals for two—although the ABA, for example, used three points for field goals made from 25 feet or more away from the basket. The point also refers, defensively, to the area at the top of the key.

POINT GUARD: Used more and more in reference to the offensive player controlling the ball and the tempo of the game most of the time. In a strict 1-2-2 offense it would be the man who directs his teammates.

POINT SHAVING: A deliberate attempt by players to hold the scoring below the predicted point spread of the two teams.

POINT SPREAD: The points given to or taken from a team in hopes of equalizing the contest for betting purposes.

POST: Another term for the pivot man's spot on the court. It is "high" when he plays near the free-throw line and "low" when he plays near the basket.

PRESS: A type of defense in which the offensive players are closely guarded from the moment the ball is thrown in bounds. The press can be full court, half court, man-to-man, or zone.

PUSHING OFF: This results in a foul—of course, it has to be detected by an official. It occurs when an offensive or defensive player pushes his opponent.

QUARTER: One of the four periods into which high school and professional games are divided.

QUINTET: A newspaper term for a basketball team since there are five players on a squad. Latin for five is *quinque*.

RACE HORSE: Coaches don't like to see their teams play this unless they are in control of the game. It involves a speeded-up pace with emphasis on the fast break.

REBOUND: A missed shot that bounces off the rim or backboard is a rebound. The men trying to get the ball are rebounders, and they are in the act of rebounding.

REFEREE: One of the officials assigned to a game. It is his job to inspect and approve all equipment, toss the ball for the center jump at the beginning of the game, and assist in calling fouls and other violations.

REJECTION: A television and radio term for a blocked shot. Used mostly after a dramatic block.

Boston's Bob Cousy, doing his thing against Nat ("Sweetwater") Clifton of the New York Knickerbockers, was without peer as a playmaker.

RIM: The metal ring, 18 inches in inside diameter, attached to the backboard.

RIM THE BASKET: When a shot heading for the basket bounces out because a portion of the ball hits the inside rim but does not go through the net.

RUNNING: Walking or taking steps with the ball without dribbling. Running with the ball is a violation that costs possession.

RUNNING GAME: Teams that have perfected the fast break play what is called a running game. It features a quick pass from the rebounder to an outlet man, usually on the side of the court. The objective is to have as many players breaking for the basket with the defense out of position. Quickness and speed often opens up a three-on-two or two-on-one situation in favor of the offensive team.

SAGGING DEFENSE: A strategy used to combat the effectiveness of a good big man by having all five defenders collapse, or sag, toward the middle.

SCOREBOARD: The device used to record the running point totals of the teams. More elaborate electrical scoreboards show elapsed time, personal fouls, team fouls, and even individual point totals.

SCORER: The man who records the points, both for the teams and for the individuals. He is the one to whom players report before coming into a game. His book is the official record of the game.

SCREEN: An offensive maneuver where one or more men set a legal block in an effort to give a teammate an open shot.

SET PLAY: When a team determines ahead of time what it wants to do in a certain situation. The team then resorts to a set play, normally very patterned, with each player carrying out a specific assignment.

SET SHOT: A popular shot in the early days of basketball, taken with both feet firmly on the floor.

SETTING (HIGH or LOW): Refers to the position taken by the center or the pivot man. A low post is when the player stations himself close to the basket. A high post is when the player moves out a bit closer to the foul line and lets the play move around him at that point.

SHAVING: *See* Point Shaving.

SHIRTS AND SKINS: A term used to describe scrimmages and choose-up games in which one side wears shirts and the other side, the skins, doesn't.

SIXTH MAN: A term used to describe a valuable substitute, usually the first man to come off the bench in a crucial situation. Frank Ramsey of Boston and John Havlicek—in his early days with the Celtics—were great sixth men. Cazzie Russell, with New York, Golden State, and Los Angeles, also was an excellent sixth man through much of his career.

SLEEPER: An easy basket. Normally the offensive player is all alone under the basket. Also called an easy bunny.

SLOWDOWN: A stalling or controlled game.

SMALL FORWARD: More and more professional teams use this type of player. He's usually a shooter but not such a strong rebounder or defensive player. The power forward normally takes those jobs. The small forward's job is to be a scorer. Some can be as small as 6'4" or 6'5", and many have excellent jumping ability.

STEAL: Intercepting a pass or taking the ball away from an offensive player is called stealing the ball.

STEPS: A floor violation. It means moving with the ball, but forgetting to dribble it.

STUFF: *See* Dunk.

SUBSTITUTE: A player who comes into the game to replace a man who has started is a substitute.

SUPERSTAR: A player of exceptional talent who can dominate play and control the direction of the game—men like Wilt Chamberlain, Bill Russell, Kareem Abdul-Jabbar, Oscar Robertson, Willis Reed, Julius Erving, Jerry West, Walt Frazier, George McGinnis, Bob McAdoo, and Rick Barry.

SWINGMAN: A versatile player who can play two different positions. John Havlicek of the Boston Celtics and Lou Hudson of Atlanta could play equally well at forward or guard. Spencer Haywood of the New York Knicks could move well between center and forward.

SWISH: A ball sailing smoothly through the net makes a soft swishing sound. Thus, to swish a shot means to make it perfectly.

SWITCH: A maneuver where defenders exchange opponents.

TAP: Also, tap-off and tip-off. A jump ball. The center jump that begins the game is called the opening tap.

TEAM: The five men who are on the court at any one time. There is usually no limit to the number of substitutes amateur teams may have.

TEAM FOUL: The total number of personal fouls (excluding player-control fouls) assessed against members of one team in a period. When the limit is reached, the opposing team is awarded a bonus free throw after each foul.

TECHNICAL FOUL: A foul assessed for disrespect to an official, unsportsmanlike conduct, or such violations as exceeding the number of allowed time-outs. One foul shot is awarded, and the opposing team is given possession of the ball at half-court.

TEN-SECOND VIOLATION: After a basket or a successful free throw, the team inbounding the ball has ten seconds in which to move the ball over the half-court line. If it does not, it loses the ball.

THIRTY-SECOND CLOCK: No longer in use in

Superstars *Rick Barry (24)* and *Walt ("Clyde") Frazier*
seem to be viewing the ball as a hot potato.

professional ball but has been considered for college ball and is used in international play. It is the same as a 24-second clock except that it's for 30 seconds. A team must shoot the ball within that time or lose the ball.

THREE-ON-ONE: A fast break where three offensive men are breaking down court against a lone defender.

THREE-POINT PLAY: A player who scores a goal but is fouled while shooting and then makes the free throw is said to have made a three-point play since he gets two points for the goal and one for the free throw.

THREE-SECOND VIOLATION: Occurs when an offensive player stands in the foul lane under his own basket for three or more seconds.

THREE TO MAKE TWO: In professional basketball, when a team has five fouls in any period, this penalty situation goes into effect for any two-shot foul. If a player misses one of his first two free throws, he is allowed a third.

TIED UP: When a player closes in on the ball handler and grabs the basketball but does not gain complete possession. The official then calls a jump ball at the nearest foul line or the tip-off circle.

TIME-OUT: A one-minute break. There are different limits as to how many each team is allowed to call during a half. Time-outs may only be called when a team has possession or when the clock is stopped, such as when the ball goes out of bounds.

TIMER: The man whose job it is to keep track of the elapsed time for games. The official time is not always kept on the scoreboard clock. Sometimes the timer also has a stopwatch.

TIP-IN: A rebound that is tapped into the basket before the rebounder has full control or possession.

TIP-OFF: *See* Center Jump.

TITLE GAME: The game that decides a championship in any classification of basketball. It could be the seventh game of a professional play-off or a single meeting between two college or high school teams.

TOP OF THE KEY: That area from the foul line to the line at the back of the foul key. When a player is in this area he is known to be at the top of the key.

TRAILER: The man who, on a fast break, follows the play downcourt so that he can receive a pass from the lead man or perhaps rebound if the shot is missed.

TRAJECTORY: The flight path of the ball. The curve of the ball as it heads toward the basket. Different players have different styles of shooting: Some shoot with a lot of arc; others shoot straighter, line-drive shots.

TRAVELING: Walking, steps, running with the ball—all violations for moving without dribbling.

TURNAROUND JUMPER: A difficult shot usually taken by a player about 10 or 15 feet from the basket. Starting with his back to the basket, the player turns, jumps, and releases the ball.

TURNOVER: Occurs when the offensive team loses possession of the ball without taking a shot and without having the other team intercept a pass. Usually comes as the result of a floor violation or a bad pass that goes out of bounds.

TWENTY-FOUR-SECOND CLOCK: Adopted in the mid 1950s by the NBA in an effort to speed up the game. A team has 24 seconds in which to shoot after it gets possession of the ball. If a shot is not taken, the ball goes to the other team. A 30-second rule is used in international play.

TWO-ON-ONE: A fast break with two offensive players driving on one defender.

UMPIRE: The official whose job it is to conduct the game and make sure the rules are observed.

UNDERNEATH: That area of the floor closest to the basket, usually between the foul lanes, where the center often plays. The percentage shots are taken from this position, and strategy dictates trying to get the ball to a player who has such good position.

UNIFORM: Each team wears a distinct uniform of different colors, with the home team usually wearing white and the visitors wearing a solid, dark color. The complete uniform consists of a sleeveless or short-sleeved jersey, shorts, knee-length socks, warm-up jerseys, warm-up jackets, and pants. Most uniforms are made of cotton or rayon. In the early days they were made of wool.

USBWA: United States Basketball Writers Association.

VIOLATION: Any infraction of the rules.

WALKING: Traveling with the ball.

WEAVE: *See* Figure Eight.

WHIZ KIDS: The nickname given to the University of Illinois players in the 1940s because of their youth and their superior, fast-breaking play.

WONDER FIVE: The nickname given to the great St. John's University teams in the late 1920s. There was also a Passaic (N.J.) High School team that won 159 straight games between 1919 and 1925 and was called the Wonder Five.

ZONE DEFENSE: A system of defense where the five players defend assigned areas of the court rather than specific opponents, and shift with the movement of the ball. The names for various zone defenses are derived from the various alignments, such as 3-2, 2-1-2, and 1-3-1.

BOWLING

ABC: American Bowling Congress. The governing body of the nation's nearly five million sanctioned men bowlers. Actually the ABC is governed by the bowlers themselves, as they elect their own officers annually.

AJBC: The American Junior Bowling Congress, composed of almost a million junior bowlers. The organization is administered by both the ABC and WIBC (Women's International Bowling Congress). The juniors are not permitted to bowl for cash prizes.

ALLEY: The surface on which the game is bowled. This term is being phased out by the more refined term *lane*.

ALL THE WAY: Finishing a game with a string of strikes.

ANCHOR: The bottom man in a team lineup, usually the most experienced and most dependable member of the team, who can most often be counted on to produce when a game depends on the last man in the last frame.

APPLE: A name given to a bowling ball. Also used in a derogatory sense. A bowler who fails in the clutch is said to "get the apple." Also known as choking.

APPROACH: The act of bringing the ball to the foul line. Also, the portion of the floor leading to the foul line. The ABC specifies an approach must be a minimum of 15 feet.

ARROWS: Markings on the lane to guide spot bowlers.

BABY SPLIT: The 2-7 or 3-10 split, the least difficult to convert.

BACKSWING: An integral part of a bowler's delivery. As a bowler approaches the foul line, he permits the ball to swing behind him in a pendulum manner, the height of the backswing usually determining the amount of momentum imparted to the ball at release.

BACKUP: A ball, rolled by a right-hander, that breaks from left to right instead of the recommended right-to-left break. It is caused by the thumb being too far to the right at the time of delivery. Not recommended for consistent scoring. Also known as a reverse.

BALL RACK: The rack that holds house balls in an establishment.

BALL TRACK: The normal route to the picket used by major-league bowlers. Because of the amount of friction and wear caused by so many bowling balls being rolled over the same route, a ball track results. The rings that appear on a ball after much use are also called ball tracks.

BEAKER: A beak hit; a ball that strikes the headpin full. Also known as a nose hit or a full hit.

BED: The boards making up the alley, or lane.

BEDPOSTS: The 7-10 split, also called the golden gate, goalposts, or fence posts. The most difficult split to convert.

BEER FRAME: When four of five members of a team strike in the same frame, the bowler who did not strike is stuck with a beer frame and must buy the beer for the team.

BELLYING THE BALL: A curve ball that curves first to the right, then back to the left toward the pins.

BEST BALL: A form of bowling tournament in which two partners bowl one ball each on adjoining lanes. If one gets a strike, his team is credited with it. If neither get a strike, the two have a choice of trying for either spare.

BIG FOUR: The 4-6-7-10 split, one of the most difficult to convert. Also called double pinochle.

BLIND: A score used for a missing bowler in a team lineup.

BLOCKING A LANE: A trick to cause high scoring by sanding and oiling a lane in such a way that a ball that normally would hit the nose stops hooking and sets in the 1-3 pocket.

BLOW: A miss.

BLOWING A RACK: Getting a strike.

BODY ENGLISH: Body gyrations after a ball has been delivered. There is no documentary evidence that a bowler has ever been aided by this.

BOOMERANG: A bowling tournament in which one frame is bowled on one lane after which the bowler moves to the next lane, etc., until he has crossed eleven or twelve lanes.

BOWLING: History fails to state who made the first 7-10 split, but bowling is generally regarded as second only to archery among the oldest sports in the world, and is the granddaddy of all games that are played with a ball. It's at least seven-thousand years old; paraphernalia for a type of bowling was found in an Egyptian tomb that dates to 5200 B.C. It may even have been that cavemen were bowlers, too. Markings on the walls of prehistoric caves suggest a game that was played by rolling stones at various objects.

As far back as the fifth century A.D., bowlers were called keglers, the name deriving from *kegle* or *kegel*, an all-purpose club used in Germany as a weapon, tool, and plaything. Gradually the shaped pin and wooden ball evolved, and rules were worked out for a variety of bowling games. The one that took hold in this country was ninepins, brought to America in the early seventeenth century by the Dutch. Ninepins became enormously popular. It soon moved indoors, and by the early 1800s there were bowling alleys up and down New York's Broadway.

But there was so much gambling connected with it that the sport was banned at one time or another in New York, Connecticut, and Massachusetts, and there is a theory that the game of tenpins was devised to get around the laws against ninepins. Whatever its origin, tenpins has been the prevailing form of bowling in the U.S. since about 1860.

In 1895 the American Bowling Congress (ABC) was created to standardize rules and equipment and promote the sport. Eventually, along came electronic equipment—AMF's Pinspotter in 1952 and Brunswick's Pinsetter in 1956—to replace pinboys and take bowling out of the dank basements and make it our biggest participant sport.

BOWLING BALL: To be approved for sanctioned competition, a ball may not weigh more than 16 pounds nor have a circumference greater than 27 inches.

BOX: A frame, one-tenth of a bowling game.

BPAA: Bowling Proprietors Association of America.

BREAK: A frame in which a bowler does not get a strike or spare. Also the moment when a ball stops sliding and begins to hook.

BRIDGE: The space between the thumb and finger holes in a ball. Also known as a span.

BROOKLYN HIT: A ball rolled by a right-hander that crosses the headpin and hits the 1-2 pocket, instead of the 1-3. Often it results in a lucky strike. Also known as Jersey hit, crossover, or cross hit.

BUCKET: The 2-4-5-8 or 3-5-6-9 cluster leave. Also called dinner jacket.

BVL: Bowlers Victory Legion, a fund-raising organization that uses proceeds to provide recreational material for hospitalized veterans.

CHANNEL: The modern term for what used to be known as the gutter; the depressed area on either side of a lane.

CHERRY PICKING: Knocking down the front pin of two left standing, such as 2 off the 8, or 3 off the 9. (The two pins are known as double wood). Also called a chop.

CHOKE: What a bowler is said to do when he fails to produce in the clutch. Also called getting the apple.

CHOP: *See* Cherry Picking.

CINCINNATI: The 8-10 split.

CLASSIC: Name given a league of major-league caliber. Also a division limited to pro bowlers in the annual ABC Championship Tournament.

CLASSIFIED: A league in which teams are allowed to have an average no higher than an agreed limit. Classified tournaments are limited to bowlers with averages no higher than a certain figure.

CLEAN FRAME: A frame in which all members of a team get a spare or strike.

CLEAN GAME: A game in which a bowler gets a strike or spare in all ten frames.

CLUTCH: A pressure situation.

CONVERSION: Knocking down all standing pins with the second ball in a frame.

COUNT: The number of pins knocked down with a ball.

CRANKER: The bowler who gives a ball an extreme twist or turn at the time of delivery.

CREEPER: A slowly delivered ball.

CROSS HIT: *See* Jersey Hit.

The pros' Harry Smith demonstrates body english.

CROSS-LANE: The recommended manner of rolling at spare leaves in a corner of the lane. Thus, for a pin in the right corner it is recommended to roll from the left corner.

CURVE: A ball that travels in an arc from the time it leaves a bowler's hand, as opposed to a hook, which travels in a straight line for part of the distance.

CUSHION: The pad at the back of the pit behind the pin deck.

DEAD BALL: The ABC declares a ball dead when any of the following occurs: (1) a player delivers a ball and attention is immediately called to the fact that one or more pins were missing from the setup; (2) a human pinsetter removes or interferes with a pin or pins before they stop rolling or before the ball reaches the pins; (3) a player rolls on the wrong lane; (4) a player is interfered with by a pinsetter, another bowler, spectator, or moving object as the ball is being delivered or before delivery is completed; (5) any pins are moved or knocked down in any manner before the ball reaches them; (6) a ball comes in contact with any foreign object.

DECK: *See* Pindeck.

DINNER BUCKET: *See* Bucket.

DIVISION BOARDS: The area where the maple boards on a lane are spliced with the pine boards, 15 feet from the foul line. The harder maple boards can withstand the dropping of the ball; the pine enables the ball to have a better roll. The pin deck, which takes a beating from the pins, is also maple.

DODO: A ball that is barred from sanctioned competition because of a lop-sided distribution of weight. The ball was legal some sixty years ago and was highly effective in the hands of an expert.

DOUBLE PINOCHLE: The 4-6-7-10 split. Also known as big four.

DOUBLE WOOD: A leave in which one pin is directly behind another, such as the 2-8 and the 3-9.

DUMPER: A bowling cheat; one who deliberately maintains a low average so that he can take unfair advantage in a league or tournament. Also known as a sandbagger.

DUROMETER: One of bowling's new gadgets. It is used to measure the hardness of a ball. The Pro Bowlers Association permits a reading no softer than a 75 rating.

DUTCH 200: A 200 score rolled on the head by a bowler alternating spares and strikes throughout the game.

ERROR: A missed spare. Also called a blow.

FAST LANE: In the East a fast lane is one on which a ball breaks sharply. In the West a fast lane is one on which it is difficult to make a ball hook.

FENCE: A row of pins left standing after the first ball, such as the 1-2-4-7. This term is useful in directing blind bowlers.

FENCE POSTS: *See* Bed Posts.

FIELD GOAL: Rolling a ball between two standing pins, such as the 7-10.

FILL: The number of pins knocked down following a spare. This number must be added to the spare before a score can be posted in that frame.

FLAT BALL: A weakly rolled ball with insufficient lift to make a strike, even though the ball is in the pocket.

FLAT LANE: A bowling lane that has been resurfaced and has no trace of a ball track.

FOLLOW-THROUGH: The act of continuing the arm swing after the ball has been delivered, thus imparting lift to the ball and causing it to hook.

FOUL: A bowler commits a foul when any part of his person encroaches beyond the foul line and touches any part of the lane, equipment, or building during or after a delivery. No pins are counted when a foul is committed.

FOUNDATION: A strike in the ninth frame, thus giving a bowler a foundation for the tenth frame. With a strike in the ninth a bowler can get 60 pins in the final two frames by striking out.

FRAME: One-tenth of a game. Also known as box.

FUDGE SHOT: Cutting down the revolutions in a delivery.

FULL HIT: A ball that hits the headpin on the nose. Also called a nose hit or a beaker.

FULL ROLLER: A ball delivered in such a manner that it rolls in a complete revolution around its middle and between the thumb and finger holes. This is in contrast to a spinner, which rolls on a small axis as it is delivered with the hand on top of the ball.

GETTING THE WOOD: Obtaining a good count on the first ball following a spare. Also used when a bowler has a wide-open split, such as two pins on one side and one on the other. It is a difficult split, and if a teammate tells the bowler to get the wood, he means for the bowler to try for two sure pins instead of trying to slide one pin over to convert the split.

GOALPOSTS: The 7-10 split. Also known as bedposts, fence posts, and the golden gate.

GOLDEN GATE: *See* Goalposts.

GRAVEYARD: A lane, pair of lanes, or an establishment noted for tough scoring conditions.

GREEK CHURCH: The 4-6-7-9-10 split leave.

GRIP: The combination of finger holes and span in a bowling ball.

GUTTER: A downgraded name for the depressed

area on either side of the lane. Now known as channel.

GUTTER BALL: A ball rolling off a lane into the channel, or gutter.

GUTTER SHOT: A ball delivered on the edge of the channel, or gutter. Some of the pro bowlers have become adept with this shot, permitting the ball to roll for several feet within an inch or two of the channel before breaking into the setup.

HALF HIT: Midway between a pocket hit and a nose hit.

HALL OF FAME: The American Bowling Congress instituted a Bowling Hall of Fame in 1941. It is located in Greendale, Wisc., and is run in conjunction with the Women's International Bowling Congress. Electors include the Hall of Fame members and bowling writers. Among the most illustrious members are Ned Day, one of the first bowlers to make extensive exhibition and match game tours; Andy Varipapa, famous trick-shot artist who once made nine strikes in a row on television; Dick Weber, the first to earn $500,000 in professional bowling; Don Carter, regarded by most experts as being the greatest bowler of all time; Hank Marino, voted by the writers as being "Bowler of the Half Century;" Floretta McCutcheon, pioneer teacher and leader of women's bowling; amd Marion Ladewig, who dominated women's bowling for two decades.

HEADPIN: The 1 pin in a setup, the pin that is at the peak of the triangle, meaning closest to the bowler.

HIGH HIT: A ball that hits the 1 pin fuller than the 3 pin in a try for a pocket-hit strike. Also known as a heavy hit.

HOLE: The 1-3 pocket, for right-handers.

HOOK: A ball that travels in a straight line for a distance and then curves toward the 1-3 pocket. The most popular delivery.

HOUSE BALL: A ball that is available to the public in an establishment. Better bowlers own their own bowling balls, drilled especially to their measurements and desires.

IN THE WOOD: A game in which the decision is still in doubt.

JERSEY HIT: *See* Brooklyn Hit.

KICKBACKS: No, it doesn't involve money. The kickbacks are the boards on either side of the pindeck, off which pins bounce back on the lane and spill standing pins. Also called sideboards or walls.

KINGPIN: The 5 pin in a setup. Also the name of an old German bowling game in which pins were set in a diamond shape with the kingpin in the middle. The object was to knock down as many pins as possible without spilling the kingpin.

KITTY: A fund collected by a team through penalties

for missed spares or low scores. Usually the kitty money is used for expenses for rolling in tournaments.

LANE: The bowling surface. To be certified a lane must measure 41 to 42 inches in width and 60 feet from the foul line to the headpin.

LEADOFF: The number-one man in a lineup.

LEAVE(S): The pin(s) left in the setup after the first ball is rolled in each frame.

LEGAL PINBALL: Pins knocked down when no foul is committed.

LIFT: What the bowler imparts to the ball with his fingers after his thumb has been removed from the hole at time of delivery.

LIGHT HIT: A ball, aimed at the 1-3 pocket, that gets more of the 3 pin than the 1 pin.

LIGNUM VITAE: The hardest and heaviest wood, which was used to make bowling balls before the hard-rubber-composition ball replaced it. Balls are also now made of plastic.

LINE: A game of ten frames. Also a term used to signify the path a bowler finds best in hitting the pocket.

LINE BALL: A ball delivered on a straight line to the pocket.

LOCKED IN: A term pro bowlers use when they are confident that they have found the best angle for hitting the pocket on a lane.

LOFTING THE BALL: Delivering the ball far out on the lane. Not recommended, since any lift or turn on the ball is dissipated when it strikes the lane after being lofted.

LOOPER: A curve ball.

MAPLES: Another name for the pins. At one time the pins were 100-percent maple. Now they are plastic coated.

MARATHON BOWLING: A freak activity, not recognized by the ABC, in which a bowler bowls as long as he can with only short breaks. Many marathon bowlers do this to raise money for a worthy cause.

MARK: A spare or strike.

MISS: Failure to make a spare. Also called a blow.

MIXER: A ball rolled with medium speed and much spin, which causes the pins to spin and knock each other down. Also, a league composed of both men and women.

NBC: National Bowling Council. Made up of various organizations in the sport and established to deal with various issues and common problems.

NOSE HIT: A ball that hits the headpin full. Also called a full hit or a beaker.

NOTHING BALL: A poorly delivered ball that appears to call for a strike but that leaves pins standing

*Don Carter, one of bowling's all-time greats, is in the
Hall of Fame.*

(often the 5 pin among them). This means the ball was weak and did not go through to the 5 pin but deflected when hitting the headpin. This happens with a spinner delivered with the hand on top of the ball.

ONE IN THE DARK: The rear pin in a double-wood situation.

OPEN BOWLING: Casual bowling, not in league or tournament competition.

OPEN FRAME: A frame in which a bowler does not get a mark.

OUT AND IN: A curve ball.

OVERTURN: A fault in which the bowler turns his hand at the moment of delivery. As a result he winds up with his hand on top of the ball. He gets a spinning ball, or a nothing ball.

PACKING: Pins knocked down after a spare.

PART OF THE BUILDING: What a bowler calls a pin that remains standing after an apparently perfect pocket hit.

PBA: Professional Bowlers Association. An organization of more than one thousand members who are the cream of the sport and who bowl for two million dollars in prize money each year. The finals of their tournaments are often carried on national television.

PENDULUM SWING: The recommended bowling approach technique in which the ball is permitted to swing under its own weight into the backswing and forward for the delivery in a smooth manner, without forcing.

PERFECT GAME: A 300; 12 straight strikes.

PIE LANE: A lane on which scoring is comparatively easy. Also known as a slot.

PINDECK: The portion of the lane on which the pins stand.

PINS: The ten objects that provide the target for the bowler. Made of wood, plastic, or a combination of both. A pin certified for sanctioned play may not be more than 15 inches in height nor measure more than 4.76 inches wide at its widest part.

PIT: The space at the rear of the pindeck into which the pins are knocked by the ball.

PITCH: The angle at which the finger holes in a ball are drilled.

PLUS AND MINUS: The method used to record the progress of bowlers in PBA tournaments. On the telescore sheets above a bowler's lane, the figures show plus and minus figures, based on a 200-average base. The pluses are in black, the minuses in red.

POCKET: The area between the 1 and 3 pins for the right-handed bowler; the place to hit for a perfect strike.

POCKET HIT: A ball hitting the 1-3 pocket for a right-handed bowler.

POINTING BALL: Aiming the ball directly at the pocket at the moment of release instead of rolling to the right and allowing for the ball to hook.

POT GAME: A bowling match in which the high scorer takes all the stakes.

PUNCHING OUT: Striking out in the last frame.

PUSHAWAY: The act of pushing the ball away from the body at the start of the approach. The pushaway gets the ball in a position to start its pendulum motion into the backswing.

PWBA: The Professional Women's Bowling Association. This is the women's counterpart of the PBA.

RAIL: Another name for split. Also known as railroad in some sections of the country.

RAKE: The part of the automatic pinsetter that sweeps away fallen pins after the first ball in a frame.

RAP: Failing to get a strike on an apparent perfect hit. Also known as a tap or a touch.

READING A LANE: A facility possessed by the better pro bowlers for determining quickly the best angle to roll for strikes.

RELEASE: The act of delivering the ball.

RETURN: The means by which the ball is returned to the bowler after a delivery.

REVERSE: *See* Backup.

RUNNING LANE: A lane on which a ball is inclined to hook sharply.

SANDBAGGER: *See* Dumper.

SCORING: A game consists of ten frames. A bowler is permitted a second ball in each frame if he does not score a strike on his first ball. A strike is scored when all the pins are knocked down on the first ball. A spare is recorded when all the pins are knocked down with two balls.

A bowler scoring a strike is credited with 10 pins, plus the number of pins he knocks down on his next two deliveries.

When a bowler gets a spare, he is credited with 10 pins plus all the pins knocked down on his next ball.

When pins are left standing after the second ball is rolled, a bowler is credited with only the pins knocked down.

A split is recorded when two or more pins are left standing after the first ball is rolled, leaving a space between two pins where a pin had been standing.

In the typical game pictured here, the bowler made a strike in the first frame. When he knocked down 10 pins on his next two balls in the second frame, he was credited with 20 pins in the first frame as well as a spare in the second frame.

When the bowler got 8 pins on his first ball in the third frame, he was credited with 18 in the second frame, but 38 is written, as the total for the two frames is brought forward.

In the third frame, he left a split with his first ball,

and on his second ball in that frame he missed both pins so was credited with just 8 pins in that frame for a total of 46.

He converted a split in the fourth frame, and it was worth 19 pins when he knocked down 9 pins on his first ball in the fifth.

The rest should be easy to follow.

BOWLING SYMBOLS

⊠ STRIKE

◩ SPARE   ⊙ SPLIT

◪ CONVERTED SPLIT   ⊟ MISS

SAMPLE GAME

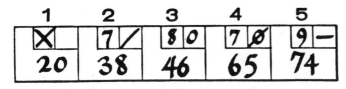

SCRATCH LEAGUE: A league in which the teams bowl on even terms, without a handicap. Handicaps are usually based on a percentage of the difference in team averages.

SEMIROLLER: A ball that rolls outside the thumb and finger holes instead of between them as does a full roller. The ball, though delivered with the hand on top of the ball, does not roll on a small axis as does a spinner.

SETUP: The ten pins standing in their regular triangular position on the pindeck. In this formation, the pins are numbered with the 1 pin standing alone at the forward point of the triangle and the rest of the pins are numbered from left to right in sequence. Thus, the setup looks like this:

```
7  8  9  10
  4  5  6
   2  3
    1
```

SHOTGUN SHOT: Firing the ball from the hip.

SIDEARM: A bowling fault; bringing the elbow away from the body so that the hand winds up on top of the ball.

SIDEBOARDS: See Kickbacks.

SLICK: A lane condition whereby the ball is inclined to skid extremely.

SLIDE: The finish of a bowler's delivery. Also, in some areas, a name for a bowling lane.

SLOT: A lane on which scoring is easy. Also a ball drilling in which two fingers are inserted into the same hole.

SLOW LANE: A lane that has the opposite characteristics possessed by a fast lane.

SOAKER: A plastic ball that is softened by being placed in a solvent for a period of time. The softer shell induces more traction on a lane. The Pro Bowlers Association has barred the soaker. The solvent is flammable.

SPAN: The distance between the finger holes and thumb hole in a ball. Also known as bridge.

SPARE: All the pins knocked down on two balls in a frame.

SPINNER: A ball delivered with the hand on top of the ball so that it spins on a small axis. A weak ball, not recommended because it is easily deflected when it hits the pins.

SPLICE: See Division Boards.

SPLIT: Two or more pins standing with at least one pin down in between. If the headpin is standing, it is not a split.

SPOT BOWLING: The recommended method of bowling; choosing a spot near the division boards, only 15 feet distant, and attempting to roll the ball over this spot consistently instead of aiming at the pocket, which is 60 feet away.

STANCE: The position taken before beginning the approach.

STRAPPING BALL: Getting all the lift possible in delivery.

STRIKE: Knocking down all ten pins on the first ball in a frame.

STRIKEOUT: Three strikes in the final frame.

STRIKE SPLIT: The 8-10 leave for a right-hander on an apparent strike hit.

STRING: Several successive strikes.

SWEEPSTAKES: A form of tournament play with awards usually made immediately after its conclusion. Normally a two-game event.

TAP: Failure to get a strike on an apparently perfect hit. Also known as a rap or a touch.

THIN HIT: A try for a pocket hit that gets a bigger piece of the 3 pin than the 1 pin.

TIGHT LANE: A lane on which it is difficult to make a ball hook.

TOPPED BALL: An overturned ball.

TOUCH: *See* Tap.

TRACK: *See* Ball Track.

TRIPLE: Three strikes in a row. Also known as a turkey.

TRIPPED 4: A 4 pin that is knocked down by the 2 pin rebounding from the kickback instead of being spilled by the action of the ball driving 2 into 4.

TURKEY: Three strikes in succession. Said to have originated in the early days of bowling when a turkey would be awarded to anyone getting three strikes in a row.

TURN: *See* Lift.

TWO-TEEN: A score of 213 through 219.

WALLS: *See* Kickbacks.

WASHOUT: Similar to a split but with headpin standing.

WIBC: The Women's International Bowling Congress, governing body of more than three million organized women bowlers.

WOOD: The pins.

WOOLWORTHS: The 5-10 split leave.

WORKING BALL: A ball that, because of the lift given to it at release, results in a strike even though the hit was not perfect. The spin of the ball is imparted to the pins, causing them to work for the bowler.

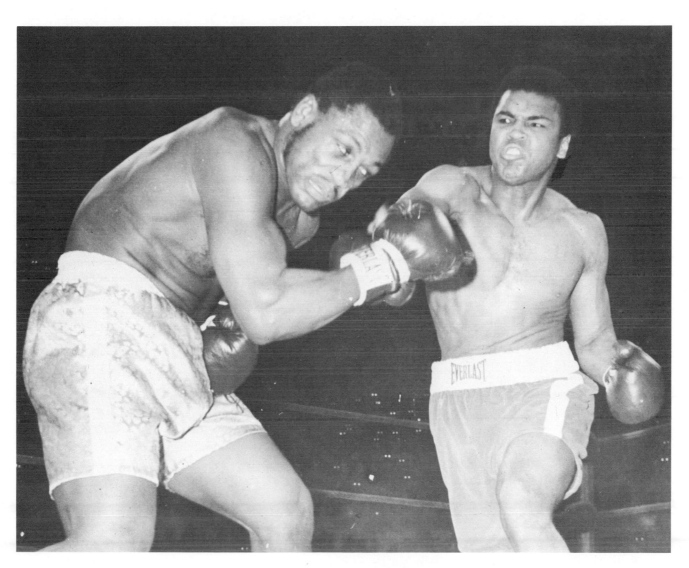

Muhammad Ali, once Cassius Clay, is on the attack against Joe Frazier in their first world heavyweight match in 1971, but it was Smokin' Joe who won the decision.

AAU: Amateur Athletic Union. As with other amateur sports, the AAU supervises amateur boxing in the United States. It sanctions matches that are held according to AAU specifications and, annually, holds national championships. On the negative side, many amateur boxing groups believe that the AAU actually restricts boxing. These groups charge that since the AAU will sanction only matches that have AAU officials, a promoter must pay at least five hundred or six hundred dollars to stage a card. This minimizes the number of matches and gives rise to unsanctioned fights. *See also* Bootleg.

ACHE: An ache is an ache in any sport, but boxing might give it an added dimension. For instance: In his dressing room after winning a hard fight, light-heavyweight Bobby Cassidy was asked by his manager, Paddy Flood, how he felt. "Okay," Cassidy said, "except my left eye aches." Flood examined the eye and said, "Yeah, I see. And the ache is getting purple."

ACT: A common ploy in which one fighter will pretend to be hurt more than he is, hoping his opponent will become rash and abandon defense in an effort to score a knockdown. Another familiar act is when a fighter who has taken a low blow grovels on the canvas, hoping the referee will disqualify his opponent or allow him time in his corner to recover (take a rest). This rule varies according to the state or country.

ALI: Muhammad Ali, once Cassius Clay. The second man to ever win back the heavyweight championship of the world (Floyd Patterson was the first). His title was stripped from him after he was indicted for refusing induction into the armed services during the war in Vietnam. He has since been cleared of the charge. He is noted for being brash, for spouting bad poetry, and for being probably the quickest heavyweight champion ever.

ALI SHUFFLE: This is a stiff-legged dance that Muhammad Ali resorts to in the ring. It might confuse his opponent, although none has ever admitted being confused. Primarily it's done by Ali to amuse his fans.

AMATEUR: The fighter who does not fight for money, but rather awards. Olympic team members must be amateurs.

AMATEUR RULES: In the United States amateur rules conform closely with those of the professional. But when an American amateur fights in an international meet, the rules radically change. In international rules a knockdown counts only as a good point, not more than a blow would earn that did not knock a man down. International rules also provide more varied and stringent penalties for rule violations.

ANNOUNCER: This is the man, usually in a tuxedo, who introduces the fighters, their hometowns, and their weights to the crowd and who, when the fight is ended, collects the slips from the officials and reveals the winner, or in the case of a knockout, the time of the knockout.

APRON: The portion of the ring that extends beyond the roped area.

ART OF SELF-DEFENSE: Also referred to as the manly art or noble art, the phrase was originally used in England in advertisements used to attract gentlemen and members of the nobility to "boxing salons" run by well-known fighters. John Broughton, one of England's early champions, ran such a salon and had as patrons the Duke of Cumberland and Lord Byron.

AUTOMATIC EIGHT-COUNT: In most professional rings throughout the world rules insist that a boxer who has been knocked down must take a mandatory eight-count. This, it is believed, gives the knocked-down fighter time to recover and hence lessen the chance of injury.

AUTOMATIC TIMEKEEPER: The clock at ringside that automatically rings the bell and tolls the minutes of a round. It was first used in California at the Peter Jackson-James J. Corbett fight on May 21, 1891. It has been adopted for years by the larger boxing arenas, but smaller houses still resort to the stopwatch and the hammer the human timekeeper uses to belt the gong.

BACKHAND: A swipe with the back of a fighter's hand, which is outlawed in both professional and amateur boxing. In the early days it was common for a fighter who missed a punch to jerk his hand back and land a backhand.

BAG GLOVE(S): In training a fighter uses several types of punching bags and must use small, pliant leather gloves to avoid abrasions—particularly from the heavy bag, which usually weighs from 60 to 80 pounds.

BALANCE: Probably the hardest thing for a trainer is to teach a budding fighter balance. In order to throw a punch correctly and deliver it with potency, a fighter must be evenly balanced on both feet. Defense depends on balance, too. Experts believe that most knockdowns are not the result of the punch, but a combination of a good punch from the aggressor and bad balance on his opponent's side.

BANDAGES: These are the wrappings that go around a fighter's hands before the hands are encased in the gloves. They are meant to protect the knuckles and hand bones.

BANTAMWEIGHT: The weight division from 113 through 118 pounds.

BAREKNUCKLE: Before the so-called modern era of sports, men in the prize ring fought bare-handed, which was as tough on hands as it was on faces. In 1867 in England the Marquis of Queensberry rules were introduced that called for gloves. The first heavyweight championship fight in which gloves were used was the John L. Sullivan-James J. Corbett fight, September 7, 1892, at New Orleans.

BARNSTORMING: In earlier days many professional boxers would travel to small towns and county fairs, set up a stall, and offer money to any hearty local who could last a certain period of time with him. The boxer seldom had to pay off. On such a tour John L. Sullivan faced 50 men and knocked out 49 of them.

BATTLING BASQUE: Paulino Uzcudon of Spain. He was an obstacle set before any heavyweight who thought he had a future in the division during the 1930s. If they got by Uzcudon, they had a chance. He boxed from 1923 until December 13, 1935, when Joe Louis knocked him out in four rounds.

BBC: The British Boxing Board of Control is a self-perpetuating organization that rules boxing in the British Isles. Being insular, it is much more powerful than other organizations that are made up with members of different countries or states and are beset with a confusion of national or territorial interests.

BELL: The gong that signals the start and end of each round.

BELLY SHOT: A punch to the stomach—usually a hook. Body punching often gets a call from a fan in the stands that "he don't like 'em there." Of course, nobody does. Belly shots are usually effective in getting an opponent to lower his guard from his face and thus give the aggressor two targets.

BELOW THE BELT: This is a foul. Until the advent of a foul-proof belt, a leather contraption that covers the lower abdomen and groin area, it led to disqualification—as it still does if considered a flagrant violation in the amateurs. In Britain a puncher who continues to hit foul will be disqualified. In most U.S. states such punches lead to penalties in points. In some states the man who is fouled is allowed a rest period before continuing the fight. One heavyweight championship was won on a punch below the belt. On June 12, 1930, Jack Sharkey, fighting Max Schmeling for the title vacated by Gene Tunney, landed a low punch and the fight and title were awarded to Schmeling.

BLACK EYE: A discoloration of the skin around the eye. According to the Oxford Universal Dictionary the term has been in the language since 1604.

BOLO PUNCH: The favorite punch of Ceferino Garcia, a popular welterweight and middleweight of the 1930s. A native of the Philippines, Garcia would whip his right in a three-quarter uppercut, a move, he said, he had learned swishing a machete in the cane fields of his homeland. The blow was later copied by Kid Gavilan, a welterweight champion in the 1950s.

BOOTLEG: Amateur fights conducted without sanction of the AAU. Since AAU sanction and AAU officials cost between five hundred and six hundred dollars for a match (the estimate comes from bootleg promoters), nonsanctioned fights are staged to provide an outlet for fighters who would not be able to fight other than in Golden Glove matches. Amateurs complain that while bootlegs give them a chance to

John L. Sullivan won the heavyweight crown at a time when they fought with bare knuckles, and lost his title to James J. Corbett in 1892 when gloves were used for the first time in a heavyweight championship bout.

fight, the officials are usually local politicians or promoters who do not understand boxing and that often the verdicts are unfair.

BOSTON STRONG BOY: John L. Sullivan, the last of the bareknuckle heavyweight champions. He was born in Roxbury, Mass., October 15, 1858. Sullivan, 5'10½", weighed 190 pounds in his better days. In 1888 in London he fought Charley Mitchell a 39-round draw that lasted 3 hours, 10 minutes, and 55 seconds under London prize-ring rules. Wearing gloves, Sullivan was knocked out by James J. Corbett in 21 rounds at New Orleans on September 7, 1892, and lost his championship.

BOTTOM: In England, a word used to denote courage. Pearce Egan, a boxing biographer of the nineteenth century, wrote, "He took a dreadful beating, but the crowd applauded his bottom." Usually when a boxing writer notes that one fighter has courage, it is because the man has taken a beating and keeps coming back for more.

BOXING COMMISSION: In the U.S. many states have commissions that have jurisdiction over boxing within their borders. In states that have no commissions cities or counties appoint their own.

BRAWLER: He is the fighter who has very little sense of boxing science and, usually, doesn't think he needs it. He churns up and makes for his opponent, trying to hit and hurt before he in turn is hit and hurt.

BREAK: The command the referee gives boxers when they are clinched or are holding. At the command "break!" the boxer should take a step backward before resuming the fight.

BRENNER: Teddy Brenner, a vice president and matchmaker at Madison Square Garden, was known as the boy promoter when he operated small arenas in the New York area. In more than twenty-five years at the Garden, Brenner has made more topnotch fights than any man in the business.

BRINE: It's not in use much any more, but once fighters would bathe their hands in brine to toughen them. Some even used it on their faces if they were prone to being cut. According to Dr. Edwin A. Campbell of the New York Athletic Commission, it was "completely ineffective—sort of an old wives' tale."

"BRING IT UP": A fighter's manager or second will yell this when his fighter gets into a stomach-punching rut. The yell usually sounds like this: "For crying out loud, bring it up!" He means that the fighter should alternate punches to the head.

BROCKTON BLOCKBUSTER: Rocky Marciano, a native of Brockton, Mass., earned this nickname by scoring 43 knockouts in 49 bouts. He won the heavyweight championship by knocking out Jersey Joe Walcott in 13 rounds on September 23, 1952, in Philadelphia. He retired undefeated in 1956. Marciano was killed in an airplane crash in Iowa on August 31, 1969.

BRONX BULL: Jake LaMotta, who won the middleweight championship from Marcel Cerdan, June 16, 1949, at Detroit, had the reputation for not being knocked down, no matter how hard he was hit. His record ended after 103 bouts when he was floored by Danny Nardico at Coral Gables, Fla., on December 11, 1952. LaMotta, in 1959, admitted to the Kefauver Crime Commission in the U.S. Senate that he had taken a "dive," meaning he threw a fight in New York with Billy Fox in 1947, in exchange for a promise that he would fight for the championship.

BROWN BOMBER: Joe Louis Barrow, the champion of the world for longer than any other heavyweight was champion, 1937-49. He won the title from James J. Braddock, June 22, 1937, and successfully defended the crown 26 times. *See also* Bum of the Month Club.

BULL: Meaning to press aggressively. "He bulled his way," a boxing person says of a man who keeps the pressure on his opponent throughout a fight. It is also used to describe great strength, e.g., "a bull of a man."

BULL OF THE PAMPAS: Luis Firpo, also known, if the boxing writer was looking for adjectives, as the Wild Bull of the Pampas. Firpo came up from Argentina to fight Jack Dempsey. With the first punch of the night he knocked Dempsey to his knees. Dempsey got up and smashed Firpo to the canvas seven times in that opening round and seven times Firpo got up. After the seventh knockdown he belted Dempsey and knocked the champion out of the ring. Hands of reporters pushed Dempsey back into the ring. Dempsey dropped his man for good in the next round.

BUM OF THE MONTH CLUB: After winning the title, Joe Louis defended it against Tommy Farr in a hard-fought 15 rounds and then embarked on what writers called the Bum of the Month Club. Between 1938 and 1941, Louis met such nonnotables as Nathan Mann, Harry Thomas, Jack Roper, Tony Galento, Bob Pastor, Arturo Godoy, Al McCoy, Red Burman, Gus Dorazio, Abe Simon, Tony Musto, and Buddy Baer—all in title defenses!

BUSTED UP: A fighter who is cut is said to be busted up.

BUTCHER'S APRON: Sometimes a punch on the nose will cause excessive bleeding, and as the fighter bleeds, his trunks will become blood spattered. And, as has always been the case, some writer will write, "His trunks were like a butcher's apron."

On the way to the heavyweight title, Rocky Marciano, the Brockton Blockbuster, *knocked out former champion Joe Louis in 1951.*

BUTT: A deliberate foul. When a fighter uses his head to hit his opponent's head.

BUTTON: An indefinite point on the side of a boxer's jaw. If this area is hit by a sharp blow, it is supposed to render the receiver unconscious. Boxing men deny any such point exists and maintain that a hard punch on any part of the jaw can be harmful. Nevertheless, the cry will remain: "Hit him on the button."

CANVAS: The covering of the ring.

CANVAS BACK: A fighter who has a record of being knocked down frequently.

CARD: The various matches scheduled for a single night in an arena are referred to as the card. Main-event fighters will be said to "top the card."

CAULIFLOWER EAR: Ears that are hit frequently over many bouts swell and form bumps that harden and stay that way. At one time it was the badge of the unsuccessful fighter, but not any more. Ear swellings are now eliminated by ring doctors with minor surgery.

CHOP: This is a punch delivered overhand that strikes an opponent with the outside part of a fist. It is delivered as if the aggressor were swinging a claw hammer.

CINDERELLA MAN: James J. Braddock. One day less than a year after he appeared on the semifinal of the heavyweight championship bout between Max Baer and Primo Carnera, he fought and decisioned Baer over 15 rounds (June 13, 1935) to win the heavyweight

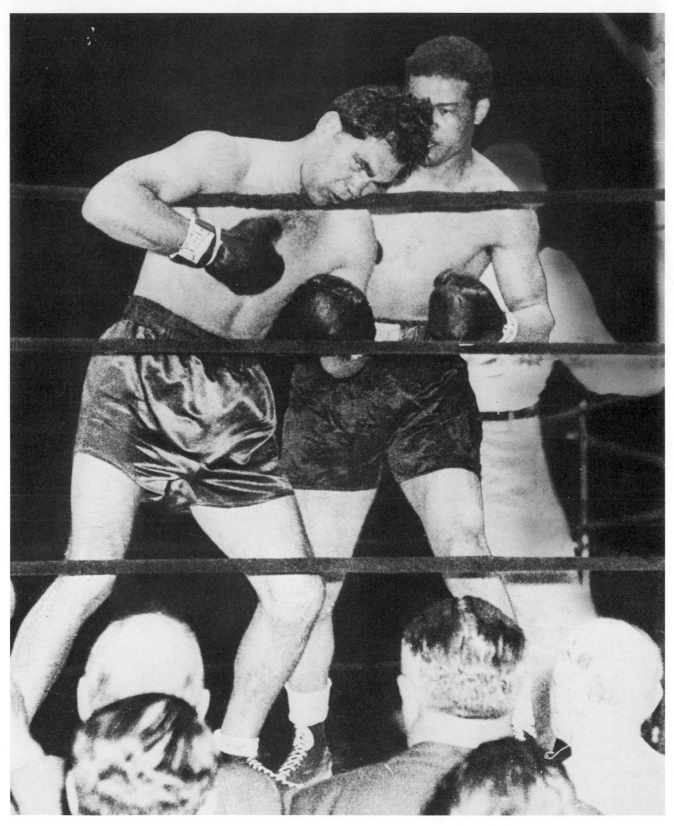

Joe Louis, the Brown Bomber, *got revenge for an earlier defeat when he knocked out Max Schmeling in one round in 1938.*

crown. Braddock, before that semifinal fight, had drifted onto the New Jersey docks as a part-time stevedore and was on relief—hence, The Cinderella Man.

CLARET: A euphemism for blood. Ted Husing, a radio broadcaster before World War II, would describe a bleeding fighter as being covered with claret.

CLAY: *See* Ali.

CLINCH: When both fighters are wrapped up in each other's arms so that neither man can throw a punch, that's a clinch. The referee will part the men, who must step back before resuming the bout. The referee will not break the men if one fighter has a hand free.

CLOCK: Not only is the automatic timekeeper or stopwatch at ringside referred to as the clock, but most large arenas have huge clocks on display so that the spectators might see how much time is left in a round. Of course, the boxers take advantage of these clocks, too. A man who is tiring, or who wants to put on a spurt near the end of a round will be said to be watching the clock. *See also* Stealing.

CLOUT: Another word for punch, but it indicates that it was a hard punch.

COLD: Has nothing to do with the weather. When a fighter says he's cold, he means he could not get himself into the fight. "He caught me cold," an early knockout victim will alibi.

CORBETT: *See* Gentleman Jim.

CORKSCREW PUNCH: In the 1920s the corkscrew punch received some publicity in the gyms as a new weapon. Turns out it wasn't a weapon of any kind. The idea was that when a man landed a punch, he should grind his fist at the point of impact. But boxing people say the impact is the thing, and the corkscrew is just so much dressing.

COUNT: When a fighter is knocked to the canvas, the referee will toll the seconds, or count. In most states and countries, a mandatory eight-count is required before the downed man can resume fighting. If the man remains on the canvas for ten seconds, he is considered knocked out.

CROWDING: A fighter who has an opponent who possesses superior speed and length of arm will crowd him, i.e., stay close to him, to minimize his opponent's assets.

CUFFING: This is almost a slap, usually delivered with an open glove, which is a violation of the rules. A cuff has little power and is often delivered to irritate an opponent or, as in Muhammad Ali's bag of tricks, used to intimidate.

CUT: A laceration of the skin. The word also applies to the share a manager received from his fighter's purse—much more painful to the fighter than a laceration.

CUT MAN: A second in a fighter's corner who is adept at stemming the flow of blood from a cut.

DANCER: Applied to a fighter who moves around the ring avoiding his opponent's attack.

DATES: A fighter's scheduled engagements—"I got me a date in Scranton the sixth."

DECISION: If a fight runs its full course, the officials, usually two judges and a referee, will hand in their cards on which they have tabulated rounds and points, and the fighter with the greater number of rounds or points (depending on the system) will be awarded the decision.

DISQUALIFICATION: A fighter can be disqualified for repeatedly fouling or for refusing to go on the offensive. The disqualified fighter, of course, loses the fight.

DIVE: When a fighter deliberately loses, he has, boxing people say, "Taken a dive." *See also* Tank.

DOG: Means a couple of things. "He's a dog," in reference to a fighter, means the man has very little ability. But "He's got a little bit of dog in him" means the fighter is more concerned with not getting hurt than with fighting. He wants to survive. Angelo Dundee, longtime trainer of Muhammad Ali, has said, "I like a fighter who has a little bit of dog in him. Guys that are nothing but brave get busted up."

DOLLAR SEAT(S): The cheapest seats in a boxing arena—regardless of what they cost.

DONNYBROOK: When two fighters flail at each other unceasingly and the fight is virtually a war, it's called a Donnybrook for no reason anyone knows, except that Donnybrook is a village near Dublin, Ireland, and when the pubs there close on Saturday nights, the streets can become lively.

DOUBLE-END BAG: A punching bag that is suspended between the ceiling and the floor.

DOUBLE UP: When a fighter uses the same punch twice in a row, he is said to be doubling up. "He doubled up with a hook."

DRAW: When a fight has gone its scheduled limit and the officials have each fighter even, the fight is called a draw, or tie.

DRESSING: The bandage a fighter wears to protect a cut.

DRESSING ROOM: Exactly that. In the dressing room a fighter dresses to fight. He will also do calisthenics in it to warm up before a fight.

DUCAT: A ticket to a fight.

DUKE: The verdict. "He copped the duke" means he won the decision.

DURHAM'S LAW: The late Yancey Durham, onetime manager of Joe Frazier, was discussing theater-television with a promoter. "We have a hundred thousand seats available," the promoter told Durham. Durham then invoked his law: "It ain't how many seats you got," Durham said. "What counts is how many rear ends you got in those seats."

EKE OUT: To barely win a fight. In a case where the two judges score a fight even and the referee gives one fighter a one-point edge, that man has "eked out" a victory.

ELBOWING: A violation that often is not detected by the referee. A man who misses a punch with his fist sometimes connects with his elbow. It is a good cutting tool.

EMERGENCY BOUT: This is a fight not on the card, but the fighters are available in the event several fights end in knockouts and the promoters wish to extend the evening for their customers.

EUROPEAN BOXING UNION: The overall authority in Europe to which all European boxing groups belong.

EVENT: A bout. Usually as in "main event."

EVIL EYE: Some seconds take advantage of a fighter's superstitions and try to spook the man by giving him the evil eye.

EVIL EYE FINKLE: An oldtime second who rose to some fame on one fight. Melio Bettina, a light-heavyweight, was to fight Gus Lesnevitch. Bettina's manager was Jimmy Grippo, a magician and hypnotist. Grippo advertised that he would hypnotize Lesnevitch and that Bettina would win. Lesnevitch's manager, Lew "The Honest Brakeman" Diamond, thereupon hired Evil Eye Finkle to offset Grippo. Finkle's man won a one-round knockout. Diamond, incidentally, was called The Honest Brakeman because the boxing fraternity alleged, "He never stole a boxcar."

FAN: Short for fanatic. One who follows boxing. Perhaps the most fanatical of all fans is Bryan Brown of London, who, *The Ring Record Book* reports, named a daughter born in 1972 after every world heavyweight champion since 1882. The girl's name is Maria Sullivan Corbett Fitzsimmons Jeffries Hart Burns Johnson Williard Dempsey Tunney Schmeling Sharkey Carnera Baer Braddock Louis Charles Walcott Marciano Patterson Johansson Liston Clay Frazier Foreman Brown.

FANCY DAN: A boxer who utilizes speed of foot and deception to make his opponent miss.

FARGO EXPRESS: A lightweight during the 1920s and 1930s who had a churning offense and fought the best in his division for eleven years, Billy Petrolle came from Fargo, N.Dak. He's a member of the Boxing Hall of Fame.

FEATHERWEIGHT: The weight division from 119 through 126 pounds.

FEINT: When a fighter makes a gesture as if he is going to throw a punch with one hand and instead throws the other, he has feinted with a left and crossed over a right.

FIGHT: What fighters do in the ring. To land punches on their opponents.

FIGHTER: Two of them make a fight.

FIGHTING MARINE: Gene Tunney, who defeated Jack Dempsey for the heavyweight title and again in a rematch, served with the Marine Corps in World War I. Tunney retired undefeated.

FIGHT OF THE WEEK: A longtime television series on Friday nights. Don Dunphy was the blow-by-blow announcer.

FIREPLUG: A squat, short fighter. "He's built like a fireplug."

FISH: An easy opponent. "He was no problem; he was a fish."

FISTICUFFS: An archaic name for boxing.

FIST(S): What occurs when a person clenches his hands. It's what fighters hit with.

FITZ: Bob Fitzsimmons defeated James J. Corbett for the heavyweight title on March 18, 1897. He lost the title to Jim Jeffries on June 9, 1899, and in 1903 won the light-heavyweight title. Another nickname for Fitzsimmons was Ruby Robert. *See also* Solar Plexus.

FIVE-POINT MUST: A system of scoring in many states. The winner of a round is given five points and his opponent four or less.

FLATTENED: A man who is knocked out is flattened.

FLURRY: A rapid delivery of many punches, one after the other.

FLYWEIGHT: The weight division up to 112 pounds.

FOOTWORK: What a fighter displays who moves quickly and scientifically on his feet. Deft feet give a boxer the opportunity to deliver a punch and step out of countering danger.

FOUL: Any punch that hits a man behind the ear or in the groin, as well as a backhand punch, lacing, or holding and hitting.

FOUL-PROOF BELT: A leather device that protects a fighter's lower abdomen and groin.

FOXES: Muhammad Ali's name for pretty women. Before a fight starts he will gaze in each direction from his corner to "count the foxes."

GATE: The money paid by a fight crowd; admissions. After the Joey Giardello-Dick Tiger middleweight championship fight at Atlantic City, December 7, 1963, the fight's publicist, Murray Goodman, announced, "The ushers stole the gate." What had happened was that ushers had opened side doors to the convention center, where the fight was being held, and allowed fans in for sums much less than the admission price.

GAUZE: The material placed upon a cut and under a dressing.

GENTLEMAN JIM: James J. Corbett, the first heavyweight champion under Marquis of Queensberry rules. He defeated John L. Sullivan at New Orleans on September 7, 1892.

GET OFF: A boxer's ability to go right to work or to start an offense is referred to as "getting off." A boxer who fights a lacklustre fight will admit later, "I just couldn't get off."

GLASS JAW: A boxer who cannot take a punch and is easily flattened is said to have a glass jaw.

GLOVES: The upholstered leather mittens that boxers must wear. The word also applies to the gloves worn to punch training bags.

GOLDEN GLOVES: A national amateur tournament held under the cosponsorship of the *New York Daily News* and the *Chicago Tribune*.

GOUGE: A flagrant foul. When a boxer gouges another boxer, he is putting the hard thumb of the glove into the other's eye. *See also* Thumbing.

GREATEST: Muhammad Ali self-description: "I am the Greatest."

GRIPPO: *See* Evil Eye.

GYM: Gymnasium. Where boxers train for fights.

GYM FIGHTER: Boxers who show great ability boxing in the gym but never seem to be able to call on that ability during an actual fight.

HALL OF FAME: Through the years great boxers of the past have had their names enshrined on the Hall of Fame record. There is no actual "hall" such as baseball has at Cooperstown, N.Y. Members of the Boxing Writers Association vote on those who are candidates for the hall.

HAMMER OF THOR: Ingemar Johansson, who won the heavyweight title from Floyd Patterson (June 26, 1959, New York) and lost it to Patterson (June 20, 1960, New York) called his right-hand punch the Hammer of Thor.

HANDLE: In boxing, unlike in horseracing, *handle* does not mean "money." It refers to a person's name, as in "What's his handle?" *See also* Moniker.

HANDLER: A man who trains a boxer or works in his corner. *See also* Second(s).

"HASN'T LAID A GLOVE ON ME": A boxer will say this between rounds to his handler if he is having a fairly easy time in the ring. When a handler tells his fighter the other man hasn't laid a glove on him, it gives

rise to what is now an old saw, "Yeah? Well, you better watch the referee, 'cause someone is beating hell out of me."

HEAD: A boxer who believes he is being butted will complain to the referee, "Watch the head." It is also used as in, "He was in over his head," meaning that a boxer was overmatched.

HEAD GEAR: This is a leather skull protector that international amateurs must wear in bouts and that all boxers usually wear while sparring in the gym. The late former welterweight champion Barney Ross was in Stillman's Gym one day, and King Levinski, who was training to fight Joe Louis, was sparring with another heavyweight. Levinski was not wearing head gear. "Look, King," Ross told him. "Without head gear you could get cut. This is a good purse for you. Why screw it up?" Levinski immediately put on head gear and started punching the speed bag.

HEAD HUNTER: A boxer who goes after the other man's head, disregarding any other target.

HEAVY BAG: A ponderous canvas or leather sack holding about 60 pounds of padding and suspended from the gym's ceiling by a chain. It is used to practice hard punching and serves to build up shoulder and arm muscles and strengthen wrists.

HEAVYWEIGHT: Any fighter weighing more than 175 pounds.

HEELING: A foul. A man is heeling who rubs the lower inside of the boxing glove on his opponent's face. It can cause cuts.

HIDE: A fighter's skin. Also, what a boxer cannot do in the ring. Joe Louis, on being told his next opponent was tricky and very fast, replied, "He can run if he wants to, but he can't hide."

HITTING ON THE BREAK: When boxers are separated from a clinch, they must step back before resuming boxing. A man who hits on the break commits a foul.

HOLDING AND HITTING: A foul. If a boxer grabs a man with one hand and hits him with the other, it is a violation, and the holder will be warned by the referee.

HOMETOWN DECISION: Fighters will complain that they can't win a decision out of town. "I beat him, but they gave him the duke. A hometown decision."

HONEST LEGS: Usually means a boxer is slow-footed. "He had larceny in his arms, but his legs were honest."

HONEY: Some seconds will serve a fighter honey and water between rounds of a bout to give him additional energy or make up for what energy the boxer has lost. Other seconds have been known to cheat—to mix the honey with brandy instead of water.

HOOK: A sidearm punch to the jaw or ribs. Right-handed fighters have left hooks and left-handers have right hooks.

HORTON LAW: Governed boxing in New York, from 1896 to 1900. It permitted bouts of any duration and a decision by the referee. It was repealed by the Lewis Law in 1900, which outlawed boxing except in membership clubs.

HURRICANE: A nickname worn by two notables. Henry Armstrong, who held the welterweight, light-weight, and featherweight titles simultaneously, was called Hurricane Henry because of his nonstop punching routine. Tommy Jackson, a heavyweight of the 1950s, was Hurricane Jackson because he threw the way Armstrong did, but with less results.

ICE: Applied to areas of a boxer's body, face or hands, to reduce swelling.

INGO: Ingemar Johansson. *See also* Hammer of Thor.

IRISH: A pride in nationality and a desire to attract Irish customers have led scores of fighters to put the word "Irish" in front of their own names. An example is Irish Bobby Cassidy.

IRISH THRUSH: Jack Doyle, supposedly the champion of Ireland, came to the United States in the 1930s to challenge American heavyweights. Doyle would sing in a pretty tenor voice before the fight, but he was inept in the ring.

ITALIAN ALP: A nickname of Primo Carnera, who won the heavyweight championship from Jack Sharkey on June 29, 1933, and lost it to Max Baer on June 14, 1934. He was 6'5¾" tall, which made him the second tallest heavyweight champion. Jess Willard was the tallest at 6'6¼".

JACOBS' BEACH: Max Jacobs was the promoter at Madison Square Garden in the 1930s and 1940s, and the area around the old Garden on Fiftieth Street and Eighth Avenue in New York was called Jacobs' Beach.

JAMMED KNUCKLES: A painful injury that occurs when a fighter's knuckle is bunched back into his hand, usually because he has hit his opponent on the head.

JERSEY JOE: Joe Walcott, who won the heavy-weight title from Ezzard Charles on July 18, 1951, in Pittsburgh, and lost it to Rocky Marciano on September 23, 1952. Walcott, whose real name was Arnold Cream, became sheriff of Camden County, N.J.

JEWEL OF THE GHETTO: Ruby Goldstein. He was a lightweight from Manhattan's Lower East Side and became a noted referee.

JUDGE: In most states and countries two or three judges are assigned to score a fight. In the United States, most states use two judges and give the referee a vote. Where a referee does not judge, as in amateur fights, three judges are used.

KIDNEY PUNCH: A punch to the kidneys. It's illegal, although boxers are seldom warned unless they actually aim at the kidney section.

KILLER INSTINCT: What fighters who seem ferocious are said to possess. Jack Dempsey was said to have it. *See also* Manassa Mauler.

KING: Don King, a black promoter from Cleveland who promoted Muhammad Ali fights in the United States, Africa, Malaysia, and the Philippines for more money than any other fighter ever received. King has said he owes his success to "OPM"—Other People's Money.

KNOCKDOWN: When a fighter is hit by a punch that knocks him off his feet.

KNOCKOUT: When a fighter who has been knocked down cannot get to his feet within ten seconds, he has suffered a knockout.

KNUCKLES: The bony points at the end of a fist with which fighters inflict harm.

LABONZ: A corruption of an Italian word for stomach. It is usually yelled by fans who are urging their favorite to go for the other fellow's midsection.

LACES: The strings that secure boxing gloves to a fighter's hands.

LACING: The illegal practice of rubbing the tight glove laces across the face of an opponent.

LEATHER PUSHERS: A term that was used for boxers in the 1920s. The term died—hopefully for good.

LEFT HOOK: *See* Hook.

LEFTY: Since most people are right-handed, left-handers, or "lefties," are considered unorthodox. They are also unpopular among right-handed fighters, some of whom are confused by the left-handed stance. Many boxers believe that lefties have an advantage over right-handed boxers since lefties are usually fighting right-handers, but right-handers see few lefties.

LIGHT-HEAVYWEIGHT: The weight division from 161 through 175 pounds.

LIGHTS: The term for the heavy and bright lights over the ring.

LIGHTS WENT OUT: A term for a knockout. A fighter will say, "I don't know what happened. All of a sudden the lights went out."

LIGHTWEIGHT: The weight division from 127 through 135 pounds.

LI'L ARTHUR: Jack Johnson, the first black heavy-weight champion. He defeated Tommy Burns for the title on December 26, 1908, at Sydney and lost it on April 5, 1915, to Jess Willard in Havana.

LIVERMORE LARRUPER: Max Baer, heavy-weight champion from June 14, 1934, when he knocked out Primo Carnera in 11 rounds, to June 13, 1935, when he lost a 15-round decision to James J. Braddock. Baer lived in Livermore, Calif.

LONG COUNT: Used to describe the tolling of 10 seconds when the toller is a slow counter. The most historic long count occurred in the second Gene Tunney-Jack Dempsey fight in Chicago on September 22, 1927. Dempsey floored Tunney but did not go to a neutral corner, and referee Dave Barry refused to count until he did. Tunney got up at the count of 9, but 14 seconds had actually elapsed.

LOOKING FOR AN EXCUSE: A fighter badly overmatched or out of condition and taking a beating might go down and out from a seemingly harmless punch. When this happens, ringsiders confide to each other: "He was looking for an excuse"—to quit, of course.

MADISON SQUARE GARDEN: There have been four of them in the past century, each described as a Mecca of boxing. And perhaps each has been. The Garden has been the display case for almost every great boxer of the period.

MAIN BOUT: The feature attraction on a boxing card.

MAKE THE WEIGHT: Boxers who fight under the heavyweight limit must make the weight, i.e., be within the weight restrictions of their division.

MANAGER: The man who directs the career of a fighter. He arranges the fights for his fighter and collects usually one-third of the fighter's purse.

MANASSA MAULER: Jack Dempsey, heavyweight champion from July 4, 1919, when he knocked out Jess Willard in Toledo, until he fought Gene Tunney, September 23, 1926, and lost a ten-round decision. A bruising, ferocious fighter, Dempsey was said to have an inherent killer instinct. He was born in Manassa, Colo., May 25, 1898. In a poll some years ago, Dempsey was voted the greatest fighter in the first fifty years of the century.

MAN OF STEEL: Tony Zale, the middleweight champion from 1941 until he lost the title to Rocky Graziano in 1947, only to regain it a year later. Zale was rugged and could absorb a lot of punches. That, and the fact he had once worked in steel mills in Gary, Ind., earned him the nickname.

MARQUIS OF QUEENSBERRY: John Sholto Douglas, who sponsored the rules that bear his name and that are the basis for all boxing contests. Before the Queensberry rules fights were fought to a finish, barefisted, and rounds were terminated only when one boxer went to the ground. The Queensberry rules call for three-minute rounds, a minute's rest between rounds, and boxing gloves.

MATCHMAKER: These are the astute students of the business who match fighters. Two of the foremost are Don Fraser, of Los Angeles's Coliseum, and Teddy Brenner, at Madison Square Garden.

MEDICINE BALL: A heavy, nonbouncing ball that fighters use to strengthen stomach muscles.

MICHIGAN ASSASSIN: Stanley Ketchel, called by many the hardest hitting middleweight of all time. He fought, knocked down, and was knocked out by Jack Johnson, who weighed 205 to Ketchel's 170. His real name was Stanislaus Kiecal. He was shot to death in 1910.

MIDDLEWEIGHT: The weight division from 148 through 160 pounds.

MONIKER: A person's nickname, or the name he may use. A "square moniker" is a person's real name. Ray Robinson, for instance, is really Walker Smith—at least that's who he was at birth.

MOUSE: A small swelling under the eye.

MOUTH: The fighter known as Muhammad Ali.

MOUTHPIECE: A rubber or plastic protector that fits in the mouth and prevents teeth from breaking.

MUSHKY: Two factotums for years at Madison Square Garden were Mushky McGee and Mushky Jackson, colorful Runyonesque characters who were frequently mentioned in sports columns.

MUSHY: Mushy Callahan was a junior welterweight champion and had a short, but colorful career. His real name: Vincent Morris Scheer.

NAIL: To punch hard. "I nailed him with a right."

NEUTRAL CORNER: There are two of them. They are the corners where the boxers do not sit. When a boxer scores a knockdown, he must retire to a neutral corner until his opponent has regained his feet.

NO CONTEST: When a fighter is obviously outclassed or can't continue a fight, a referee rules "no contest," as if the fight has never happened. Under the Frawley Law, 1911-20, decisions were forbidden in New York, and all fights that went the distance were declared "no contest." Bets were paid off on consensus opinions of sportswriters.

NO DECISION: *See* No Contest.

NO-FOUL RULE: With the advent of the foul-proof leather protector, a no-foul rule was instituted by many commissions. This deals almost exclusively with low blows when a fighter is given time to recover. *See also* Low Blow.

ONE-ARMED FIGHTER: This does not refer to amputees, but rather to fighters who favor one hand. For instance, the fraternity will say of a fighter who relies mostly on a left jab and/or a left hook, "He uses his right hand to wave good-bye with in bus depots."

ONE HAND FREE: *See* Clinch.

ONE-TWO PUNCH: This is a classic combination of punches. It can be a left jab followed immediately by an overhand right, or a left hook followed by a right.

ORCHID MAN: The nom de guerre of Georges Carpentier, a French light-heavyweight who fought

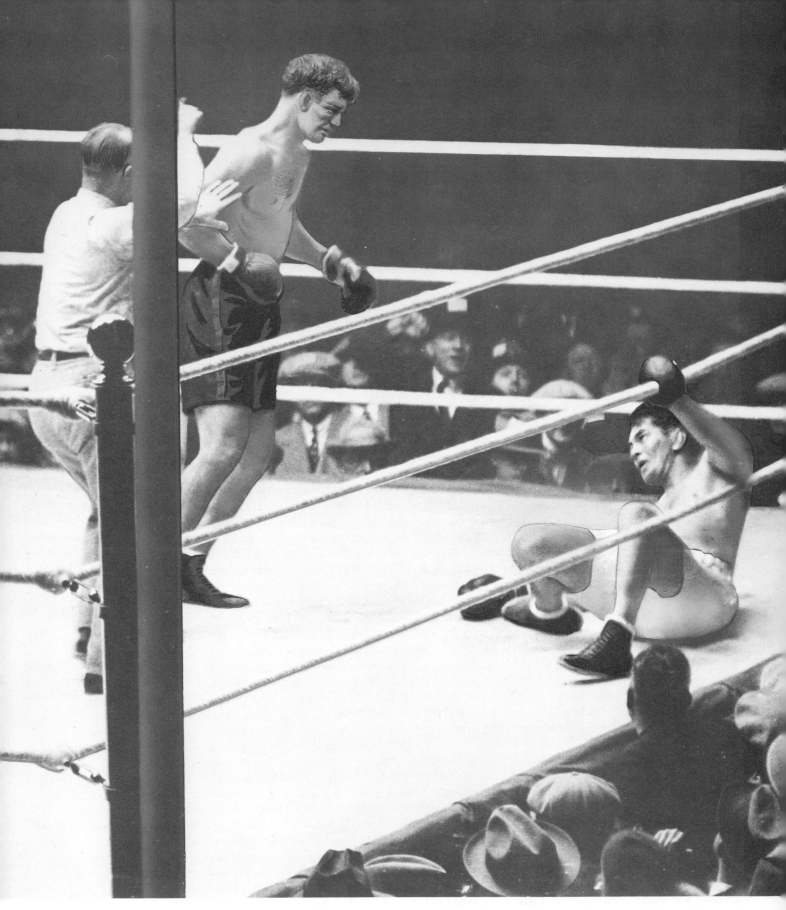

Gene Tunney has Jack Dempsey down in the historic long count *fight in 1927.*

Jack Dempsey for the heavyweight title on Boyle's Thirty Acres in Jersey City, N.J., on July 2, 1921. Publicity pumped into the fight made it the first million-dollar gate ever—$1,789,238. Dempsey punched Carpentier out in four rounds.

ORTHODOX: A right-handed fighter who leads with his left is called orthodox. *See also* Lefty.

OUTDOOR FIGHTS: Fights not held within an arena. Once ball parks were almost exclusively used for big fights because they could accommodate more fans. This usage has died out, however, with the advent of television. Rain, which often postponed outdoor fights, would raise havoc with television or closed circuit schedulings. The last outdoor fight of note was in Kinshasa, Zaire, when Muhammad Ali regained the heavyweight title from George Foreman on October 30, 1974.

PAL: Initials of the Police Athletic League, which maintains gyms in many cities and sponsors amateur competition.

PEA: A person in the fight business, when appraising a fighter's courage, will, if the fighter hasn't passed his test, remark that the fighter has a heart like a pea. Meaning, of course, that it's small.

PEEKABOO: This was a style that Floyd Patterson's manager, Cus D'Amato, devised to keep Patterson's head out of danger. Patterson fought with his gloves in front of his face. It was good enough to win the heavyweight title twice for Patterson, but not good enough to keep him from being knocked down. Patterson was knocked down 16 times in championship bouts.

PENALTY: Both amateur and professional boxing rules allow the referee to penalize a fighter points for violation of the rules.

PHAINTIN' PHIL: Phil Scott, an English heavyweight, earned this nickname during the late 1920s, when he developed a propensity for going down on the canvas from punches that didn't seem necessarily harsh.

PHILADELPHIA JACK O'BRIEN: One of the fine early boxers. He boxed from 1896 until 1912 and won the light-heavyweight championship by stopping Bob Fitzsimmons in 13 rounds at San Francisco, December 20, 1905. O'Brien's real name was Joseph Hagen.

PIER SIXER: An all-out brawl. Derived, apparently, from fights on the docks. *See also* Donnybrook.

PIVOT PUNCH: This was outlawed many years ago. A man throwing a pivot punch would suddenly turn his back to an opponent and then, whirling in a pivot, punch his opponent.

PLUGGED TICKET: Free tickets to a fight. The management will give some tickets away to the faithful, but these are punched with holes to make sure they are not sold.

POINTS: The score officials give boxers after each round. The systems vary, but the boxer with the most points usually wins.

POTAWATOMIE GIANT: Jess Willard. He won the heavyweight title from Jack Johnson in Havana, April 5, 1915, and lost it to Jack Dempsey in Toledo, Ohio, July 4, 1919. He was the tallest man to hold the title. He was 6'6¼". He came from Potawatomie County, Kans.

POUND FOR POUND: A measure that fight people use when appraising fighters. For instance, it was commonly said that Ray Robinson was the best fighter ever, pound for pound.

PRELIMINARIES: The fights that precede the semifinal and the main event. Also known as the undercard.

PROMOTER: The person who runs the boxing show.

PUG: Short for pugilist, the uncommon name for one who indulges in boxing.

PUGILISM: Boxing. It's taken from the Latin.

PUG UGLY: A man who has been a fighter and has a disfigured profile.

PUNCH-DRUNK: The label pinned on a former boxer who appears to be shuffling on his feet and talking incoherently. But a panel of New York doctors who had been associated with the Boxing Commission and had examined thousands of fighters among them, were agreed that they had never seen a punch-drunk fighter.

PURSE: The amount of money a boxer receives for fighting.

PUSH HIM OFF: A frequent expression of a second who wants his fighter to keep the other man away and in punching range.

PUSHOVER: An easy fight in which one man had little trouble with his opponent.

QUEENSBERRY RULES: *See* Marquis of Queensberry.

RABBIT PUNCH: A blow delivered deliberately to the back of an opponent's neck. It can cause severe damage and is considered a foul.

RATINGS: Boxing groups throughout the world issue monthly ratings, usually the top ten boxers in each division. The ratings are useful in considering contenders to the various titles.

REFEREE: The "third man in the ring." He is the official in charge of the fight, and in many states and countries he has a vote on the decision.

RESIN: The substance that is rubbed into the canvas so that the boxers will not slip when the canvas gets wet from perspiration, blood, or water.

RIGHT HOOK: *See* Hook.

RING: The so-called square circle in which boxing contests are held. It is an area between 24 and 16 feet on each side and has either three or four strands of ropes around it to confine the fighters to the inside-the-ring area.

RING LIGHTS: The large electric lights that are over the center of the ring.

RINGSIDE: The seats immediately adjacent to the ring. It originally meant that, but of late promoters have been extending what is called ringside on their tickets to include up to the first fifty rows of seats.

ROADWORK: The running a boxer does while training for a fight. Usually a boxer will run or jog about four miles a day while seriously training.

ROPE-A-DOPE: Muhammad Ali unveiled this strategy against George Foreman in their fight in Zaire. Ali leaned against the ropes, kept his gloves in front of his face with his arms protecting his chest and ribs, and allowed Foreman to punch at will. Foreman punched long enough and hard enough to become fatigued, and Ali, unhurt, won the title.

ROPES: *See* Ring.

ROUND(S): The three-minute segments into which a fight is broken. Preliminary bouts are usually 4, 6, or 8 rounds. Main bouts are 10 or 12 rounds, and all championship fights are scheduled for 15 rounds.

RUBBING TABLE: An upholstered, waterproof table in dressing rooms on which a fighter is massaged, usually before a fight.

SAVED BY THE BELL: For years a knocked-down or even unconscious fighter could be saved from defeat if the bell ending the round sounded before the count of ten was tolled. In many areas now, however, the bell cannot save a fighter, and the count continues even after the bell. This does not apply to the last round, because when that bell rings, the fight is over.

SCAR: The trace of a healed wound. On fighters these are often apparent around the eyes.

SCAR TISSUE: When the wounds have been many, scar tissue will build up around a fighter's eyes, making him susceptible to cuts. Surgery is used to remove this tissue.

SCHOOLING: Teaching a fighter to adopt a style or, with amateurs, to learn the basics.

SCIENTIFIC: What boxers are called who are quick and talented rather than just brawlers.

SCRATCH: In the bareknuckle days fighters had to "toe the scratch," i.e., come up to a line drawn across the ring before fighting.

SECOND(S): The men in a boxer's corner. They will attempt to staunch the flow of blood, sponge the fighter between rounds, and offer him advice. *See also* Cut Man.

"SECONDS OUT": The referee calls this when the seconds or boxer's aids, have not left the ring as the warning signal sounds to indicate there are ten seconds left before a round begins.

SHADOWBOX: When a fighter trains, he sometimes spars with himself and is said to be boxing his shadow.

"SHAKE HANDS AND COME OUT FIGHTING": At the beginning of a bout, after the referee has instructed the fighters in the rules of the contest, he will have them touch gloves and tell them, "Shake hands and come out fighting."

SHELL: A fighter who is trying to avoid punches will crouch, holding his hands near his head—i.e., go into a shell.

SHINER: *See* Black Eye.

SKIP ROPE: In training a fighter will ease off from a training session with a few minutes of skipping rope. It is meant to make him quicker on his feet. Some boxers, such as Willie Pep and Ray Robinson, became virtuosos at skipping rope and invariably drew applause for their performances.

SLAPSY: Maxie Rosenbloom was called Slapsie Maxie, mostly because of his hit-and-run approach to fighting. In sixteen years of professional boxing he scored only 18 knockouts in 289 fights. Light-heavyweight champion from 1932 to 1934, Rosenbloom became a featured player in movies as well as a nightclub comedian. One night when a drunk was heckling him during a nightclub appearance, Rosenbloom said to the heckler, "I've had two hundred fights, what's your excuse?"

SLIP: A boxer who deftly avoids blows is said to be slipping the blows. The word also applies to a boxer who falls in the ring. If the referee decides the man was not punched down, he will call it a slip and no count will be made.

SMELLING SALTS: A preparation of carbonate of ammonia that is held under a fighter's nose to revive him or make him more alert.

SMOKIN' JOE: The nickname of Joe Frazier, who won the heavyweight championship in an elimination bout with a 5-round knockout of James Ellis in New York on February 16, 1970. A year later he defeated Muhammad Ali in 15 rounds but lost his title to George Foreman in 2 rounds at Kingston, Jamaica, January 22, 1973.

SMOTHER: A fighter who presses his body into that of his attacker or grabs the attacker's arm and will be said to smother the punches of his opponent.

SNAP IT OFF: A really effective punch is not delivered simply by throwing a fist, but rather by putting a jolt onto the punch through a snapping of the wrist. Seconds who watch for such things will command a fighter who is pushing his punches to snap it off.

SOLAR PLEXUS: An unprotected part of the body between the ribs and just under the breastbone. Bob Fitzsimmons knocked out Jim Corbett with a solar-plexus punch during their championship fight.

SPAR: In training a fighter will work out in the ring with another fighter, but not with the intent to hurt. They go through the motions of battle, i.e., they spar.

SPARRING PARTNER: Someone one spars with.

SPECIAL(S): The police at boxing bouts who are hired by the promoter to keep order and are not usually part of the regular police force.

SPEED BAG: A small punching bag hung head-high that a fighter punches to improve the speed of his punches.

SQUARED CIRCLE: The ring. Once men fought in circles formed only by onlookers. With the advent of the Marquis of Queensberry rules, the circle was squared.

SQUARE MONIKER: *See* Moniker.

STANDING COUNT: When a man is punished by blows and is not retaliating, a referee might give him a standing count of eight, just as if the man had been knocked down. This is more prevalent in amateur bouts than in professional ones.

STAND-UP BOXER: A man who fights from an erect position rather than crouching.

STEAL THE ROUND: Fighters who stay on the defensive until the final seconds of a round are said to be trying to steal the round—impress the officials.

STICK: A jab. Seconds will yell to a fighter, "Stick 'em, stick 'em," meaning jab, jab.

STONE: In Great Britain a boxer's weight is determined by stones and pounds. A stone is 14 pounds; therefore, a fighter weighing 160 pounds would be said to weigh 11-stone-6.

STOOL: The four-legged (sometimes three-legged) seat that is put into the corner between rounds for the fighter to rest on.

STRAIGHT LINE: This might be the shortest distance between two points, but a boxer who is said to fight in a straight line is one who can be confused by an opponent who moves from side to side.

SUBSTITUTE: When a fighter cannot go on because of illness or any other reason, a promoter might insert a substitute for him.

SUGAR RAY: Ray Robinson, born Walker Smith, who fought professionally from 1940 to 1965. He had 202 bouts and won 175 of them. Rated by many as the best boxer ever, "pound for pound," Robinson was welterweight champion once and five times was the middleweight champion. He attempted to win the light-heavyweight division by fighting Joey Maxim, June 25, 1952, in New York, but was stopped in the 14th round when the intense heat so fatigued him that he was unable to continue. Robinson was ahead on points at the end. While still a teen-ager, too young to get an AAU card to box, he borrowed the card of an older boy named Ray Robinson and used the name all through his career. He was labeled Sugar one night after an amateur fight in Watertown, N.Y., when the local sports editor, Jack Case, wrote: "This Robinson is as sweet as sugar."

SWAB: A small bit of cotton rolled on the end of a thin stick. This is used to daub at a fighter's cuts between rounds or to cauterize a bleeding nose.

SWEET SCIENCE: An archaic term for boxing and the title of a book on the subject by the late A.J. Liebling.

TAKE A COUNT: A knocked-down fighter often wants to get up immediately. Sometimes this is rash, and his corner will advise him to take a count, i.e., wait until eight or nine to allow himself a rest before getting up. A fighter who is knocked out will be said to have taken the count.

TALE OF THE TAPE: The comparative weight and measurements of two opponents.

TANK: A woeful word in boxing. "He went in the tank" means the fighter deliberately lost or did not try to win a fight.

TANK TOWN: Any small town with a small boxing club.

THREE-KNOCKDOWN RULE: A rule that is almost universal in professional boxing. A fighter who is knocked down three times in one round is automatically ruled to be technically knocked out and loses. The rule is usually waived in championship fights.

THRILLA IN MANILA: This was the advertised name of the heavyweight championship fight between Muhammad Ali and Joe Frazier in Manila, September 30, 1975. It turned out to be a "thrilla," too. Ali won on a technical knockout after 14 rounds.

THROW IN THE TOWEL: Once a fighter's seconds would terminate a fight if their man was being beaten badly by throwing a towel into the ring. It is no longer allowed by most commissions.

THUMBING: The act of putting the thumb of a boxing glove in an opponent's eye. It's painful and illegal.

TIME CLOCK: *See* Clock.

TIMEKEEPER: The man who operates the time clock and counts the seconds of a knockdown.

TKO: Technical knockout. When a referee decides a man can no longer continue to fight, he is ruled to be technically knocked out. When a fighter is cut badly, a ring doctor might tell the referee to end the fight.

TOE THE LINE: Coming up to the scratch in bareknuckle fighting.

TOY BULLDOG: Mickey Walker, former welterweight and middleweight champion, known for his tenacity and disregard of an opponent's weight. He often fought top heavyweights, giving away as much as 40 to 50 pounds.

TURNED AROUND: A left-handed fighter is sometimes turned around, i.e., made to adapt a right-handed style. One reason for this is that left-handers find it difficult to get fights because right-handers like to shun them. *See* Lefty.

20-SECOND RULE: A rule, adopted by some commissions, that allows a fighter who has been knocked out of the ring 20 seconds to reenter the ring or be counted out.

TWO-TON-TONY: Tony Galento, a beer keg of a man, a heavyweight who fought from 1929 to 1943. He fought Joe Louis for the heavyweight championship on June 28, 1939, and was knocked out in four rounds, but not before he sent Louis to the canvas once.

UNCROWNED CHAMPION: A term given a man the fight business thinks has earned a championship but hasn't gotten it. On April 29, 1959, Billy Graham, according to the press and ringsiders, easily outpointed Kid Gavilan for the welterweight championship. But the officials gave Gavilan the fight, and Graham earned the billing as the uncrowned champion.

UNDERCARD: *See* Preliminaries.

WALKER AWARD: An award given annually by the New York Boxing Writers Association to the person deemed to have done the most for boxing in the previous year. Named after former New York mayor James J. Walker.

WALKER LAW: A law that went into effect in New York State in 1920 and serves as the model for international boxing codes. It provided for a commission to oversee boxing and allowed decisions in fights.

WALK-IN: A free ticket to the fight that allows the holder to "walk in" but does not guarantee the holder a seat. Usually the holder of a walk-in ticket will tip an usher for a vacant seat.

WALK-OUT BOUT: A fight that is held after the main event. It allows patrons to watch a fight and avoid the rush to leave the arena.

WALKOVER: An easy fight in which one man has almost no problems.

WARNING: A referee will warn a fighter who has fouled that if he does it again, he will be penalized. *See also* Penalty.

WARNING BUZZER: Ten seconds before the beginning of a round the timekeeper will sound a buzzer, which directs seconds to leave the ring.

WBA: The World Boxing Association. One of the two international boxing groups, almost always at odds with the World Boxing Council.

WBC: The World Boxing Council, the second of the two international groups.

WELTERWEIGHT: The weight division from 136 through 147 pounds.

"WE WUZ ROBBED": Joe Jacobs's plaint when his fighter, Max Schmeling, lost the decision and his heavyweight title to Jack Sharkey in New York, June 21, 1932. The decision was questionable, but it stood. And Jacobs screamed for all the world to hear, "We wuz robbed."

"WHAT, AGAIN?": Referee Arthur Donovan officiated at most of Joe Louis's title fights, and when his name was announced, the crowd would predictably yell, "What, again?"

WILLIE O' THE WISP: A nickname given Willie Pep, born William Papaleo. Pep, a former featherweight champion, had 241 fights and won 229 of them. He was considered one of the perfect boxing stylists.

WIPE THE GLOVES: When a knocked-down fighter rises, the referee will wipe the man's gloves on his shirt to remove resin.

WITHHOLD THE PURSE: In the event of speculation that a particular fighter's effort was not what it should have been, a commission will withhold the man's purse until an investigation clears the fighter.

ZIGZAG: On April 17, 1939, during his Bum of the Month parade, Joe Louis fought Jack Roper in Los Angeles and knocked out Roper in one round. After the fight Roper told the audience who had heard the fight on radio, "I zigged when I should have zagged."

FOOTBALL

Immortalized by Grantland Rice, Notre Dame's Four
Horsemen *featured, from the left, Don Miller, Elmer
Layden, Jim Crowley and Harry Stuhldreher.*

AAFC: The All-America Football Conference, a pro league that operated from 1946 through 1949. The AAFC was the brainchild of Arch Ward, sports editor of the Chicago Tribune, who had also started the College All-Star charity football game and baseball's All-Star game.

The original teams were the Brooklyn Dodgers, the Buffalo Bisons, the Chicago Rockets, the Cleveland Browns, the Los Angeles Dons, the Miami Seahawks, the New York Yankees, and the San Francisco 49ers. Most of the franchises were well financed; more than 100 players defected from the National Football League, and the AAFC hired Jim Crowley, one of the Four Horsemen of Notre Dame, as its commissioner.

The salary was heavenly for the top players, but the competing leagues cut up the pie so many ways that few teams profited. An exception was the Cleveland Browns, coached by Paul Brown and peopled with a goodly number of World War II veterans. The Browns also were among the first clubs to sign black players, notably fullback Marion Motley and guard Bill Willis. Cleveland dominated the AAFC with a 52-4-2 record, all four championships, and in 1946 an average of 57,000 fans a game.

Other franchises were not as profitable. The Miami Seahawks became the Baltimore Colts after one season; the Chicago franchise, later to be known as the Hornets, could not compete with two NFL franchises entrenched in the same city and went through four owners

and nine coaches in four seasons. By 1949, league losses were estimated at $4 million.

In 1950, there was a survival of the fittest, with three AAFC teams—the Browns, the 49ers, and the Colts—joining the NFL. For the Browns there was nothing lost in the transition: They defeated the Los Angeles Rams, 30-28, for the championship in their first year in the NFL.

ACROSS PATTERN: A route for a pass receiver in which he cuts diagonally from one side of the field to the other. This pattern is most successful against zone defenses, sometimes causing confusion among the defenders when the receiver crosses from one coverage zone to the other.

AERIAL: A Forward Pass.

AERIAL CIRCUS: Press-agent argot for an offensive team that frequently passes. This type of attack was once the hallmark of the Southwest Conference, but with the professionals' bent for the pass, it is no longer the unique property of any geographical area. The term was first applied to coach Ray Morrison's Southern Methodist University teams of the early 1920s.

AFC: See NFL.

AFL: The American Football League, a league formed to rival the National Football League (NFL) in 1960. The original teams were the Boston Patriots, the Buffalo Bills, the Denver Broncos, the Dallas Texans, the Houston Oilers, the Los Angeles Chargers, the New York Titans, and the Oakland Raiders. Joe Foss, former governor of South Dakota, was named commissioner. At the start Foss came close to becoming the commissioner of nothing when a franchise in Minneapolis rejected the AFL and accepted an NFL offer to become an expansion team in 1961.

Four of the original teams—New York, Dallas, Los Angeles, and Oakland—were competing head to head with NFL clubs. Pro football had previously failed in Buffalo and Boston. The AFL founders had money to lose—and lose it they did, approximately $4.6 million the first year, $1 million alone by Dallas multimillionaire Lamar Hunt. The AFL obtained a modest television contract ($150,000 a team), innovated a two-point conversion by passing or running, and featured teams that didn't know the meaning of the word *defense.*

The AFL didn't raid the NFL for players, accepting NFL rejects, Canadian Football League talent, and free agents. College seniors, however, enjoyed a run on the bank because the AFL and NFL furiously tried to outbid each other over premium draft choices. Litigation became part of the game plan because a number of players—the most famous was Heisman Trophy winner Billy Cannon of Louisiana State—signed with both leagues.

AFL teams could be found playing almost anywhere: the New York Titans taking to the rickety Polo Grounds, the Oakland Raiders playing in San Francisco, Houston using a high school field, and Denver making a home out of a minor-league baseball park. The first year the average attendance was 16,000 a game. Individually there were problems (the Titans' paychecks bounced, and the league had to assume operation of the team) but collectively the league progressed steadily, and in 1965 the National Broadcasting Company signed a five-year contract to televise AFL games for $36 million. "People have stopped asking me if we are going to make it," said commissioner Foss.

Still, the two leagues had to push each other toward merger. After the 1965 season the New York Giants of the NFL signed place-kicker Pete Gogolak of the AFL's Buffalo Bills. The AFL named Al Davis, an acknowledged infighter, as its new commissioner, and Davis's first mission was to pirate several of the NFL's top quarterbacks, including John Brodie of the San Francisco 49ers. That depolarized both sides.

Starting with the 1966 season, they agreed to a common college draft, and on January 15, 1967, the Green Bay Packers of the NFL defeated the Kansas City Chiefs of the AFL in the first Super Bowl, 35-10. In 1970, the leagues were singular on all fronts, playing interlocking schedules under the same commissioner.

A FORMATION: An offensive alignment, now obsolete, that was popularized by Steve Owen and his New York Giants in 1938. If there would be a marriage between the shotgun and the single-wing formations, the offspring would be the A formation. With an unbalanced line the quarterback is the only back standing on the strong side, slightly to the right and several yards behind the center. The fullback is the deep back, a few yards behind the quarterback and directly behind the center. The blocking back and wingback line up even with each other, a couple of yards behind the line, the blocking back between the tackle and center, the wingback outside the end. Mel Hein, the Giant center, could snap the ball to the blocking back, the quarterback, or the fullback. The A is different from the single wing because when the backs are strong left, the line is unbalanced right, and vice versa. Besides being an effective running formation, the A also enables a team to use its fullback as a passer.

AGAINST THE GRAIN: A technique used by running backs who, when they see their planned direction crowded with tacklers, cut back and head into the flow of tacklers that might not be as heavily populated.

ALIGNMENT: The positioning of players in either a defensive or offensive formation.

ALL-AMERICAN TEAM: The first All-American team was selected in 1889 by Casper Whitney, leading authority on sports, big-game hunter, and part-owner of the publication *The Week's Sport.* Walter Camp, another football expert, helped Whitney pick the team and gave All-American players national recognition by selecting teams for *Harper's Weekly* and *Collier's* magazine. Before long everybody—wire services, coaches, newspapers, individual writers—began picking All-American teams.

There are also Little All-American teams, for the small colleges, and high school All-American teams. At a time when eligibility rules were looser than they are today, Frank Hinkey, a 150-pound end from Yale, was an All-American four years running. Among those who made "consensus" All-American for three years: back Red Cagle of Army (1927-29), end Bennie Oosterbaan of Michigan (1925-27), end Wes Fesler of Ohio State (1928-30), back Doc Blanchard of Army (1944-46), and back Doak Walker of Southern Methodist (1947-49).

The flaw in modern All-American teams is that none of the selectors can see all of the qualified players. But the immense interest in the teams persists, even though hundreds of All-Pro players were never All-Americans as undergraduates.

ALLEY-OOP: A lob pass from a quarterback to a tall

receiver, usually near the end zone. So named because of its successful use by the San Francisco 49ers in the late 1950s, with Y. A. Tittle throwing and R. C. Owens catching. The 6′3″ Owens, a former basketball player, had remarkable leaping ability and could jump into the midst of several defenders and usually come up with the ball.

ALL-PRO: The professional equivalent of the collegiate All-American teams. Until 1972 the National Football League recognized the Professional Football Writers of America's All-Pro team as its official All-Pro, but since then the NFL lists a number of teams—those selected by the writers as well as wire services and news syndicates. All-Pro teams are generally more reliable than All-American teams because there are fewer players to judge and the selectors usually see most of them. But the players themselves sometimes complain about perennial choices at unseen positions (in particular, offensive linemen) being based more on reputations than accomplishments. The All-Pro's All-Pro was Jimmy Brown, the Cleveland Browns' fullback who was selected in eight of his nine years in the NFL.

ANKLE WRAP: A bandage, usually consisting of tape, that is wrapped around the ankles of most players prior to a game or practice, protecting them from injury.

ARMCHAIR QUARTERBACK: Coaches despise them, wives tolerate them, but they are the lifeblood of the game. The fan who sits in his chair before a television set and calls strategy as though it were his team. The same guy at the game becomes a grandstand quarterback.

ASSIGNMENT: The job a player is given on each play, such as blocking, running a pass route, performing a pass coverage, etc.

ASTROTURF: *See* Synthetic Surface.

AUDIBLE: A change of the original play at the line of scrimmage by the quarterback after he looks over the defense and decides the play called in the huddle won't work. Also known as check-off or automatic. Audibles are also called on defense, usually by the middle linebacker.

AUTOMATIC: *See* Audible.

AUTOMATIC FIRST DOWN: For certain penalties a first down is awarded to the offense even if it hasn't gained the necessary yardage. This occurs on all defensive fouls except these: offside, encroachment, delay of game, illegal substitution, excessive time-outs.

AX: A block a defensive man executes on a wide receiver to nullify him from the play as he tries to run downfield.

BACK: A player stationed behind the line of scrimmage on offense or defense. On offense there are four backs, most commonly called the quarterback, the halfback, the fullback, and the flankerback, or wingback. These descriptions may vary, however, according to formations. On defense the number of backs is unlimited, but they usually include linebackers, cornerbacks, safeties, and halfbacks. Cornerbacks and safeties can be loosely referred to as halfbacks.

Good offensive backs possess three skills—ability to run with the ball, block, and catch passes. Because of the increased sizes of all pro players, few offensive backs weigh less than 200 pounds. Defensive backs, who must be good tacklers, adept at defending against the pass and proficient at anticipating plays, come in various sizes, but cornerbacks and safeties are smaller than linebackers and defensive linemen.

BACKER: If you're a player or an inveterate fan, this is another name for a linebacker. If you're a general manager with a franchise that's in trouble, a backer is an angel with dollar signs in his eyes.

BACKFIELD: The area behind the line of scrimmage. On defense it is called the secondary. On offense the backfield consists of four backs. *See also* Back.

BACKFIELD IN MOTION: A five-yard offensive penalty that is called when a back (1) in motion moves forward more than one yard beyond his starting position, or (2) fails to pause one second after a shift or huddle. Also, a team is permitted to have only one man in motion on the same play.

BACK JUDGE: One of the officials who operates on the same side of the field as the line judge, 15 to 17 yards beyond the line of scrimmage on the defensive team's side. The back judge concentrates on the path of an end or back, observing legality of potential blocks or of action taken against them. He is prepared to rule from a deep position on holding or illegal use of the hands and has primary responsibility to make decisions involving the sideline on his side of field—whether a pass receiver or runner is in or out of bounds, for example.

A back judge makes decisions regarding catching, recovery, or illegal touching of a loose ball beyond the line of scrimmage; assists in covering the action of the runner, including blocks by teammates and that of defenders; calls clipping on punt returns, and together with the field judge rules whether or not field-goal attempts are successful.

BACKPEDAL: Running backward, usually at a slow pace, with the eyes remaining on a developing play. This act is usually practiced by defensive backs.

BACKWARD PASS: A pass in which the receiver is behind the passer. If the pass is not caught, the ball is in play, as opposed to being an incompleted pass, which would be the case if the receiver were in front of the passer.

The All-Pros' All-Pro was Jimmy Brown of the Cleveland Browns.

BALANCED ATTACK: An offense consisting of a fairly equal number of running and passing plays.

BALANCED LINE: An offensive line with three players on each side of the center.

BALANCED T FORMATION: A T formation with a balanced line.

BALL: The ball must have four panels of leather covering a rubber bladder and must be smooth on the outside except for seams or laces. The ball's dimensions are 11 to 11¼ inches in length, approximately 6¾ inches in width, 28 to 28½ inches around lengthwise, and 21¼ to 21½ inches around the middle. It must weigh 14 to 15 ounces and must be inflated to 12½ to 13½ pounds. The ball is now longer and more streamlined than it used to be, a concession to the forward pass. In another era, the ball was more oval shaped and rounder, making it easier to kick and drop-kick.

BALL BOY(S): The sideline people who, during a game, follow the line of scrimmage with a spare football should the game ball become wet or a long pass or kick bounce out of play. In training camps a ball boy is responsible for all of the team's footballs, which are usually transported in a rack on wheels or carried in a large cloth bag.

BALLCARRIER: A player who legally runs with the ball, usually a back, but also a receiver when he catches the ball, a defensive player who intercepts a pass, a player who returns a kick, etc.

BALL CONTROL: An offensive system predicated on short-yardage gains, either through runs or short passes. Exponents of this attack may be coaches who believe in using up a lot of time on the clock and who may be trying to hide a weak defense by keeping their offensive unit on the field as much as possible. Ohio State's teams under Woody Hayes are the epitome of ball-control football at the collegiate level; Vince Lombardi's Green Bay Packers were the professional counterpart.

BELLY SERIES: An offense in which the basic play is a direct hand-off by the quarterback to a running back going into the line. The quarterback will hold the ball in the runner's belly for at least a full count before either completing the hand-off or withdrawing it and giving the ball to another back. The quarterback may also keep the ball himself and have the option of running or passing. While confusing the defense with deft ballhandling, belly-series teams are also more susceptible to fumbling. The belly series was popularized by coach Earl (Red) Blaik at West Point in the mid-1950s.

BENCH: The sideline area where nonparticipating players sit. During the days when football was an endurance sport and eleven men usually played most of the game, a bench warmer (a player not playing) was held in low esteem. Eventually, though, football evolved into a game of specialists, and bench strength—a large number of useful substitutes—has become an important asset.

Now two-platoon football is universal, and coaches use a different 11 players on offense from those on defense. Professional roster limits exceed 40 men, and colleges are allowed to have even more than that in uniform.

Probably the most memorable incident regarding the bench took place in the 1954 Cotton Bowl game, when Alabama fullback Tommy Lewis instinctively leaped off the bench and tackled Rice's Dicky Moegle, touchdown bound and streaking down the sideline. Officials penalized Lewis and gave Moegle the touchdown. "I guess I was just too full of Alabama," Lewis said. Rice won the game, 28-6.

BIRDCAGE: A type of player's facemask, usually worn by a lineman, that has three horizontal bars plus a vertical bar running from the chin all the way to the forehead of the helmet. One of the few offensive players to ever wear a bird cage was Rudy Bukich, quarterback for the Chicago Bears.

BLESTO: *See* Scouting Combine.

BLIND SIDE: The side of a player turned away from approaching opponents. When blocked or tackled from the blind side, a player can be easily hurt, and this tactic is a leading cause of injuries.

BLITZ: When one or more linebackers or defensive backs rush through the line of scrimmage with the intent of causing havoc in the offensive backfield. Blitzing is exciting but risky, leaving the defense vulnerable. If the offensive team is passing, the blitz may help a defensive man get to the quarterback before he can pass the ball to an uncovered receiver. A blitz is also called a dog or a red dog.

BLOCKING: A means of protecting the ballcarrier by moving defensive men out of his path. Once uncomplicated and done either from a crouch or by throwing a player's entire body at an opponent, blocking has now become quite sophisticated. There is a different type of block for practically every kind of play.

BLOCKING BACK: A position in the offensive backfield that is virtually passé. The blocking back in the era of single-wing football was the back who would have to do the important blocking on running plays. In the T formation the blocking back has been replaced by the guard pulling out of the line. Blocking backs are obscure players, seldom touching the ball. One of the most famous was Forest Evashevski, who blocked from 1938 to 1940 for Tom Harmon, the All-American tailback at Michigan. Fullbacks do much of the blocking in modern offenses, but they are not referred to as blocking backs.

BLOCKING CALL: As the quarterback reaches the line of scrimmage, the offensive linemen will call out to one another what type blocking is to be used, and what men are to be blocked, for a particular play.

BLOWN DEAD: When the referee blows his whistle, officially stopping the play and making the ball dead.

BLUE CHIPPER: A college coach's term for a recruit who has can't-miss qualifications. Blue-chip players are courted by hundreds of colleges and virtually have the pick of the country regarding where they want to enroll.

BOMB: A long pass of 35 yards or more, designed to create a quick touchdown. Daryle Lamonica, when he was quarterback for the Oakland Raiders, was known as The Mad Bomber because of his penchant for throwing the bomb.

BOMB SQUAD: *See* Special Teams.

BONUS PLAYER: A player who receives a bonus for signing with a professional team. Bonus players have come a long way since Willie Heston, a halfback from Michigan, signed for $600 with Canton in 1905. Joe Namath signed with the New York Jets for an estimated $400,000 after leaving the University of Alabama. Those who did even better were Texas linebacker Tommy Nobis with the Atlanta Falcons and Texas Tech halfback Donny Anderson with the Green Bay Packers. Both reportedly received bonuses of $600,000.

Namath, Nobis, and Anderson signed when the National Football League and American Football League were competing for players, but since the merger the days of the boxcar bonus diminished, although the short-lived World Football League did give players additional bargaining power on a much more limited basis.

Sometimes established players look at bonus rookies and wonder what talents they possess to command such hefty payments. "If Namath was worth four hundred thousand dollars without playing a game, then I'm worth a million," said Frank Ryan, quarterback for the Cleveland Browns. When Anderson steamrollered Fred Williamson of Kansas City in the Super Bowl, Green Bay teammate Fuzzy Thurston said: "Donny must have hit him with his wallet."

BOOT: To kick the football. A punt or kickoff is a boot.

BOOTLEG: A term, borrowed from the Prohibition era, used to describe the quarterback faking a hand-off to another back and carrying the ball himself, which is hidden on his hip, around either side of the line. Bob Waterfield of the Los Angeles Rams and Frank Albert of the San Francisco 49ers were masters at running the bootleg. It is also called the keeper play.

BOUNDARY LINE(S): The chalk lines that encompass the rectangular playing field. A player stepping on or over these lines is said to be out of bounds.

BOWL GAME(S): Postseason games among the top collegiate teams, which are selected by the bowl games' individual committees or through contracts the bowls have with the various leagues and conferences (the Big Ten champion perennially plays in the Rose Bowl).

Bowl games were the invention of James A. Wagner, who after presiding over the Tournament of Roses festival in Pasadena, Calif., added a football game to the gala. Michigan defeated Stanford, 49-0, in the first Rose Bowl game on January 1, 1902. Bowl games, traditionally reserved for New Year's Day, have proliferated, and now there are games as early as November. They almost always cause controversy, because prestige-minded bowl committees are eager to land the top teams, but sometimes they have been burned by signing a team before the end of the season and then seeing the selection get embarrassed in its concluding games.

Bowl games are sources of substantial revenue for the schools. Big Ten gross receipts for the 1973 Rose Bowl game, which are divided among the member schools, fell just short of $1.4 million. Ohio State received $264,000 alone for its expenses, which include the tab for the school's "official party"—the president and officials of the university, state officials, mayors, and legislators. Ohio State actually went $9,000 over its expense allowance, but the school considers that an investment, since a team that consistently attends bowl games is an easier seller when coaches seek out recruits.

Recently there has been a proposal that the major bowl games be used as vehicles to determine the number-one college team, settling that issue through an elimination tournament instead of relying on the subjective views of wire-service polls. The proposal was killed, however, at the NCAA convention in 1976. *See also* Super Bowl.

BREAD-AND-BUTTER PLAY: A team's favorite play, the one that it relies on for yardage in a crucial situation.

Joe Namath of the New York Jets was a bonus player out of the University of Alabama.

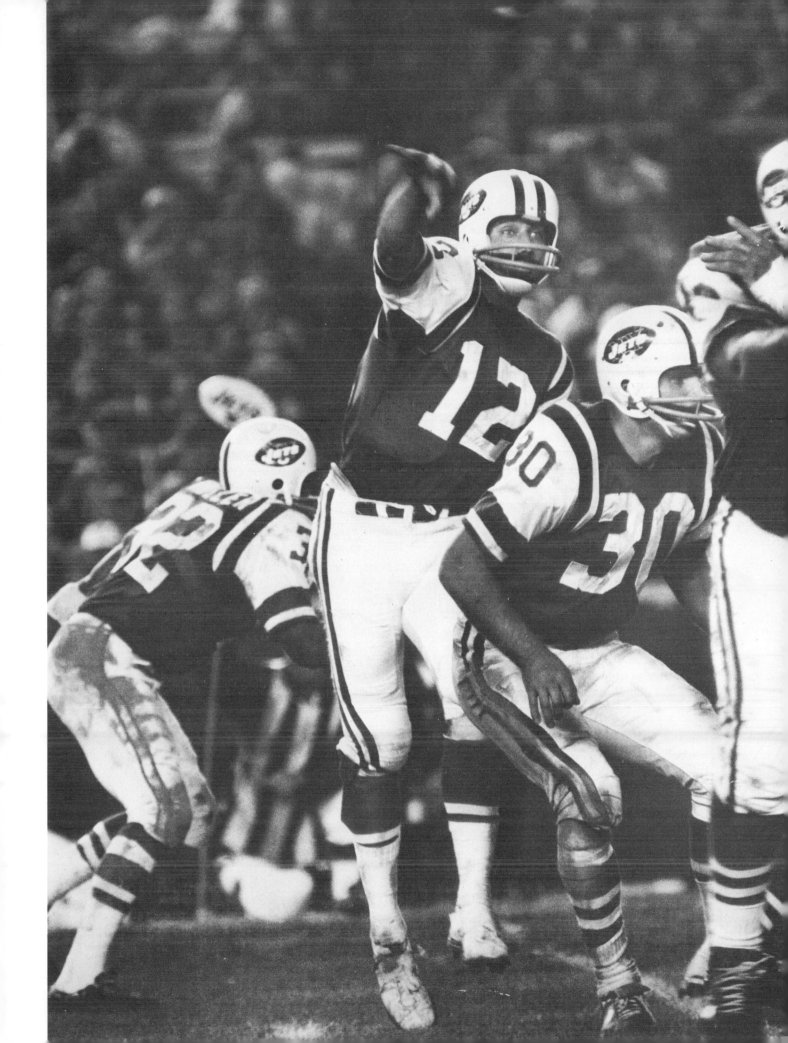

BREAKAWAY BACK: A runner with extraordinary speed that makes him a threat to go for a touchdown any time he carries the ball.

BREAK DOWN: What coaches do with film of a game, dividing it into offensive and defensive sections for more particular review purposes.

BROKEN-FIELD RUNNER: A ballcarrier with the ability to weave his way through an open field or a large area where players are spread out instead of congested. The best broken-field runners usually return kickoffs and punts, since the requirements frequently call for impromptu running.

BRUSH BLOCK: A block in which the blocker just brushes his man, impeding him slightly. Usually used on screen passes, allowing the defenders to rush the passer but taking them away from the intended receiver so that he will have more time to run once he catches the quick pass.

BUCK: A charge into the heart of the line by a ballcarrier seeking short yardage.

BULLET PASS: A pass thrown with high velocity. Not always an asset, because some quarterbacks are accused by receivers of throwing the ball too hard.

BUMP AND RUN: Defensive ploy by a cornerback to slow up a pass receiver as he leaves the line of scrimmage. After the bump the cornerback then continues in pursuit of the receiver. This defense was popularized by coach Hank Stram with the Kansas City Chiefs.

BUTTONHOOK: A pass pattern in which the receiver goes straight into the secondary, as if to get behind it, then slows his pace abruptly and hooks back toward the center of the field.

CAB SQUAD: *See* Taxi Squad.

CADENCE: The rhythm with which the quarterback calls the play at the line of scrimmage just prior to the center snap. Regular cadence might be something like "Hut one, hut two, hut three," and the ball would be snapped on the count of three. A variation would be "hut...hut-hut-hut...hut-hut." Cadence is important for the smooth execution of a play, but it is also important for the quarterback to vary his cadence so the defense line doesn't share the rhythm.

CALL: The quarterback's choice of play in the huddle. Or the coach's from the sidelines. Also, a decision by an official.

CANADIAN FOOTBALL LEAGUE: A league lesser in caliber than the National Football League but probably the equivalent or more of major college football in quality. Teams include British Columbia, Calgary, Edmonton, Hamilton, Montreal, Ottawa, Saskatchewan, Toronto, and Winnipeg. At the end of each season the winners of the Eastern and Western conferences play for the Grey Cup, a title trophy that was donated by Governor-General Earl Grey in 1909.

Because of rules designed to encourage offense, Canadian football is more wide open, with more scoring, than the American brand. In Canada there are 12 men on a side, including a fifth back called the flying wing; each team gets only three downs; and the field is 110 yards long. Many American players have been successful in Canada, including Heisman Trophy winner Johnny Rodgers of Nebraska. The Canadian teams abide by small quotas of American players and recognize NFL contracts, which makes them less than full-fledged competitors of the NFL.

CAPTAIN: The team leader. On the field there is at least one offensive and one defensive captain, and the referee will refer all decisions to him. The captains can be appointed by the coach or elected by teammates, which is almost always the case in college. Some teams use different captains for each game.

Alex Hawkins, a handyman for the Baltimore Colts, was once sent to the field with captains Johnny Unitas and Gino Marchetti for the pregame meeting with the officials and captains of the opposing team. Hawkins was the leader of the specialty teams, and since they had been doing an effective job, coach Weeb Ewbank felt they deserved representation. After going through the formalities of introducing Unitas and Marchetti, the referee said, "And this is Captain Hawkins." One of the rival captains said, "Captain who?" Forever after, Hawkins was called Captain Who by his Colt teammates.

CARRY: A running assignment by a ballcarrier. Also called a rush.

CATCH: The act of legally holding on to the football, whether it is kicked, passed, or lateraled. There is no time limit that governs a legal catch, it is the discretion of the official to determine if a player has possession. Both of a receiver's feet must be in bounds for a reception to be considered a legal catch in the pros. One foot suffices in college. Masters of the sideline pass have been Ray Berry of the Baltimore Colts and Fred Biletnikoff of the Oakland Raiders.

CATCH-UP FOOTBALL: The style a team adopts when it falls behind by a large margin. This means abandonment of original strategy and use of more reckless tactics.

CENTER: The player stationed in the middle of the offensive line, between the guards. He passes the ball between his legs, usually to the quarterback but sometimes to other backs, depending on the formation. A center must also snap the ball on punts and field goals, and the trend has been toward using specialists for these assignments. A center is also required to block after he snaps the ball, and this can be a rugged task because frequently he is being challenged by the opposition's middle linebacker.

Although few centers make the Hall of Fame—as did Chuck Bednarik, Mel Hein, George Trafton, Bulldog Turner, and Alex Wojciechowicz—the position turns out the true iron men of the game. While the average longevity of a professional football player is about five years, there were 14 centers in the National Football League in 1974 who had ten years or more of seniority.

Jim Otto of the Oakland Raiders, who drew more attention than most centers because he wore 00 for a uniform number, played fifteen years and 210 consecutive games before retiring in 1975. Dick Szymanski, a center for fourteen years with the Baltimore Colts, explains the staying power of the men who play that position: "It's speed. Centers don't have to move laterally, and therefore they don't have to be as fast as the rest of the offensive linemen. As most players get older, they lose speed, and centers get even slower. But since a center doesn't have to have much speed in the first place, it's not a factor."

CEPO: See Scouting Combine.

CHAIN CREW: The men who operate the first-and-10 chain on the sidelines. One holds a stick at each end of the chain, and the third man holds a post indicating the number of the down and the position of the ball. When the ball is too close to the first-down spot for the referee to tell whether or not it has made it, the chain will be brought on to the field for a measurement.

CHALK TALK: See Skull Session.

CHEAP SHOT: A blow delivered to a player who is not in a position to defend himself. Players who revert to such tactics are called cheap-shot artists. The line between cheap-shot artists and aggressive players who like to intimidate is minuscule. Johnny Sample, a journeyman cornerback, was called a cheap-shot artist, and although he denied the reputation while active, he later wrote a book called *Confessions of a Dirty Football Player.*

CHECKOFF: See Audible.

CHIP SHOT: A golf expression that has come to be used for a short field-goal attempt, usually inside 20 yards.

CHOKE: Act of failing in a crucial situation because of an emotional letdown. Also called getting the apple, or swallowing the apple.

CHUCKING: A defensive back's technique, usually by use of the forearms, to prevent a receiver from running his regular pattern. The defensive man makes contact near the line of scrimmage and is legally entitled to one chuck before the ball is thrown.

CIRCUS CATCH: A sensational catch of a pass, usually in midair as by a high-wire performer. If you're one of those coachly types who doesn't know anything until he sees the films, check the pictures of the 1976 Super Bowl and the circus acts performed by Lynn Swann of the Pittsburgh Steelers.

CLAWS: Scouting jargon for a receiver with good hands for catching passes.

CLEAT: A football shoe with a studded bottom, especially designed for traction on grass fields.

CLIFF-HANGER: A close, dramatic game decided in the final minutes. So called because it produces tension akin to hanging from a cliff.

CLOTHESLINING: Tackling the opponent across his neck with the arm, creating a choking effect and one that jars the head. Only the Santa Monica Freeway causes more whiplash. The clothesline is a legal but lethal tackle, among the most aggressive and savage in football, but also the most risky because if the ballcarrier anticipates it, it is easy to dodge the defensive man. Some leading clotheliners of days past were Fred Williamson of the Kansas City Chiefs and Dick ("Night Train") Lane of the Los Angeles Rams and Detroit Lions.

CLUBHOUSE LAWYER: Not Nick Buoniconti, who has studied law while playing for the Miami Dolphins. A clubhouse lawyer is the coach's bête noire, a locker-room second-guesser who never keeps his opinions to himself, isn't averse to argument, and can destroy a team's morale.

COACH: The man in charge of a team on the field. He hires a staff of assistants, organizes practices, decides on what players to keep and use, and at the college level must beat the stumps for the players he tries to recruit. Some pro coaches are also the team's general manager, but regardless, the success or failure of the team rests on the coach's shoulders.

Knute Rockne of Notre Dame was psychologist, orator, master strategist, innovator—considered by many to be the greatest coach ever. Rockne, killed in a plane crash, had a record of 105-12-5 and established the Notre Dame image, which is still being perpetuated.

Before Rockne, there was Amos Alonzo Stagg, who coached for an incredible fifty-five years at the University of Chicago and College of the Pacific. Almost as durable was Glenn ("Pop") Warner, who coached for forty-four years. Other innovative coaches were Fielding ("Hurry Up") Yost of Michigan, Bob Zuppke of Illinois, Percy Haughton of Harvard, Frank

Coach *Vince Lombardi's* teams ran to daylight as they
sought to prove that winning is the only thing.

Cavanaugh of Fordham, and Jock Sutherland of Pittsburgh.

Lou Little of Columbia was hailed as the master of the upset after his teams surprised Stanford in the 1934 Rose Bowl and stopped Army's long unbeaten streak in 1947. Other top coaches in the midlands were Bernie Bierman of Minnesota; Don Faurot of Missouri; and Frank Leahy and Ara Parseghian, who imitated Rockne's success at Notre Dame.

College coaching evolved into an era of salesmanship instead of innovation, however, and with recruiting becoming the name of the game, those who rose head and shoulders above the others were Bud Wilkinson of Oklahoma; Woody Hayes of Ohio State; John McKay of Southern California; Paul ("Bear") Bryant of Kentucky, Texas A&M and Alabama; Joe Paterno of Penn State; Bo Schembechler of Michigan; Frank Kush of Arizona State; Darrell Royal of Texas; Dan Devine of Arizona State, Missouri, and Notre Dame; Frank Broyles of Arkansas; and Ralph ("Shug") Jordan of Auburn.

The highest tribute to the excellence in college coaching has come from the National Football League, which annually dips into the campus ranks for some of its top jobs. Among these have been Johnny Ralston of the Denver Broncos, Chuck Fairbanks of the New England Patriots, Lou Holtz of the New York Jets, Tommy Prothro with first the Los Angeles Rams and then the San Diego Chargers, Dan Devine with the Green Bay Packers, and Don Coryell with the St. Louis Cardinals.

The Pro Football Hall of Fame includes these members who were recognized mainly for their coaching: George Halas, Curly Lambeau, Jimmy Conzelman, Paddy Driscoll, Steve Owen, Paul Brown, and Vince Lombardi. Halas single-handedly ran the Chicago Bears for more than fifty years; Lombardi is one of the game's most quoted coaches (e.g., "Run to daylight" and "Winning isn't everything, it's the only thing"); Brown has won championships with the Cleveland Browns of the All-America Conference and with the Browns of the NFL.

No doubt the Hall doors beckon for the likes of Tom Landry of the Dallas Cowboys and Don Shula of the Miami Dolphins, but make it or not, the best of the contemporary coaches likely would agree with Rockne when he said: "A coach and his system are just as good as his players—and not an iota better. Give me great players and they can win without a system. Bad ones can't win with the best coaching in the world."

COACHES' GRAVEYARD: A university or pro football team with a tradition for costing coaches their jobs. The University of California was once considered a coach's graveyard. So was Ohio State—before Woody Hayes exploded the theory. In the pros, clubs like the Houston Oilers, the San Diego Chargers, and the New Orleans Saints have the graveyard reputation.

C.O.D.: A scout's abbreviation for change of direction. A favorable quality in a player who is adept at reversing his field without sacrificing maneuverability and speed.

COFFIN CORNER: Where the sideline meets the goal line, the last two or three yards where punters sometimes try to kick the ball, thus avoiding a touchback, minimizing the risk of a return, and forcing the offense to start deep in its own territory. The coffin-corner kick was revived in the National Football League in recent years when missed field goals from beyond the 20-yard line were returned to the line of scrimmage. Teams began disdaining long field goals and opting for coffin-corner punts.

COLLEGE ALL-STAR GAME: The annual August exhibition game in Chicago between the best graduating college seniors and the previous season's NFL champion. The series began in 1934 as a *Chicago Tribune* promotion and companion piece to the All Star baseball game. The game, played every year except in 1974 because of an NFL players' strike, has drawn more than three million fans and produced more than $13 million for charities. Since the All-Stars' upset of Green Bay in 1963, the game has turned into a mismatch, the pro team usually winning in a romp. Pro coaches reluctantly accept the game; the All-Star players they've drafted are late reporting to training camp, and they risk injury in the game.

COMEBACK: A maneuver by the receiver in which he will stop short of his defensive man and reverse his direction, going back toward the line of scrimmage. Sometimes the tactic is involuntary, e.g., when the quarterback underthrows the ball.

COMMISSIONER: The official in charge of the league or conference. Although he is supposedly the representative of both the owners and the players, there has seldom been a question that the commissioner owes his allegiance to the owners—the men who hire him. Alvin (Pete) Rozelle, one of the strongest commissioners in any sport, admitted in 1976 that his office was sliding more and more in the direction of NFL owners because of continued litigation over labor disputes.

Rozelle, after more than 20 ballots, had been a compromise choice for commissioner in 1959 after Bert Bell died of a heart attack at a game. Rozelle, who had been general manager of the Los Angeles Rams, makes an estimated $200,000 a year. He has led the league through competition from the rival American Football League, a successful merger, lucrative television contracts, gambling and drug scandals, and recurring labor problems.

The NFL's first commissioner was Elmer Layden, one of the Four Horsemen from Notre Dame, who was elected in 1941. Before Layden the titular head had been designated a president, starting with Jim Thorpe in 1920. The first commissioner of the American Football League was Joe Foss, a World War II flying hero and twice governor of South Dakota. Shortly after Al Davis replaced Foss, the AFL and NFL merged, and Rozelle emerged as the game's sole commissioner.

CONFERENCE: A league of teams playing games among themselves to establish a champion at the end of the season. Games against outside teams are called nonconference. The Western Conference was the first college league, formed in 1896 and consisting of Wisconsin, Michigan, Minnesota, Purdue, Northwestern, Illinois, and Chicago. The conference is now unofficially but popularly known as the Big Ten. In pro football the NFL is made up of the American and National conferences, each conference broken down into two divisions.

CONTAIN MEN: On a kickoff, the two outside men on the kicking team are responsible for forcing the kick returner into running to the inside of the field.

CONVERSION: The point after touchdown.

CORNERBACK: The third line of defense, behind the line and the linebackers. Cornerbacks are primarily pass defenders, but they must also be skilled in open-field tackling. Good cornerbacks can be effective in jarring the ball loose from runners because once the offensive back leaves the scrimmage area, he has a tendency to loosen up. Cornerbacks usually weigh between 190 and 210 pounds and frequently are former track and field men who can outrun most of the other players. One of the best modern cornerbacks was the Green Bay Packers' Herb Adderley, a former champion hurdler.

CORNER FLAG: A small flag with a pliant staff placed where the goal line joins the sideline. A back who heads for the flag is trying to make it for the end zone.

CORNER PATTERN: A pass route, popular with tight ends, in which the receiver will run down the field 10 to 15 yards, then angle diagonally toward the outside in the direction of the corner flag.

COUNT: The sound and cadence of the quarterback calling signals at the line of scrimmage. There are long counts and short counts, and a player who improperly anticipates will be jumping offside.

COUNT SYSTEM: A passer throwing to a receiver after a certain number of seconds.

COVERAGE: The defense's attempt to stop a receiver from catching a pass or a kick returner from running with a punt or kickoff. Popular pass coverages are the zone, man-to-man, and a combination of the two.

COVERAGE UNIT: The team assigned to handle coverage.

CRACKBACK: A near clip on a block just beyond the scrimmage line in which a wide receiver catches an unsuspecting linebacker at knee level. Because the blocker is usually a fast man, he can generate tremendous speed; and this combined with the element of surprise, since the linebacker is usually following the flow of the ball, can cause serious knee injury. A recent rule change has disallowed the crackback block by ends.

CRADLE OF COACHES: Generally thought to be Miami University of Oxford, Ohio, which has been a feeder system for major colleges and professional teams. Miami coaches who moved on to larger jobs include Paul Brown, Ara Parseghian, Bo Schembechler, Weeb Ewbank, Paul Dietzel, Woody Hayes, Carmen Cozza, Bill Mallory, John McVay, Johnny Pont, Jim Root, Doc Urich, Clive Rush, and Jerry Wampfler. Robert T. Howard, former sports publicist at Miami, gave this explanation for the school being such a successful training ground: "The thing that has kept this tradition going has been the caliber of the men, the caliber of training they got at Miami, and the caliber of help they gave one another."

CRAP-ROLL SPIKE: A folk rite instituted by Harold Carmichael of the Philadelphia Eagles. After he catches a touchdown pass Carmichael takes the ball in one hand, pretending it's a pair of dice, bends to one knee in the end zone, and rolls the ball as though he were shooting craps. Such shenanigans make the defense seethe, but when you're as big as Carmichael (6'8" and 225 pounds), you don't worry about the other guy's hard feelings.

CRASHING END: A defensive end whose primary job is to rush full speed toward the center of the play, breaking up interference or putting pressure on the passer. Most of the time an end will play back slightly, prepared to hand-fight anyone coming his way.

CRAWLING: A five-yard penalty against a runner for crawling with the ball after the whistle. It is a seldom-seen violation and seldom called when seen.

CROSSBAR: The horizontal bar that connects the goalposts, or uprights. It is 18 feet 6 inches long and 10 feet off the ground.

CROSS BLOCK: A block on a linebacker or cornerback that is thrown after two offensive linemen cross, in an attempt to create doubt in the defensive man's mind about where the block is coming from.

CRYING TOWEL: The coach who always moans about losses, injuries, lack of material, lack of money—even a *high* national rating—is a man who uses the crying towel.

CURL: *See* Buttonhook.

CUT: The coach's distasteful job of reducing the team to roster limit. In a different sense, a cut is a sharp change of direction while running. Still differently, to cut is to block low, around the knees, or to body block.

CUT DOWN: To tackle a man low and cleanly so that he drops immediately as though he had been cut down. Also, a low, neat downfield block that cuts down the defensive man.

DEAD BALL: A ball no longer in play, signaled dead by the referee's whistle.

DECEPTION: The trick of making the defense think a play is going one way when it's actually moving in the opposite direction. Percy Haughton, the old Harvard coach, had an ingenious way of testing a trick play in practice. He would scent a ball and let Pooch, his wife's cocker spaniel, smell it. At practice, if the ball was hidden so well that Pooch would chase a player without the ball, Haughton knew he had a play that would work. You'll have to admit, it beats litmus paper.

DECOY: A receiver who goes downfield to lure defenders away from the planned target. Because top receivers frequently draw double coverage, they make the best decoys.

DEEP BACK: In the I formation, a back at the rear of the I, farthest away from the center.

DEEP SECONDARY: The line of defense farthest away from the line of scrimmage, usually consisting of two safety men. When a receiver is told to go deep, it means at least as far as the deep secondary.

DEFENSE: The team that does not have the ball and is trying to stop the offensive attack is on defense. In simplest terms, the best defense is the defense that works. If a team is graced with an outstanding linebacker, it might want to build its defense around him. Defensive formations change throughout a game, either based on what the offense might do or to confuse the offense.

In the early days of football defense was a mob of men following the ball, but now the approach is more studious, and a well-oiled defense can be beautiful to watch. Most defenses are numbered according to the number of players a coach assigns to each layer. The 5-2 defense, for example, consists of five players on the line, closest to the line of scrimmage, with two linebackers close behind. This is a passing defense, with the rest of the defense scattered about the secondary according to the type of pass coverage that is being used.

The 4-4 defense is popular at many colleges, with four men on the line and four linebackers backing them up. This is a flexible defense, for the linebackers can fill holes in the line if they see a running play or drop back for pass coverage if the offense takes to the air. The standard pro defense is the 4-3, with two ends and two tackles on the line and three linebackers.

DEKE: A hockey term gaining some acceptance in football. *See* Fake.

DELAY: When a player hesitates a moment before moving at the snap of the ball. The delay is designed to confuse the opponent and detract from his timing, and it might be used by a receiver, a ballcarrier, or an offensive or defensive lineman.

DELAY OF GAME: It is a 5-yard penalty if the offensive team doesn't run a play within 30 seconds (25 for the colleges) after the referee signals the ball in play. There are other instances of delay of game—a fake injury, or players slow to line up following the completion of a play—but taking too much time in the huddle is the most common. A rare delay of game would be a team being late for the start of a half, and this is a 15-yard penalty.

DESPERATION PASS: A bomb, thrown late in the game, with the team's fastest receiver usually the target. The play is no surprise, but occasionally it will work for a touchdown—to wit, Roger Staubach's last-second heave to Drew Pearson in a 1975 play-off game, giving the Dallas Cowboys a victory over the Minnesota Vikings—a victory the Cowboys needed en route to the Super Bowl.

DIPSY DOO: Chicanery; some sort of trick play or series of plays.

DIRTY PLAY: Frequently this kind of football, designed to injure and a violation of the rules, is not far removed from overly aggressive play. Dirty play includes hitting a man from behind, piling on top of a ballcarrier after the whistle has blown, hitting a man when he is out of bounds, and punching an opponent.

DISQUALIFICATION: The ejection from the game of a player who has committed a serious violation of the rules. His team is also penalized 15 yards. There is automatic disqualification for (*1*) striking an opponent with the fist; (*2*) kicking or kneeing an opponent; (*3*) striking an opponent on the head or neck with the forearm, elbow, or hands; and (*4*) entering a game a second time with illegal equipment. Disqualification may be ordered by an official if he feels that any of these fouls is flagrant: (1) roughing the kicker, (2) roughing the passer, (3) malicious unnecessary roughness, (4) unsportsmanlike conduct, and (5) committing a palpably unfair act.

DIVE: A back's attempt to score from short yardage by diving over the line of scrimmage into the end zone. Defensive linemen are usually stacked up in a low stance on goal-line situations, and diving over the top can be an effective way of gaining the necessary yardage.

DIVE PLAY: *See* Quick Opener.

DOG: *See* Blitz.

DOGGING IT: Taking it easy; not playing up to ability. Also known as jaking it.

DOG ON THE FIELD: It seems as though no football game has ever been played without this type of amusing delay. There's nothing that makes an official more human than to see him chasing a dog off the field so play can resume. Cornell graduate Henry Schoellkopf left a large endowment to his alma mater, including money for the school's Schoellkopf Field, with the stipulation that dogs would always be free to roam the campus.

DOOMSDAY DEFENSE: An imaginative description of the intrepid defenses constructed by coach Tom Landry, who quickly built an expansion team, the Dallas Cowboys, into a contender and a Super Bowl champion.

DOUBLE COVERAGE: Assigning two players to cover one receiver on pass coverage. Usually a cornerback and a safety man will double up, and a receiver can get no greater tribute than to earn this kind of treatment.

DOUBLE FOUL: A foul by each team during the same play. Regardless of the violations, one penalty nullifies the other and the down stays the same.

DOUBLEHEADER: Two pro exhibition games for a single admission, as they do in baseball. Conceived in 1962 by Art Modell, owner of the Cleveland Browns, the doubleheader annually drew capacity crowds to Cleveland's Municipal Stadium. But they don't have the twin bills anymore.

DOUBLE-TEAM: A block in which two offensive men try to move a defensive lineman out of the play. Most frequently used when a single lineman is having trouble blocking a heavier defender. On the double-team the man who plays in front of the defender is called the post man and he sets the opponent up. The other blocker comes in at an angle and is the drive man who does the heavy moving work.

DOUBLE WING: An offensive formation that places two set backs spread out wide at opposite sides of the field.

DOWN: A unit of action in the game that begins with the snap of the ball and ends when an official whistles the ball dead, signifying that the play is over. The offensive team gets four downs in order to advance the ball 10 yards. When 10 yards are gained, a first down is ruled, and the offensive team receives four more downs.

DOWN AND IN: A receiver's pass pattern that extends straight down the field and then inward toward the center of the field at a 90-degree angle.

DOWN AND OUT: Same as down and in, except the receiver goes outward toward the sideline at a 90-degree angle.

DOWNFIELD: Technically, the area one yard past the line of scrimmage. Offensive linemen are not allowed to move into this area on a pass play unless they are sustaining a block. On running plays to one side of the field linemen on the other side are usually required to throw a downfield block or a block on a defensive halfback that might spring the ballcarrier loose.

DOWN LINEMAN: Any lineman, usually on the defense, who operates out of a three-point stance. An exception might be an end who plays off the line slightly and in an upward position, or a middle guard who plays from a crouched position.

DRAFT: A method of choosing collegiate seniors for professional teams. Because the draft is based on the previous year's won-lost record, with the worst teams drafting first and the best clubs picking last, it is designed to be a talent equalizer. The ideal falls short of reality, however, since some teams abuse the draft. Other teams thrive on it.

The Pittsburgh Steelers until the 1970s were notorious for drafting players who wouldn't make the team. But the Steelers won successive Super Bowls largely through talent obtained in the draft. The Dallas Cowboys, Pittsburgh's opponent in the 1976 Super Bowl, are another draft-conscious team. Vince Lombardi perhaps used the draft better than any other coach. Not only did the Green Bay Packers usually cull top prospects from the college ranks, but Lombardi, sensing when many of his veteran players had passed their peaks, would trade them to other clubs in exchange for draft choices. Thus when Green Bay went to draft, it would own more selections than the average team, which picks about 20 players.

Then there is a coach like George Allen, who abhors rookies and the draft in interchangeable order. Allen usually trades away his top draft picks for veteran players, his theory being that you don't have to train

O. J. Simpson got caught in the draft by Buffalo.

veterans. Allen, with the Washington Redskins, carried this practice to such an extreme that he was caught trading draft choices he didn't even own, for which the team was fined by the league.

Bert Bell introduced the draft in 1935, in order to end expensive bidding among the teams. The National Football League Players Association has challenged the legality of the draft, but the courts have wavered on the issue. If it weren't for the draft, for example, O. J. Simpson probably would have remained in California, where he played collegiately. When Simpson was drafted by the Buffalo Bills, he complained about the ugliness of the city and the cold climate. But Simpson put up with Buffalo and was instrumental in reviving the Bills as a contending team.

In the first draft in 1936, the first player chosen was Jay Berwanger, an All-American halfback from the University of Chicago. The Philadelphia Eagles sold the rights to Berwanger to the Chicago Bears, but when the player and Bears owner George Halas couldn't come to contract terms, Berwanger went into private business, where he became the president of his own company.

The competition in the draft and the pressure from the teams to pick successful players have made scouting of the colleges a full-time job for the pro clubs. Small schools receive as much attention as the monolithic universities. For a sporting event that comes with no final score, the draft is a popular conversation piece for fans everywhere, speculating about what players their favorite teams will pick.

There is another kind of pro draft, held whenever the NFL expands by adding new teams. These added teams are stocked in part through players from rosters of the existing teams, who are allowed to protect most of their regulars. This is known as an expansion draft.

DRAW PLAY: A running play that apparently begins as a pass, with the quarterback fading back after taking the center snap. But as he fades, the quarterback will slip the ball to a back running up the middle. When the defense is overloaded against the pass, this can be a big-gain call. It is used in obvious passing situations to keep the defense off guard. Many middle linebackers feel the draw is their toughest play to handle, because they are vulnerable to blocks from offensive tackles coming in from the blind side.

DRIFT: The flow of the play. Linebackers sometimes make instinctive tackles because they "caught the drift of the play." Also, a player who drifts away from the offensive formation hopes to go unnoticed, so he'll be a target for a screen pass, a reverse, or some trick play.

DRILL: Another word for a practice session. Also, within that session, drill is a description for a specific type of activity—e.g., a passing drill, kickoff-return drills, field-goal drills, etc. Also, when a passer drills a ball, he is throwing it with both velocity and accuracy.

DRIVE: The ability in a back to keep moving forward after he is hit. In a lineman, the ability to move an opponent out of position through sheer strength. During a game a drive is an offensive team's series of plays, from the time it gains possession of the ball until it either scores or loses possession. When a team takes the ball from its own 20-yard line to a touchdown, it might be said that "the scoring drive covered 80 yards in twelve plays."

DROP-BACK QUARTERBACK: A quarterback who takes the center snap and immediately fades back into the pocket, about six or seven yards deep, to set up and attempt a pass. As opposed to other types of quarterbacks, such as the roll-out variety or the scrambler.

DROPKICK: A kick given to the ball as it rebounds after having been dropped from the hands to the ground. Once an art, the dropkick is obsolete. Points after touchdown can still be drop-kicked, but the only time you'll see one tried is by a harried kicker after a busted play.

DUCK WALK: An outmoded practice exercise in which the player would reach down and grab his ankles and waddle around. Catching the spirit of the thing, some players would also quack like ducks as they did the exercise. Coaches later learned that the duck walk was in fact harmful to the knees.

DUMMY: A piece of equipment used to give a player practice in blocking, tackling, and timing. Tackling dummies can be heavy bags suspended from a platform. There are charging sleds padded with foam rubber and attached to a platform that absorb the contact of anywhere from two to ten charging linemen.

The New York Giants used to have a huge inflated dummy that the players called Mike the Bartender, which was placed on either side of the line to take the place of a defensive lineman during a passing drill. The Giants paid $5,000 for a battery-powered dummy that swiveled around, lit up, and fired out at a real player. "Son," Jimmy Patton said to a rookie one day in training camp, "some night you'll be asleep and that thing is going to come walking across the grass, right up into your room to get you."

Practice dummies were invented in 1889 by Amos Alonzo Stagg when he rolled up a mattress and suspended it from a chain in a gym.

DUMMY SCRIMMAGE: A drill that imitates the

actual plays called during a game except that the players run through the blocks and tackles without making hard contact. Usually pads aren't worn in dummy scrimmages, which are the opposite of all-out live scrimmages that resemble a game in most ways.

DUMP: Throwing an intentional incompletion. When the quarterback's receivers are all covered and the linemen are charging him hard, he will sometimes dump the ball so he won't be tackled behind the line of scrimmage. There is a penalty for this called intentional grounding of a pass, but it isn't called often, particularly on the slick quarterbacks who can dump the ball while appearing to be actually trying to hit the receiver.

EAT THE BALL: When a quarterback is back to pass and finds his receivers covered and can't or won't run with the ball, he allows the defense to tackle him, thereby doing what is called eating the ball. Quarterbacks who throw anyway to avoid the yardage loss sometimes regret it because passes thrown when receivers are covered are likely to wind up being intercepted.

ELIGIBLE: In college, being scholastically and athletically qualified to play a sport. During different eras college players have had either three or four years of football eligibility. Often when a player transfers from one school to another, he forfeits a year of eligibility.

ELIGIBLE RECEIVER: On offense there are five players eligible to catch a pass—three backs and two ends. Tackles and guards can be eligible, too, if any of them lines up as an end. A player must notify the referee of this so the defense can be told that a man with a noneligible number on his uniform is going to be eligible. All defensive players are eligible to catch (intercept) a pass.

ENCROACHMENT: When a player moves across the neutral zone and makes contact before the ball is snapped. This is a five-yard penalty.

END: On both offense and defense, the players stationed at both ends of the line. Offensive ends are more commonly known as wide receivers or tight ends. Some think the term "tight end" is suggestive. Jackie Smith, veteran tight end of the St. Louis Cardinals, tried to open a suburban bar and name it after his position. The ruling body thought this was in poor taste and wouldn't grant a license under that name. Ergo, Jackie Smith's Bar.

A tight end is more a blocker than a pass catcher. A wide receiver is the reverse. Defensive ends must be big and mobile—their job takes them in all directions: They must rush the passer, provide help for the tackles on plays run to the inside, and be able to fight off end runs

until help arrives from the linebackers and others in the secondary.

Alabama's Don Hutson, a 195-pounder who could run 100 yards in 9.8 seconds, was the first of the great pass-catching ends. Hutson, after starring in the 1935 Rose Bowl, became a pro standout with the Green Bay Packers. Some tight ends who could also catch the ball have included the Detroit Lions' Leon Hart, a 260-pounder who also played fullback; Green Bay's Ron Kramer; and Richard Caster of the New York Jets.

END AROUND: A trick play in which an end, after lining up in his regular position or a step or two behind it, will circle back and take a hand-off from a back and continue running with the ball around the opposite end.

END LINE: The base line of the field, also the back line of the end zone. It is located ten yards behind the goal line.

END OVER END: A kick in which the nose of the ball rotates. Usually said of kickoffs.

END SWEEP: A run in which the back, with the help of additional blocking from a guard pulling out of the line, will try to circle either of the defensive ends. The difference between this play and a simple end run is that on the latter the guard does not pull.

END ZONE: The ten-yard area between the goal line and the end line, which is where a ballcarrier must reach with any part of the ball in order to be credited with a touchdown.

EXCESSIVE TIME-OUTS: Each team is allowed three time-outs per half. Any more than that draws a five-yard penalty, although in most instances a referee will not allow a team to take an extra time-out.

EXECUTION: Applying blackboard plans, which call for a touchdown on every play, to the field. In other words, putting theory into practice. When practice strays from theory too often, the head coach faces a different kind of execution.

EXHIBITION GAME: National Football League hirelings may smoke, drink, and even bum with women who do, but the expression "exhibition game" should never pass their lips if they value their jobs. To Pete Rozelle, a game that doesn't count is called a preseason game. The exhibition season is simply preseason. But Park Avenue semantics aside, an exhibition game is generally a contest between casts of hundreds, many of whom won't be around when the season starts. Nevertheless, clubs charge regular-season prices for exhibitions, which usually draw large, if not sellout, crowds. Although fans are unable to use exhibitions as a gauge for what to expect during the championship season, the preseason games are vitally important for rookies trying to make the team.

EXPANSION DRAFT: *See* Draft.

FACEMASK: The plastic structure that is attached to the helmet for protection of the face. A far cry from the days when players didn't even wear helmets, few players play without facemasks today. One of the exceptions was Tommy McDonald, the little receiver for the Philadelphia Eagles.

FADE: Moving in a clear, precise pattern at less than full speed. Usually used to describe the quarterback, who fades into the pocket after taking the center snap on pass plays.

FAIR CATCH: A catch of a punt, signalled by a raised arm, in which the receiving player may not run back the ball and may not be tackled by the coverage team. After a fair catch the receiving team puts the ball in play from scrimmage at the point of the catch. If a fair catch is dropped, the ball is free for both teams. If the punt returner signals for a fair catch and does not touch the ball, it still belongs to his team. An untouched ball after a fair catch that rolls into the end zone is still a touchback for the receiving team. Many punt returners take pride in seldom calling for a fair catch; giving up a chance to return the kick is a blow to their macho.

FAKE: A move designed to deceive the defense. A back will fake, or feint, trying to throw a tackler off-balance. In this sense a fake is also called a juke or a deke. Quarterbacks fake hand-offs to draw the defense out of position. Eddie LeBaron, a 5'8" 170-pound quarterback for the College of the Pacific and the Washington Redskins, was one of football's greatest faking quarterbacks. LeBaron would frequently warn referees of what he was planning to do so they wouldn't prematurely whistle the play dead.

FAR SIDE: A term used by broadcasters, meaning the side of the field farthest away from them and/or the camera.

FIELD GENERAL: The quarterback, as though he were an army officer on a battlefield, is considered the field general, the man who has command of the offensive field action.

FIELD GOAL: A ball kicked above the crossbar and between the uprights after being snapped from center and held on the ground by a holder. A field goal is worth three points. Especially during the times when the goalposts were located on the goal line, the field goal has been a popular scoring vehicle for the pros, and a good kicker has become *de rigueur* for college teams since the NCAA increased the size of the goalposts.

Answering a lingering complaint that teams were becoming too dependent on field goals, the National Football League in 1974 returned the goalposts to the back of the end zone, ten yards from the goal. The NFL also approved a rule that gives the ball to the defensive team at the line of scrimmage if a field goal is missed from beyond the 20-yard line. Field goals missed from the 20-yard line or closer are still returned to the 20.

The trend in the pros has continued to be toward soccer-style kickers, many of them foreign players who kick from the side instead of facing the ball head on. The Gogolak brothers, Pete and Charley, were among the first of these. At Princeton Charley Gogolak kicked 16 field goals in a season, and 6 in one game. Jim Bakken of the St. Louis Cardinals kicked 7 field goals in one game.

The New Orleans Saints' Tom Dempsey, who has only one hand and a stub for a toe, was permitted by the NFL to use a special shoe, and he kicked a 63-yard field goal against the Detroit Lions in 1970. Ray Guy of Southern Mississippi kicked a 61-yard field goal against Utah State in 1972. To show how important the kicking game is to the pros, Guy was drafted by the Oakland Raiders, but because Oakland still had George Blanda at the time, Guy was restricted to just punting. Blanda holds the record for lifetime field goals in the pros with more than 300 to his credit.

When Lou Groza and Paul Hornung and Ken Strong were kicking, they also played regularly, but a kicker is a kicker is a kicker nowadays, and some players, defensive linemen in particular, detest these undersized specialists. Pete Gogolak would always defend his specialty, once saying: "People think we're not athletes, that we just loaf around at practice and just show up for games. That's bullsmoke. I underwent extensive weight programs to strengthen my legs during the off-season, and to stay sharp you have to do the same thing during the season."

FIELD JUDGE: A game official who takes a position between 22 and 25 yards downfield from the scrimmage line, near the center of the field but favoring the side occupied by the head linesman. He concentrates on the path of the end or back on his side, observing the legality of his potential blocks and of actions taken against him. He is prepared to rule from the deep position on holding or illegal use of the hands by the end or back, or on defensive infractions by players guarding him. The field judge times the 30-second interval between plays; makes decisions

Nobody has kicked as many field goals *as George Blanda, the ageless Oakland Raider.*

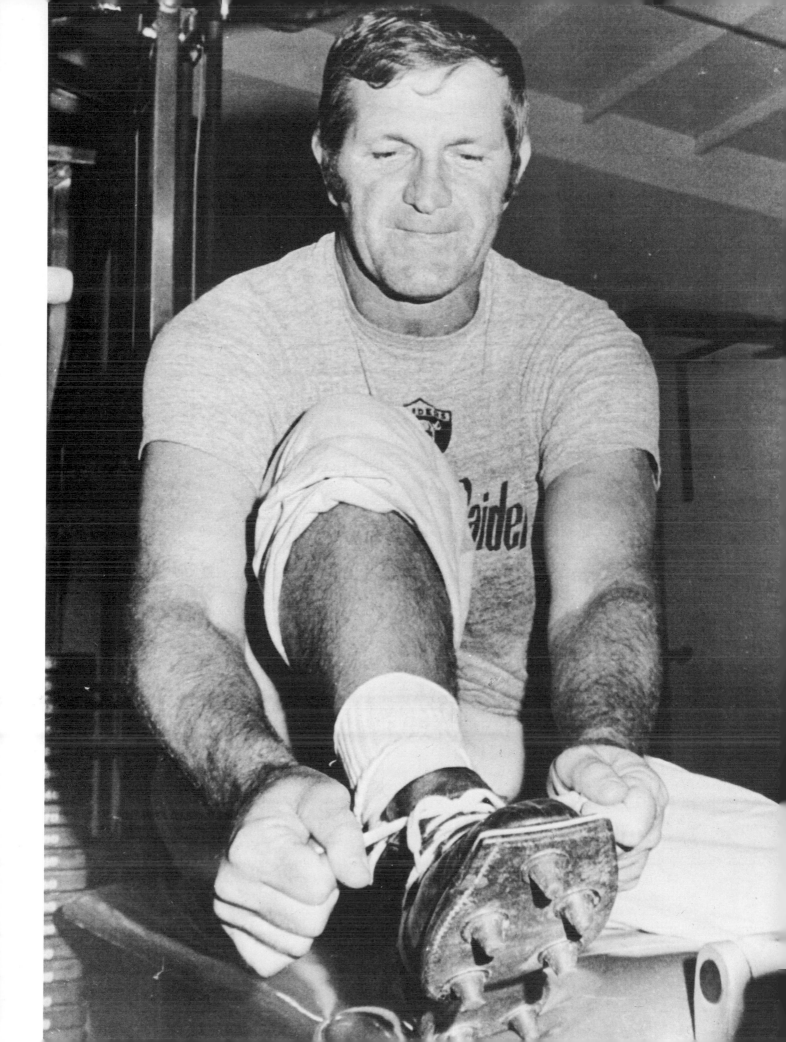

involving catching, recovery, or illegal touching of a loose ball beyond the line of scrimmage; is responsible to rule on plays involving the end line; calls pass interference, fair-catch infractions, and clipping on kick returns; and, together with the back judge, rules whether or not field-goal attempts are successful.

FIELD POSITION: The point on the field where the offensive team assumes control of the ball. The closer to the opponent's goal, the better the field position, because a team away from its own goal normally can be more selective in the plays that it uses. Coaches are constantly striving for "good field position," which is loosely defined as anywhere from their own 40-yard line or closer.

FIFTH-DOWN GAME: A game in 1940, played in a blizzard in Hanover, N. H., in which Cornell defeated Dartmouth, 7-3, by scoring a touchdown on an illegal fifth down because of an official's error. Cornell, which came into the game with an 18-game unbeaten streak, was trailing, 3-0, and had been stopped by Dartmouth on the 1-yard line on fourth down with less than a minute to play. But referee Red Friesell, confused because he had penalized Cornell for an illegal substitution, allowed Cornell an extra down. Cornell scored a touchdown and kicked the extra point.

Films of the game, however, revealed Friesell's error, and Cornell immediately wired Dartmouth that the game would go into the record books as a 3-0 Dartmouth victory. The referee, now dead, lived forever with the haunting nickname of Fifth-Down Friesell. There have been other instances of teams mistakenly getting five downs, but none as famous or meaningful as Dartmouth-Cornell.

In 1968 in a National Football League game, the officiating team headed by referee Norm Schachter, considered a top official, mixed up the downs. Commissioner Pete Rozelle suspended the crew from working in the playoffs.

FIFTH MAN IN THE BACKFIELD: Praise for a defensive player who makes so many tackles behind the line of scrimmage that he is called the fifth man in the backfield—the other team's backfield.

53 DEFENSE: Another name for the four-linebacker defense, coined by the Miami Dolphins because their extra linebacker, Bob Matheson, wore uniform number 53. The defense developed by accident, with Matheson sent in as a substitute in a passing situation. He had the option to rush the passer or play the pass, and he handled the assignment so well that coach Don Shula made the 53 a regular defensive alignment when it appeared that the other team might pass. Then many of the other National Football League teams began using four linebackers in similar situations.

FIGHT TALK: Few coaches shake down the thunder from the skies like Knute Rockne did at Notre Dame. Al Conover, when he coached at Rice, threw a chair through a locker-room window at halftime, hoping it would inspire his team. Conover forgot that he was on the road, and the school sent him a bill for the damages. "What price inspiration?" Conover may have been asking a few years later when he was fired by Rice.

"If a team isn't ready for a game, anything I tell them right before isn't going to help," claims Duffy Daugherty, the former Michigan State coach. "Our job is to get them ready during the week, not five minutes before they take the field."

FILL: When a lineman blocks, filling in the gap left by another lineman who has pulled out to lead interference.

FIRE OUT: An offensive lineman's quick move off the line at the snap and into his blocking assignment.

FLAG: An official's marker, which he throws at the spot of an infraction of the rules. Flags have been various colors in various leagues, but the National Football League has been using yellow flags in recent seasons. The corner flag is a red marker where the sideline meets the goal line at the four corners of the field.

FLAG PATTERN: A pass route in which the receiver will take off in the direction of the corner flag.

FLAKE: A player who is goofy, kooky, eccentric. As some of the players say, a flaky player doesn't play with a full deck. The consummate modern flake was Joe Don Looney, who bounced from team to team in the National Football League. Looney would physically attack practice dummies in anger. He refused to throw his dirty clothes in a bin "because no sign is going to tell me what to do."

Fred Dryer of the Los Angeles Rams enjoys his reputation as a flake—he used to sleep in his Volkswagen bus instead of renting an apartment, and at the 1975 Super Bowl he and teammate Lance Rentzel showed up at a press conference dressed as a couple of reporters out of the 1930s, with press cards in their hat bands, etc. Steve Wright drove coaches to distraction wherever he played. In Washington he irked George Allen by saying: "What you want, all that jumping around after a play, is what I call false hustle. But if it's false hustle you want, it's false hustle you'll get."

FLANKER: A running back who takes a position to the far left or right of the quarterback to function as a pass receiver. The difference between a flanker and a split end is that the flanker will usually line up a yard or two behind the line of scrimmage, on the opposite side of the field.

FLARE: A quick pass in which the receiver will take a few steps downfield and then take a step or two right or left in anticipation of the quarterback's throw.

FLAT: The area to the side and a few yards beyond the line of scrimmage where a receiver, sometimes a back, will move to accept a short pass.

FLEA FLICKER: A forward pass in which the receiver laterals to a teammate after the completion. Also, a pass play in which the receiver laterals back to a teammate behind the line of scrimmage and he throws a second pass. Coach Bob Zuppke of Illinois is credited with devising the flea flicker, so named because of the quick flicking action of a dog trying to rid himself of fleas.

FLIP-FLOP: When an offense uses a wide receiver on either side of the field, depending on the situation. Hence, a defense doesn't know from one play to the next which side of the field the wide receivers will be on. With the popularity of the zone coverages, flip-flopping of wide receivers has been a source of less concern for a defense.

FLOAT: To throw a pass softly. Also, for a back, to move in graceful, deceptively easy strides.

FLOOD A ZONE: To send two or more receivers into one area so that there are more receivers than defenders to cover them.

FLOP-ON: A scout's derogatory term for a player who will be late joining in on a tackle, trying to gain some of the credit.

FLOW: The direction of a play and the route most of the offensive players seem to be taking.

FLY: A pass pattern in which a receiver will run straight down the field, hoping to beat the defensive man by simply outrunning him.

FLYING WEDGE: A formation that was long ago abolished because it caused too many injuries. The rest of the offensive team would gather around the ballcarrier in a wedge-shaped formation and move down the field deflecting tacklers along the way. Players in the wedge, and players who assiduously tried to break it, such as Pudge Heffelfinger of Yale, would subject themselves to inevitable injury. Teams still use a distillation of the flying wedge on kickoff returns, except that they just call it the wedge and only three or four blockers are involved. A member of the kicking team who is considered effective at breaking through the blocking is referred to as a wedge buster.

FLYING WING: The 12th man, the extra back, in Canadian football who is used primarily as a pass receiver.

FOOTBALL: A field game in which the two contesting teams, consisting of 11 men on a side, try to kick or carry the ball to or through their opponents' goal

Jim Thorpe, the Carlisle Indian, was a star halfback in the United States Football Association, the first pro league in football.

or goal line. American football is a spin-off of rugby. In football, however, one side is allowed undisputed possession of the ball at the moment it is put in play, players may run ahead of the man with the ball to prevent his being tackled, the forward pass is permitted, and the play is more systemized and formal than rugby.

The object of football is to score the most points in a specific amount of time, which is 60 minutes in professional and collegiate football, broken down into four quarters of 15 minutes apiece. Scoring is accomplished by (1) a touchdown, which is six points; (2) an extra point or conversion, one point; (3) extra points, two points; (4) a field goal, three points; and (5) a safety, two points.

A touchdown is scored when a player runs across the goal line, or catches a pass or recovers a fumble in his opponent's end zone. An extra-point try is allowed following a touchdown and is scored by kicking the ball through the goalposts and above the crossbar, or passing or running it in. Two extra points, permitted in collegiate football, are scored following a touchdown when a team runs or passes the ball into the end zone from the 3-yard line. A field goal is scored by place-kicking or drop-kicking the ball from scrimmage through the goalposts and above the crossbar. A safety is scored when an opposing player is tackled in his own end zone, or when the ball goes beyond the end line of the offensive team on its own impetus—e.g. a bad snap from center.

In college football a game can end in a tie, but professional teams allow a 15-minute overtime period if the game is tied after the fourth quarter, with the first team scoring being the winner. If neither team scores in the extra period, then the game is ruled a tie.

In the early nineteenth century the two lower classes at Harvard played an annual game called Bloody Monday, at which they pushed a ball over a line, using as many players as they wished and observing few rules. The game of football as it is known today evolved from this competition. A loose kind of soccer also existed, and in 1869 Princeton challenged Rutgers to what is generally considered the first intercollegiate football game.

Actually, the game more resembled soccer than football, and with both teams using 25 men on a side, Rutgers won, six goals to four. After a few colleges adopted the same sport, football's breakthrough came in 1874 when McGill University in Canada challenged Harvard to three games, two at Cambridge, Mass., and one at McGill, with rugby rules prevailing. The games at Cambridge resembled soccer and the game at McGill

was more like rugby, and Harvard adopted a game that combined features of both.

Early football was such a power game, contingent on brutality by both sides, that in 1905 President Theodore Roosevelt ordered colleges to tame down the competition or suffer federal intervention. The result of this ultimatum was a more wide-open game, and in 1906 the forward pass was introduced. Schools did not embrace the forward pass, however, until 1913, when an unheralded school from the Midwest used the weapon against a much bigger West Point team to score a monumental upset.

West Point, looking for a breather on its schedule, had offered Notre Dame $1,000—just about enough to transport 15 players—to come to New York and play. Knowing the Army game was ahead, Notre Dame quarterback Gus Dorais and his end, Knute Rockne, developed their passing routine at a vacation resort the summer before the season started. Against Army Dorais alternated passes to Rockne and another receiver as Notre Dame scored a 35-13 victory. In addition to popularizing both the game and the pass play, the victory had an uplifting effect for schools with small players everywhere, and it also marked the emergence of Notre Dame as a football power.

Professional football reportedly started in 1898 when teams from two western Pennsylvania towns, Latrobe and Jeannette, played a challenge game. The Latrobe team, sponsored by the city's YMCA, allowed its players to share profits from admission charges. Latrobe hired John Brailler, who later became a dentist, to play quarterback for a one-game fee of ten dollars.

Pittsburgh-area companies began sponsoring teams, pro football spread to the Ohio communities of Canton and Massillon, and the first organized league was formed in 1920. It was called the United States Football Association. Jim Thorpe, the great halfback from Carlisle, was the president and the league's star player. In 1921 the group of teams changed its name to the National Football League. When Red Grange, the famous Illinois halfback, turned pro in 1925, the NFL's popularity grew enormously.

FOOTSTEPS: The sound, usually imaginary, of an approaching defensive player, which a receiver is said to hear before he drops a pass.

FOREARM SHIVER: A defensive lineman's technique of fighting off a blocker by the use of an upward blow with the forearm.

FORFEIT: Failure to appear in time for a game or refusal to continue playing can cause an official to declare the other team the winner. The score of a forfeited game is 1-0.

FORMATION: An alignment of players in a set offensive or defensive pattern. When the quarterback lines up just behind the center for a short snap, it is called the T formation. Punt formation is when the team kicks the ball with the kicker lined up several yards behind the center. Football has evolved into a highly complex game consisting of a myriad of formations.

40-YARD DASH: The distance that most football teams use to measure the speed of their players, or potential players. The theory is that football players are seldom required to run more than 40 yards on a single play. The closer to four seconds a player can run the 40, the better his speed.

FORWARD PASS: An overhanded throw, usually by the quarterback, to one of his five eligible receivers—the other three backs and the two ends. Also called a pass, an aerial, and a pitch. The pass was legalized in 1906, and in 1933 the National Football League legalized passing from any spot behind the line of scrimmage.

The change in the size of the ball, from blimp-shaped to a more streamlined style, has coincided with the popularity of the pass play. No one really knows who threw the first pass (there is the hoary joke crediting Adam, shortly after the arrival of Eve), but the first great passer was Gus Dorais of Notre Dame. Little Davey O'Brien of Texas Christian was averaging 25 passes a game in 1937 while most other teams seldom threw 10. Nowadays, 30 or 40 passes a game, for pros or colleges, is not considered unusual.

Few teams survive without an accomplished passer, although Ohio State has been a long-standing exception. Woody Hayes, Ohio State's irrascible coach, has had this to say about the pass: "Three things can happen when you throw [completion, incompletion, and interception], and two of them are bad." Veteran football observers cite Sammy Baugh of the Washington Redskins as the greatest passer ever, but the NFL's record books include so many names that a debate on the subject would be interminable.

FORWARD PROGRESS: When a ballcarrier is stopped and pushed back, the referee will place the ball at the spot called forward progress, the point where the defensive man started moving the offensive player in a backward direction.

FORWARD WALL: Another name for the offensive line.

FOUL: A violation of the rules.

FOUR HORSEMEN: "Outlined against a blue-gray October sky, the Four Horsemen rode again. In dramatic lore they are known as Famine, Pestilence, Destruction and Death. These are only aliases. Their real names are Stuhldreher, Miller, Crowley and Layden." Grantland Rice, writing for the *New York Herald Tribune* on October 19, 1924, immortalized the Notre Dame backfield with that lead on a story that described the school's 13-7 victory over Army at New York's Polo Grounds.

Rice's story is probably the most memorable single piece ever written about football. Purists say that Rice's bombastic style, while typical of his day, would not survive a copy editor's pencil today. Actually, the idea of comparing Notre Dame's backfield with the Four Horsemen belonged to George Strickler, later to become sports editor of the *Chicago Tribune* but a student publicity director for Notre Dame at the time. Strickler had seen a Four Horsemen film, starring Rudolph Valentino, four or five times, and in a conversation about the precision of the Notre Dame backfield he interjected the remark that they "are just like the Four Horsemen."

After Rice wrote the story, Strickler embellished the reference by hiring four broken-down livery-stable plugs and taking publicity pictures of the backs in the saddle. The Notre Dame linemen took umbrage to the spate of publicity for the backs, and center Adam Walsh coined another label for the ages when he said: "We are just the seven mules. We do all the work so that these four fellows can gallop into fame."

FRANCHISE: The license, issued by a league, to operate a team in that league. The New York Giants' franchise, now worth approximately $25 million, was purchased in 1925 by Tim Mara for $500. Art Rooney bought the Pittsburgh Steelers' franchise for $2,500, money he had won at a race track, in 1933.

FREE AGENT: Players who are undrafted coming out of college or veteran players who have exercised the option clause in their contract, i.e., played a year without a contract and freed themselves to negotiate with other teams. Every year rookie free agents will be invited or will wangle their way into training camps, and it is a coaching windfall if any of them makes the team.

FREE BALL: A fumble that may be recovered and advanced by either the offense or defense.

FREE KICK: A kick that is required following a safety and which may be attempted after a fair catch of a punt. Following a safety the team scored upon must also give up the ball, putting it into play with a free kick, a punt, from its own 20-yard line. After any fair catch the receiving team, without interference, is allowed to attempt kicking a field goal.

FREE SAFETY: One of the defensive team's safety

men who is given no special assignment, being able to help where needed, strive for the interception, and when the play is called, blitz the quarterback. Willie Wood of the Green Bay Packers and Larry Wilson of the St. Louis Cardinals were two of the game's premier free safeties.

FREQUENCY CHART: A scouting tool used by teams to determine what percentage of plays an opponent has been using on offense and what formations the opponent has been using on defense.

FRONT FOUR: The defensive line, consisting of two ends and two tackles, most commonly used by professional teams. Rosey Grier was a tackle in two front fours known as the Fearsome Foursome—first with Dick Modzelewski, Jim Katcavage, and Andy Robustelli for the New York Giants; later with Merlin Olsen, Deacon Jones, and Lamar Lundy of the Los Angeles Rams.

For a time, the Minnesota Vikings' front four of Jim Marshall, Carl Eller, Alan Page, and Gary Larsen played under the theatrical name of the Purple People Eaters because of the color of the team's uniforms. The Pittsburgh Steelers' famed front four of L. C. Greenwood, Dwight White, Joe Greene, and Ernie Holmes has been known as the Steel Curtain.

FULLBACK: The power back or workhorse whose main job is to gain short yardage between the tackles. The fullback is normally the biggest, roughest player in the backfield, and every era has had a standout, starting with Ted Coy of Yale. Other memorable fullbacks include Jarrin' Jawn Kimbrough of Texas A&M; Tank Younger of the Los Angeles Rams; Bronko Nagurski of the Chicago Bears; Ernie Nevers, Stanford's Gray Ghost who, as a pro, scored 40 points in one game; Doc Blanchard of Army; Marion Motley and Jimmy Brown of the Cleveland Browns; and Larry Csonka of the Miami Dolphins and New York Giants.

FULL HOUSE: An offensive backfield in which all three running backs are set behind the line and inside the ends.

FUMBLE: The loss of possession of the ball by the ballcarrier. Fumbles are free balls and can be recovered by either team.

GAIN: The amount of yardage a ballcarrier picks up on a play, as measured from the line of scrimmage.

GAMBLING DEFENSE: A defense filled with stunts and blitzes, which looks for big losses, fumbles, and interceptions. Teams that play gambling defenses are usually trying to compensate for a lack of experience or a shortage of ability.

GAME PLAN: The strategy a coach outlines for a certain game, based on his scouting reports. Resource-ful coaches will change their game plans if they notice the opponent changing its tendencies.

GAMES: *See* Stunts.

GANG TACKLING: When two or more defensive players hit a runner at the same time. Gene ("Big Daddy") Lipscomb, 6'6" and 288 pounds, was referred to as a one-man gang tackler when he played in the National Football League.

GAP: The space between two offensive linemen.

GAP DEFENSE: A defense in which the linemen station themselves in the gaps rather than directly opposite offensive players.

GAP-EIGHT: The classic goal-line defense in which an eight-man line is used, filling every gap in the opponent's offensive line.

GARBAGE DEFENSE: Formations in which the spacing is so wide, the alignment so weird, and the execution so tricky that they defy the conformist way of playing football.

GLUE-FINGERED: A term used to describe a receiver who is so sure-handed that he appears to be wearing glue. A similar expression is sticky-fingered.

GOAL LINE: The line in front of each team's end zone which must be reached or crossed in order for a team to score a touchdown.

GOAL-LINE DEFENSE: A defense, close to its own goal line, which uses more men than usual on the line to prevent power plays up the middle.

GOAL-LINE STAND: When a team using a goal-line defense rises to the occasion and prevents its opponent from scoring from short yardage. Columbia stopped Stanford at the goal line so often in the 1934 Rose Bowl that Columbia end Red Matal said: "We always knew where to line up; we just found our footprints in the mud from the last stand and dug in all over again."

GOALPOSTS: Two poles at opposite ends of the field, connected by a crossbar. The poles are called uprights and are 18 feet 6 inches apart in professional football, 23 feet 4 inches apart in college. The crossbar is 10 feet above the ground, and the uprights can extend 20 feet or more above the crossbar. Concerned about overemphasis on the field goal, the National Football League in 1974 moved its goalposts back to the end lines, ten yards back of the goal line and where they have always been in college ball.

GOAL TO GO: An expression that indicates that the offensive team must score a touchdown within its four downs or give up the ball. "Third down and goal to go on the seven" means that the offense needs seven yards for a touchdown.

GOLDEN STAIRS: A New York Giants' play in the early 1950s, designed to propel fullback Eddie Price

Mean Joe Greene (75) was a menace as a member of Pittsburgh's front four.

A powerhouse fullback *was Larry Csonka of the Miami Dolphins.*

over the goal line from a short distance away. One lineman would kneel, another would crouch in front of him and the center would stand up straight, as Price would run up their backs as if climbing a staircase. The Cleveland Browns foiled the play in the 1950 play-off for a divisional title when they built their own stairs on the defensive line, with Bill Willis, a top guard, meeting and resisting Price at the top.

GO 60:   To play a full 60-minute game. With platoon football hardly anyone plays an entire game anymore. One of the last of the 60-minute players was Chuck Bednarik of the Philadelphia Eagles.

GRASS DRILL: A warmup in which the players run in place and then, on a coach's signal, hit the ground on their stomachs, backs, or sides. In other words, they make contact with the grass.

GREATEST GAME EVER PLAYED: A superlative frequently applied to the Baltimore Colt-New York Giant National Football League title game in 1958, when the Colts defeated the Giants in an overtime period, 23-17, with Alan Ameche's touchdown. Purists argue that the game might have been the most dramatic ever played, and a game that gave the sport lasting impact, but they add that great it was not, to wit: The teams played eight minutes before either side made a first down. There were eight fumbles, the Giants losing possession four times.

GREY CUP: The trophy emblematic of the championship in the Canadian Football League, donated by Governor-General Earl Grey in 1909.

GRIDIRON: Another name for the football field. The field was first referred to as a gridiron, or grid, when it was lined in checkerboard fashion, making it resemble the branding iron called a gridiron.

GRIND IT OUT: When an offensive team moves down the field with small, steady chunks of yardage.

GROUNDING: Intentionally throwing a pass on the ground to avoid being thrown for a loss. The penalty is 15 yards plus loss of down.

GUARD: The offensive linemen stationed on each side of the center. On defense a middle guard is the player who is in the center of a five-man line, between the two tackles. In the early days guards were literally guards because their job was to guard the center. Guards are no longer the largest players on the team because now they are required to pull out of the line and lead the blocking on end sweeps. Classic pulling guards were Jerry Kramer and Fuzzy Thurston of the Green Bay Packers.

GUN-SHY: Said of a player who lives in fear of getting hit and consequently acts timidly.

HALF: Two 15-minute quarters make a half. Two halves, interrupted by a 20-minute intermission, constitute a game.

HALFBACK: Halfbacks are victims of streamlining. It used to be there were two halfbacks in every offensive backfield, one on each side of the fullback. Now you're lucky to find one, since pro football uses the generic term "running back," which can mean either the fullback or the halfback. A halfback also masquerades under the noms de gridiron of wingback, flanker back, tailback, and slotback. Defensive halfbacks are still there, but they're called cornerbacks and safety men. The classic offensive halfbacks, the ones with the silky outside moves—like Glenn Davis, Red Grange, Jim Thorpe, Beattie Feathers, Gale Sayers, and O. J. Simpson—might not be called halfbacks anymore, but a star by any position is just as beautiful.

HALFTIME SHOW: Some day somewhere one of the television networks will skip the game and stage an entire four-quarter strut-off between the Apache Belles and the Kilgore (Tex.) Rangerettes. The halftime show to end all halftime shows is still at the Orange Bowl, where no cost is spared to entertain the fans.

HALL OF FAME: The Professional Football Hall of Fame is located in Canton, Ohio, where the National Football League was organized in 1920. The league recognized Canton as the official parthenon in 1961, and the hall was dedicated two years later. Seventeen charter members were elected to the hall in 1963 by a national board of selectors, representatives from the media in cities where professional football is played. Annual elections are held, with inductions conducted late in the summer, followed by an exhibition game between two pro teams. The collegiate Hall of Fame is relatively obscure, located temporarily in New York City. The first batch of inductions came in 1951, when 52 men were honored by a selection committee. Now there are more than 200 members, with the selection committee considering men who have been away from the game for at least ten years.

HAMMER: Fred Williamson, cornerback of the Kansas City Chiefs, was a cause célèbre prior to the playing of the first Super Bowl in 1967. Williamson predicted that with his hammer tackle, which was actually a forearm smash, he would personally destroy the Green Bay Packers. In the second half the unintimidated Packers gave Williamson some of his own medicine and the Kansas City player, knocked unconscious, was carried from the field. He was revived in time to witness the finish of Green Bay's 35-10 victory.

HAND-FIGHTING: A technique used by defensive ends to fend off blocking linemen.

HANDKERCHIEF: A synonym for the flag that officials throw on penalties.

HAND-OFF: The exchange of the ball between quarterback and running back.

Red Grange was a legendary halfback, *first at the
University of Illinois and later as a pro.*

Halfback, *running back, call him what you will, Gale Sayers of the Chicago Bears was one of the best, as exemplified on this 96-yard touchdown run against the Minnesota Vikings.*

HAND SLAP: A legal maneuver, providing the defensive end only does it once on each play, in which he slaps his line opponent's helmet with gusto as he tries to rush the quarterback. Deacon Jones of the Los Angeles Rams had the reputation of being one of the most effective hand-slappers in pro football.

HANG A PASS: When the ball is thrown so softly that it appears to be suspended in the air, just waiting for someone to intercept it.

HANG IN EFFIGY: When a team's slump exasperates alumni and fans, a rough, dummy imitation of the coach, properly labeled, is strung up from the nearest tree or post available. When Sid Gillman coached the San Diego Chargers, he said that "our fans are realistic. If there's going to be a hanging, it'll be the real thing, not effigy."

HANG TIME: The number of seconds the ball kicked by a punter stays in the air before the opposition can make a catch for the runback. Good hang times are anything more than four seconds, because by that time the coverage team should be far enough down the field to contain the runback. Donny Anderson, when he punted for the Green Bay Packers, seldom averaged 40 yards a kick, but because of his consistently good hang times coach Vince Lombardi never considered replacing him.

HANG UP THE CLEATS: A figurative expression that signifies a player quitting the game—taking his football shoes and hanging them on the wall for a remembrance.

HARD-NOSED: A tough player, one unafraid of going head to head with an opponent.

HASHMARKS: The inbounds markers, intersecting lines that run from one end of the field to the other and determine where the ball is spotted for each play that isn't in the center of the field. In 1972 the National Football League owners approved a rules change in which the hashmarks would be moved closer to the center of the field, a distance of 23 yards 1 foot and 9 inches from the sideline. The purpose was to bring more running back to the sport, giving backs a chance to reach the outside.

HAT: What a player sometimes calls his helmet.

HEADHUNTER: A vicious tackler, a defensive man whose first target is the opponent's head.

HEAD LINESMAN: *See* Linesman.

HEIDI GAME: In 1968 the New York Jets were beating the Oakland Raiders, 32-29, in a late-season game seen by most of the country on television. With two minutes to play, National Broadcasting Company executives decided to preempt the finish so that *Heidi*, a children's movie, could start on time. Irate fans multiplied by thousands, flooding station switchboards, when the Raiders scored two quick touchdowns to win the game, 43-32. Network officials regretfully said that it would never happen again.

HEISMAN TROPHY: The John W. Heisman Trophy—awarded each year to the college player who, in the estimation of the New York Downtown Athletic Club, "is the most outstanding in the United States"—is named in honor of the coach who was the first athletic director of the club.

Although the Heisman sometimes is criticized because the sportswriter voters do not equally represent all areas of the country, the winner becomes an instant celebrity. He is a player who usually is drafted on the opening rounds by the pros and commands several thousand dollars extra in bonus money because he's a Heisman winner.

Archie Griffin, the durable Ohio State halfback, became the first player to win the Heisman two straight years in 1974-75. The first Heisman winner, Jay Berwanger of the University of Chicago in 1935, didn't play pro ball. Some Heisman winners tried the pros and failed miserably, such as Terry Baker of Oregon State, John Huarte of Notre Dame, and Gary Beban of UCLA. Only two linemen have ever won the Heisman—end Larry Kelley of Yale in 1936 and Notre Dame end Leon Hart in 1949.

Prepping a player for the Heisman can become a slick advertising campaign that any Madison Avenue hotshot would be proud of. One year at Notre Dame publicity man Roger Valdiserri pulled out all the stops in pumping quarterback Joe Theismann for the Heisman. "How do you pronounce your name?" Valdiserri asked Theismann. "Theezman," the quarterback said. "Well," Valdiserri said, "from now on it's going to be Thizeman, as in Hizeman." Despite the help from Valdiserri, Theismann didn't win the Heisman.

HIDDEN-BALL TRICK: As rare as the whooping crane, the hidden-ball trick, in which a player would hide the ball under his jersey, used to be a favorite play of schools like Carlisle. Now such a play would call for an unsportsmanlike-conduct penalty.

HIGHTOPS: Football shoes that cover the ankle. Few players wear them anymore, one of the reasons being that many of the games are played on synthetic surfaces that require special shoes. Johnny Unitas was one of the last players to continue wearing hightop shoes.

"HIKE": What used to be the signal from the quarterback to the center to snap the ball. "Hike" has been replaced by "hut" as the snap command.

HIT: Any form of contact—a blocker hitting a defender, a tackler hitting a ballcarrier, a passer hitting his receiver when the throw is completed.

HOAXES: For football hoaxes to top all football hoaxes, the Plainfield Teachers College caper in 1941 easily wins first prize. Plainfield, the creation of a stockbroker named Morris Newburger, never existed, but Newburger had New York newspapers believing the school played and won all its games, with John Chung, a Chinese halfback, leading the way. Newburger phoned in fictitious scores, related that Chung ate bowls of rice between halves for extra energy, and the public prints fell for it. Toward the end of the season Newburger was exposed, and he promptly flunked Chung and the rest of the team out of Plainfield and canceled the rest of the schedule.

HOLDER: The player, frequently a quarterback, who holds the ball on field-goal kicks.

HOLDING: An offensive or defensive foul, called when an official rules that a player is illegally using his hands to contain an opponent. Many players say that offensive holding could be called against linemen on almost every play, meaning that there's a thin line between good blocking and a penalty. In 1974 the National Football League changed the penalty on

Archie Griffin of Ohio State won the Heisman Trophy *twice.*

holding from 15 yards to 10 when the violation occurs in the area of the line of scrimmage and three yards beyond.

HOLE: The spot on the line that is opened by blockers so runners can move through with the ball.

HORN: One of the officials, a linesman, used to carry a horn that he would blow if he saw a violation. Players were accustomed to continuing the play if they heard the horn, since the sound did not carry the authority of a whistle.

HORSE COLLAR: *See* Necktie Tackle.

HUDDLE: The gathering by either the offensive or the defensive unit away from the line of scrimmage to call its signals for the next play. Bob Zuppke of Illinois is credited with devising the huddle.

HURDLING: When a ballcarrier leaps over another player who is still on his feet. Although the rule prohibiting hurdling has been on the books since 1906, the penalty is rarely called.

ICEBERG: *See* Snow Job.

I FORMATION: A T formation in which the quarterback, directly behind the center, is followed in a line by the three other backs—the halfback, the fullback, and the tailback. The I was popularized by coaches like Tom Nugent at Virginia Military Institute and the University of Maryland, and John McKay at Southern California in the early 1960s. The Kansas City Chiefs under Hank Stram also used the I effectively.

ILLEGAL: Anything not allowed by the official rules.

ILLEGAL MOTION: An offensive back moving before the ball is snapped or not getting into a set position one second before the snap. A five-yard penalty.

ILLEGAL PROCEDURE: A violation, caused when an offensive lineman charges or moves in such a way as to make the defense believe that the ball has been snapped. A five-yard penalty.

IMMACULATE RECEPTION: A description of Franco Harris's touchdown reception that enabled the Pittsburgh Steelers to beat the Oakland Raiders in the final minute of their 1972 play-off game. The ball bounced off the Raiders' Jack Tatum and ricocheted into Harris's hands as he trailed the play. Harris ran the ball in for the touchdown. Tatum and the Raiders argued that the ball had touched a Steeler receiver first, which would have made Harris's catch illegal.

IMPETUS: A player's action that gives momentum to the ball.

INBOUNDS: When the player or the ball remains within the sideline stripe.

INCOMPLETE PASS: A forward pass is not complete, and the ball and the clock become dead when the ball (1) strikes the ground or goes out of bounds, (2) strikes the goalpost or crossbar, (3) is caught by an offensive player after touching another offensive player first, or (4) is caught by a receiver who doesn't have both feet in bounds. In college only one foot must be in bounds.

INDIVIDUAL PLAYER FORM: A scouting form which lists all the pertinent information on a prospect, including grades from scouts for individual techniques and attributes that range from 0 to 3.1, 0 being the best. No player has ever been judged a 0 on his composite. The information on the form is fed into a computer, which evaluates it and comes up with a composite rating.

INELIGIBLE RECEIVER DOWNFIELD: When an interior offensive lineman runs downfield on a pass play. A 15-yard penalty.

INFLUENCE BLOCK: Not a block at all, but the pretense of blocks by several offensive linemen, designed to deceive the opposition into thinking a play is going to be run in a certain direction. Actually, the play moves in the opposite direction.

INJURY CATEGORIES: Subject to a fine, National Football League clubs are required to report injuries twice a week to the league office. The relative seriousness of the injuries is specified by these categories: probable (player is likely to play), questionable (status uncertain), doubtful (probably won't play), definitely out (won't play).

INTERCEPTION: A forward pass caught by a defensive player.

INTERFERENCE: When an offensive blocker or blockers move ahead of a ballcarrier to remove potential tacklers from the path. In a different sense, the act of illegally hindering an opposing player trying to catch the ball—whether a pass receiver, a defensive man trying for an interception, or a punt returner who has signaled for a fair catch.

INTERIOR LINEMAN: An offensive lineman other than the ends.

INTERSECTIONAL: A college game played between teams from different geographical regions. The first intersectional game was Harvard-Michigan in 1881.

IRON MAN: A player who plays a full 60-minute game frequently. In 1926 Brown had an entire team of iron men, 11 players going the distance in three games.

ISOLATION: When the offensive team is able to get a defensive back into a one-on-one coverage against one of its pass receivers.

IVY LEAGUE: A group of some of the nation's oldest colleges, so named by Caswell Adams of *The New York Herald Tribune* in the 1930s. He was inspired by the ivy-covered school buildings on many of the campuses. Although the colleges had played each other for years, it wasn't until 1956 that formal league play began among Yale, Harvard, Columbia, Dartmouth, Princeton, Penn, Brown, and Cornell.

JAKING IT: *See* Dogging It.

JAM: A legal act by a defensive back or linebacker when he pushes a receiver to the inside as he leaves the line of scrimmage. The idea is to delay the receiver from promptly running his pattern. Jamming is legal as long as it comes before the ball is put into the air.

JIMMY THE GREEK: James ("Jimmy the Greek") Snyder is a Las Vegas publicity man who handicaps college and professional games in a syndicated newspaper column. Snyder calculates point spreads—in theory, the number of points the inferior team would need to play the superior team evenly.

JOP: An acronym for jump on the pile. A jump-on-the-pile player, a derogatory description by a scout, is a man who will come along after a tackle has already been made and jump on the ballcarrier.

JUKE: *See* Fake.

JUMP: When a lineman or back moves prematurely, jumping the count, and draws an offside, illegal-motion, of illegal-procedure penalty.

KAMIKAZE: *See* Special Teams.

KEEPER: *See* Bootleg.

KEYING: When a defensive player uses the movements of an offensive player to determine his own movements. Cornerbacks, for example, will frequently key on split ends.

KF-79: Lou Little's reverse play that scored the only touchdown in Columbia's 7-0 victory over heavily favored Stanford in the 1934 Rose Bowl. Fullback Al Barabas faked to the left halfback, who ran around the right end with interference. Barabas, keeping the ball, hid it on his hip and ran alone for 17 yards without being touched.

KICKER: A player who kicks the ball—either the punter, kickoff man, or field-goal kicker.

KICKING: Propelling the ball with the foot.

KICKING TEAM: The unit, either offensive or defensive, whose responsibility is to handle the play on a kickoff or punt.

KICKOFF: With the ball either resting on a kicking tee or lying flat on the ground, a kick that starts either half or follows a touchdown or field goal. For years college and pro teams kicked off from the kicking team's 40-yard line, but in 1974 the National Football League changed the spot to the 35-yard line, intending to discourage touchbacks and revive crowd-pleasing runbacks.

KILLING THE CLOCK: When the offensive team uses running plays designed to protect a lead and use up a maximum amount of time.

KNEE: When a player is said to have a knee, it means he has a serious knee injury. Knee injuries are the most prevalent in football, and knee operations are also common. Pro players say, with support from some doctors, that artificial surfaces have increased the number of knee injuries. Joe Namath of the New York Jets has had two of the worst knees in the game. One teammate said, "Joe has a twenty-two-year-old body and seventy-year-old knees."

LAMBERT TROPHY: A trophy furnished by a New York jewelry firm that is annually presented to the best collegiate team in the East.

LANES: Areas assigned to special team members, pass receivers, or pass rushers in the execution of their duties.

LATERAL PASS: An underhanded pass thrown backward. The difference between a forward pass and a lateral pass is that a dropped or errant lateral is not incomplete, it is in play. A forward lateral, in which the receiver is not behind the thrower, is illegal and will draw a five-yard penalty.

LEAD BLOCK: The driving block by a lineman in a double-team lead post-block.

LETTERMAN: In college, a player who accumulates enough playing time in games to receive an award, a monogram of the first letter in his school's name. Letters are frequently sewn to a player's campus sweater, which is called a letter sweater. Awarding letters is an old custom, dating back to the days when Amos Alonzo Stagg coached at the University of Chicago in 1904.

LIMP LEG: A ploy by ballcarriers and defensive linemen in which they offer their leg as a target without putting weight on it. When the opponent lunges for the leg, they quickly draw it away. Jim Thorpe was a master of the limp leg.

LINEBACKER: Originally called a roving center, a linebacker is a defensive player who plays behind the defensive line, alertly guarding against the run or the pass. Linebackers must be heavy, reasonably quick, and have instincts that tell them whether the play will be a run or a pass. Dick Butkus, nonpareil of the middle linebackers, said he could sometimes tell what a quarterback was going to do by the position of his feet as he stood behind the center calling signals.

Teams will usually use two, three, or four linebackers, depending on the situation. The middle linebacker frequently calls defensive signals and is that rare defensive player who can achieve superstar status. Some of the great linebackers have been George Connor of the Chicago Bears, Mel Hein of the New York Giants, Bulldog Turner of the Chicago Bears, Ray Nitschke of the Green Bay Packers, and Sam Huff of the Giants. Nitschke was part of the great linebacking crew that also included Dave Robinson and Lee Roy Caffey, a trio rivaled in the 1970s by Andy Russell, Jack Ham, and Jack Lambert of the Pittsburgh Steelers.

LINE JUDGE: In pro football, an official who straddles the line of scrimmage on the side of the field opposite the head linesman. The line judge keeps the time of the game as a backup for the scoreboard clock operator. With the linesman he is responsible for offside, encroachment, and actions on the scrimmage line prior to or at the snap. The line judge observes the movements of the wide receiver on his side after the snap. The line judge must rule on the flight of the ball when it's in his area and must determine whether the passer is behind or beyond the line of scrimmage. He also observes the actions by blockers and defenders on his side of the field.

LINEMAN: A player positioned on the line of scrimmage. On offense there must be seven men on the line of scrimmage. On defense there can be any number.

LINE OF SCRIMMAGE: The imaginary line that stretches straight toward both sidelines from the position of the ball between plays.

LINESMAN: The official with primary responsibility for ruling on offside, encroachment, and actions on the scrimmage line prior to or at the snap. The linesman is positioned on the scrimmage line on the same side of the field as the field judge. The linesman is responsible with the referee for keeping track of the number of downs and is in charge of the mechanics of the chain crew. The linesman must assist in determining the forward progress of the ballcarrier and in signaling to the referee or umpire regarding what point the ball has reached. Also called the head linesman.

LIVE BALL: A ball that is legally free-kicked or snapped and continues in play until the down ends.

LIVE COLOR: The signal used by the quarterback to alert the offensive team that an automatic, or change in play, is being called at the line of scrimmage. Before the snap the quarterback might say something like "red, thirty-two . . ." If red isn't the live color, the call means nothing. But if red is the live color, it's an indication that the original play, the one called in the huddle, has been switched.

LIVE SCRIMMAGE: A practice session or practice game in which there is full physical contact as there might be in a regulation game.

LOAF OF BREAD: When a ballcarrier carries the ball away from his body, inviting a fumble, it is said that he carries it like a loaf of bread.

LOLLIPOP: A pass thrown softly, hanging in the air, that might be easy to intercept.

LONELY END: A stratagem devised by coach Earl ("Red") Blaik at Army in 1958 in which a receiver, Bill Carpenter, was usually stationed as a flanker close to the sideline, not participating in the team's huddle but picking up the signal for each play from the way the quarterback placed his feet. Army went undefeated that year, leading the nation in passing, and in 1959 Carpenter was named All-America.

LONG COUNT: A lengthy signal call by the quarterback at the line of scrimmage, designed to either pull an impatient defensive line off side or to interfere with the defense's timing.

LONG MAN: The receiver running the deepest pattern on a pass play.

LONG YARDAGE: A situation in which the offense faces a considerable distance before it can make a first down. Estimates vary, but long yardage is generally considered to be five or more yards on third down, eight or more yards on second down.

LOOK: The name for the appearance of an offense or defense. In reading offenses or defenses it is important to recognize the look of the opponent's formation.

LOOK-IN PASS: A short pass pattern, usually designed for the tight end, in which he will run diagonally for a few yards toward the center of the field, then look up for the quick throw. Timing between the quarterback and the receiver is what makes the look-in effective, and when the defense is caught unaware, the play will sometimes net gains of 10 to 20 yards.

LOOK-OUT BLOCK: A missed block by an offensive lineman, who in chagrin will yell "Look out!" to his backs as the opponent races in to make the tackle.

LOOPING: When a defensive lineman is having trouble getting past a blocker, he may try sidestepping the man, moving toward the developing play in an arc, or loop, instead of taking the straight route.

LOOSE BALL: A live ball not in possession of any player. When a loose ball is on the field, players who spot it will yell "Ball! Ball!" to alert their teammates to the situation.

LOSS OF DOWN: Certain play situations cost a team a down in addition to, or instead of, yardage. A loss of down with no loss of yardage occurs when (*1*) a second forward pass is thrown behind the line of scrimmage, (*2*) a forward pass strikes the ground, goalpost or crossbar, (*3*) a forward pass goes out of bounds, (*4*) a forward pass is first touched by an eligible receiver who has gone out of bounds and returned, (*5*) a forward pass is touched or caught by a second eligible receiver before it is touched by the defense, and (*6*) a forward pass accidentally touches an ineligible receiver on or behind the line of scrimmage.

A 5-yard penalty and loss of down are assessed when a forward pass is thrown from beyond the line of scrimmage. A 15-yard penalty and loss of down are assessed when (*1*) a forward pass is intentionally or accidentally touched by an ineligible receiver beyond the line of scrimmage, (*2*) a forward pass is intentionally touched by an ineligible receiver on or behind the line of scrimmage, and (*3*) a passer is called for intentionally grounding a forward pass.

LOW-CUTS: Low football shoes, where the top stops short of the ankle, were first used mostly by backs, but now they are worn by almost everybody in the game, replacing the hightop style.

MAIN MAN: What pro players call the superstar, the bellwether, of their own team.

MAN IN MOTION: The method of having a back

Army's lonely end, *Bill Carpenter (87), had to pick up his signals the hard way.*

running in another spot, parallel to the line of scrimmage, after the rest of the offensive unit has gone to a set position but before the snap of the ball. The purpose of the man in motion is to confuse the defense and to force the defensive team out of its set formation before the play is run.

MAN-TO-MAN: A type of defensive pass coverage in which each defender, usually a back, is responsible for a certain receiver regardless of where the receiver goes on the field.

MASCOT: An animal corresponding with a school's or a team's nickname is often paraded around the field and along the sidelines during a game as an inspirational device, for good luck, or just to add to the pageantry. Navy for years has been represented by its goat, Bill XVIII at last check. Attempts have been made before

the Army-Navy game to kidnap (goatnap?) the Navy mascot.

The Southern California Trojans are represented by a rider outfitted in ancient military panoply, riding a horse. The Baltimore Colts hire a horseman to ride a colt around the field during their games. The Cincinnati Bengals even have a caged tiger at their home games. Sometimes, a person will dress in an animal costume and perform as the team's mascot at games.

MEAT GRINDER: The middle of a mass-interference blocking tactic into which valiant defensive men sometimes throw themselves to break up the play.

MESSENGER: A player sent from the sidelines by a coach to deliver a play to the quarterback. Paul Brown, when he coached the Cleveland Browns and the

Cincinnati Bengals, called every play from the bench and rotated a pair of guards as his messengers. Other coaches will rotate players at other positions as their messengers. The colleges recently approved a rule that required a substitute to remain in the game for at least one play, eliminating the practice of coaches using players as nothing but messengers.

MIDDLE LINEBACKER: *See* Linebacker.

MIDFIELD: The 50-yard line, or the area in the general vicinity of the 50.

MISDIRECTION: An offensive tactic designed to befuddle the defense, when a back and several blockers will head in one direction, but the ball will be given to another back who will take off in the opposite direction. The Miami Dolphins, who felt they couldn't handle the Minnesota line one-on-one in the eighth Super Bowl, beat the Vikings partly because of successful use of misdirection.

MOMENTUM: An intangible that coaches and players frequently mention, but are hard pressed to define. Momentum is that moment in the game when a certain play or misplay will give a team a psychological lift. Momentum in a single game is capable of shifting from one team to the other.

MONDAY MORNING QUARTERBACK: A second-guesser, a fan who the day after the game has all the reasons why his team or a certain player failed.

MONDAY NIGHT FOOTBALL: In 1970 the National Football League signed a contract with the American Broadcasting Company to play one nationally televised game every Monday night during the season. The result was a broadcasting phenomenon, as thousands of life-styles on Monday nights were changed because of the game on the tube. Audience ratings have been sensational. Coaches look at playing on Monday nights with mixed feelings. They dislike the games because it leaves them with less preparation time for the game the following Sunday. On the other hand, players in the Monday night games are frequently more emotionally aroused because they know the players from the rest of the league are watching their performance. Other broadcasters handling the games have changed, but the Monday night game became a weekly soapbox for Howard Cosell, the diffuse color man who was wont to make the game secondary to his own circumlocutions.

MONEY PLAYER: A player at his best in the important games, with the most money at stake. Shortly after Paul Hornung had served a one-year suspension by the National Football League for betting on games, the Green Bay star had a big day against the Baltimore Colts. A reporter asked Packer coach Vince Lombardi after the game to rate Hornung as a money player. If the reporter didn't recognize the nuances of the question, Lombardi did. "Er—" the coach said, "couldn't you think of a more delicate way to phrase that question? It still doesn't sound proper to refer to Hornung as a money player."

MONSTER MAN: A combination linebacker-defensive back who is not part of the assigned defense but has the privilege of roaming at will and positioning himself where he thinks he is needed. One of the premier monster men was George Webster of Michigan State.

MONSTERS OF THE MIDWAY: A nickname for the Chicago Bears during their heyday in the 1930s and 1940s when they were not only winning a lot of games but were physically punishing as well.

MOUSETRAP: *See* Trap Blocking.

MOUTHPIECE: A rubber protection worn inside the mouth, devised in 1948 by Fred Moffett, the Berkeley (Calif.) High School football coach who saw one of his players die from a blow to the mouth in a game. Not as many college and professional players wear mouthpieces as the players in high schools, where in many states the piece of equipment is mandatory. A mouthpiece can keep a player from biting his tongue and chipping or breaking teeth.

MOVING POCKET: A changing area where a quarterback will fade after taking the center snap on a pass play. Usually the pocket will be several yards directly behind center, but with a moving pocket the quarterback is allowed to shift to either side, and his blockers are expected to slide with him. Hank Stram, when he coached the Kansas City Chiefs, sometimes favored a moving pocket.

MUFF: The touching of a loose ball by a player in an unsuccessful attempt to obtain possession. The difference between a muff and a fumble is that neither side can advance the recovery of a muff.

MULTIPLE FOUL: More than one penalty on the same play. When the penalties are called against both teams, the play is nullified and the down repeated.

MULTIPLE OFFENSE: An offensive system, popularized by coach Clarence ("Biggie") Munn at Michigan State, in which a variety of offensive formations and systems are used.

NAIA: The National Association of Intercollegiate Athletics, an organization of the country's smaller colleges.

NAIL: To tackle. Nailing to the ground is the same as tackling.

NAKED REVERSE: Nothing sexy here. Entire offensive team shows movement one way and final ballcarrier takes hand-off in opposite direction alone (naked).

NCAA: The National Collegiate Athletic Association. The governing body for college football and other sports. The NCAA was founded in 1905 as the Intercollegiate Athletic Association, and the name was changed to NCAA in 1910. The NCAA controls and establishes college rules, including television policy, bowl selecting procedures, and recruiting.

NEAR BACK: The backfield man closest to the side of the field toward which the play is going.

NEAR SIDE: A term used by broadcasters meaning the side of the field nearest them and/or the camera.

NECKTIE TACKLE: A high tackle in the area of the necktie—around the neck or top of the shoulder pads. Also called a horse collar.

NEUTRAL ZONE: The one-yard area between the line of scrimmage for the offensive team and where the defensive team lines up.

NFC: *See* NFL.

NFL: The National Football League, professional football's oldest, biggest, and most durable league, which was founded on a sweltering fall afternoon in 1920 by a group of men in Canton, Ohio. They met in an automobile showroom, some of them sitting on running boards (romantics like to say that the beginning took place in a garage).

The original name was the American Professional Football Association, and each man paid $25 for a franchise. The most prominent single force behind pro football was George Halas, originally a playing coach for the Decatur (Ill.) Staleys, a team sponsored by a furniture store. Halas moved the Staleys to Chicago in 1921, changed the name to Bears, and became a living legend as owner, player, and coach of the team.

The Bears, Green Bay Packers, New York Giants, Washington Redskins, and other teams produced standout performers, such as Sid Luckman, Sammy Baugh, George McAfee, Don Hutson, and Joe Stydahar, in the 1930s and 1940s. By the 1950s a new breed of swift-running, pinpoint-passing superstars, like Jimmy Brown, Hugh McElhenny, Otto Graham, and Johnny Unitas, had arrived on the scene. The NFL has survived competition from other leagues notably the All-America Conference from 1946 to 1949, the American Football League (AFL) from 1960 to 1966, and the World Football League (WFL) in 1974 and 1975. The NFL and the AFL agreed to merge in 1966 (starting regular-season competition in 1970); the WFL went bankrupt after only two seasons. After four seasons in existence a few of the All-America teams joined the NFL.

In the 1970s, pro football was generally considered to be America's number-one sport, moving ahead of baseball with predominantly sellout crowds and weekend television audiences of some sixty-five million. The NFL-AFL merger produced two NFL conferences, the American and the National, whose winners meet annually in the Super Bowl. In 1976 the American Football Conference (AFC) consisted of fourteen teams: Baltimore, Buffalo, Cincinnati, Cleveland, Denver, Houston, Kansas City, Miami, New England, the New York Jets, Oakland, Pittsburgh, San Diego, and Tampa Bay. The National Football Conference (NFC) also consisted of fourteen teams: Atlanta, Chicago, Dallas, Detroit, Green Bay, Los Angeles, Minnesota, New Orleans, the New York Giants, Philadelphia, St. Louis, San Francisco, Seattle, and Washington. Each conference was broken down into three divisions—Eastern, Central, and Western.

NICKEL DEFENSE: The placing of one extra defensive back in the secondary when expecting a pass.

NICKNAMES: Sporting names for school teams, professional teams, and players. The derivations range from the founder of a school (the Yale Elis, after Eli Yale) to an animal (Denver Broncos) to something indigenous to the area (San Francisco 49ers) to an area's industry (Nebraska Cornhuskers). Sometimes a team will take on a nickname during a specific era—e.g., Louisiana State's Chinese Bandits; Navy's Team Called Desire; and the Washington Redskins' Over the Hill Gang. Individual nicknames can become more a part of a person than his given name—Bulldog Turner, Night Train Lane, Big Daddy Lipscomb, Cannonball Adderley, Tank Younger, etc.

NO-BRAINER: *See* Snow Job.

NO-HUDDLE SERIES: After a group of plays is called, a team will run them in succession without calling a huddle. This is usually a time-saving device that is part of the two-minute drill.

NOSEMAN: In college football, the middle guard on the defense, the player who plays directly across the offensive line from the nose of the ball.

NOSE OF THE BALL: The ball's farthest forward point. This end of the ball determines how far the team in possession has advanced.

NUMBER: The numeral worn on the back of a player's jersey for identification purposes by fans, officials, and other players. Numbering players was the idea of Karl Davis, who was in charge of the sale of football programs at the University of Pittsburgh in 1908. Davis got the idea from watching track athletes perform with numbers on their backs, and he would change the numbers of the Pitt players every week.

In 1915 wearing numbers was written into the rules. In professional football there is a standardized numbering system according to positions—80-99 for ends; 70-79 for tackles, 60-69 for guards, 50-59 for centers, and 1-49 for backs. On a scrimmage play, at least five offensive players with numbers 50 through 79 must line up on the line of scrimmage.

Jim Otto, long-time center of the Oakland Raiders, was permitted to wear his 00 number in spite of the rule. College and pro teams give players the ultimate honor when they retire their numbers, never permitting another player to wear them. Such recognition was accorded Red Grange with his 77 at Illinois and Tommy Harmon with his 98 at Michigan. Terry Hanratty, the Notre Dame star who has played in the pros for the Pittsburgh Steelers, was once asked if his college number had been retired. "If they retired the numbers of all the greats at Notre Dame," Hanratty said, "there wouldn't be any numbers left."

NUTCRACKER: A practice drill in which an offensive and a defensive lineman face each other with a back stationed behind the offensive player. The defender must fight off the block and then tackle the back, who tries to run past him while staying inside of an area defined by two dummies spaced about ten feet apart. This is a severe training-camp exercise for young defensive linemen. It is also known as the Oklahoma drill.

OFFENSE: The team that controls the ball. An offense is also the name for that team's attack. On a kickoff the offensive team is the one receiving the ball.

OFFICIALS: The men appointed by either the competing schools or the league to enforce the rules during a game. College games usually have five officials—a referee, a linesman, an umpire, a field judge, and a back judge. The National Football League uses a sixth official, a line judge. For details of their duties see individual listings.

OFFICIAL TIME-OUT: A stopping of the clock, without charging a time-out to either team, for the purpose of measuring for a first down, administering to an injured player, discussing a rule with a coach, etc.

OFF LINEMAN: Another name for the weak-side lineman, a player who isn't on the side the play is directed toward.

OFFSIDE: A penalty called when a player is offside, i.e., when any part of his body is beyond his scrimmage or free-kick line when the ball is snapped. A five-yard penalty.

OKIE DEFENSE: A defense originated by Bud Wilkinson at the University of Oklahoma. It is especially effective against the tricky option offenses.

Wilkinson started with what was called the seven-box defense and changed it into the 3-4-4 Okie. The corner men in the seven-box were moved off the line, and the ends played from a standing position to become what amounted to linebackers. The advantages of the Okie over the standard 4-3 pro defense are that (1) there are two middle linebackers instead of one; (2) there are five short-pass zone defenses instead of four, making it difficult for receivers to find the gaps or seams, and there are still three men left to cover deep routes; (3) any two linebackers can blitz, making it a five-man rush, and there are still two linebackers left to protect for the run and a free safety to play the ball; (4) if either of the inside linebackers blitz, it is much the same as a 4-3, but with the element of surprise; (5) the linebackers can stack behind the three down linemen, forcing offensive blockers to react quickly when these stacked linebackers move in either direction from their hidden positions. The New England Patriots were one of the first National Football League teams to use the Okie.

OKLAHOMA DRILL: *See* Nutcracker.

ONE-ON-ONE: Single pass coverage, where a defensive man is isolated with a receiver. Teams with superlative receivers figure to profit when they can get them in one-on-one coverage.

ONSIDE: The opposite of offside; a player lining up on his legal side of the line of scrimmage. An onside kick is a kickoff in which the ball is placed flat on its side. The purpose is to make the return hard to handle and perhaps make the receiving team fumble. The disadvantage is that the kick will not travel as far or as high as the end-over-end type. On a kickoff the ball must travel ten yards from the spot it's kicked, thereby becoming a free ball.

OPTION: A play called by the quarterback in which he has the choice, as he runs along the line of scrimmage toward the end, of either passing, running with the ball, or lateraling to a trailing back.

OUTLAND TROPHY: An annual award, presented by the Football Writers Association of America to college football's most outstanding interior lineman. George Connor of Notre Dame was the winner of the first Outland in 1946, and no one has ever won the trophy twice. Since the Heisman Trophy is usually presented to a back or end, the Outland is the highest award for a player who labors in the game's trenches.

OUT OF BOUNDS: When the ball or a player with the ball goes past the sideline or past the end line beyond the goal line. The clock is stopped when the ball or a player with the ball goes out of bounds.

OUT PATTERN: A pass route in which the receiver breaks to the outside, in the direction of the sideline.

OVERSHIFT: When the defensive team moves extra players to one side to counter additional strength by the offensive team.

OVER-THE-HILL GANG: A name for several of the teams George Allen formed while coach of the Washington Redskins in the 1970s. Using few rookies, Allen signed retreads from other teams and traded draft choices for veterans. One of these teams played in the 1973 Super Bowl.

PAPER LION: George Plimpton spent several weeks in the Detroit Lions' training camp, occasionally as a participant, and wrote a book called *The Paper Lion*, considered one of the best nonfiction works done on football. The book was later converted into a movie.

PASS: *See* Forward Pass, Backward Pass, or Lateral Pass.

PASS RATING(S): The National Football League has used a variety of ways to statistically rank its passers, most of them inscrutable to passers and public alike. The latest ranking system is based on performance in four categories—percentage of completions, percentage of touchdown passes, percentage of interceptions, and average yards gained per passing attempt. The point allocation is from 0.000 to a maximum of 2.375. The maximum allocation is given to a quarterback reaching or topping the standards of 77.5 for completion percentage, 11.9 for touchdown percentage, no interceptions, and an average gain of 12.5 yards per pass. Former quarterback Frank Ryan, who has a doctorate in mathematics, might understand, but he's in the minority. And you have to question a system that ranks Milt Plum of the Cleveland Browns with the best rating in the history of the league—110.4 in 1960.

PATTERN: The route a receiver runs on a pass play.

PAY DIRT: The end zone. Scoring a touchdown is reaching pay dirt.

PENALTY: A punishment for violating the rules. It may be meted out in yardage, by depriving a team of a down, or by ejecting a player from the game.

PENETRATING DEFENSE: A defense that tries to prevent a gain and force a loss or mistake on every play. Sometimes penetrating defenses will play the man instead of the ball.

PEP RALLY: An inspirational gathering of fans, players, and coaches the day or night before a game. The team is introduced, and there are cheers, music, and speeches.

PERIOD: *See* Quarter.

PERSONAL FOUL: A penalty call against a player when he (*1*) runs into or roughs the kicker, (*2*) runs into the passer, (*3*) trips, or (*4*) clips.

PICK PLAY: When two receivers crisscross in front of a defensive man, one receiver taking the other receiver's defender out of the play.

PICKUP: A gain in yardage by the offensive team.

PILEUP: The mass of players that results from a runner hitting into the center of the line on a short-yardage attempt.

PILING ON: The act of jumping on a downed man after the whistle has blown. A 15-yard penalty.

PINCH BLOCK: *See* Double-Team.

PIT: The battle area at the line of scrimmage, where offensive and defensive linemen go head to head. Also called the trenches.

PITCHOUT: A play in which the quarterback takes the snap and makes a quick underhanded lateral to a back on the run to start a rushing play.

PIVOT MAN: The offensive center.

PLACE-KICK: A kick, either for a field goal or an extra point, that is preceded by a holder accepting the center snap and placing the ball in a position to be kicked.

PLATOON: A term, adapted from army argot for fighting squadron, that refers to either the offensive or defensive unit. Unlimited substitution was first permitted in 1941, paving the way for specialists who could play on either the offensive or defensive platoon.

PLAY: The formation and resultant action that the offensive and defensive leaders call before each center snap.

PLAY-ACTION: A passing play with the appearance of a run, created when the quarterback fakes a hand-off to a back going into the line.

PLAYBOOK: A pro football player's most sacred possession, a book containing a complete set of instructions, diagrams, team policies, and plays. To lose it means an automatic fine, and when a player is cut from a team, he is immediately told to turn in his playbook. Carl Sweetan, an itinerant quarterback, was once accused of trying to sell his Los Angeles Ram playbook to the New Orleans Saints.

PLAYER REPRESENTATIVE: A member of the National Football League Players Association, the players' union, who is the link between the other players on the team and management. In recent years the union has accused NFL clubs of deliberately trading player representatives—Kermit Alexander, John Mackey, and Tom Keating to name three—but the charge has never been substantiated.

PLUNGE: A short-yardage play calling for a back, usually the fullback, to hit the middle of the line. Also called a line buck or smash.

POCKET: The blocking wall behind the line of

scrimmage that is set up for the quarterback as he fades and tries to spot an open receiver.

POCKET QUARTERBACK: A drop-back passer who stays in the pocket and refuses to run with the ball even if there are no receivers open.

POINT-A-MINUTE TEAMS: From 1901 to 1905 Fielding ("Hurry Up") Yost's University of Michigan teams had a 55-1-1 record and averaged 564 points a season, almost a point a minute.

POLICEMAN: A rugged player on a team whose secondary duties include the protection of teammates from unnecessary roughness by the opposition.

POLL: A ranking of the top collegiate teams. The Associated Press in 1936 began to poll its member sportswriters around the country to determine the top ten teams of the year. In 1950 United Press started its top-ten poll, using a board of coaches as its experts. Now both wire services conduct weekly polls and wait until after the bowl games to make their final rankings. Neither system is infallible; the voters don't see all of the teams, and some of them still have regional prejudices.

POLY TURF: *See* Synthetic Surface.

PONY BACKFIELD: A quartet of undersized backs who still do a powerful job. Among the most famous of the pony backfields was Michigan State's 1953 combination of Tom Yewcic, LeRoy Bolden, Billy Wells, and Evan Slonac.

POP: A hard hit. The name is derived from the sound of pads colliding during fierce contact.

POSSESSION: When a player holds the ball long enough to give him enough control to perform any act common to the game.

POST BLOCK: The sustaining block by a lineman in a double-team blocking situation.

POST PATTERN: A pass route in which the receiver goes straight down the field and cuts across the field at an angle that will take him in the direction of the goalposts.

POSTSEASON: Games played, either in college or the pros, after the end of the regular schedule. In college this would mean bowl games. In the pros there are play-off games, conference title games, and the Super Bowl.

POWER I FORMATION: The I formation in which two backs line up in single file behind the quarterback, and the third is positioned as a close flanker or wingback.

POWER RUNNER: The strong, battering runner on the team, usually the fullback, who is capable of gaining extra yards even after he has been hit by a tackler.

PRAYING COLONELS: The Centre College team which scored a monumental upset over West Virginia in 1919 when its coach, Uncle Charley Moran, asked the players to kneel in prayer during the halftime intermission when Centre, nicknamed the Colonels, trailed, 6-0. Two years later, Centre, led by Bo McMillin, upset a Harvard team that hadn't lost in 28 games.

PRESEASON: *See* Exhibition Game.

PRESS BOX: The area high atop a stadium that is assigned as a working area for the media representatives who are covering a game. Not all press boxes are sanctuaries. At Kezar Stadium in San Francisco, where the 49ers used to play their games, a reporter was told by a seatmate that his typing was disconcerting. The complainant turned out to be the city dog catcher.

PREVENT DEFENSE: A defensive formation aimed at stopping long passing gains. The defense pulls back, leaving itself open for short gains, since the tactic is usually pulled late in the game when the offense is expected to be using desperation plays.

PRIMARY RECEIVER: The first man the passer is looking for.

PRO: Anyone who plays the game for money. A pro, or a real pro, is a complimentary description of a veteran player who can be counted on to produce in clutch situations in big games. The first recorded incident, according to the National Football League, of a player being paid for his services was on November 12, 1892, when William ("Pudge") Heffelfinger received $500 from the Allegheny Athletic Association to play against the Pittsburgh Athletic Club.

PROBATION: A penalty imposed upon a college by the NCAA for failure to obey rules, usually in the area of recruiting. A common penalty would be making a school ineligible for extra money from playing in bowl games or on televised games. Paul ("Bear") Bryant, taking over as head coach at Alabama, announced a five-year plan: "First year, a .500 season. Second year, a conference championship. Third year undefeated and fourth year, a national championship." Someone wanted to know about the fifth year. Bryant winked and said, "Why, in the fifth year, we'll be on probation, of course."

PRO BOWL: The National Football League's post-season All-Star game. Originated in 1951, it used to pit the Eastern Division against the Western, but now it's the American Conference against the National. Once a Los Angeles fixture because it was a promotional vehicle of the *Los Angeles Times*, the game is now played in a different NFL city every year. The Pro Bowl has become an anticlimax to the Super Bowl and an awfully hard sell. The 1976 game in the New Orleans Superdome drew less than 35,000 fans. Regardless, being named to a Pro Bowl team is a treasured honor for a player. Each player on the winning team receives $2,000, while the losers get $1,500.

PROGRAMS: Listings of the players' numbers and articles and pictures of the teams haven't always been as sophisticated as they are now, but programs for the fans in the stadiums have been hawked almost since the sport began.

PRO SET: A T formation with a tight end, wide receivers spread eight to ten yards on each side, and the halfback and fullback lining up parallel to one another behind the quarterback. The pro set is a passing formation, most common among National Football League teams, and puts extreme pressure on the defense to cover a couple of fleet ends.

PROTECTION: Blocking for the quarterback, giving him enough time to release a pass. Blockers are expected to give a quarterback a minimum of three seconds to throw a pass after he takes the snap. In dummy practices a three-second clock is used on the sideline, buzzing at the end of the time to remind the quarterback that he should have already thrown the ball if a receiver was open.

PULLOUT: When an offensive lineman, usually a guard, pivots after the snap and runs parallel to the line in an effort to lead the blocking for a ballcarrier running to the outside.

PUMP: The forward-backward motion of a quarterback's arm as he fades to pass and tries to spot an open receiver.

PUNT: A scrimmage kick that the offensive team will use either when it is deep in its own territory with no prospects of a first down or when it wants to put the opposing team at a disadvantage deep in its own territory. Punts are usually fourth-down plays, although college teams still occasionally inject the surprise element of the quick kick on the third down. A punt is kicked out of the hands or after a short drop, but the ball must not touch the ground.

Punters stand 15 yards behind the line of scrimmage, so their blockers have enough time to stop charging defensive players who want to block the kick.

PURSUIT: Following a play to its conclusion, even if the defensive man might not seem to have a chance to make the tackle at first. A defender who doggedly chases a ballcarrier until the play is whistled dead is said to have good pursuit.

QUAB: A scouting acronym meaning quickness, agility, and balance, categories in the prospect's individual player form.

QUARTER: A 15-minute frame of playing time in a game. Two quarters make a half, and four quarters, or two halves, make a game. At the end of the first and third quarters, the teams exchange goals, and play resumes without interruption. At halftime, the team that lost the pregame coin flip gets the choice of goals or whether to kick or receive. A quarter is also known as a period.

QUARTERBACK: The offensive player who usually takes the snap from center, which initiates each play. Quarterbacks frequently call plays and have the most to do regarding their execution. They can keep the ball and run, pass, or hand off to a running back. About the only offensive function a quarterback is exempt from performing is the block, mainly because a quarterback is usually smaller than the defensive players and susceptible to injury.

Quarterbacks know the best of times and the worst of times, and the frightening thing about their occupation is that they never know when fortune will frown. They are either (1) deified, (2) despised, or (3) tolerated, and seldom is it the latter. Their careers are fickle; they can have the world on a string one moment, and be sucking the fuzzy end of the lollipop the next. Few quarterbacks go to sleep with both eyes shut. There are more losers than winners, and no one yet has blamed the right guard.

Coaches might say that defense is the name of the game, but try telling that to the quarterback. Try telling that to the fan. A quarterback can be booed in one town, cheered in the next, which is what happened in the dichotomous career of Sonny Jurgensen with the Philadelphia Eagles and the Washington Redskins. A quarterback can be hated by one coach and loved by another, which is what happened to Fran Tarkenton in his roller-coaster career as a Minnesota Viking, first under Norm Van Brocklin, himself a former quarterback, then under Bud Grant.

Not even the great quarterbacks are spared the ignominy of the catcall. In Baltimore Johnny Unitas would hear, "We want Cuozzo." Sonny Jurgensen once said that playing quarterback is "like holding group therapy for 50,000 people a week." The booing of Don Meredith in Dallas turned so vicious that Tom Landry, the head coach of the Cowboys, would send out his defensive team for pregame introductions. When Meredith took an early retirement and turned to broadcasting, he went to Dallas to cover a game. In the middle of the first half the fans began the roundelay of "We want Meredith." "No way you'll get me out there again," Meredith said in the booth. Once scarred, and eventually all quarterbacks are, they never close up the wounds.

QUICK COUNT: A play run off on a number count sooner than expected, to catch the defense off guard.

QUICK HUDDLE: A series of plays called so quickly in a huddle that the defensive team is either kept off balance or exhausted. It is the method of a lighter, faster team looking for an edge, such as the great Oklahoma teams in the 1950s.

QUICK KICK: A punt, usually on a down before the fourth, which is made unexpectedly so that the extra yardage with the roll of the ball will put the other team in a disadvantageous field position. The quick-kick formation has the original look of a normal alignment, but right before the snap the punter will backpedal into position, hoping to launch the kick before the defense can move a kick-return man into position.

QUICK OPENER: A dive play in which the back hits the hole as soon as it opens, hoping to pick up some short yardage.

QUICK RELEASE: Said of a quarterback when he can get his pass off with a snap of the wrist.

QUICK WHISTLE: When an official whistles a play dead and players on one of the teams feel that the runner's forward progress hadn't stopped.

RATING POINTS: *See* Pass Ratings.

READING A DEFENSE: An intangible but paramount ingredient for a successful quarterback, who when he reaches the line of scrimmage should be able to spot tendencies and indicators in the defensive alignment that will tip him off as to what the opposition is planning. A good reading quarterback will be able to call automatics and counter the defense.

RECEIVER: Any player who is a target for a forward pass. They come in all shapes and sizes and might be a tight end, a wide receiver, a halfback, or a fullback. Some of the great professional receivers have been Don Maynard, Raymond Berry, Lance Alworth, Del Shofner, Don Hutson, Elroy ("Crazylegs") Hirsch, Charley Taylor, Bobby Mitchell, and Tommy McDonald.

RECEPTION: The catching of a forward pass.

RECOVERY: The claiming of a fumble, either by a fumbler or the opposition.

RECRUITING: The most difficult, yet the most necessary, job of a collegiate coach. The hypocrisy and vagaries of recruiting have driven many a coach away from the game at the college level. Coaches must spend most of their off-season time with their staffs coaxing, selling, motivating high school seniors into thinking their particular school is the one and only. Coaches scout high school games during the season to get lines on players and rely heavily on tips from bird dogs, alumni, and friends. Sometimes coaches and alumni offer recruits more than the NCAA allows in the way of financial aid, and high school transcripts have even been doctored so a poor student is able to matriculate.

But recruiting has been a part of the game since 1897, and with no substitute it is not likely to disappear.

RED DOG: *See* Blitz.

REDSHIRT: The college policy of withholding a player from competition for a year, even though he is attending classes, so he will be eligible in his fifth year at the school, not having obtained enough credits to graduate. Redshirting is sanctioned by the NCAA and is usually done when a coach has a surplus of talent at the same position, or when a player is injured before the season starts. Redshirts attend practice and used to wear red practice jerseys, although that procedure has been largely discontinued. Some conferences don't allow redshirting, while their coaches wail that this puts them at a disadvantage when they play a school that does.

REFEREE: The official who has general oversight and control of the game. He stands at the rear of the offensive backfield and when the play has ended, gives all signals for fouls and is final authority for rules interpretations. The referee determines legality of the snap, observes the deep backs for legal motion, and observes the quarterback during and after a hand-off or pass. During kicking situations, the referee has primary responsibility to rule on kicker's actions and whether there has been roughing of the kicker.

RELEASE: The passer's action of throwing the ball. In a different sense, the blocker's act of leaving his block and heading for another assignment. On a screen pass, for example, a blocker might be told to hold fast for two counts and then release.

RETURN: The act of running with a kickoff, punt, or pass interception. Also called runback.

REVERSE: A play that calls for a back to start running wide and then hand off to another back or end coming from the opposite direction. The defense might be fooled into following the original back and not be able to right itself until the ballcarrier has run for a sizable gain. A double reverse consists of two hand-offs, with the eventual ballcarrier moving in the same direction as the first man with the ball.

ROLL-OUT: A play in which the quarterback circles back to either side of the line of scrimmage, waiting for a passing or running opening to develop.

ROSTER: The list of players on a squad.

ROTATION: In a zone defense the deep backs and sometimes the linebackers make a synchronized move in the direction of the offensive team's strength.

ROUGHING: Excessive contact with a player on offense or defense. The penalty for roughing is 15 yards and in certain cases is an automatic first down if committed by the defense.

ROVER: *See* Monster Man.

ROZELLE RULE: Slang for what the National Football League and Commissioner Pete Rozelle refer to as the player-compensation rule. Under the rule if a player satisfies his contractual obligation to a team, then plays a year without a contract and signs with another team, the second team owes the original team compensation for having lost the player. If the two teams cannot agree on compensation after a reasonable length of time, the commissioner steps in and arbitrates the compensation. The Rozelle rule has been seldom used, but it has been struck down in the lower courts and has frequently been a bane in labor negotiations between management and the players' union.

The players have contended that the threat of the Rozelle rule, more than the use of the rule itself, restricts their mobility. According to no less a source than Rozelle, the Rozelle rule was coined by John Elliott Cook, the lawyer for quarterback Joe Kapp when he jumped from the Minnesota Vikings to the New England Patriots and got involved in a lengthy lawsuit with the NFL that he eventually lost.

RUGBY FOOTBALL: A game that allows rugged running and tackling and that was the forerunner of American football. Rugby was named after the school in England where William Webb Ellis first picked up a ball and ran with it.

RULES: A set of playing regulations. Rules in both college and the National Football League can be amended and changed after individual rules committees give recommendations.

RUNBACK: *See* Return.

RUNNING BACK: A halfback or fullback who carries the ball is generally called a running back.

RUNNING QUARTERBACK: A quarterback who is adept at running and often plans his attack around his ability to use the option play. Not the same as a scrambler, though, because a running quarterback's actions are planned.

RUN TO DAYLIGHT: When a ballcarrier, seeing an unplanned opening, ignores the play and heads for the unoccupied spot. The phrase was coined by Vince Lombardi, who used to always give the advice to one of the Green Bay Packers' top backs, Jim Taylor.

RUSH: *See* Carry.

RUSHING: The statisticians' word for running. A common postgame figure is net yards rushing, which means the amount of ground a ballcarrier has gained after his losses have been deducted. A rushing average is based on yard per carry. An average of 4 or more is considered good.

SACK: The tackling behind the line of scrimmage of a quarterback attempting to pass.

SAFETY: The situation in which the ball is dead on or behind a team's own goal if the impetus comes from a player on that team. Two points are scored for the opposing team. The team giving up the points must then put the ball in play via a free kick from its own 20-yard line. Also, a safety man.

SAFETY BLITZ: An all-out rush of the quarterback by the free safety man. The safety blitz was refined by safety Larry Wilson of the St. Louis Cardinals through the theories put forth by one of his coaches, the late Chuck Drulis.

SAFETY MAN: One of the two deepest defensive backs, the strong safety and the free safety. *See* Strong Safety and Free Safety.

SAFETY VALVE: *See* Secondary Receiver.

SALARY: Professional salaries usually rise dramatically each time there are rival leagues competing for players. At one time Jimmy Brown of the Cleveland Browns was the National Football League's highest-paid player, making an estimated $75,000 a year. In 1972 the NFL Players Association announced these salary averages: entire league, $28,000; kicking specialists, $22,300; quarterbacks, $42,000; defensive backs, $25,500; offensive linemen, $26,600; linebackers, $26,700; receivers, $29,100; and running backs, $33,500.

A number of players now make more than Jimmy Brown's ceiling. About two dozen players earn in six figures annually, with Joe Namath's $450,000 estimate being the highest. Other high-salaried stars in recent years include Johnny Unitas, John Brodie, Sonny Jurgensen, Roman Gabriel, O. J. Simpson, Fran Tarkenton, and Alan Page.

SCALPER: A person who attempts to sell tickets for more than their listed price. Scalpers abound at big college games, such as bowl games, and at professional play-off games and the Super Bowl. Somehow the expert scalpers obtain large numbers of tickets at regular costs and then sell them at five times that price or more. Scalping is illegal in most states.

SCATBACK: A small but fast runner.

SCORING: Registering points through touchdowns, extra points, field goals, and safeties. A professional record that may last for a long time is George Blanda's point total, which was at 2,002 through the 1975 season. In the collegiate ranks, Glenn Davis of Army scored 354 points in four seasons, and Steve Owens of Oklahoma scored 336 in three years.

SCOUT: A person, sometimes an assistant coach, assigned to watch the games of other teams or potential players. Collegiate scouts watch their future opponents and also look at high school games so they can evaluate recruits. Professional scouts watch other pro teams as well as college teams for purposes of drafting. A scout's information is written down in a highly detailed scouting report. Teams also scout other teams and players through the use of film, which is usually exchanged on a reciprocal basis. Teams will also scout their own scouts in order to determine what prejudices, weaknesses, and hang-ups might color a particular report.

SCOUTING COMBINE: A cooperative among several professional teams in which they supply a variety of information on collegiate prospects to a central agency that correlates it with information from its own scouts, feeds all the data into a computer, and then distributes the results to all teams involved. Scouting combines were the brainchild of Dan Reeves, late owner of the Los Angeles Rams. The Rams, San Francisco 49ers, and Dallas Cowboys formed the first combine, called Troika. When the San Diego Chargers joined the group, the name was changed to Quandra.

The combine named BLESTO originally stood for the Chicago Bears-Detroit Lions-Philadelphia Eagles-Pittsburgh Steelers Talent Organization. When the Minnesota Vikings joined, it became BLESTO-V. When three more teams joined, it grew to BLESTO-VIII. Another pro combine is CEPO, for Central-Eastern Personnel Organization. Some teams informally participate in these combines, supplying only partial information and receiving in turn limited print-outs.

A few teams, such as the Oakland Raiders and the Cincinnati Bengals, have refused to participate in a combine, choosing rather to accrue their own information and make independent judgments. In the final analysis, of course, any team must make a judgment based on something the computer can't furnish—the size of the player's heart.

SCOUT TEAM: A team of reserve players who impersonate the next opponent during the week's scrimmages.

SCRAMBLER: A quarterback who intends to pass but is forced out of the pocket and then dodges and runs until he either finds a receiver or is tackled. The quintessential scrambler has been Fran Tarkenton of the Minnesota Vikings. Tarkenton insists, however, that when he scrambles, it's never with the intention of running, he's just buying time until a receiver can get open. For all his scrambling, Tarkenton has seldom been injured and will be remembered as one of the most durable of the pro quarterbacks.

SCREEN PASS: A deceptive pattern intended to fool the defense into thinking a deep pass is developing, while the blockers let linemen penetrate deep into the backfield. Meanwhile a wall of blockers forms for a back, who takes a lob pass from the quarterback with the hope of penetrating a vulnerable defense.

SEAL: To close off a hole in the line that has been made for a ballcarrier.

SEAM: The imaginary line in a defense where coverage for one part of the secondary stops. Receivers sometimes try to get open by crossing the seams of a defense.

SECONDARY: The area past the defensive line, occupied by the linebackers, cornerbacks, and safety men.

SECONDARY RECEIVER: A receiver to whom the quarterback looks when his primary receiver is covered. Also called safety valve.

SECOND EFFORT: When a player seems to be stopped but gives it a last-gasp thrust, good for additional yardage. Or when a tackler appears to be blocked out of the play, or when he is blocked to the ground, yet comes on and still makes the tackle.

SEMIPRO: A semiprofessional player who may or may not be paid. The most famous semipro sandlot player was Johnny Unitas, making seven dollars a game for the Bloomfield Rams, near Pittsburgh. Unitas got a tryout with the Baltimore Colts, capitalized on an injury to incumbent quarterback George Shaw, and became one of the game's greatest passers.

SENIOR ABILITY FORM: *See* Individual Player Form.

SEQUENCE: A pattern of plays run during the course of a team's single possession of the ball.

SERIES: The number of plays a team runs during a single possession of the ball.

SET BACK: A back who does not go in motion prior to the snap.

SEVEN BLOCKS OF GRANITE: The Fordham University line in 1937, which allowed no touchdowns to an enemy runner all season. The stars were Ed Franco and Alex Wojciechowicz. The only blemish on the team's record was a scoreless tie with Pittsburgh.

SEVEN MULES: The name for the offensive line that played in front of Notre Dame's Four Horsemen.

SHIFT: A change in position by either the offensive or defensive players after the teams have reached the line of scrimmage. The offensive team is required to reach a set position one second after any shift.

SHINE BLOCK: A coaching expression for a block at the shoe tops, right near the opponent's shoeshine.

SHOESTRING TACKLE: A shoe-top or ankle tackle, the most effective way of stopping a power runner.

SHORT YARDAGE: A generality for a down-to-go situation in which the offensive team needs very little yardage to make a first down.

SHOTGUN: A passing formation in which the

King of the scramblers, Fran Tarkenton had two careers with the Minnesota Vikings.

quarterback will position himself seven or eight yards behind the center to take a direct snap. The quarterback thereby starts in the pocket and is ready to throw the ball. The backs line up close behind the line, and the receivers are split, giving the quarterback a good chance to find any of five men in the open. The shotgun cannot be used for an entire season because it prohibits a balanced attack; there is no potential for a screen, trap, or draw; and the quarterback is a sitting duck for the defense should he be forced to run the ball. Coach Red Hickey got short-term mileage out of the shotgun with the San Francisco 49ers in 1959, and in 1976 the Dallas Cowboys went to the Super Bowl while intermittently using the shotgun.

SHOVEL PASS: A quick pass, either backward or forward, so termed because the passer looks as though he's throwing it with a shovel. Also called a shuffle pass.

SIDELINE: The line on either side of the field that runs lengthwise from end line to end line. Each sideline is 120 yards long, counting both end zones.

SIDELINE PASS: A pattern in which the receiver goes straight out and cuts quickly and sharply in a 90-degree fashion toward the sideline. Usually thrown to the side of the field the offensive team is closest to, the sideline pass is hard to defend, impossible to intercept if thrown with precision, and an effective method of stopping the clock because after the completion the receiver will either be carried out of bounds by his own momentum or be pushed out of bounds.

SIDESWIPE: To block or tackle with vigor from the side.

SIDEWINDER: *See* Soccer-style Kicker.

SIGNALS: The call of an offensive or defensive play, either in a huddle or at the line of scrimmage. Also, the actual act of the quarterback calling numbers and codes at the line of scrimmage, with the center scheduled to snap the ball on a certain signal.

SINGLE WING: An offensive formation that is so named because one of the halfbacks acts as a wingback and is stationed just outside an end. There is really no quarterback in this formation; the blocking back, fullback, and tailback are all one to seven yards behind the center, and one of them takes a direct snap to start the play. The strengths of the single wing are that two offensive men will be blocking each of the key defensive men on every play; an unbalanced line gives the offense extra impetus in the direction the play is going; the blocking back can be used as a blocker on running plays and, unlike a quarterback, does not hand off the ball; and congestion of the players means greater deception. The weaknesses: Plays are slow in developing, and there are seldom any long runs and passes. Doc Sutherland at the University of Pittsburgh was one of the leading exponents of the single wing.

SITTING ON THE BALL: *See* Killing the Clock.

SKILL POSITIONS: Other players will disagree, but coaches refer to quarterback, receiver, and running back as the skill positions because they require skills apart from the basic abilities that are required to play the game.

SKULL SESSION: When players sit in a classroom and either watch movies or plays being diagrammed by a coach on a blackboard. Also called a chalk talk.

SLED: *See* Dummy.

SLEEPER PLAY: Unsportsmanlike though legal, this is a pass play in which the receiver, often someone who has just entered the game, will try to linger inconspicuously along the sideline, hoping the defense will not notice him, so he can sprint down the field for a pass when the ball is snapped.

SLOTBACK: A backfield man stationed in the slot, the area between the outside of the tackle and the split end. A team that lines up with a slotback is in the slot-formation.

SMASH: *See* Plunge.

SNAP: The centering of the ball that starts the play. The center is also called the snapper.

SNOW JOB: A game in which one team wins easily, by a substantial score. Also called iceberg or no-brainer.

SOCCER-STYLE KICKER: A place-kicker who approaches the ball from an angle and kicks with the side of his foot.

SOFT HANDS: A compliment for a receiver who seems to hang on to most balls he gets close to, whether they're thrown soft or hard.

SPEARING: Charging a player while he's down and ramming him with the helmet. A violation which brings a 15-yard penalty.

SPECIALIST: A player who specializes in one area of the game, e.g., a kicker.

SPECIAL TEAM(S): The teams used for kickoffs and punts, either on offense or defense. Usually they are made up of reserves who hope to show through their aggressiveness that they're capable of playing regularly. This zeal to knock somebody down has resulted in synonyms such as bomb squad, suicide squad, and kamikazes. Coaches put a lot of importance in the specialty teams. George Allen of the Washington Redskins and some other coaches have hired assistant coaches whose lone responsibility is training the specialty teams. Head coach Chuck Noll of the Pittsburgh Steelers has handled his own specialty teams himself.

SPECIMEN: When a scout refers to a prospect as a specimen, he is referring to the player's physical ability with regard to the game.

SPIKE: A modern fad in which the scorer of a touchdown slams the ball to the end-zone turf with as much gusto as possible, causing referees to duck and opposing teams to be further chagrined. There are variations of the standard spike, such as the crap-roll spike and an outright toss of the ball into the stands, which usually results in a fine equivalent to the cost of the ball. Isaac Curtis of the Cincinnati Bengals has refused to spike, instead making his touchdown trademark the nonchalant act of tossing the ball over his shoulder after he's crossed the goal. One time Dave Smith of the Pittsburgh Steelers, running unmolested to the goal in a nationally televised game on a Monday night, was so eager to spike that he misjudged the end zone and slammed the ball down before he reached the goal. What Smith had was a fumble instead of a touchdown.

SPILL: To tackle a man with a block. Also called a dump.

SPINNER: A back in the single-wing formation whose job is to execute a half or complete spin as a means of deception.

SPIN-OFF: When a ballcarrier shakes a tackle by spinning away at the moment of contact.

SPIRAL: A perfectly thrown pass in which the ball travels in a straight path with a clockwise rotation. Many punts will also travel in a spiral.

SPLIT END: An end stationed at the line of scrimmage but spread apart a few yards from the other linemen to enable him to get downfield faster.

SPOTTER: A coach stationed in the press box who will note variations and tendencies in offenses and defenses and relay by phone the information along with suggestions to the head coach on the bench. Another kind of spotter is an aide to a television or radio broadcaster who assists in pointing out ballcarriers, blockers, and tacklers.

SPRING PRACTICE: A five- or six-week period of practice for college teams during the spring, frequently concluded with an intrasquad game.

SPRINT-OUT: *See* Roll-out.

SPY: Devious coaches will sometimes send a representative to a rival team's practice, hoping to pick up some useful information. Sometimes these spies are so assiduous that they will climb a tree or pole with binoculars. Coaches are paranoid about spies, constantly checking an otherwise vacant practice area or stadium during practice to see if any interlopers have made their way in.

SQUARE-IN: A pass pattern favored by tight ends in which they head straight down the field for 10 to 15 yards, then make an abrupt turn in the direction of the center of the field.

SQUARE-OUT: Same as a square-in, except the turn is in the direction of the sideline.

STACK: A defense in which the linebackers play directly behind their linemen instead of in the gaps.

STANCE: A player's position before the ball is snapped.

STATUE OF LIBERTY: A trick play of yore in which the quarterback stands with his arm cocked as though to pass and another back circles behind the quarterback, snatches the ball, and takes off running.

STICKUM: What the players call an adhesive substance which pass receivers rub on their hands before a game.

STIFF-ARM: When a runner, trying to ward off tacklers, sticks out his arm, extending the heel of the hand and trying to keep a defender from reaching him, usually by putting his hand on the would-be tackler's helmet.

STRAIGHT-ARM: *See* Stiff-Arm.

STREAK: Any number of consecutive victories or losses.

STRIP THE BALL: The art of taking or knocking the ball out of a ballcarrier's grasp.

STRIP THE INTERFERENCE: When a defensive player throws himself at some blocking interference, thereby removing those men and leaving the ballcarrier vulnerable to other tacklers.

STRONG LEFT: When the tight end lines up on the left side of the line.

STRONG RIGHT: When the tight end lines up on the right side of the line.

STRONG SAFETY: The safety man who plays the offense's strong side, usually covering the tight end.

STRONG SIDE: The side of the offense where the tight end and flanker line up. Since most teams are right-handed, this is generally the right side. One of the more recent successful teams that was left-handed has been the Oakland Raiders, with their left-handed quarterback, Kenny Stabler.

STUNTS: A defensive ploy of sending linemen off in different angles or moving linebackers to confuse the offensive line. Also known as games.

STUTTER STEP: The shuffling of the feet quickly by a ballcarrier to give the appearance that he is going to stop. Effectively done, the stutter step can throw a tackler off-stride. The stutter step can hardly be taught; you either have it or you don't. Gale Sayers had it.

SUBMARINE: A defensive lineman's charge in which he goes in low, anticipating a plunge and hoping to tangle up the legs of everyone concerned. It is a gamble, since once he is committed, the submarining lineman takes himself out of the play.

SUBSTITUTE: A player who relieves one of the regulars.

SUCKER SHIFT: A shift devised by the offense to deliberately throw the defense off side. Officials can penalize the offensive team if they recognize it. One of the best sucker shifts was frequently used by coach Frank Leahy's teams at Notre Dame.

SUDDEN DEATH: In pro football a fifth 15-minute period is played if the score is tied at the end of four quarters. The first team to score in the extra period is the winner, and if neither side scores in the 15 minutes, the result is recorded as a tie.

SUICIDE SQUAD: *See* Special Teams.

SUPER BOWL: The playoff game to determine the championship of the National Football League. Originally conceived to pair the titlists from the now-defunct American Football League against the NFL when the two leagues cemented a merger, the game now pits the winner of the American Football Conference playoff against the winner of the National Football Conference playoff. There is no permanent site for the game, but it is always played on a neutral field.

The first Super Bowl, at the Los Angeles Coliseum on January 15, 1967, was won by the Green Bay Packers, who beat the AFL's Kansas City Chiefs and repeated in 1968 against the Oakland Raiders. The AFL achieved parity with the New York Jets' dramatic victory over the Baltimore Colts in 1969, followed by the Chiefs' triumph over the Minnesota Vikings in 1970, the last game before the two leagues became one.

No team has won the Super Bowl three times, but the Miami Dolphins (1972, 1973) and the Pittsburgh Steelers (1974, 1975), along with the Packers, own two titles. Other winners have been the Baltimore Colts (1971) and the Dallas Cowboys (1972). In the first 10 games, AFL or AFC teams had won seven titles.

Named unwittingly by the daughter of AFL founder Lamar Hunt, who one day explained to her father that she called her toy rubber ball a "super ball," the title game has become a yearly spectacle watched by 75 million TV viewers.

SUPERSTITION(S): Like most athletes, football players have their superstitions, rituals they believe will enhance their victory chances. Buddy Parker, when he coached the Pittsburgh Steelers, feared the number 13. He would not stay on the 13th floor of a hotel. In Baltimore once Parker was given a room on the 11th floor and thought he was safe. As he unpacked, though, it hit Parker that the number of his room was 1102; those digits added up to 13. Parker went to the desk and asked for another room. Paul Brown always used to wear a brown hat when he coached. Mike Manuche, a New York restaurateur, would take the same route to games, arrive at the same time, wear the same clothes, and give his ticket to the same usher when the Giants were winning. When the Giants went through a long losing streak, Manuche tried all combinations in trying to right his favorite team.

SWEEP: *See* End Sweep.

SWING PASS: A pass thrown immediately out to the side, with a back coming out of the backfield as the receiver.

SWIVEL-HIPPED: A tricky, shifty runner who appears to fake tacklers out of position by the way he moves his hips as he runs with the ball.

SYNTHETIC SURFACE: More and more the game is being played on something that isn't God's grass. The Astrodome in Houston was one of the first fields with a synthetic surface, using a product called AstroTurf. Other popular synthetic fields are made of Tartan Turf and Poly Turf. The Orange Bowl in Miami made a unique switch in 1976, removing its Poly Turf field and returning to natural grass. Players abhor synthetic surfaces, saying they cut into their longevity and cause more injuries, especially to the knees. Some medical surveys substantiate this, but such a thing is hard to prove, and in many instances the team managements

have no choice, since they play in municipally owned stadiums, multi-sport facilities that use synthetics because they are easier to maintain. The players refer to synthetic surfaces as rugs.

TACKLE: To bring a ballcarrier to the ground, either forcing at least one of his knees to touch the ground, or stopping his forward progress long enough so that in the referee's estimation the ball should be whistled dead. A tackle is also a position on either the offensive or defensive line. Offensive tackles play between the guards and the ends and in the pros frequently weigh 260 pounds or more. On defense, tackle has become a glamor position, with Alan Page of the Minnesota Vikings becoming the first defensive player to be named Most Valuable Player in the National Football League in 1971. Defensive tackles need to be as big or bigger than their offensive counterparts, for it is the tackle who is concerned with fighting off the double-team block.

TACKLE-ELIGIBLE PASS: A play in which the end drops back into the backfield and becomes a flanker, making the tackle the outermost man on the offensive line and thus eligible for a pass.

TAILBACK: The role of the tailback has changed. In the days of the single-wing formation, he was a part of almost every play, giving his team a pass-run threat. A tailback in the I formation is the deep man in the I, whose main assets are running and blocking.

TARTAN TURF: *See* Synthetic Surface.

TARZAN-JANE: A scout's description of a player who was originally impressive but later turned into a disappointment. "He's a Tarzan-Jane," a scout will say. "The first time I saw him he looked like Tarzan, but it turned out he was a Jane."

TAXI SQUAD: Players who are officially cut from a pro team but remain with the team for practices. The players draw pay and remain under contract but are not eligible for the games until they are reactivated. The term began in Cleveland when Art McBride, original owner of the Browns, gave these extra players jobs driving a fleet of cabs he owned. When the National Football League trimmed its roster limit a few years ago, the taxi squad became extinct. Also called band squad or cab squad.

TEE: A three-pronged, hard-rubber stand used by kickers to prop up the ball for kickoffs.

TELEGRAPHING: A bad habit by a quarterback in that he looks directly at the receiver he intends to throw to, thereby tipping off the defense as to which way he's going with the ball.

T FORMATION: A formation introduced by Ralph Jones of the Chicago Bears in 1931 which revolutionized football. In the T formation, the line is balanced and the quarterback stands with his hands under the center for a snap of just a few inches. From this position, the quarterback can either hand off, pass, or run the ball himself. The T formation allows for speed, with great fakes and maneuvers by the backs; the backs are running at full speed or close to full speed when they take a hand-off; there is room for quick openers and fast play development; double-team blocking is not necessary because of the speed with which the play develops; a pocket for pass protection is easily formed; backs can choose the open hole; the center becomes a more effective blocker, since he can snap the ball without looking for the quarterback; and more men can be sent in motion. Without a versatile quarterback, however, a man who can both pass and handle the ball well, the T can be a liability. Also, the T does not give a team the power on short-yardage situations that it might gain from the single wing, and the quarterback is useless as a blocker once he hands off. Sid Luckman of the Bears was one of the first great T-formation quarterbacks, and there have been hundreds since then.

THREE-MAN FRONT: The Okie defense, adopted by teams like the Houston Oilers and the New England Patriots in the early 1970s. Only three men occupy the defensive line, a middle guard and two ends, with the man missing becoming in effect a fourth linebacker. There is intense pressure on the three-man front to rush the passer and fight off the run, but by the same token it is difficult for the passer to find a receiver open.

THREE-POINT STANCE: The traditional position for a lineman, in which his feet form two of the points, and the third is either hand providing support in front of his body.

THREE YARDS AND A CLOUD OF DUST: A team that relies on a ground attack, preferring to grind out short yardage and consume time on the clock. This has been the description of all of Woody Hayes's teams at Ohio State.

THROWING TO A CROWD: When a passer throws a ball to a receiver even though it appears that he is well covered. A dangerous tactic that can lead to an interception.

TIGHT END: The end who lines up close to the tackle, usually entrusted with blocking responsibilities instead of primarily catching the ball.

TIME-OUT: When the clock is not running. Officially, teams are allowed three time-outs per half, and they try to hoard them in the event they need to kill the clock in the final minutes.

TIMING: The ability of a passer and receiver to work together so that the passer knows where a receiver will be on a certain pattern and the receiver knows when the ball will be thrown. There is also timing involved in a hand-off between a quarterback and a running back.

TIP: When a lineman gives away a play by some unknown gesture or movement, such as the way he is shifting his weight at the line of scrimmage. Quarterbacks can also sometimes tip plays by their posture just before the ball is snapped.

TOTAL OFFENSE: The combined rushing and passing numbers, after losses have been deducted, for either a team or an individual. To inflate a player's numerical value, some teams will also add receiving, punt-return, and kick-return yardage to the rushing and passing figures.

TOUCHBACK: When a ball is dead on or behind a team's own goal line, provided the impetus came from an opponent and provided it is not a touchdown or a missed field goal. A touchback results in the ball being brought out to the 20-yard line for the start of a series of downs. For example, a team's kicking the ball out of the other team's end zone on a punt or kickoff would be ruled a touchback, and the team opposite the kicker would receive the ball at its own 20. A touchback counts for no points and is not to be confused with a safety.

TOUCHDOWN: When any part of the ball, legally in possession of a player inbounds, is on, above, or over the opponent's goal line, provided it is not a touchback. A touchdown counts six points and entitles the scoring team a chance to try for the point after touchdown (pro) or two points after touchdown (optional in college ball).

TOUCH FOOTBALL: A brand of football with rules similar to tackle football, except that instead of tackling, a ballcarrier is stopped by being tagged any place beneath the belt. Tackle teams use the touch system in light-contact drills. Another form of touch is flag football, in which a tackle is scored when flags, inserted in the belts of all players, are pulled from their person.

TRADE: An agreement between two teams in which they will exchange players, money, draft choices, or combinations of any of the three.

TRAFFIC: The flow of blockers, ballcarrier, and potential tacklers. When a defender is said to be caught in traffic, he has become so entangled in a stream of players that he is unable to make the tackle.

TRAINER: An assistant to the team physician who is responsible for routine medical help such as bruises and muscle pulls. The trainer also tapes ankles, hands, and other parts of the player's body prior to a practice or game.

TRAINING CAMP: A preseason period in which players compete for positions on the team, coaches evaluate personnel, and teams refine much of the strategy they intend to use during the season. A professional training camp, usually held in an isolated area away from where the team plays, begins in July. Colleges hold two camps, a spring session and then preseason training starting in August.

TRAINING TABLE: A special table or area at training camp where the players and coaches meet to eat together. Training-table meals are usually high in protein and calories to make up for the great amounts of energy expended during practice.

TRAP: To catch the ball on a short hop just after it's hit the ground. A trapped ball by a receiver might look like a completed pass from the stands, but it is not legal.

TRAP BLOCKING: A block in which the offense lures a defender across the line of scrimmage only to have him impeded from the blind side by an offensive player from the other side of the line. This leaves a big hole for the ballcarrier to run through. Also called mousetrap blocking, and a mousetrap play is a running attempt in which there is trap blocking.

TRAVELING SQUAD: The number of players who make a trip with a team to an out-of-town game. College limits are determined by the NCAA; professional teams are allowed to travel with as many players as they dress in uniform for home games.

TRIPLE OPTION: A play in which the quarterback has three choices—to run the ball himself, pass the ball after faking the run, or hand it off to another back.

TRIPLE THREAT: A back who can run, pass, and kick.

TRY FOR POINT: The attempted conversion after a touchdown has been scored.

TURK: The nickname for the person, usually an assistant coach or a team manager, who must notify a player that the head coach wants to see him, a prelude to his being cut from the team.

TURNOVER: When the offensive team loses possession of the ball through a fumble or pass interception.

TURN THE CORNER: When a back running with the ball has stopped running parallel with the line of scrimmage and has made his cut upfield.

TWEENER: Scouting lingo for a player who is considered too large to play one position but too small to play another.

TWO-MINUTE DRILL: A set of plays designed to consume as little time as possible so that a team can attempt to move down the field in the final minutes of a game. A grand master at working the two-minute drill was Johnny Unitas, quarterback for the Baltimore Colts.

TWO-MINUTE WARNING: In professional football, a time-out by the referee to inform both benches that only two minutes, or slightly less than two minutes if the clock cannot be stopped in time, remain in a half.

UMBRELLA DEFENSE: A formation originated by the New York Giants in 1950 that consisted of a six-man line, a lone linebacker in the middle, and four defensive halfbacks fanned out like an umbrella. The four-man backfield has since become standard in pro ball.

UMPIRE: One of the game officials whose prime responsibility is to rule on players' conduct and actions on the scrimmage line. The umpire lines up in the defensive backfield, approximately four or five yards behind the line of scrimmage. He checks for false starts by offensive linemen, for the legality of contact by offensive linemen and by defensive players as they attempt to ward off blockers, and for interior linemen moving illegally downfield on a pass play. He also rules on incomplete or trapped passes when the ball is thrown overhead or short.

UNBALANCED LINE: When one side of the offensive line has more players on it than the other. This alignment was indigenous to the single-wing formation but is sometimes also used with the T formation.

UNDEFEATED, UNTIED, UNSCORED ON— AND UNINVITED: Sportswriters' reference to the 1932 Colgate team, which did not receive a bid to a postseason bowl game.

UNDERNEATH: A pass receiver who will catch the ball short of the deep men in the defensive backfield.

UNDERTHROW: A pass that is not thrown as far as it was intended. Occasionally this can be a blessing for the offensive team when a receiver leaves his defender and comes back to catch the ball.

UNIFORMS: The uniform, which started in one form or another in 1875, has evolved into a helmet, usually with a face bar; a jersey; pants with thigh and knee pads; long stockings; and cleated or rubber-tipped football shoes. The padding includes hip pads, shoulder pads, rib pads, forearm pads, and hand pads that are taped in place. Most modern padding is made of plastic and foam rubber.

UNIT: The team of 11 players that is on the field at any given time, such as the offensive unit, the defensive unit, the field-goal unit, the kicking unit, etc.

UP BACK: In a two-running-back offense, the back closer to the line of scrimmage.

VARSITY: The regular team in college. As distinguished from the junior varsity, which is made up of players who are striving to make the regular team, and the freshman team.

VEER: A triple-option offense developed by Bill Yeoman at the University of Houston. Usually the tight end will block someone in the secondary instead of a man on the defensive line. The quarterback, vital to the successful running of the veer, will take the ball from under center like a T-formation quarterback, but then he has a choice of keeping the ball, passing it, handing off, or pitching out to his backs who are veering in the same direction he is. The veer caught on and was being used by approximately 20 percent of the major college teams in the early 1970s.

WAIT BLOCK: A block in which the offensive player will hesitate, usually a full count, before making contact with the opponent.

WAIVER: The legal action frequently taken on a pro player when he is cut from the squad. The player is placed on a waiver list, and the other teams, starting with the team with the poorest record, are allowed to claim him for a certain price, usually around $100. If the player is unclaimed by the rest of the teams, he is free to bargain for himself as a free agent. There are also recallable waivers, after which the original team may pull the player back and retain him when he is claimed. Sometimes teams will put a player on recallable waivers just to see what other clubs in the league are interested in him, and then try to make a trade.

WALK-OFF: The distance marked off by an official in assessing a penalty.

WALK-ON: In either college or pro ball, a player who comes to the camp uninvited and persuades a coach to give him a trial. This would be a player without a scholarship in college or an undrafted free agent in the pros.

WALL: The formation of blocks along the sideline on a punt or kickoff return. The blockers string themselves in single file and block inward, trying to spring the ballcarrier loose for a long gain. Wall and forward wall are also names for the offensive line.

WATCH-CHARM GUARD: A small speedy offensive guard, expert at pulling out of the line and leading end sweeps. Practically nonexistent now. One of the most famous watch-charm guards was Bert Metzger, who was a 153-pound All-American at Notre Dame in 1930.

WEAK SAFETY: The safety man who plays the weak side of the offense. He is also called the free safety because he is free to play the ball or his choice of men.

WEAK SIDE: The side of the offense away from the tight end and flanker. Usually the left side, since most teams move to the right. Paul ("Bear") Bryant used to call his weak-side linemen weak guard, weak tackle, and so on, but he dropped the designation when a player's mother wrote: "Why do you call my son a weak tackle? He weighs 220 pounds and I don't call that weak."

WEAVE: To thread one's way through a broken field in a back-and-forth pattern.

WEDGE: Usually four men on a kickoff return whose prime responsibility is to provide immediate protection for the return man.

WEDGE BUSTER: Any defensive player skilled at breaking up the offensive team's blocking wedge on a kickoff return.

WFL: The World Football League, a league that attempted to break the monopoly of the National Football League in 1974, but after less than two full seasons collapsed in bankruptcy. The WFL was the brainchild of Gary Davidson, a lawyer who had started other upstart leagues in basketball and hockey. Unable to obtain a major television contract, the WFL lured few NFL stars away, and the stars who were scheduled to play for the WFL once their NFL obligations were met either wound up with breach of contract or broke the contracts themselves.

The WFL originated several rules variations designed to capture the public—e.g., touchdowns counted seven points and were followed by an "action point" that could not be kicked and had to be attempted by either passing or running. The WFL started with twelve teams, many of which padded attendances, were unable to pay their players or their bills, and were even faced with legal confiscation of the team uniforms. After the WFL disbanded in 1975, one franchise remained, the Memphis Southmen. Owner John Bassett had persuaded three Miami Dolphin stars—Larry Csonka, Jim Kiick, and Paul Warfield—to jump to his team for a package totaling $2 million. The Dolphin defectors and the rest of the team continued to get paid beyond the league's demise, Basset hoping that he would eventually be given an NFL franchise.

WHISTLE: The signal from a referee or another official that the play has ended.

WHOA BACK: Now archaic, the whoa back was Amos Alonzo Stagg's term for a back who delayed and sort of reared like a horse before starting to run on the old spinner play.

WIDE RECEIVER: A receiver who splits from the tackle on either side of the line, spreading out several yards from the rest of the offensive unit so he can more easily run a pass route.

WILD-CARD SUBSTITUTION: A step toward unlimited substitution in 1959 in which a so-called wild-card player could be inserted or removed from the lineup at any time. Eventually the college rules were changed to permit unlimited substitution.

WILD-CARD TEAM: The National Football League's designation for a team that does not finish in first place in any of the divisions, but has the best record of the runner-up teams in a conference and thereby qualifies for postseason play-offs. In 1976 the Dallas Cowboys, a wild-card team, became the first such to

Wrong-Way Riegels *sets out...*

1

reverses his direction...

2

as teammate Lom pursues...

3

and Riegels is finally caught.

4

reach the Super Bowl. They lost to the Pittsburgh Steelers.

WIND SPRINTS: A traditional drill at the end of a practice in which players line up according to position and run a series of dashes of between 20 and 50 yards.

WINGBACK: Originally a halfback in the single- or double-wing formation, a wingback is now a halfback out of any formation who splits out to the side, primarily as a flanker-type pass receiver.

WINGED T FORMATION: A T formation that includes a wingback.

WIN ONE FOR THE GIPPER: Supposedly George Gipp, one of Notre Dame's greatest players, on his deathbed asked Knute Rockne to ask a future team to win a game in his honor. Former players of Rockne's say he used this inspirational crutch more than once, but it is certain that eight years after Gipp's death in 1920 the coach did relay the player's message to his team at halftime. Notre Dame went from a scoreless tie to a 12-6 victory over undefeated Army. Trivia buffs are aware that George Gipp's role in the movie of Rockne's life was played by Ronald Reagan.

WISHBONE: A formation attributed to Darrell Royal at the University of Texas in which the fullback lines up a few yards closer to the quarterback and the halfbacks are the deep backs in parallel, giving the overview of a wishbone. The quarterback has four options—to hand off, toss laterally to another back, keep and run, or pass. The formation requires a versatile quarterback. The drawback to the wishbone is that plays take longer to develop, and long passes are limited because with a tight end there is only one wide receiver, as opposed to two in the pro set.

WOLVES: People who snarl because their team isn't winning. They may be alumni, fans, bettors—anyone who can put the heat on a losing coach.

WORKHORSE: A back who carries the ball most of the time, averaging 20 or more attempts a game.

WRONG-WAY RIEGELS: Roy Riegels, center for the University of California, ran 63 yards with a fumble, but in the wrong direction, against Georgia Tech in the 1929 Rose Bowl. A teammate, Benny Lom, caught Riegels at the 1-yard line and turned him around, but he was tackled at that point by Tech's Frank Waddey. When Lom attempted to punt out of his end zone on the next play, his kick was blocked, and the safety made the difference in Georgia Tech's 8-7 victory.

X'S AND O'S: Symbols used in diagramming plays. The *O*'s are the offensive players, and the *X*'s represent the defense.

YARD CHAIN: The link chain, ten yards long, that connects the two portable posts used in measuring first downs.

YARD LINE: Any spot on the field where the ball or players are positioned, such as the 5-yard line, the 50-yard line, etc.

ZIG AND ZAG: An irregular pattern used by a ballcarrier in evading blockers once he breaks into the open field.

ZONE DEFENSE: A pass coverage in which the defensive backs are responsible for certain areas of the field instead of specific receivers.

When a golfer, Jack Nicklaus here, explodes sand and ball out of bunker, it's a blast.

ACE: A score made on a hole with one stroke. Also called a hole-in-one.

ADDRESS: The position taken just before hitting the ball. Also known as addressing the ball. Pro Gene Littler is noted for addressing the ball in good form.

AMATEUR: A golfer who plays for fun. If he wins a tournament, an amateur may accept a prize of small retail value. If he accepts money for winning or teaches the game for pay, he becomes a professional. In 1976 there were an estimated 16.5 million amateur golfers in the United States.

AMATEUR SIDE: The lower side of the hole on a sloping green. A ball putted to this side will rarely fall into the cup but will drift away with slope. Opposite of pro side.

APPROACH: Being within hitting distance of a par-four or par-five green. Also known as approach shot.

APRON: A two- to three-foot ring of grass surrounding the green. Usually turf is allowed to grow a half inch higher than the surface of the green. Also known as fringe.

AWAY: The ball farthest from the hole. The player whose ball is away hits or putts first.

BACK DOOR: The rear of the cup as the player looks at it. A putt that goes in the back door is one that rims one side of the cup before it topples in at the back.

BACK SIDE: The last nine holes of a course. Opposite of front side.

BACKSPIN: A reverse spin put on the ball by skilled players when hitting approach shots. Spin serves as "brakes" and "bite" when ball hits green.

BACKSWING: The part of the swing that begins with the club being taken away from the ball. Backswing is completed when the hands reach the top of swing.

BALL: The object hit by a golfer. In the United States the ball must have a diameter of 1.68 inches. Its weight must be 1.62 ounces. It is formed with a center of steel, or a frozen liquid pellet, or a rubber ball. Rubber thread is wound tightly around the center and encased in a cover of balata, a refined rubber. Balls made in one piece out of plastic materials came on the market in the late 1960s. The diameter, weight, and velocity of balls are tested annually by the United States Golf Association. British-made balls are slightly smaller and lighter than those made in the United States.

BALL MARKER: The penny or dime used to spot the position of the ball on the green while it is being cleaned or removed from another player's line of putt. Texans, the joke goes, use silver dollars for ball markers.

BANANA BALL: A struck ball that veers right instead of going straight. Its route curves like a banana.

BERMUDA: Not the island. It is a type of hybrid grass that is used widely on courses in the South. It cannot survive northern winters.

BEST BALL: The lowest score made on a hole by any player on a team, which is recorded as the team's score.

BIRD: One stroke under par for the hole. Also known as birdie. This is an American contribution to the game, for it was first used by a golfer at Atlantic City (N.J.) Country Club early in this century. He described his three-stroke play on a par-four hole as a bird. At the time "bird" was slang for something rare.

BLAST: When a golfer explodes sand and ball out of a bunker. Also known as an explosion. If it can be avoided, it's not the shot to hit when the wind is blowing into golfer's face.

BLIND HOLE: These unpopular holes occur on hilly courses where a player cannot see the landing area for his drive, or the green for his approach.

BOGEY: One stroke over par on a hole.

BOLD: Describes a putt that is hit further than required. Arnold Palmer, one of the best-known bold putters, plays this type of game to make sure the ball at least reaches the hole.

BUNKER: A depression filled with sand. Some courses, like Augusta (Ga.) National Golf Club, have grass bunkers. The term originated in Scotland where grazing sheep inadvertently helped design the first seaside golf courses. The first bunkers were holes where the flock gathered for protection from strong winds. Over the years the huddling sheep rooted out all the grass and left nothing but sand.

CABBAGE: A heavy rough.

CADDIE: One who carries a player's clubs. A player may confer with caddies about the distance to the green or the contour of the putting surface.

CARRY: The distance the ball must travel in the air to reach its target. The 16th hole at the Augusta (Ga.) National Golf Club is a par three measuring 190 yards, and the player must carry over a pond that lies between the tee and green.

CASUAL WATER: A temporary gathering of water anywhere on the course. In winter snow and ice are considered casual water. A player may remove the ball from casual water without penalty, but he may not move it closer to the hole.

CHIP SHOT: A very short shot onto the green.

CHOKE: To grip down on the handle, or to move hands closer to club head. And, as in other sports, to fall victim to pressure.

CLOSED STANCE: When the left foot is positioned more forward than the right foot. This shifts the left shoulder forward and appears to close off the line of sight to target. Closed stance helps induce a shot to bend left. Opposite of open stance.

CLUB: What one hits the ball with. There are many clubs, each designated by a name and/or number. Wooden-headed clubs are generally called woods; all others are irons. Also, a club is an organization of golfers.

CLUB HEAD: The hitting end of the club. Strangely, the head has these parts: sole, heel, toe or nose, neck, and face.

COURSE: The area where golf is played, usually 9 or 18 holes. There were more than eleven thousand courses in the United States at the start of 1976.

CUP: A round hole in the green, 4¼ inches in diameter and about 10 inches deep. The cup itself is made of metal or plastic and serves as a liner inside of the hole.

CUT SHOT: This shot requires skill and strength, as the player must bring the club into and across the ball to impart forward motion with a sideward spin. The spin causes the ball to land softly with virtually no forward movement.

DIMPLES: The indents on the surface of the ball. Dimples give the ball stability as it rides through the air. If you want to appear "in," you can stump many golfers by asking them to guess the number of dimples in a golf ball. The answer: 360.

DIVOT: A hunk of grass and dirt cut out of the ground during a swing. Considerate golfers find their divots and place them back. Pressed down lightly with foot, most divots will grow in again.

DOGLEG: A fairway that bends right or left rather sharply. To cut the dogleg is to take the shortest route and avoid going around the turn. Generally, however, a tree or pond stands in the elbow of the bend discouraging all but the strong-backed golfers.

DOUBLE BOGEY: A score of two over par for a hole.

DOUBLE EAGLE: A score of two on a par-five hole, or three under par. Golf's most famous double eagle was scored by Gene Sarazen in the last round of the 1935 Masters on the 520-yard 15th hole. After a strong drive Sarazen hit a number-4 wood some 230 yards into the hole. It enabled him to tie Craig Wood for the lead. Sarazen won the next day's play-off.

DOWN: The number of holes (in match play) or number of strokes (in stroke play) a player is behind his rival.

DRAW: A control shot hit so the ball drifts leftward during its flight. Useful for bending shot around trees. Also, draw is term for pairings or sequence in which golfers play.

DRIVE: A ball hit from the teeing area. Also known as tee ball.

DRIVER: The heaviest club in the set. Also called the number-1 wood. Used to get maximum distance. Better players will sometimes use the driver to hit off the fairway for second shots on long holes.

DUB: A poorly executed shot. Golfers have used other terms to describe poor shots, but they could never be seen in print.

DUCK HOOK: Any shot that almost immediately curves hard left at a discouragingly rapid rate.

DUFFER: A common name for a golfer who is not a skilled player. Also called hacker.

EAGLE: Two strokes under par on a hole—e.g., a score of two on a par four or three on a par five.

EXPLOSION: *See* Blast.

FACE: The surface of the club head that hits the ball. Also, the wall of a bunker.

FADE: When the ball drifts toward the right at the end of its flight. Opposite of draw. Jack Nicklaus and Bert Yancey normally hit fades, while most other pros hit a draw.

FAIRWAY: The area between the tee and the putting green. The grass is cut, ½″ to ⅝″, so that the ball sits on top of the turf and is therefore easier to hit.

FAN: To miss the ball completely. Sometimes called a whiff. To miss the ball is embarrassing enough, but under the rules a fan counts as a stroke.

FAT: To hit ground slightly behind the ball before hitting the ball. Usually results in the ball traveling a shorter distance than expected and golfer losing control of the ball.

FIELD: All players in a tournament.

FLAGSTICK: A slim steel or aluminum pole placed in the hole on the green to show its location. The flag at the top bears the number of the hole. Also known as pin or flag.

FLANGE: A protrusion on the bottom of the club head, extending from the sole.

FLAT SWING: When a golfer's swing is relatively horizontal. Lee Trevino, winner of the U.S. and British Opens, has a flat swing.

FLIER: Ball hit out of high, rough, or wet grass. It usually sails without backspin and often goes farther than expected.

FOLLOW-THROUGH: The portion of the swing after the ball has been hit. Johnny Miller, one of the best players of the 1970s, has excellent follow-through.

"FORE": A cry of warning that a ball is headed for a human target. If you hear "fore," cover your head with your arms and crouch down. Also used as "Fore, Please" at tournaments as a request for quiet.

FORESWING: The portion of swing that begins when the hands start their descent, bringing the club into the ball.

FOUR-BALL: A match in which two players count their better ball against the better ball of a rival two-man team.

FOURSOME: A match in which two players hit one ball in a match against two other players. This form of play is often used in international team matches. Also, popularly used to mean any four people golfing together.

FRIED EGG: A ball buried in a bunker. The ball protrudes slightly above the sand like an egg yoke. The fried-egg image is enchanced by the ring of sand around the ball.

FRINGE: *See* Apron.

FROG'S HAIR: Long grass allowed to grow at the edge of a bunker or water hazard.

FRONT SIDE: The first 9 holes of an 18-hole course.

GIMMIE: A putt so short, perhaps up to 18 inches, that it can be holed without effort and is conceded in friendly games. Under the rules of golf, all putts must be holed out. The expression is a contraction for "Will you give it to me?" When Dwight D. Eisenhower was president, many of his golfing friends conceded putts much longer than the normal gimmie distance, apparently out of respect for his office. One day the president golfed with Ben Hogan, the steely professional champion. The first time the president had a three-foot putt, he looked to Hogan for word that it was a gimmie. But Hogan, a stickler for the rules, was intently studying the countryside.

GOLF: The best definition of the game is given in *Rules of Golf*: "The game of golf consists in playing a ball from the teeing ground into the hole by successive strokes in accordance with the rules." Although several countries claim that golf was started within their borders, it is generally agreed that it is a Scottish game. Golf reached new levels of skill and popularity in the United States starting after World War II.

GRAIN: Grass grows in one direction, and this is its grain.

GRAND SLAM: Achieved by Bobby Jones, an Atlanta, Ga., attorney in 1930 when he won, in order, the British Amateur, U.S. Open, British Open, and U.S. Amateur. The Pro Grand Slam is considered to be the Masters, U.S. Open, PGA championship, and British Open. Ben Hogan, in 1953, came closest to turning in this record by winning the Masters, U.S. Open, and British Open. The ladies have their version of the Grand Slam too. In 1961 Mickey Wright won the Titleholders, the Open, and the LPGA Championship—a Grand Slam.

GREEN: The putting surface of each hole on the course.

GRIP: The end of the club shaft, which is covered with leather or some other material by which club is held. Also refers to the grasp a player makes on the club.

Ben Hogan (left) wouldn't concede a gimmie to Ike
Eisenhower, President of the United States.

GROUND UNDER REPAIR: That portion of the course not in normal condition. It is usually marked, and a player may remove his ball from designated area.

HACKER: *See* Duffer.

HALFSWING: A shortened backswing, used because the player feels it is not necessary to make a full swing to generate power for a full hit.

HALVED: Match-play expression. Used when each side has played a hole in the same number of strokes. Also, when a match has ended in a tie after 18 holes.

HANDICAP: The number of strokes given to the less skilled player so his score may be adjusted to the level of par. Handicap is determined by using a complicated formula. Professionals do not have handicaps.

HAZARD: Any bunker, pond, river, or ditch designed to make life interesting and miserable for the golfer on his way to a hole.

HEEL: The part of the head nearest the shaft.

HOLE: Same as cup. Also used to describe each of the units on an 18-hole course.

HOLE-HIGH: When a ball is hit to the green and it stops on an imaginary line with the hole off to either side.

HOLE-IN-ONE: A ball hit into the hole with one stroke on a particular hole. Same as ace.

HOLE OUT: To complete play on a hole by getting the ball into the cup.

HONOR: The right to hit first from the tee. To start, it is determined by the pairing or by a toss of a coin. Thereafter, the honor is given to the man with the lowest score on the last hole.

HOOK: A ball that curves to the left. Opposite of slice.

IN or **IN NINE:** The second nine holes of a course. The first nine holes are often called the out nine.

INSERT: The small portion of a wooden club head's face. It is the area that comes into contact with the ball.

IRON: Generally, any club with a metal head. Long irons are numbers 1, 2, and 3. Middle or medium irons are numbers 4, 5, and 6. Short irons are numbers 7, 8, and 9. As the club number increases, so does the angle of loft on the club face.

LIE: The position of the ball as it rests on any part of the course. Also, the angle between ground and shaft when the club is rested on ground in its usual position. Tall players require clubs with shafts more vertical than those for shorter players. Hence, there are clubs with an upright lie and those with a flat lie.

LINE: The direction in which the player plans the ball to follow after it is hit. Same as line of flight or line of putt.

LINKS: A term that goes back to Scotland and the early days of the game. Only tees, fairways, and greens were grass and appeared to be links of green against a background of sand and varied colored underbrush.

LIP: The edge or rim of the hole.

LOFT: The elevation of the ball in flight. Also, the angle at which the club face is set back from the vertical. A driver has an almost vertical face, with little loft; a sand wedge is laid back to face and is almost horizontal.

LPGA: The Ladies' Professional Golf Association. It conducts the women's golf tour.

MARKER: Objects on teeing grounds that set the forward limit from which to drive. Often they are made to resemble golf balls. Also, a person who records a player's score for tournament purposes.

MARSHAL: The person who controls spectator traffic at a tournament.

MATCH PLAY: A form of competition where each hole is considered separately (in contrast to cumulative total of strokes) with the side making the lowest score winning the hole. The side that wins the greatest number of holes wins the match. A match ends when a player is more holes ahead or "up" than there are holes left to play. Example: A player may win by 3 and 2, which means he had won three more holes than his opponent, and since only two holes were left to play, there was no chance he could lose.

MEDALIST: The player with the lowest score in a tournament qualifying round. This player usually receives a medal, hence the name.

MEDAL PLAY: A term that should not be used but often is as another expression for stroke play.

MONEY WINNINGS: In pro tours, the amount of money won up to a certain point, or for a calendar year, or for a career.

MULLIGAN: A second chance at the start of a round. Not permitted by *Rules of Golf*, but most amateurs will grant each other a Mulligan. If a golfer's first drive is wild, he may "take a Mulligan." The first stroke is not counted, and he hits another ball. The second one always counts. The origin of the term is unknown but probably stems from a wild-hitting Irishman. Some clubs have their own terms instead of Mulligan. A few predominately Jewish clubs have jokingly changed it to Shapiro.

NASSAU: Competition in which a point is alloted for scoring on the first nine holes, the second nine, and the over-all round.

NECK: Where the shaft joins the head of the club. Same as socket.

NET: The net score, after one's handicap is deducted.

NOSE: *See* Toe.

Bobby Jones drives in the British Open in 1930, one of the four titles that made his grand slam.

Mickey Wright won a grand slam too—the Titleholders, Open and LPGA.

OPEN: A tournament open to both amateurs and professionals.

OPEN STANCE: When the left foot is positioned farther back than normal and turns golfer's shoulders more toward his target. Usually results in ball going to the right.

OUT or **OUT NINE:** The first nine holes of a course.

OUT OF BOUNDS: The area outside the playing course. A ball hit out of bounds costs two penalty strokes.

PAIRINGS: The schedule of tee-off times for all players in the field.

PAR: The number of strokes a good player should take to hole out his ball on each hole. Par includes two putting strokes on every green.

PAR FIVE: A hole measuring 471 yards or more, with the green reachable in three shots. There are a few par-six holes in the U.S., but these are considered as freaks.

PAR FOUR: A hole measuring from 251 to 470 yards. Par allows for two shots to reach green.

PAR THREE: A hole with a green reachable in one shot; 250 yards is the arbitrary limit of distance.

PENALTY: The stroke or strokes added to score for any rules violation.

PGA: Professional Golfers' Association of America, the organization of male pros, with headquarters in Palm Beach Gardens, Fla. PGA also includes a Tournament Players Division, which comprises those players on national tour. There are some eight thousand PGA members.

PIN: *See* Flagstick.

PITCH: A short shot onto the green. Some pitches are highly lofted shots planned to drop the ball on target with little roll. Pitch-and-run shots are those where the ball is flipped to the green and allowed to roll toward the pin.

PITCHING WEDGE: A specially designed club with a heavy flange, used for pitching the ball.

PLUGGED LIE: Occurs in sand or rain-soaked ground. The ball buries itself on impact.

PRO: A professional, one who earns money through golf.

PRO SIDE: The high side of the cup when hole is cut into sloping green. A ball putted to this side of the cup will often drop in as it stops on the lip.

PROVISIONAL BALL: When a ball is placed in play after an original ball is believed to have been lost or is hit out of bounds.

PULL: A ball that goes left of target with little or no curve.

PUNCH: A shot kept low to keep the ball out of the wind, or to keep it below tree branches.

PUSH: A ball that goes right of target with little curve.

PUTT: A stroke on the green. Some players will putt from off the green.

PUTTER: A club made especially for putting. Often this is a player's favorite club. Bobby Jones's putter was affectionately called Calamity Jane. Many golfers get angry with their putters when their games go sour. Many years ago a pro used to punish his putter after bad rounds either by shoving it in a creek or pond and screaming "Go ahead...drown!" Or when he was driving away from the course, he'd open the car door and drag his putter on the road.

QUAIL HIGH: A shot that flies low to the ground, as a quail flies. Lee Trevino is a quail-high hitter.

RAINMAKER: A ball hit so high that players joke that it will go through the clouds and make rain. Jack Nicklaus hits rainmakers regularly.

R AND A: Royal and Ancient Golf Club of St. Andrews, Scotland. The R and A is to the rest of the world what the USGA is to the United States.

RECOVERY SHOT: *See* Trouble Shot.

ROUGH: A place where no golfer wants to land. Technically, grass not mowed to fairway height, which is ½" to ⅝". There are actually two areas of rough—the rough adjoining fairway grass that has been cut to two inches in length; the rough approximately 10 feet from fairway that is allowed to grow five to eight inches in length.

RUN: The distance the ball rolls on the ground after its flight has ended. A run-up shot is one deliberately hit to run for a distance greater than its flight.

SAND TRAP: *See* Bunker.

SAND WEDGE: A club with a heavy flange, especially designed to slide through sand under the ball and help pop it out of the bunker. Developed in the 1930s, the sand wedge has been credited with helping to lower scores. Bobby Jones played before the development of the sand wedge and used a 9 iron to get out of most bunkers.

SCRATCH: An amateur who plays at par and receives no handicap.

SHAFT: The longest part of the club.

SIDE: Members of a team. Also, the front or back part of the course.

SKULL: An error in hitting a chip or pitch; when the club hits only the top, or skull, of the ball. The cover of the ball is usually cut.

SKY: A hit under a ball that sends it sky high with little forward advance. Like a pop fly in baseball.

SLICE: A shot that curves to the right instead of going straight. Opposite of hook.

SMILIE: When a ball is hit incorrectly, the edge of the club often cuts the cover of the ball. Since the ball is round, the cut curls like a smile.

SNAKE: A long putt that twists over several contours and goes into the hole.

SNAKE KILLER: A badly hit shot that bounces over the ground.

SOCKET: The opening in the neck into which the shaft is fitted.

SOLE: The bottom of a wooden club head. The sole plate is metal. Also, the act of placing the club on the ground behind the ball at address is known as soling the club.

SQUARE STANCE: When both feet touch an imaginary line that is parallel to the intended line of flight.

STONY: To hit a ball within gimmie distance of the flagstick.

STROKE: The motion of a club made with intent to hit the ball.

STROKE PLAY: When every stroke taken by a player is recorded hole by hole. The player with the lowest number of strokes at the conclusion of the round or tournament is the winner.

STYMIE: The player's position when a tree or some other object stands between his ball and his target.

SWING: A player's stroke.

TEE: The peglike device on which the ball rests for driving. Also, the area from which a ball is hit first on each hole.

TEE BALL: *See* Drive.

TEXAS WEDGE: Texans were first to exploit the use of the putter when hitting from off the green. Flat ground between the ball and the pin is a must for this shot.

TOE: The part of club head farthest from the shaft. Same as nose.

TOP: To hit only the upper half of the ball.

TOUR: The national PGA tour.

TOURNAMENT: Any form of golf competition.

TROUBLE SHOT: Any shot necessary to get a player out of the rough, etc. Also known as recovery shot. Arnold Palmer is one of the game's most spectacular recovery players.

UNPLAYABLE LIE: A ball that comes to rest in a position from which it is not possible to make a recovery shot, as between rocks or in the branches of a bush. The player takes a penalty stroke and removes the ball.

UP: The number of holes (in match play) a player is ahead of his rival.

UPRIGHT SWING: When the club head is taken back and almost vertically upward. Al Geiberger, 1966 PGA champion, has a fine upright swing.

USGA: United States Golf Association, an organization of private and public golf clubs in this country. Also serves as overseer of rules.

WATER HOLE: Any hole on which water is a factor—a creek, pond, or lake. Some timid golfers use "water balls" here. These are old, scuffed balls, or maybe smilies, that would not be missed if they splashed out of sight.

WEDGE: A club with a heavy flange.

WHIFF: *See* Fan.

WOOD: Any club with a wooden head.

WORLD GOLF HALL OF FAME: Located in Pinehurst, N.C., the Hall of Fame opened to the public in September, 1974. It contains exhibits of golf history in addition to plaques honoring the greats of the sport. Chosen by the nation's golf writers, members include Tommy Armour, Patty Berg, Walter Hagen, Bobby Jones, Byron Nelson, Jack Nicklaus, Francis Ouimet, Arnold Palmer, Gary Player, Gene Sarazen, Sam Snead, Harry Vardon, Mickey Wright, and Babe Didrikson Zaharias.

YIPS: A psychophysical malady that afflicts golfers. A form of nervousness on the greens. It causes players to miss makable putts. Extreme cases have been known to hit themselves on the head with their putters after missing an easy one. Ben Hogan suffered through the yips and once described his feeling: "I think I lose a pint of blood every time I try to putt."

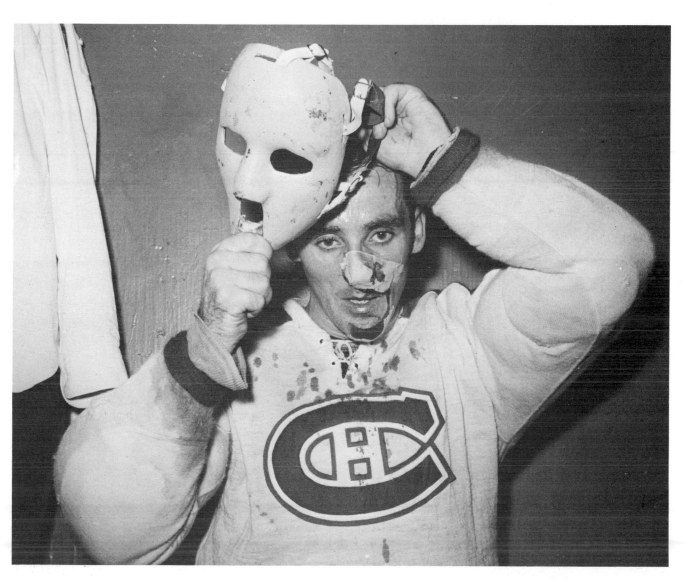

Bloodied but unbowed, Montreal's Jacques Plante donned a mask in 1959 during game against New York Rangers, and popularized use of protective device.

AHL: The American Hockey League, which was founded in 1936 when the old International League merged with the Canadian-American League. It is considered pro hockey's top minor league, being equal to a Triple-A league in baseball. It has undergone many changes in recent years due to big-league expansion; four former AHL cities—Philadelphia, Washington, St. Louis, and Buffalo—now have teams in the NHL. The AHL launched its 1975-76 season with eight teams—Nova Scotia, Rochester (N.Y.), Providence (R.I.), and Springfield (Mass.) in the Northern Division; and Richmond (Va.), Hershey (Pa.), Baltimore (Md.), and New Haven (Conn.) in the Southern Division.

ALL-STAR GAME: Most hockey leagues stage these drab affairs at midseason. They are drab because the players involved disdain contact for fear of being injured in a game that means nothing in the standings. Even the pay is poor. For the National Hockey League All-Star game each member of the winning team gets $500; the losers get $250 apiece. Payments to those competing in the World Hockey Association All-Star game are $300 (winners) and $200 (losers). That's chicken feed to players earning as much as $2,000 per game for regular-season combat.

The format for matching the NHL All-Stars has been revised several times since the game was introduced in 1947. It once pitted the defending Stanley Cup champion team against a collection of All-Stars from the five other teams in the league. But that was long before expansion. Now it brings together the best of the two conferences: The Wales vs. the Campbells. The WHA All-Star game is East vs. West. Members of the news media select the nucleus of the All-Star teams in both leagues.

ASSIST: The point awarded to a player or players for helping set up a goal. No more than two assists are awarded on a single goal.

ATTEMPT TO INJURE: A match penalty is imposed on any player who deliberately attempts to injure an opponent, official, coach, etc., in any manner.

AVCO WORLD TROPHY: The World Hockey Association's version of the Stanley Cup. Avco Financial Services presented the trophy to the WHA in the league's first season (1972-73). It is awarded to the league's play-off champion. The New England Whalers were its first winner; the Houston Astros claimed it the next two seasons and the Winnipeg Jets won the trophy in 1976.

BACKCHECKING: An attempt by players returning to their defensive zone to harass and regain the puck from the opposition.

BACKHAND SHOT: When a right-handed player shoots from his left side (or vice versa), using the back of his stick's blade.

BANANA BLADE: *See* Curved Stick.

BARREL: The net. "It was my turn to go in the barrel." The term was popularized by former goaltender Lorne ("Gump") Worsley.

Perennial performers in the National Hockey League All-Star game, Bobby Hull (left) of the Chicago Black Hawks and Gordie Howe of the Detroit Red Wings ended their careers in the World Hockey Association.

BOARDING: Causing an opponent to be thrown violently into the boards by means of a body check, charging, elbowing, or tripping.

BODY CHECK: Using the body to slow down or halt an opposing puck carrier.

BOX DEFENSE: This is employed by a team playing shorthanded (minus a penalized player). The remaining four skaters on the defensive team form a box in front of their netminder (two up front, two in the rear).

BREAKAWAY: One of hockey's most exciting plays, the breakaway occurs when a puck carrier breaks into the open with no opposing player to stop him except the goaltender.

BUTT-ENDING: A foul in which a player jabs the handle of his stick into an opponent's body.

CAGE: The steel-framed goal located at either end of the rink. Also known as the net. It measures six feet long by four feet high. Attached at the rear is a nylon-mesh net.

CALDER TROPHY: Awarded annually in the NHL to the league's outstanding rookie (first-year player). The winner is selected by members of the Professional Hockey Writers' Association. It honors Frank Calder, president of the NHL from 1936 until his death in 1943, and carries a monetary award of $1,500.

CAMPBELL BOWL: Awarded annually to the team finishing with the most points in the NHL's Campbell Conference at the end of the regular season.

CENTER: Normally the playmaker on an offensive line, the center has two other forwards, called wings, as teammates on his line. His main duty on defense is to protect that area in the center of the defensive zone known as the slot.

CENTER ICE: That 60-foot-long portion of the rink that separates the offensive zone from the defensive zone. The neutral zone is separated by the center line into two 30-foot sectors. In an official-size rink, each zone measures 60 feet in length, 85 feet in width. There is an additional 10 feet of clearance behind each goal, bringing the total length of the playing surface to 200 feet.

CHARGING: An illegal maneuver in which a player takes two or more steps or strides and willfully crashes into an opponent.

CLEARING: When the puck is passed or shot away from the front of the goal or any congested area.

CORNERS: These are actually curved sections of the boards in the corners of the rink.

CREASE: The area in front of the goal marked off by a thin red line. It measures eight feet by four feet and is considered the goaltender's private preserve. A goal scored by an unimpeded player from the crease is disallowed.

CROSS-CHECKING: An illegal check delivered with both hands on the stick and no part of the stick on the ice.

CURVED STICK: Also known as a banana blade. Curved sticks were popularized by Stan Mikita and Bobby Hull of the Chicago Black Hawks in the early 1960s. They originally took regular sticks and achieved a suitable curve in the blade by bending them under the doors of hotel rooms and leaving them there overnight. The maximum curvature allowed under pro rules was reduced from one inch to one-half inch in 1970. The change was instituted at the insistence of goaltenders, who claimed the extremely curved sticks caused the puck to "dance" like a knuckleball in baseball.

DEFENSEMAN: This player is just what his name implies—a defender. Most NHL teams carry five defensemen; some carry six. They work in tandem, one defending the left side of the defensive zone, the other defending the right side. They are generally bigger men than the forwards, and they like to throw their weight around.

DEFLECTION: When a defending player uses his body or his equipment (stick, pads, skates) to block a shot. When a deflected shot flies into the crowd, some fans attempt to catch the puck with their bare hands—an extremely foolish practice. It is wiser to pay $1.50 for a puck at the souvenir stand than to risk permanent injury caused by a deflected shot.

DEKE: Short for decoy. If an attacker pretends to shoot one way, hesitates, and then shoots another way, he has used a deke or has deked his opponent.

DRAW: Should not be confused with a tie game. The draw takes place during a face-off between opposing players. The player who succeeds in directing the puck to a teammate wins the draw.

ELBOWING: A minor penalty is imposed on any player who uses an elbow to foul an opponent.

FACE-OFF: To resume play, the puck is dropped by a linesman between two opposing players, normally centers, who face each other. They attempt to gain control of the dropped puck with their stick or to direct it to a teammate.

FLIP PASS: To hoist the puck off the ice while passing to a teammate. This is a legal pass.

FORECHECKING: Checking or harassing opponents in their own defensive zone while trying to regain control of the puck; an important part of any game. The Montreal Canadiens have always been blessed with great forecheckers—fast, strong skaters in the tradition of Jean Beliveau and Henri Richard. The Philadelphia

Flyers, led by Bobby Clarke, are loaded with excellent forecheckers.

FOREHAND: A shot delivered from the front end of the stick's blade and from the player's natural shooting position.

FORWARD(S): The three principal attackers—the center and two wings, or wingmen. They work together on a line, and under normal circumstances they enter and leave a game together. Each NHL team employs at least three forward lines working in shifts. They are shuttled in and out of the game at any time and without the benefit of a time-out.

FREEZING THE PUCK: All pucks are frozen before a game to remove some of their resiliency. This is legal. However, when opposing players succeed in pinning the puck against the boards with their sticks or skates so as to halt the action, this is called freezing the puck and a face-off ensues.

GAME MISCONDUCT: This penalty involves the suspension of a player for the balance of the game, but a substitute is permitted to replace him immediately. Automatic fine: $50.

GOAL: A goal is credited to a player who succeeds in propelling the puck into the opponents' net. If the puck is inadvertently put into the net by a member of the defending team, the player on the attacking side who last played the puck is credited with a goal. Phil Esposito ranks as the most consistent goal scorer of modern times. He scored a record 67 goals in 78 games in the 1970-71 season and averaged 62.5 goals a season for the next four years.

GOALIE: *See* Goaltender.

GOAL JUDGE: One goal judge is stationed behind each net to rule on goals scored. If a puck enters the net legally, the goal judge flashes a red light. He can be overruled by the referee. Goal judges are hired by the home team and generally are unpaid. Most NHL clubs reward them with two free tickets to each game they work, plus meal money in some instances.

GOAL LINE: It is a red line, two inches wide, that is painted on the ice between the goalposts and extends across the width of the rink.

GOALTENDER or **GOALIE:** The most valued member of any hockey team. It is his job to block, glove, kick, or bat away all shots aimed at his net. He must also be a man of great courage, for he is called upon to handle up to 50 shots a game, many of which are fired at him at speeds ranging up to 120 miles per hour. Also known as netminder.

HALL OF FAME: Located in the Canadian National Exhibition Park on the shore of Lake Ontario in Toronto, the Hockey Hall of Fame building was opened on August 26, 1961. It was constructed with funds provided by NHL teams. The hockey exhibits on view in the building are provided and financed by the NHL and the Canadian Amateur Hockey Association. Those players and officials voted into the Hall of Fame normally have retired five years prior to their election, but in exceptional cases this period of retirement may be shortened by the election committee. Example: Gordie Howe became a member in 1972, the year after he retired from the Detroit Red Wings, and then became the Hall's only active player by joining Houston of the WHA.

HART TROPHY: Awarded annually to the NHL player adjudged to be most valuable to his team. The winner selected by the Professional Hockey Writers' Association receives a $1,500 cash award. The trophy honors the memory of Cecil Hart, former general manager-coach of the Montreal Canadiens.

HAT TRICK: A player who scores three goals in one game is said to have fashioned a hat trick. In hockey's infancy, a hat would be passed among the fans to collect money for a three-goal scorer. In later years, fans greeted such a performance by flinging their hats onto the ice. The expression hat trick may have derived from cricket. As a reward for taking three wickets with three successive balls, the bowler received a new hat from his team.

HEADMANING: This term has nothing to do with bossing or heading a team. It is used to describe a forward pass in hockey. When a player relays the puck to a teammate skating ahead of him it is called headmaning the puck.

HIGH-STICKING: A player is not permitted to raise his stick above his shoulders. A face-off is called if the stick is carried in this manner, or a penalty is imposed if the stick is used in this manner to check an opponent.

HOCKEY: The sport of ice hockey was born in Canada in the 1870s. It was played first by youngsters on frozen ponds who borrowed some of the rules of field hockey and adapted that sport to the ice.

The derivation of the word "hockey" remains cloudy to this day. The Mohawk Indians always claimed it came from the Indian word *ho-ghee*, meaning "it hurts." The French insist it is derived from *hoquet*, a crooked stick once used by shepherds.

One of the first recorded ice-hockey games with rules was played in 1879 when two teams of students from McGill University in Montreal took to the ice, 30 on a side. The resulting mob of 60 youngsters swirling about the ice with sticks in their hands created mayhem and chaos; the McGill students eventually rewrote the rules so that only 18 players were permitted on the ice at a given time—9 to a side.

By the time the first league of amateur players was

formed in Montreal in 1885, the game became a seven-man sport. It now was vying with lacrosse as Canada's national game. And below the Canadian border, in the state of Michigan, hockey had become popular in factory towns by the turn of the century.

Oddly, hockey's first professional team was introduced in the United States, not in Canada. A dentist named J. L. Gibson gathered together a collection of Canadian imports in 1903, brought them to Houghton, Mich., a copper town in the state's Upper Peninsula, and named the team Portage Lakes.

The following year the International Pro Hockey League was organized. Teams in this league began playing six-man hockey, principally as a money-saving device, and it remains a six-man game to this day.

Canada established its first professional league in 1908 when the Ontario Professional Hockey League was formed. Two years later, the National Hockey Association began play. The four-team NHA drafted a new charter and changed its name to the National Hockey League in 1917 when the sport finally became "big league." The NHL, free of competition for more than a half century, finally was confronted with a rival when the World Hockey Association was founded in 1971 and launched player raids on the NHL.

HOLDING: When players use their hands to hold an opponent or his stick. Another minor infraction; the penalty: two minutes in the penalty box.

HOOKING: When a player uses the blade of his stick to halt an opponent. A minor penalty.

ICING THE PUCK: To deliberately shoot the puck from behind the center red line across the opponents' goal line. This is illegal and calls for a face-off in the defending zone of the guilty team. An exception: Players are permitted to ice the puck when their team has a man in the penalty box.

INTERFERENCE: When a player impedes the progress of an opponent who is not in possession of the puck. A two-minute penalty is imposed for this infraction.

LADY BYNG TROPHY: Awarded annually by the NHL to the player exhibiting "the best type of sportsmanship and gentlemanly conduct combined with a high standard of playing ability." The original trophy was donated in 1925 by Lady Byng, wife of Canada's governor-general at the time. After Frank Boucher of the New York Rangers won the award seven times in eight seasons, he was given permanent possession of the trophy, and Lady Byng donated another trophy in 1936.

MAJOR PENALTY: A five-minute penalty for such infractions as fighting, drawing blood, etc., and at the referee's discretion, can also be imposed for such infractions as charging, boarding, cross-checking, high-sticking, etc. No substitute is permitted for a player serving a major penalty, and he must complete the entire sentence regardless of how many goals the opposing team scores during his absence.

MASK: The mask is considered the goaltender's most important piece of equipment. Clinton Benedict of the old Montreal Maroons was the first to wear one, in the 1929-30 season. Jacques Plante popularized its use while playing for the Montreal Canadiens in the 1960s. Only a handful of goalies have declined to wear the mask. Lorne ("Gump") Worsley used to say, "My face is my mask," but he finally surrendered and wore one briefly before retirement in 1974.

MASTERTON TROPHY: Awarded annually to the NHL player "who best exemplifies the qualities of perseverance, sportsmanship and dedication to hockey." It was donated by the Professional Hockey Writers' Association in 1968 to commemorate the late Bill Masterton of the Minnesota North Stars, who died on January 15, 1968, of injuries sustained in a game against the Oakland Seals.

MATCH PENALTY: A match penalty involves the suspension of a player for the balance of the game and an automatic fine of $200. A substitute player is permitted to replace the penalized player after ten minutes playing time has elapsed.

MINOR PENALTY: A two-minute penalty for lesser infractions, it automatically terminates if the opposing team scores a goal while the penalized player is in the penalty box.

MISCONDUCT PENALTY: Involves removal from the game for a period of ten minutes and an automatic fine of $50. A substitute is permitted to replace a player serving a misconduct penalty.

NETMINDER: *See* Goaltender.

NEUTRAL ZONE: The center portion of the rink bounded by the blue lines that separate the offensive zone from the defensive zone. Also known as center ice.

NHL: The National Hockey League, which was organized in 1917 with four teams that played a 22-game schedule. The pioneer teams were the Montreal Wanderers, the Montreal Canadiens, the Toronto Arenas, and the Ottawa Senators. Toronto was the only team that played its games on artificial ice.

The Boston Bruins became the first United States team to join the NHL, gaining membership in 1924. Two years later, three other U.S. teams were awarded franchises the New York Rangers, the Chicago Black Hawks, and the Detroit Cougars (now the Red Wings).

During the late 1920s and through the 1930s, the league membership fluctuated between eight and ten teams. Other U.S. cities represented by NHL teams

Maurice ("Rocket") Richard of the Montreal Canadiens came by his nickname through his explosive play.

during this period included Pittsburgh, Philadelphia, and St. Louis. New York had two teams (the Rangers and the Americans), and Montreal was represented by the Canadiens and the Maroons.

From 1942 until 1967 the NHL operated as a six-team league. Those teams—the Canadiens, Maple Leafs, Bruins, Rangers, Black Hawks, and Red Wings—formed the Eastern Division when the NHL doubled its membership in 1967.

The six expansion teams that formed the Western Division were the St. Louis Blues, the Philadelphia Flyers, the Pittsburgh Penguins, the Minnesota North Stars, the Los Angeles Kings, and the Oakland (later California) Seals. When Buffalo and Vancouver were awarded expansion franchises in 1970, they were placed in the Eastern Division, and the Black Hawks shifted to the Western Division.

The NHL continued to expand into virgin territory—awarding franchises to Atlanta and Long Island in 1972 and to Kansas City and Washington, D.C., in 1974. By this time the league had 18 teams, each of whom played 80 games. They were split into four divisions operating in two conferences. Twelve of the 18 teams qualified for the Stanley Cup play-offs, which now run until late May.

NICKNAMES: Hockey players, like athletes in other sports, inherit nicknames early in their careers, and many fans soon forget their given names. How many know that Rocket Richard was christened Joseph Henri Maurice Richard?

And how about King Clancy? There are few hockey followers aware that when this Hall of Fame defenseman attended grade school he signed his examination papers Francis Michael Clancy.

Rocket Richard inherited his nickname on the strength of his explosive nature and his style of play. And it seemed quite proper that when his younger and smaller brother, Henri, joined him on the Montreal Canadiens, he would become the Pocket Rocket.

When Bernie Geoffrion was playing junior hockey, a sportswriter watched him banging pucks off the sideboards of a rink with ferocious intensity and dubbed him Boom Boom. Emile Francis became Cat because of his catlike movements as a goalie and Camille ("The Eel") Henry drove rival defensemen into a rage by slithering in and out of their grasps.

Down through the years, hockey also has had many famous forward lines. There was Boston's Kraut Line, Toronto's Kid Line, Detroit's Production Line, Chicago's Scooter Line, and, more recently, Buffalo's French Connection Line.

NORRIS TROPHY: Awarded annually to the NHL's outstanding defenseman, this prize carries a cash award of $1,500. It honors the memory of James Norris, a one-time owner of the Detroit Red Wings and father of Jim Norris, who owned the Chicago Black Hawks until his death in 1966. Should be renamed Orr Trophy. Bobby Orr won it for the eighth straight year in 1975. Orr's streak was snapped in 1976 by Dennis Potvin of the New York Islanders, but Orr had an excuse. He missed all but ten games during the 1975-76 season because of knee surgery.

OFFSIDE: There are many variations of an offside play in hockey. The principal rule to remember is that no player of an attacking team is permitted to precede the puck into the attacking zone. Upon violation of this rule, play is stopped and the puck is faced-off in the neutral zone.

PENALTY KILLERS: Specialists who are used to harass the opposition and prevent a goal while one of their teammates is serving a penalty. The forwards employed on this specialty team normally are swift skaters and tireless forecheckers; the defensemen also must be quick, alert, and tireless backcheckers.

PENALTY SHOT: On certain infractions, specifically when a player in control of the puck in the attacking zone has no opponent in front of him other than the goaltender and is fouled from behind, a penalty shot is awarded to the fouled player. It sets up the most exciting play in hockey. The fouled player takes the ice alone, is given the puck at mid-ice, and skates in for one free shot at the rival goalkeeper.

POINTS: In determining the team standings in professional hockey leagues, two points are awarded for a victory, one point for a tie. Points also mean those two positions just inside the opposition blue line and close to the sideboards. The attacking defensemen normally take these point positions when their team is in control of the puck in the opposition's zone.

POKE CHECK: To dislodge the puck from the puck carrier by stabbing at it with the blade of the stick. It's legal.

POWER PLAY: Another exciting part of the game, the power play is employed when a team has a manpower advantage. Normally, the attacking team will employ four forwards and one defenseman during a power play, using the extra forward as a pointman.

PRINCE OF WALES TROPHY: Awarded annually to the team with the most points in the NHL's Prince of Wales Conference at the end of the regular season. Accompanying the trophy is a monetary award totaling $52,500, based on 21 units of $2,500 each. The Montreal Canadiens have won this trophy, donated in 1924 by the Prince of Wales, a record 19 times.

PUCK: What one hits with the stick. The puck used in hockey games is made of vulcanized rubber. It is one

The Norris Trophy for the NHL's outstanding defenseman was a cinch for a healthy Bobby Orr of the Boston Bruins.

inch thick, three inches in diameter, and weighs between five and one-half and six ounces.

PUCK SENSE: What a player has who possesses excellent anticipation.

PULL THE GOALIE: If a team is behind in the waning moments of the game, the coach will often replace the goaltender with an extra skater, leaving the net of the trailing team vacant. Such a maneuver, although risky, provides an exciting finish.

RAGGING THE PUCK: Keeping the puck in constant motion and away from pressing rivals. It is similar to dribbling in basketball.

REEFING: Illegal use of a stick on an opponent. It is a modified form of spearing and/or slashing.

RINK: Hockey's playing surface. An official rink is 200 feet long and 85 feet wide. It is surrounded by a wooden wall known as the boards, which extend no less than 40 inches and no more than 48 inches above the level of the ice surface.

RINK RAT: A person, normally young, who spends most of his waking hours at a rink, loafing or doing odd jobs.

RIVER HOCKEY: *See* Shinny.

ROSS TROPHY: Awarded annually to the player who leads the NHL in scoring at the end of the regular season. It honors Arthur H. Ross, former general manager-coach of the Boston Bruins.

RUSH: When a team launches an attack up ice.

SAVE: What a goaltender is credited with when he prevents a shot from entering the net.

SHIFT: The period of time spent by a player on the ice at a given time. If he makes five appearances during a period, he is said to have taken five shifts.

SHINNY: A game of shinny is similar to a pick-up game, or informal game, in baseball. Its derivation is unknown, but it came into being during the early days of hockey when youngsters would gather on frozen ponds or lakes or rivers and choose sides.

SHOTS: The shots on goal are reported at the end of each of the three periods of play and totaled at the end of the game.

SLAP SHOT: A forehand shot taken by a player who first winds up by bringing the stick far back and then swings quickly forward, slapping at the puck with the front blade of the stick. Old-timers frown on such a shot because of the time needed for the windup, but it is used by all the great scorers of today. Bobby Hull has been the most feared practitioner of this shot in recent years.

SLASHING: A minor penalty is imposed on any player who seeks to impede the progress of an opponent by slashing with his stick.

SLOT: The slot is the center area in the attacking zone extending from the goalmouth to approximately 35 feet

out. It is the duty of the defensemen to keep this "no man's land" free of traffic.

SNOW THROWER: Not an endearing term, it is used to describe a timid player who makes sudden stops on the ice to avoid body contact. The stops cause his skates to throw snow.

SOLO DASH: A player who single-handedly carries the puck from his team's defensive zone, across the neutral zone, and into the attacking zone, performs a solo dash.

SPEARING: One of hockey's most flagrant and dangerous fouls, it is produced by stabbing an opponent with the point of the stick blade. A minor or major penalty can be imposed for this infraction, and it includes an automatic $25 fine.

SPLITTING THE DEFENSE: A puck carrier who skates between two opposing defensemen is splitting the defense.

STANLEY CUP: The oldest professional sports trophy in North America. It was purchased for £10 ($48.50) in 1892 by Lord Stanley of Preston, then Canada's governor-general, and presented to the amateur hockey champions of that country. Engraving costs and alterations have increased its value in recent years to approximately $20,000. Since 1910, when the National Hockey Association (a forerunner of the National Hockey League) took possession of the Cup, it has been the symbol of professional hockey supremacy, being awarded annually to the winner of the NHL play-offs.

STICK: What makes the puck go. The stick, made of wood, must be a minimum of 55 inches in length from the heel to the end of the shaft, and not more than 12½ inches from the heel to the end of the blade. The blade of the stick may not be more than 3 inches in width at any point or less than 2 inches. All edges of the blade must be bevelled. The curvature of the blade of the stick shall be restricted so that the distance of a perpendicular line measured from a straight line drawn from any point at the heel to the end of the blade to the point of maximum curvature may not exceed ½ inch.

The blade of the goalkeeper's stick may not exceed 3½ inches in width at any point except at the heel where it may not exceed 4½ inches in width. The goalkeeper's stick may not exceed 15½ inches in length from the heel to the end of the blade. The widened portion of the goalkeeper's stick, extending up the shaft from the blade, may not extend more than 24 inches from the heel and not more than 3½ inches in width.

STICKHANDLING: The art of carrying the puck along the ice with the stick. One of the smoothest stickhandlers of all time was Bill Cowley of the Boston Bruins. Buffalo's Gil Perreault and Philadelphia's Bobby Clarke rank high among current stickhandlers.

SWEEP CHECK: To lay the stick flat on the ice and with a sweeping motion attempt to dislodge the puck from the puck carrier.

TRIANGLE: When a team is forced to play two men short, the three remaining skaters on the ice deploy in a trianglelike defense in front of their goaltender. Also known as a diamond defense.

TRIPPING: Self-explanatory. A minor penalty is imposed on any player guilty of this infraction.

VEZINA TROPHY: Awarded annually to the NHL goaltender(s) on the team with the fewest goals allowed during the regular season. It honors the memory of Georges Vezina, one of the outstanding goaltenders of all time, and carries a monetary reward of $1,500.

WHA: The World Hockey Association. Founded in 1971 as pro hockey's second major league, the WHA soon became the bane of NHL club owners but the salvation of many players, some of whom were paid enormous salaries to turn their backs on the older league. These included Gordie Howe, Bobby Hull, and Frank Mahovlich. The bidding for talent also helped escalate the salaries of NHL superstars who remained faithful to their teams.

The WHA launched its first season (1972-73) with twelve teams—New England, New York, Cleveland, Ottawa, Winnipeg, Edmonton (Alta.), Quebec, Chicago, Philadelphia, Houston, St. Paul, and Los Angeles.

Some dropped by the wayside—notably New York and Chicago. Other franchises were shifted—Philadelphia to Vancouver and later to Calgary (Alta.), Ottawa to Toronto, Los Angeles to Detroit to Baltimore and later to oblivion.

Other cities were granted franchises—Indianapolis, Cincinnati, Denver, and Phoenix—enabling the WHA to launch its fourth season (1975-76) with fourteen teams. But the attendance at most WHA games has remained disappointing, the number of reverse "jumpers" (WHA to NHL) has kept growing, and there have been club owners in both leagues who felt a merger was imminent.

WING or **WINGER:** One of the two players on the forward line playing on either side of the center. The area the wings patrol is either right or left wing.

WRIST SHOT: Propelling the puck off the blade of the stick with a flicking motion of the wrist. Gordie Howe used this shot to establish his numerous scoring records.

ZAMBONI: The trade name for the ice-cleaning machine found in most rinks. It is derived from the name of the manufacturer.

ZONE: All rinks are divided into three zones—the offensive zone, the neutral zone (center ice), and the defensive zone.

The closest an American male has come to a gold medal in alpine skiing was in 1964 when Billy Kidd took second place (silver) in the Winter Olympics at Innsbruck, Austria.

ABSTEM: The stem motion of the downhill ski used in ATM (American Teaching Method) to initiate turns; opposite of the uphill stem of the Austrian short swing and the American System of the 1960s.

ADVANCED SKIER: One who can wedel and connect carved-finish turns.

ADVANCED TURN: A turn that begins with a slide and finishes in a carve. Also called a carved-finish turn.

AERIAL: A freestyle jump; taking to the air from a jump in order to perform a specific trick or stunt while airborne.

AFD: Antifriction device. A fixed slippery plate or swiveling mechanism that allows the boot to move when forced by toe release.

AIRPLANE TURN: The act of swiveling skis in the air after a takeoff assisted by poles or a mogul; a jump taking a new direction before coming down; a deliberately extended hop turn. It's a standard hot-dog trick.

ALLAIS METHOD: A teaching method of the 1940s that flowed from the belief that sideslip and parallel form are the best means for reaching expert parallel skiing, as opposed to Arlberg, which uses stem and stem christie to progress toward parallel.

ALLAIS TECHNIQUE: The earliest parallel technique, systematized by Emile Allais from the technique spontaneously invented by the Austrian Toni Seelos.

ALPINE: High mountain country. Also, the downhill recreational and competitive sport, as opposed to nordic.

ALPINE COMBINED: The score for a combination of alpine events, which determines the FIS (Federation International de Ski) world championship, as opposed to Olympic or World Cup championships.

ALPINE PARK: An open slope with widely spaced trees or groups of trees.

ALPS: A Central European mountain chain, the most intensively developed ski terrain in the world; from the Swiss for "mountain meadow."

AMERICAN PARALLEL METHOD: The current official name for Foeger method, a direct parallel method using full hop.

AMERICAN STYLE: A style that leans toward hot-dog or freestyle skiing (freestyle was invented in the U.S.)—a loose, eclectic free way of skiing.

AMERICAN SYSTEM: The official U.S. method and technique during the 1960s. An adaptation of the Austrian short swing, it was replaced by GLM and ATM in the 1970s by PSIA.

AMERICAN TECHNIQUE: Today a meld of short swing and avalement.

ANGULATION: Bending the body over the outside ski of the turn for weight shift and edge control. It has two elements: upper-body angulation—bending down and toward the outside ski from the waist—and lower-body angulation—bending the knees toward the inside ski. Extreme angulation, or comma, was often called for in the days of leather boots and close parallel; today's wide track and plastic boots eliminate the need for all but a slight lower-body angulation and moderate upper-body angulation.

ANTICIPATION: Standard avalement turning power; a movement of the upper body down in the direction of the coming turn, twisting from the waist without blockage at the end of a preceding turn, as opposed to standard rotation that is initiated from a traverse with conscious blockage.

APRÈS-SKI: Anglicized usage of the French for "after skiing". A festive or relaxing time that includes sunning, drinking, dancing, partying, and eating.

AREA: A lift-serviced terrain not necessarily at a resort; it may or may not have base lodge and other amenities.

ARLBERG: The first effective skiing method, originated in 1907 by Hannes Schneider operating out of Hotel Post in St. Anton in Austria's Arlberg Pass. It is the first "ladder" of progressive steps by which novices could approach intermediate and expert levels. It consists of snowplow and stem turns first developed by Mathias Zdarsky, combined with Christiania or christie turns developed in Norway. Schneider invented the stem christie, a steered turn ending in a slide and a traverse. Beyond that lies the expert turn, the pure or parallel christie.

ARTIFICIAL SNOW: Real snow, but made by snow making, a process that atomizes water and freezes it into flakes. Compressed air is jetted at a steam of water, breaking it up into small drops that freeze as the air expands and cools. Some current snow-making machines dispense with the compressed air.

ATM: The American Teaching Method, which is characterized by wedge (gliding-stem) turns, as opposed to the hard-edged carving stems of Zdarsky, Arlberg, and short swing. ATM uses a short standard five-foot teaching ski. A wide-track wedge and steered foot-swivel turns are employed. It leads more directly to avalement and lateral projection than does the American system.

AUSTRIAN METHOD AND TECHNIQUE: Current in the 1950s and 1960s in American ski schools, but largely replaced by ATM and GLM in the 1970s. Developed from Arlberg by Austrian racers and elaborated by Stefan Kruckenhauser, it features reverse turning, in which mid-body muscles turn the skis against the inertia of the upper body. It is a more sophisticated application of Newton's laws of inertia and action-reaction than the rotation turning power of Arlberg. Also known as the Austrian system, Austrian reverse, modern Austrian, short swing, wedel.

AVALANCHE: A rapid descent of loose snow or slab after separating from the existing cover; its own weight overcomes the adhesion forces that previously stabilized the slope.

AVALANCHE CONTROL: Historically, the erection of avalanche barriers and the issuing of avalanche danger warnings. It can include the use of explosives to trigger a potential avalanche before skiers use the area

and the closing of runs until an avalanche danger is past (preferred by European resorts, which have relatively more avalanche-prone terrain than U.S. resorts). In the U.S. any run not marked closed is open. In Europe any trail not packed out is closed, except for guided parties.

AVALANCHE PATROL: Trained ski patrolmen and U.S. Forest Rangers, responsible for avalanche control at ski resorts.

AVALEMENT: A full-blown technique whereby the skier keeps a constant pressure on the skis for better control. Elements of the technique were developed largely by the French in racing. *Avalement* means "swallowing" in French; so named after the most obvious movement of the technique, absorbing (swallowing) moguls by a flexion (pulling up) of the legs followed by an extension as the skis pass the crest. It is currently the chosen technique for dealing with moguls, powder, and steep slopes. The sit-back unweighting motion causes skis to jet ahead. An early form of avalement was called jet turns; another precursor, the serpentine wedel, has, like the jet turn, been subsumed into the technique along with anticipation, the turning-power element. Also called compression technique.

BACK COUNTRY: Liftless mountains or rolling terrain suitable for ski touring and ski mountaineering. Also called boondocks, bush, or pukkabush.

BACK SCRATCHER: A freestyle aerial, an exaggerated tip drop in which the tails of the ski come up close to the back.

BAGGIES: Loose, long ski pants snugged around the ankles, used widely before stretch pants arrived in the 1950s.

BALLET: A freestyle event; smoothly executed figures blended into a continuous, aesthetically exciting run on smooth snow, as opposed to freestyle mogul skiing, which is done through a mogul field.

BASE: The bottom of a measured vertical of a mountain or terrain. Also that part of an area containing the base lodge and parking lot. Also, the bottom of the ski excluding edges. Also hard-packed snow lying immediately under the new snow or loose snow.

BASE BOX: *See* Base Lodge.

BASE LODGE: The building that contains heat and provides shelter and food for skiers during skiing; it has no overnight facilities.

BASHER: A fast-moving skier. The term connotes carelessness of personal safety.

BASIC TURN: In ATM and GLM, a concept replacing the "ladder" of progressive turns as a teaching concept. It consists of either a foot-swivel turn with both skis (GLM) in parallel or a steered foot swivel (ATM) in a wedge. The turn is raised to higher levels by introducing weight shift, closer parallel, and carving, rather than introducing turns with new names and attributes, as in the short swing and American system. The emphasis is on passing through quickly without drill in exact positions.

BASKET: A flat device near the tip of the pole to inhibit pole point from sinking into snow.

BATHTUB: A depression made by a skier falling backward and scooping out or compacting snow as he slides. Also called sitzmark.

BEAR TRAP: An archaic alpine toe iron, heavier than the ones used on cross-country skis. Having no release features, it holds the boot to the ski, in combination with heel cable, toe strap, or other fastening device.

BEGINNER: A skier who can make a basic turn, as opposed to a novice, who cannot. Also called bunny.

BEVELING: Rounding the ski edges for a specific purpose, as to make it easier to turn or cure hooking.

BINDING: The device for holding the boot to the ski.

BLOCKAGE: The sudden contraction of mid-body muscle to stop rotation so as to transfer rotational energy to the lower body and skis.

BLUE ICE: Terrain with a good percentage of ice; at times the term is applied to extensive boiler plate. It calls for extremely good edge control. It can be made suitable for reasonable skiing by grooming machines.

BOARDS: *See* Ski.

BOGNERS: The generic name for stretch pants, first made in the 1950s by the German firm of Bogner.

BOILER PLATE: A hard white opaque base caused by snow under compression by skis (as opposed to ice, which is caused by melting and refreezing). Known as ice in the West, where varieties of hard surface are not categorized further.

BOOGEYING: Freestyle; to go all out on a mogul run. Any all-out joyous run.

BOONDOCKS: Back country; liftless terrain far from settlements.

BOOT: The skier's footwear. Alpine boots are hard, high, and relatively stiff on the sides for easy edge control. They are made mostly of plastics and artificial leathers, as opposed to leather, which was formerly used. The much lighter cross-country variety is lower, with a flexible sole and sides. Mountaineering boots fall in between in weight and stiffness.

BOTTOM: The base; the bottom surface of the ski including edges.

BOWL: A trail with steep skiable sides or an open slope with rising sides.

BREAKABLE CRUST: This covering gives way under a skier's weight, dropping him to looser snow under crust. Also known as junk.

BULLWHEEL: The large horizontal wheel around which the cable of a lift passes in order to reverse direction.

BUNNY: A skier in the beginning stages, applied particularly to women or skiers dressed in nonfunctional clothing.

BURRING: Small sharp dents in the edge caused by striking rock ice. It increases drag unevenly and may cause the ski to hook or slide erratically. It is cured by squaring the edges.

BUSH: *See* Back Country.

BUSHWACKING: Skiing off-trail, in back country, particularly through woods or brush. Also, getting caught off-trail in a resort and having to make one's way back to open terrain.

CABLE CAR: An aerial tram carrying passengers in a large car or cars hung on cables.

CAMBER: Bottom camber is the bridgelike arch built into the ski that allows it to lie flat under the skier's weight and so track well. Side camber is the twin side curves cut into the ski as viewed from above, making the ski narrower at the waist and wider at shovel and tail.

CANADIAN SYSTEM: A method and technique, much like the American, used by the Canadian Ski Instructors Association as standard, which employs wide-track foot-swivel turns from wedge position at beginner level.

CANTING: Placing wedge-shaped slices under the boot or binding to keep the skis flat when a skier is in a normal running stance. It makes it equally easy for the skier to edge or flatten the ski for quick edge control otherwise distorted by bowleggedness or tilting boot shafts.

CANYON: A steep-sided trail. Also called a bowl.

CARVED-FINISH TURN: *See* Advanced Turn.

CARVED TURN: A turn in which the ski is bent into a bow under the skier by carving pressure and follows the arc of the bow in the snow without sliding. It makes tracks no wider than the distance between the outside edges; the skis are said to be holding. Also, the carving part of a stem christie or advanced modern turn, coming before or after a sliding segment of a combination turn.

CARVING: Cutting through the turn in the shape of the ski bend; not sliding. A pure carved turn is carved from beginning to end.

CARVING PRESSURE: The thrust needed to bend an edged ski into an arc for carved turning, provided by extension, momentum of the skier, weight shift (such as lateral projection), centrifugal force in the turn, or gravitational pull toward the bottom of the hill, acting separately or together. Pressure normally will build up as the skier carries any edged ski around to horizontal traverse.

CATWALK: A narrow connecting trail.

CHAIRLIFT: A line of cable-hung chairs carrying one or more passengers up the slope.

CHATTER: The repeated act of holding and releasing rapidly. Common on boiler plate or ice where it is easy to overedge.

CHEATER(S): Easy-turning skis.

CHECK: A momentary deceleration to a near stop; a fast uphill christie and edge set to brake speed and/or provide a stop in order to reverse the swing of the skis. It is currently avoided in favor of avalement and lateral projection.

CHRISTIE: The historic name for sliding turn. The term derives from Christiania (now Oslo), the capital of Norway, where the turn was first recognized as a technique. It was developed principally in the Telemark region, particularly by Sondre Norheim, and it became part of the Arlberg technique.

CLOSE PARALLEL: An expert form of parallel skiing in Arlberg and short swing, executed with knees and ankles locked. This form has been replaced by wide track as advantageous; except as a style it is not required for expertise in avalement.

COMBINATION TURN: A turn that uses both sliding and carving; it is usually more advantageous than pure sliding or pure carving.

COMMA POSITION: The extreme angulation used in the short-swing method for weight shift and weighting the downhill ski in a traverse. It is passé with modern boots and technique.

COMPRESSION TURN: Flexion-extension; pulling the legs up and extending them with the advantage of always maintaining some pressure on the skis and of producing satisfactory carving pressure over rough terrain and at high speed.

CONCAVE: A railed bottom, correctable by flat-filing in tuning.

CONVEX: When the edges and the sides of the base are below the level of the middle of the base; an unstable condition for the ski, correctable by flat-filing. Slight concavity is used in freestyle ballet ski for quick foot-swivel turns.

CORN or **CORN SNOW:** A loose surface snow that has large glistening grains made from a process of agglomerating smaller grains through melting and refreezing. It is principally met with on warm slopes during spring skiing; it is very easy to ski.

COUNTER ROTATION: Deliberate rotation of the upper body away from the direction of the turn in order to get greater upper body angulation. In early short swing, it was used to increase the turning power of the

reverse through Newton's law of action and reaction, but now it is only used this way in off-balance situations, having been replaced by the anticipation turn.

COVER: The total measured amount of accumulated snow at a representative spot in the terrain; the amount of snow on the ground.

CROSS-COUNTRY: Recreational and racing forms in nordic skiing. Skiing uphill and down over suitably rolling terrain less abrupt and demanding than alpine terrain. Cross-country uses skis and equipment that is lighter and less rugged than that for alpine skiing. The recreational form is known as touring, and the racing form is called cross-country racing.

CROSS-COUNTRY RACING: A series of competitions normally run in distances that are multiples of 5 kilometers up to 50 kilometers (30 miles), using gear lighter and more fragile than for touring. *See also* Marathon.

CROSSOVER: A freestyle ballet trick; picking up one ski and putting it down on the far side of the ski remaining on the snow by crossing one leg behind the other.

CRUD: Hard-to-ski snow; snow that is mushy or of irregular consistency; any off-trail snow that is not corn or powder. Also called junk, mashed potatoes, or breakable crust.

CRUST: A thin skin of snow that is harder than the snow underneath and that coheres. It may or may not hold the weight of a skier. It is formed by the melting and freezing of the upper cover.

DAFFY: An exaggerated walking-motion freestyle aerial.

DARK GLASSES: Optimally optical-grade glass or plastic dark lenses shaped much like ordinary glasses, serving to cut the glare and intensity of light. They cause less distortion of peripheral vision than goggles, but they give less protection against wind and flying snow.

DAY LODGE: A base-lodge-type facility, also known as warming hut.

DEEP POWDER: A cover of 12 inches or more of powder over loose snow or base.

DISPLACE: To foot-swivel skis into an angle in the direction of travel. This is necessary to start sliding turns, as in a stem motion in stem Christie, a heel thrust in short swing, or a foot twist in GLM.

DOUBLE CHAIR: A cable-hung seat for two side by side, the basic element of a chairlift.

DOWN: An organic insulator made of feathers for quilted parkas or warm-ups. The best quality is eiderdown, which comes from the eider duck. Down surpasses synthetic insulation, but it is more expensive.

DOWNHILL: Alpine skiing, recreational or racing. It is the fastest and riskiest of the alpine events, the skier often averaging over 50 miles an hour during a course a mile and a half long or longer.

DOWNHILL SKI or **DOWNHILL EDGE:** The ski or the edge of a single ski that is nearest the bottom of the hill.

DOWN-UNWEIGHTING: Taking pressure off the skis by a rapid crouch or by pulling up the legs. It is used for unweighting in anticipation, as opposed to up-unweighting used in short swing, Arlberg, and Allais.

EDGE: The metal or hard material bounding the bottom sides of the ski. It forms right-angle corners, enabling the skier with proper edge control to slide or to hold at will.

EDGE ANGLE: The angle made by the bottom of the ski (measured across the waist) and the underlying snow.

EDGE CONTROL: The ability to go from sliding to holding at will by tilting the ski to the required edge angle.

EDGE SET: Skis displaced and edged hard to perform a check. Also, suddenly increasing edge angle to execute carving pressure at the end of the turn; or inducing a brief spiral carve.

EDGING: Usually means enlarging the edge angle. "Edging less" is to decrease the edge angle, thus increasing the chance of sliding; "edging harder" increases the edge angle and decreases the chance for sliding.

EGG POSITION: Called *l'oeuf* in French, this is the optimal racing tuck—head down, back horizontal, wide track, elbows in. The position serves to reduce air drag.

EXPERT SKIER: A skier who can wedel, do avalement or lateral projection, ski deep powder or crud, and handle a good head of speed under the given condition.

EXPOSURE: The direction faced by a slope or terrain. Northern exposure provides longer-lasting, drier snow through colder temperatures. A southern exposure is warmer skiing, all other things being equal, but it ices up because temperatures go above freezing and fall again. Most resorts stress northern exposures.

EXTENSION: Thrusting the legs forward and to the side while straightening the body from the flexion position. It increases carving pressure on the skis in avalement.

FALL LINE: Straight down the steepest pitches on the slope or terrain; the direction taken by an imaginary free-rolling frictionless ball down a terrain or from a given point on the terrain.

FALL-LINE TURNS: Turns made without shallow traverse, normally alternating, twisting about the fall line like a snake down a stick.

FANNY PACK: A small belt bag used by ski patrol to carry first-aid equipment.

FIRST DESCENT: The first descent of a given very difficult or extremely demanding terrain, such as Mt. McKinley or the Eiger; skiing's equivalent of "first ascent" in mountaineering.

FIS: Federation International de Ski, the international governing body for ski racing, accredited by the International Olympic Committee.

FLAT-FILING: Using flat metal files or other abrasive means to plane off the bottom of the ski smoothly in order to improve its performance.

FLAT LIGHT: Light striking snow at a low angle, making contours hard to discern and increasing the risks of falling.

FLAT SKI: A ski set at minimum edge angle; opposite of overedging.

FLEX: The index of resistance of the ski to bending; stiff flex bends hard, soft flex bends easily.

FLEXION: Pulling the legs up to decrease pressure on the ski without losing contact with the snow; a form of down-unweighting. Flexion together with sitback provides the unweighting element of avalement.

FLEXION-EXTENSION: A compression turn, the double movement of avalement that is used partly to unweight (flexion) and partly to provide edge control and the additional thrust needed for producing carving pressure (extension) in flat terrain. It is also used to "swallow" irregular terrain, such as moguls.

FLEX PATTERN: The variation of flex along the ski. Modern flex pattern calls for a soft tip and a stiffer tail, enabling the ski to turn easily yet track well.

FLIP: An inverted aerial; the skier's head goes lower than his feet, as in a somersault. Another freestyle trick.

FLUSH: A series of close gates set with all poles in the fall line, thus delineating it. It must be skied with short, alternate turns. Flushes were where racers first began to develop wedel, which led to the reverse techniques that followed—short swing and avalement.

FOEGER METHOD: The American parallel method, invented by Walter Foeger in the 1950s, which used full-length skis and a hop unweighting.

FOG LENSES: Yellow or yellow-orange lenses for glasses or goggles that are used to help discern contours in flat light or fog.

FOOT-SWIVEL TURN: The essential element of the down-unweighted reverse turns, from beginner to expert, forming the core of modern method and technique. It displaces the skis to allow the sliding or combination turn to begin. Also called heel thrust (in short swing) and foot twist (in GLM).

FOREST SERVICE RANGER: Employee of the Agriculture Department in the Forest Service Division.

FORWARD PRESS: The recovery from sitback in avalement; part of the extension phase.

FORWARD SIDESLIP: The easiest mode of traveling downhill without traversing or turning; a form of sliding.

FREESTYLE: A three-event competition judged on form that includes mogul skiing, ballet, and aerials.

FRENCH METHOD: The Allais method updated by Jean Vuarnet and Georges Joubert during the 1950s and 1960s by a system that eventually, in the 1970s, yielded avalement.

FROZEN GRANULAR: A grainy, rather hard base whose surface can be handily marked by ski tracks, as opposed to boiler plate and ice. It is sometimes a euphemism for boiler plate in ski reports.

GATES: Paired poles in slalom and giant slalom. Contestants pass between all pairs.

GELANDE: American for *Geländesprung*, a terrain leap or quick jump using poles to aid takeoffs, to avoid obstacles, or for fun.

GELANDE CONTEST: A competition scored on form and distance over an artificial gelande jump. This was the forerunner of freestyle aerials.

GELANDE TURN: A jump turn or hop turn with poles. An airplane turn.

GEMÜTLICH: Pleasant atmosphere; ambience, especially during après-ski.

GESCHMOZZLE START: A group start in a race, used mostly in marathons, as opposed to going off one at a time against a stopwatch.

GETTING IT ON: A hot-dog expression for "going great" or performance beyond normal due to heightened or altered consciousness.

GIANT SLALOM: An alpine event like slalom, but with gates set farther apart and allowing greater speed.

GLADE: A slope with trees at least a good number of which are far enough apart so as to act as a natural slalom down its length.

GLIDING STEM: *See* Wedge.

GLM: The graduated-length method, invented by Clif Taylor and refined by Karl Pfeifer, which involves a series of teaching skis beginning with a three-foot length and progressing through four- and five-foot lengths. The basic turn is a foot-swivel parallel; there is a slight element of GLM in ATM in that ATM uses a short teaching ski that can later be traded for a longer ski.

GODILLE: French for wedel.

GOGGLES: Lenses with a fitting that snugs around the face to keep wind and snow from hitting the eyes. They may be fitted with a series of lenses—dark, yellow, and plain.

GONDOLA: A cable lift with enclosed cars that are loaded stationary off the cable and then clamped to the cable for going uphill.

GORILLA: The method for supplying visual distinction between technique and style in basic ATM and GLM turns; a deliberately unaesthetic, unstylish wide-track crouch with arms hanging while making foot-swivel turns.

GRANULAR: Old snow agglomerated into loose dense grains on top of base; improperly called heavy powder in some reporting.

GROOMING: Making changes in the contour and texture of the snow to improve skiing, particularly for intermediates and below. It involves breaking up crust, scoring ice patches, and packing out loose snow or deep powder; it is usually done by tractorlike over-the-snow vehicles known as cats. Also, off-season care for trail beds, such as removing obstacles and planting legumes.

GROOVE: Slot running the length of the bottom to improve tracking. Also, a hot-dog expression for "feeling great."

HARD BASE: The normal optimal condition for skiing, provided there is a shallow layer of loose or softer snow on top.

HEAD-TO-HEAD: Competition through dual slalom or dual giant slalom courses; the usual form in professional skiing competition, sometimes used by FIS or amateur racers.

HEADWALL: A steep pitch, usually 30 degrees or more. Also called *Steilhang*.

HEAVY POWDER: A misnomer for loose snow or granular; by definition powder is light.

HEEL CABLE: Formerly the most common form of binding, used in combination with a toe release or bear trap. Used now only in mountaineering or inexpensive rental skis, it has been replaced by modern step-in release bindings with heel and toe release.

HEEL RELEASE: The element of a release binding that lets go of the heel of the boot when twist forces become stronger than normal. It is usually restricted to letting the heel rise in a forward fall.

HELICOPTER: A complete 360-degree turn in the air with skis horizontal. In this aerial the skier lands in the original direction of travel.

HELICOPTER SKIING: Skiing that is serviced by whirlybird up the mountain above lift terminals or in back country, an effective but expensive way of getting to fresh powder.

HERRINGBONE: A method for climbing straight uphill; skis at a 45-degree angle to the fall line are lifted up and put down edged, one at a time, forming a characteristic track like a herring skeleton. It is faster but more tiring than sidestepping.

HILL: A mountain, slope, or terrain.

HOLDING: Skis traversing or carving, not sliding or running; skis edged and going in the direction pointed.

HOOKING: Skis swiveling unbidden into a turn, an undesirable characteristic that is curable by flat-filing and beveling the forebody edges. Also, deliberate or unconscious edging of the inside ski to start a turn, as in scissors christie. Also, a racing technique in which the shovel of the inside ski is edged and pressured to spiral the end of the turn, a precursor of the racing step turn.

HOP: Extreme up-unweighting in which the skis leave the snow. It relieves all pressure from the skis during displacement.

HOP TURN: A turn in which the skis are displaced in the air. It was used in the 1950s and 1960s as a preferential way of handling steep slopes but was replaced by avalement in the 1970s as the technique of choice; it is used today mostly in junk. *See also* Airplane Turn and Gelande Turn.

HOT DOG: A freestyle competitor, trick skier, or original noncomformist.

ICE: Snow that has melted and refrozen in clear sheet; it is differentiated from snow by its lack of texture. In the West, however, ice is synonymous with boiler plate.

ICE PATCHES: Melted and refrozen snow surrounded by greater amounts of snow.

INERTIA: Resistance to accelerated motion possessed by all solid bodies, and, likewise, resistance to deceleration, according to Newton's law of inertia. Specific applications include the reverse turn, where the lower body makes use of the inertia of the upper body as a resistance from which to begin the foot swivel.

INSIDE EDGE: The edge of a given ski that is nearest the center of a turn.

INSIDE SKI: The ski nearest the center of a turn.

INSTRUCTOR: A ski teacher with training in method, hopefully.

INTERMEDIATE SKIER: A skier who can make a stem christie on full-length skis or a parallel turn on five-foot teaching skis.

J-BAR: A cable-hung series of vertical arms that end in a **J** shape at the lower end, allowing skiers to lean back and be towed uphill.

JEANS: Ski jeans, used extensively for skiing because of low cost and durability, especially under warm-up pants.

JET TURN: A down-unweighted turn in which the down-unweighting principally takes the form of a quick sitback, causing skis to jet, by Newton's law of action and reaction.

JIGBACK: A lift with two passenger cars that reverse direction for every cycle, as a tramway or cable car, as opposed to a gondola, which keeps the same direction.

JUMP: An artificial or natural takeoff. Also, the act of taking to the air, as in a gelande, hop turn, airplane turn, nordic jump, or freestyle aerial.

JUMPING: The act of taking a jump. Also, the nordic competitive event which with cross-country forms the nordic combined. Length and form count for score.

JUMP SUIT: An outer garment that combines the functions of jacket and pants, covering body from neck to ankles. It may be a warm-up or a windbreaker.

JUMP TURN: A generic term for turns such as the hop turn, gelande turn, airplane turn, etc.

JUNK: Heavy or very inconsistent snow, usually found off-trail, which is unfavorable to easy skiing. Also known as crud, mashed potatoes, or unbreakable crust.

KICK TURN: A standing turnabout maneuver involving pointing skis 180 degrees from previous direction in a single move for each ski.

KNICKERS: Ski pants snugged at just below the knees, as opposed to baggies or bogners, which snug around the ankle. *See also* Lederhosen.

LATERAL PROJECTION: A sophisticated expert maneuver developed to produce maximum spiral carve at the end of a short turn.

LAYOUT: A flip with the body fully extended, as opposed to in a tuck.

LEDERHOSEN: Leather shorts with suspenders, native to the Alps. They are useful in warm-weather skiing.

LIFT LINE: Skiers waiting for a ride on a lift.

LINE: In racing, the planned path through the course. A good line will put the racer through the course with minimum loss of time in his turns and yet not accelerate him so much he loses control. In recreational skiing, it generally means to ski in the fall line or to pick a good line through a mogul field.

LINER: An inside mitten or glove used under a mitten cover.

LONGIES: Long-underwear suit or pants favored by those who eschew warm-up pants.

MAINTENANCE: The care of terrain, snow, and lifts. Also, the care of personal ski equipment.

MAMBO: A snakeline series of connected turns in the fall line initiated by anticipation without pole plant or edge set.

MARATHON: A cross-country race from point to point rather than a fixed multiple of five kilometers. It is generally for non-FIS racers.

MASHED POTATOES: Soft junk; snow with high water content in above-freezing weather.

MAZE: A winding boundary for a lift line, made of strung ropes or snow fence.

METHOD: A series of specific steps and options used in teaching skiing.

MITTEN COVERS: Heavy fingerless hand cover-

A hot dog skier is a freestyler, a nonconformist.

ings with thumb separate from palm. They are used extensively where rope tows abound to save wear and tear on gloves.

MOGUL BASHING: A fast run through the moguls, featuring bun drops or mogul explosions as skier's body hits mogul tops and showers snow in all directions. Also called boogeying.

MOGUL EVENT: The freestyle competition that involves tricks done in running a mogul field.

MOGUL(S): Round snow mounds formed by the double action of skis pushing snow to the front and to the inside of the turn combined with fall-line turns, which cut the rolls into distinct mounds with sides and a top and bottom face, as skier after skier follows the same tracks.

MOUNTAIN: A natural rock formation of considerable size that is already suitable for skiing or is rendered so.

MOUNTAINEERING: Making ascents and descents in back country with the view and the tour as important as the downhill running. It was the original alpine skiing, never as popular as touring or recreational alpine skiing. It calls for a cross between nordic touring and alpine equipment.

MOUNTING: The process of attaching ski binding to skis.

NEW SNOW: Snow that has fallen within 24 hours and is in reasonably dry, loose condition.

NORDIC: That division of recreation and racing on skis that involves touring, cross-country, and jumping, as opposed to alpine.

NORDIC COMBINED: A method of combining scores in cross-country racing and jumping to pick a nordic-combined winner, or skimeister, e.g., the annual winner of the Holmenkollen.

NOVICE: A person on skis who cannot make a turn at will.

NSAA: The National Ski Area Association, a trade association of ski-area owners and operators.

OFF-TRAIL: Unprepared ungroomed snow outside the normal bounds of skiing on a particular descent.

OLD SNOW: Any snow that has been on the ground over 24 hours.

OPEN SLOPE: A wide slope cleared of obstacles generally admitting of a large number of different widely separated paths for descent from top to bottom.

ORIENTEERING: A touring competition in which skiers are timed in following instructions and compass directions over a previously unknown course.

OUTRIGGER: A hot-dog or freestyle turn with one leg extended sweeping close to the snow.

OUTSIDE EDGE: The edge of a ski farthest from the center of a turn.

OUTSIDE SKI: The ski farthest from the center of a turn.

OVEREDGING: The loss of edge control by enlarging the edge angle too much. It causes the ski to chatter or snap in the turn and begin to track, or it prevents the ski from starting into the turn.

PACKED OUT: Snow that is sufficiently compacted to make sliding turns easy for a beginning skier.

PACKED POWDER: A misnomer (powder is unpacked by definition) referring to loose snow packed by skis or grooming vehicles but not yet compacted to a hard base.

PARALLEL: Moving skis positioned side by side, tails and tips equidistant. Parallel may be close or wide track.

PARALLEL METHOD: Teaching without explicit use of stem or wedge turns.

PARALLEL TECHNIQUE: Skiing with skis parallel without having to employ stems. With skis five feet long or shorter it denotes an intermediate; with skis longer than five feet, an advanced skier.

PARALLEL TURN: A turn made with skis parallel during the entire turn. It may be a parallel christie (sliding) or a carved parallel; it may be long, as in giant slalom turns, or short, as in wedel; it may be in the fall line, as in wedel, or traverse to traverse, as in Arlberg.

PARKA: A jacket designed for skiing. It may be quilted for warmth, or it may be a windbreaker.

PISTE: French for "trail."

PITCH: A section of slope that descends evenly. It may be steep (over 22 degrees), or it may be easy, or intermediate.

POLE: The item a skier holds in each hand. Poles help with unweighting, reverse turning and climbing; and they act as a pivot for a turn. Before 1900 long single balance poles were the norm.

POLE PLANT: Thrusting the point of the pole into the snow to increase the inertia of the upper body for down-unweighted reverse or anticipation. Also for up-unweighting in short swing, hop turns, or Arlberg.

POMA LIFT: A cable-hung arm ending in a small platter, which the rider places between legs to be pulled uphill. It was invented by Pomagalski.

POWDER: Light, dry snow uncompacted by time or man.

PROFESSIONAL: A skier who races for cash prizes.

PSIA: The Professional Ski Instructors Association, the national instructors' organization in the United States.

QUADRUPLE CHAIR: A chair lift with cable-hung chairs, each of which is capable of carrying four passengers.

RACER CHASER: A ski-equipment maker's representative who follows a race circuit to promote the use of the manufacturer's products by racers and to service the equipment of these racers. Girls following the race circuit have also been known as racer chasers or racing groupies.

RACING STEP TURN: A racing turn utilizing the advantages of a single step with the inside ski at the end of the turn.

RACING TECHNIQUE: Technical maneuvers aimed at maximizing speed as a first priority over a given race course or terrain.

RACING TURN: A turn using racing technique, whether in a race or not.

RAILED BOTTOM: A concave bottom made by ice wearing away the base at the center. It may result in hooking and erratic behavior. It is cured by flat-filing.

RELEASE BINDING: A binding with features that enable the skier to free himself in most situations where the ski might otherwise cause an injury.

RELEASING: Flattening the skis so that they will slide, not hold, usually expressed as "releasing the edges."

RESCUE: Succor by the ski patrol, Forest Service, or mountain rescue outfits rendered to injured, lost, or stranded skiers in the back country, aloft in stalled lifts, or somewhere on the slopes or trails.

RESORT: An area with a resort village or at least a hotel; not applied to a ski area with nothing but a base lodge.

REVERSE: The turning power of the Austrian short-swing system. At first believed to derive primarily from an active countermotion of the upper body or shoulders (*Gegenschulter*), it was later refined to a technique whereby mid-body muscles and legs twist the skis into the turn against the inertia of the upper body fortified by pole plant, making possible much shorter, more decisive, rapidly executed turns than are possible with rotation.

ROPE TOW: Essentially two pulley wheels, one at the top and the other at the bottom, that carry an endless rope loop driven by an intervening drive wheel. It was the first form of ski lift and is still used extensively; it operates at a relatively low cost.

ROTATION: A technique built around an act of preswinging the arms and upper body in the direction of the turn as the skier traverses; the skier then blocks this motion by isometric contraction and, pivoting on a pole, transfers the rotational energy to the lower body and skis, which have been freed by unweighting to swing into the turn. This method has been generally supplanted by the reverse technique.

ROYAL CHRISTIE: A freestyle turn with the outside ski extended to the side and behind the skier.

RUN: A trip down the given terrain referred to. Also, the act of running.

RUNNING: Skis traveling in or near the fall line with pressure equal or nearly so on both edges so there is little tendency to hold or slide.

SAFETY STRAP: A device to tether the ski to the skier's leg after it has been released by the binding.

SCHUSS: Running a given terrain without turning.

SCHUSSBOOMER: A skier going all out, or too fast for given conditions, often endangering fellow skiers.

SCISSORS CHRISTIE: A turn in which the inside ski is toed out to pull the skier into the turn and both skis are brought parallel during the slide. Although it is the original sliding turn, it is considered a faulty turn today. *See also* Hooking.

SHAFT: The uppermost portion of the boot, supporting the lower leg above the ankle.

SHALLOW TRAVERSE: Traversing nearly horizontally across the hill, primarily a means of maintaining slow speed or finding a better line.

SHARPENING THE EDGES: Squaring the edges.

SHORT SWING: *See* Austrian Method and Technique.

SHOVEL: The widest point of the ski, just behind the tip.

SIA: Ski Industries of America, the national trade organization of manufacturers.

SIDE CAMBER: The side curve of the ski from the shovel to the tail. It forms a narrow waist located under binding. Also known as sidecut.

SIDECUT: *See* Side Camber.

SIDESLIP: In a straight sideslip the skier slides downhill at right angles to the ski direction. More usual (because it's easier) is the forward sideslip where the skier proceeds on a path forward at less than right angles to the direction of the skis. This is a means of slow descent without accelerating.

SIDESTEPPING: Climbing a hill sideways by edging hard, moving one ski after the other upward. It leaves a ladderlike track, and it's easier but slower than the herringbone.

SILVER: The wax used on the ski for wet spring snow.

SINGLE CHAIR: Only one passenger to a chair on each cable arm; the original form of chairlifts, now outmoded.

SITBACK: An unweighting move in avalement; a quick bend in the knees and hip with ankles fixed, using a high back boot for support. It causes the skis to unweight partially and jet. It is also used in ballet without the usual forward-press recovery.

SITZMARK: *See* Bathtub.

SKATING: Going across the flat or down an easy slope with skating motions of the skis.

SKATING TURN: Going around a turn by means of skating motion.

SKI: A board-shaped device with a bent-up tip to facilitate travel across snow. It was made more than 4,500 years ago in northern Europe and was refined in Norway during the 1800s to nearly its modern shape and length.

SKIING: Using skis for sport, war, travel, or work.

SKI PATROL: An organized rescue unit, paid or volunteer, whose main function is to minimize the effect of injuries on the slopes and to transport skiers to medical aid.

SLAB: Snow compressed into an adhering soft crust.

SLALOM: An alpine event in which skiers race between a series of slalom poles or gates that set the course limits. The modern slalom race has about 60 gates. *See also* Giant Slalom.

SLIDING: Skiing in a sideslip or sliding turn, as opposed to running or holding; skidding; skis point away from the direction of travel, making tracks wider than the distance between the outside edges of the ski.

SLIDING TURN: A curving forward slide or sideslip that cuts a track or swath wider than the distance between the outside edges. It can serve as a braking maneuver and to execute a quicker change of direction.

SNOW: A loose or solid cover already frozen into crystals or flakes before touching down. It includes powder, boiler plate, junk, crust, slab, and loose snow, but not ice.

SNOW CONDITIONS: A description of snow and ice on a given terrain.

SNOWMOBILE: An over-the-snow vehicle of one- or two-passenger capacity, used in area maintenance and transport, and for an occasional rescue. It also lays cross-country trails and packs them out.

SNOWPLOW: When both skis are pushed out at the tails in stem motion. In the Arlberg and short-swing snowplow, the skis were edged. It was used to come to a stop by the Arlberg novice. Its use in ATM is now limited to the beginner during the brief period before he learns the wedge turn to better accomplish the same purpose. Also called a double stem.

SNOWPLOW TURN: Turning in snowplow position. In the Arlberg, this was the beginner's turn, followed by the stem.

SNOW REPORT: A snow-condition report in the news media.

SNOW SNAKE: An invisible pest that bites the tips of the skis and causes skiers to fall.

SPIRAL: An expert turn during which the radius shortens, tending to build forward speed. It can be during a slide or a carve.

SPLIT ROTATION: A combination of rotation and reverse in the same turn, one following the other.

SPREAD EAGLE: A jump with arms and legs artfully akimbo. Another freestyle aerial.

SPRING SKIING: End-of-season conditions characterized by soft, easily skied, wet, or corn, snow. A time for shedding long johns and getting tan.

SQUARING THE EDGE: Filing the edge so that its bottom face is plane with the base and the side face of the edge forms a plane at right angles to the bottom.

STANCE: A basic or "home" position for a given technique; the usual running position.

STEERED TURN: A wide-track turn in which the turning power is supplied mostly to the ouside ski, as in the Arlberg stem or the ATM wedge.

STEILHANG: German for "headwall," a very steep pitch.

STEM: To take stem position by shoving the tail of one ski outward so that the tips are closer than the tails. It is used as a braking maneuver in Arlberg.

STEM CHRISTIE: *See* Arlberg.

STEM TURN: A turn in which the tails are farther apart than the tips.

STUNT: A risky trick, difficult even for an accomplished freestyle skier; a made-up challenge, as opposed to a standard freestyle trick.

SYSTEM: The method plus the technique of a particular school, e.g., the American System of the 1960s.

TAIL: The back of the ski.

TAYLOR METHOD: A progression of foot-swivel turns first on three-, then four-, then five-foot skis. This parallel method was invented by Clif Taylor during the 1950s and was systematized at Killington, Vt., in 1965-66 by Karl Pfeiffer. Also known as GLM.

T BAR: A series of cable-hung vertical arms with the lower end in the shape of a **T**, which can pull two skiers up the slope at a time.

TECHNIQUE: The means—in body movement, muscle power, and dynamic forces—of accomplishing maneuvers essential or convenient to descent.

THREE-SIXTY: A basic ballet turn; spinning on sliding skis through 360 degrees, a full circle.

TIP: The front of the ski, including the shovel.

TIP DROP: Dropping the tips of the skis below the tails in flight. Another freestyle aerial.

TIP PULL: The precursor of anticipation and split rotation.

TOE CLAMP: A device to hold the boot fast.

TOE IRON: Cross-country or alpine toe binding. Also called a bear trap.

TOE RELEASE: A mechanism located at the front of a release binding that frees the boot toe during a fall, usually by swinging out to either side.

TOE STRAP: A strap that holds down the toe of the boot in toe iron. With toe iron and heel cable this comprised the alpine bindings of the 1930s and 1940s.

TOURING: A contemplative, noncompetitive form of cross-country; reveling in uphill and downhill travel over rolling country optimally less abrupt and precipitous than alpine country. Touring equipment is sturdier than cross-country racing, but it weighs two-thirds less than alpine equipment.

TRACK: The traces left by the passage of the ski through or over snow. Also, a warning to overtaken skier by overtaking skier to hold course. Also, the ability of the ski to hold a straight course.

TRACKED UP: Snow cut by ski tracks, as opposed to new snow.

TRAIL: The path of descent defined by trees, bushes, or obstacles. Also, a packed-out path in loose snow on an open slope. It differs from open slope in having definite shape discernible to the skier during descent.

TRAM or TRAMWAY: A jigback cable lift with two large cars carried through the air; cables that reverse direction every cycle.

TRAVERSE: Any straight path not in the fall line. Also, to go across the hill, as opposed to straight down, to avoid obstacles, ice, or merely to kill speed.

TRAVERSE TO TRAVERSE: A system that makes traverse an integral part of descent, each turn ending in a shallow traverse.

TRICK: A style maneuver, part of freestyle competition. It falls into standard freestyle categories of ballet, aerial, and mogul.

TRIPLE CHAIR: A lift with cable-hung chairs in series, each capable of holding three passengers.

TUCK: Egg position or racing tuck used in downhill. Also, legs and arms drawn in during a flip, as opposed to extended in a layout.

TUNING: Bringing out the potential of a ski; curing faults made in manufacture or caused by wear. This is done by flat-filing, squaring the edges, beveling, and filling scratches with wax.

TURKEY: A tourist skier at a resort.

TURN: To cause change in the direction of travel; to brake or decelerate. It is normally performed on alternate sides during descent, as in wedel.

UNBREAKABLE CRUST: Melted and refrozen top layer of cover strong enough to hold the weight of a skier underway.

UNWEIGHTING: Easing the pressure on the bottom of the ski to displace it or to apply carving pressure.

USSA: The United States Ski Association, a consumer association made up of individual skiers and ski clubs.

VERTICAL: The difference in feet above sea level between the top and bottom of a terrain, mountain, run, race course, or lift. The highest lift-serviced verticals in Europe are 6,000 feet; in the U.S., 4,000. A vertical of about 3,000 is considered desirable to make a major resort; under 2,000 indicates a secondary area.

VORLAGE: German for forward lean; the Arlberg stance.

WAIST: The narrowest part of the ski, located under the binding and boot.

WARMING HUT: A small day lodge with no or minimal food service.

WAX: A slippery substance applied over the base to fill in scratches. It makes the ski go faster and slide more smoothly.

WEDEL: A connected series of short reverse turns in the fall line. Also, the act of creating same.

WEDELN: German verb form of wedel; American writers usually use "wedel" as both noun and verb.

WEDGE: When the skis are sliding in stem position, a maneuver that replaces the stem and the snowplow of the short swing in ATM. Also called gliding stem.

WEDGE TURN: The basic ATM turn; a wide-track-steered stem with skis sliding; a steered turn with foot swivel.

WEIGHT SHIFT: When the weight on the outside ski stabilizes the latter part of the proper turn. The weight shifts from the outside ski in one turn to the new outside ski in the next. Also, properly executed, weight shift creates carving pressure.

WHEELIE: A hot-dog or freestyle turn, made in a sitback position without a forward-press recovery. The ski tips are jacked into the air and pivoting on the tail.

WIDE TRACK: A stance developed by French racers, with skis four or more inches apart rather than in close parallel. It adds leverage to foot-swivel turns and cuts wind resistance.

WINDBREAKER: A single-weight, closely woven cloth that breaks the passage of the wind.

WIND CRUST: Slab; a soft crust.

WINTER OLYMPICS: The winter version of the Olympic Games, first held in Chamonix, France, in 1924, with only nordic events. Alpine events were added in 1936 in Garmisch, Germany. America's first skiing medalist in the Olympics was Gretchen Fraser, who won a gold and a silver in 1948. Andrea Mead came up with two golds in 1952, Penny Pitou two silvers in 1960, Jean Saubert two bronzes in 1964, and Barbara

Cochran a gold in 1972 to highlight U.S. achievements, which haven't been many over the years. The men have never taken skiing gold for the U. S. teams; in fact, Billy Kidd and Jimmy Heuga, with a silver and a bronze, respectively, in the slalom in 1964, have been the only U. S. male medalists in Alpine events. Bill Koch did win a silver medal in cross-country in 1976. The most notable of the Olympic skiers have been Austria's Tony Sailer and France's Jean-Claude Killy, each of whom won three Olympic gold medals in 1956 and 1968, respectively.

WORLD CHAMPIONSHIPS: Competitions held every even-numbered year by the FIS. In Olympic years they are scored on the results of the Olympic competitions and are called Olympic championships. In non-Olympic years, they are run as a separate event and referred to as World Championships.

WORLD CUP: A season-long competition based on preselected races held preponderantly in Europe. It determines season championships for men and women as well as the international team championship (Nations Cup).

Gretchen Fraser became America's first skiing gold medalist in the Winter Olympics *in 1948 at St. Moritz, Switzerland.*

Pelé, *the Brazilian-born Babe Ruth of soccer, began a new career with the New York Cosmos of the North American Soccer League.*

ADVANTAGE RULE: A rule by which the referee stops play after a foul if the offending team gains an advantage. Sometimes, however, it is penalizing the wrong team to stop play—e.g., if a defender deliberately handles the ball to bring it under control but only succeeds in deflecting it to an opponent who is well placed for a shot at goal. To stop play at this moment would penalize the attacking team by allowing the defenders time to regroup. In such a case the referee would ignore the handling offense and allow play to continue.

AGGREGATE SCORE: The combined scores of two home-and-home games. Playing at home before the hometown fans is considered a big advantage in soccer, particularly in international club competitions. For this reason most international games at the club level are played on a home-and-home basis, and the scores from the two games are added together. A team losing 1-2 away from home but winning 2-0 at home wins by an aggregate score of 3-2. In some competitions if aggregate scores are tied, goals scored away from home count double.

ASSOCIATION FOOTBALL: Soccer's official title. Back in the 1860s the word "football" was being used in England for two different sports. To distinguish the two the terms "Rugby football" (because rugby was first played in the town of Rugby) and "association football" (because the first soccer rules were drawn up by the London Football Association) were used. It is believed that the word soccer is a corruption of the abbreviation "assoc.," just as "rugger" became the commonly used word for rugby.

BACKHEEL: To pass the ball backward with the back of the heel. It is a highly deceptive pass, particularly if performed at speed, as the ball travels in the opposite direction from the way the passer is moving and looking.

BALL: The spherical object the players use in a game. It must be made of leather or "other approved materials," which include various forms of plastic. It must have a circumference of 27 to 28 inches, weigh between 14 and 16 ounces, and be pumped up to a pressure of 15 pounds per square inch. If the ball should burst during a game, play is restarted with the new ball at the point where the old one was last played. If a kick results in a goal and a burst ball, the goal does not count. It is assumed that the moment the ball was kicked it started to deflate and was therefore no longer a regulation ball.

BALL IN AND OUT OF PLAY: For the ball to pass out of play, *all* of it must be over *all* of the sideline or goal line (the lines are about five inches wide). Thus, a ball on the line is in play. Even a ball resting on the ground just outside the touchline is still in play if any part of it is projecting over the line. Similarly, a goal is not scored until all of the ball has passed over all of the goal line. A shot that hits the crossbar and bounces down onto the goal line and then out is not a goal.

BALLPLAYER: A player who is especially skilled at controlling and moving with the ball.

BALL WINNER: A rather euphemistic term used to describe hard-tackling players, usually midfielders and usually lacking in constructive skills.

BANANA SHOT: A hard shot at goal in which the ball is kicked off-center, giving it a spin that makes it curve in flight. It is usually used on free kicks near the goal to "bend" the ball around a defensive wall.

BAR: The crossbar of the goal.

BEND: To kick the ball so that it curves in flight. It is done by kicking the ball off-center, making it spin.

BICYCLE KICK: *See* Overhead Kick.

BLIND SIDE: The side of a player that is farthest from the ball. A defender watching an attack develop on his right must also be aware of movement on his left, his blind side, in case an attacker should sneak behind him to receive a pass.

BOOT: To kick the ball clumsily and aimlessly. Hence the term should not be used simply as an alternative for "kick," and it should never be used in the form of "booters" to mean soccer players or "the booting game" to mean soccer.

BOX: The penalty area (the 18-yard box). Also, less frequently, the goal area (the 6-yard box).

BREAKDOWN PERIOD: The period immediately following a change of ball possession. Soccer is a game in which, like hockey, possession is constantly and abruptly passing from one team to the other. The team gaining possession must immediately switch from defense to attack, the team losing possession from attack to defense.

CALLING: Shouting on the field by soccer players to let a teammate with the ball know that they are backing him up or running alongside him to receive a pass. In a rapidly moving game like soccer the player with the ball does not usually have the time to look all around him to note exactly where his teammates are positioned. This is particularly true for those playing behind him.

CANNONBALL SHOT: Any very fast, powerful shot on goal. The hardest shooters in soccer can make the ball travel at more than 70 miles per hour.

CAP: To select a player to play for his country's national team. The phrase comes from the British custom, still observed, of awarding such players an elaborately decorated cap, complete with a large dangling tassel.

CARPET: The playing surface. A team that specializes in ground passes is "keeping it on the carpet."

CATENACCIO (kat-ten-AH-cho): A defensive system, perfected by Italian clubs in the 1960s. It employs a single extra-deep fullback who plays behind a line of three or four fullbacks. He is called the *libero*, or sweeper, or freeback. His main job is to provide cover for the defenders in front of him.

CAUTION: *See* Yellow Card.

CENTER: To pass the ball from near the touchlines into the opposing goalmouth. Also called crossing the ball.

CENTERBACK: *See* Tactics.

CENTER CIRCLE: A circle of ten yards radius marked out around the center spot of the field. It has only one official function—at the moment of a kickoff players on the team not taking the kick must be ten yards from the ball; so they must stay out of the circle.

CENTER FORWARD: *See* Tactics.

CENTER HALF: *See* Tactics.

CHALLENGE: To approach a player who has possession of the ball with the apparent intention of tackling him. In fact, a tackle may not come. The idea is to force the player in possession to commit himself, either to pass or to run with the ball.

CHARGE: Physical contact with an opponent in an attempt to force him off the ball. The charge must be a shoulder-to-shoulder contact. If the elbows, hands, or hips are used or if the charge is made from behind or with unnecessary roughness, it is illegal. Although shoulder-charging the goalkeeper when he is holding the ball is permitted by the international rules, most countries do not allow it.

CHIP: A short, lofted pass made with only a small movement of the kicking foot and no follow-through. The foot is jammed underneath the ball, which is made to rise steeply in the air. The chip is used in passing to lift the ball over a nearby defender.

CLEAR: To kick or head the ball away from the goalmouth, thus killing an immediate threat to the goal.

CLOGGER: A player who tackles roughly, aiming more for his opponent's legs than for the ball.

COIN TOSS: Before each game a coin is tossed, and the winner has the choice either of ends or the kickoff. In soccer, possession at the kickoff means virtually nothing, so that the captain winning the coin toss will invariably select which end he wishes to defend.

COLLEGE: Soccer has been played in American colleges since the end of the nineteenth century. Indeed, the famous 1869 Rutgers-Princeton game that is supposed to have marked the birth of football was clearly a soccer game, being played with a round ball. A great surge of interest in college soccer came in the 1960s and the NCAA (National Collegiate Athletic Association) now runs national championships in three divisions. There are also Junior College and NAIA (National Association of Intercollegiate Athletics) championships.

NCAA DIVISION I WINNERS

1959	St. Louis University
1960	St. Louis University
1961	West Chester State University
1962	St. Louis University
1963	St. Louis University
1964	Navy
1965	St. Louis University
1966	San Francisco University
1967	Michigan State University St. Louis University co-champions
1968	Michigan State University University of Maryland co-champions
1969	St. Louis University
1970	St. Louis University
1971	*Howard University
1972	St. Louis University
1973	St. Louis University
1974	Howard University
1975	San Francisco University

*Title vacated by NCAA due to alleged use of ineligible players.

CORNER KICK: What the attacking side is awarded when a defending player kicks the ball over his own goal line (other than into the goal). The ball is placed in the corner area and kicked, usually in the air, so that it will reach the opposing goalmouth, where attackers are hoping to head or kick it into the goal, the defenders to clear it.

COVER: To back up a teammate in defense.

CROSSBAR: The horizontal bar that forms the top of the goal.

CROSS-SHOT: A shot on goal made from the right side toward the left of the goal, or vice versa.

CUP: Soccer has an abundance of competitions in which the winner receives a large cup—e.g., the World Cup, the Intercontinental Cup, and the European Cup. It all started in England in 1871 with the Football Association Challenge Cup Competition. Most soccer-playing countries now have a cup tournament played in addition to the regular championship. These are knockout competitions, with the winner going through to the next round and the loser eliminated. The all-or-nothing aspect of cup games gives them a glamor that the regular league games often lack. *See also* European Cup and World Cup.

DANGEROUS PLAY: This is not defined in the rules, and it is up to the referee to decide what is and what is not dangerous. Two common examples are high kicking, particularly when an opponent is trying to head the ball, and kicking at the ball when it is held by the goalkeeper.

DEAD BALL: When play has been stopped by the referee and the ball is not moving. All free kicks have to be taken from a dead ball.

DECOY: An attacker who indulges in much running about without the ball, trying to make the opposing defense believe that he is about to receive a pass. Decoy running is also called off-the-ball running.

DIAGONAL RUNNING: An attacking maneuver. Although the most direct way to goal for an attacker is straight down the field, it is not usually the most successful. Attackers do much of their running diagonally across the field, rapidly interchanging positions. This creates problems of marking for the defense and makes it easier for the forwards to control passes coming through from midfield.

DIPPER: A long, hard shot at goal that suddenly dips downward in its flight. It is top spin that makes the ball dip; hence dippers are usually shots taken on the volley when the kicker can get his foot well over the ball.

DIRECT FREE KICK: A kick awarded against a team that has committed one of the nine serious fouls. A goal can be scored directly from the kick. If the foul was committed within its own penalty area, the team has a penalty kick awarded against it. All opposing players must be at least ten yards from the ball when the kick is taken.

DRIBBLE: To run with the ball under control, tapping it ahead with the inside or the outside of the foot, and taking it past opponents by tricking them with feints, body swerves, and tricky footwork.

DROP BALL: Soccer's equivalent of basketball's jump ball. When the referee has stopped the game—e.g., to allow treatment of an injured player—he will restart it by dropping the ball between two opposing players. They must let it touch the ground before they attempt to kick it.

ELEVEN: This is the number of players on a soccer team, and the word, or the Roman numeral XI, is sometimes used to mean team.

EQUIPMENT: Players wear a shirt, shorts, stockings, and what the rules insist on calling boots. In fact the old soccer boots—heavy, ankle high, with hard reinforced toes—went out of style years ago. Today's "boots" are low-cut, lightweight shoes of supple leather, allowing a much more delicate control of the ball. Some players wear shin guards, flexible shields that cover the front of the leg between the ankle and the knee; they are tucked down inside the socks.

EUROPEAN CUP: Started in 1956, this is the most successful of the international competitions for clubs. It is held yearly and involves the champion clubs from over thirty European countries.

EUROPEAN CUP WINNERS

1956 Real Madrid (Spain)
1957 Real Madrid (Spain)
1958 Real Madrid (Spain)
1959 Real Madrid (Spain)
1960 Real Madrid (Spain)
1961 Benfica (Portugal)
1962 Benfica (Portugal)
1963 Milan (Italy)
1964 Inter (Italy)
1965 Inter (Italy)
1966 Real Madrid (Spain)
1967 Celtic (Scotland)
1968 Manchester United (England)
1969 Milan (Italy)
1970 Feyenoord (Netherlands)
1971 Ajax (Netherlands)
1972 Ajax (Netherlands)
1973 Ajax (Netherlands)
1974 Bayern Munich (West Germany)
1975 Bayern Munich (West Germany)
1976 Bayern Munich (West Germany)

In 1960 a similar competition was started in South America, thus opening the way for championship games between the European and South American winners. This is the International Cup, and the winner can truly claim to be the champion club of the world.

INTERCONTINENTAL CUP WINNERS

1960 Real Madrid (Spain)
1961 Peñarol (Uruguay)
1962 Santos (Brazil)
1963 Santos (Brazil)
1964 Inter (Italy)
1965 Inter (Italy)
1966 Peñarol (Uruguay)
1967 Racing Club (Argentina)
1968 Estudiantes (Argentina)
1969 Milan (Italy)
1970 Feyenoord (Netherlands)
1971 Nacional (Uruguay)
1972 Ajax (Netherlands)
1973 Independiente (Argentina)
1974 Atlético Madrid (Spain)

FIELD: Under international rules the playing area in soccer can vary greatly in size, but the length (100 to 130 yards) must always be greater than the width (50 to 100 yards).

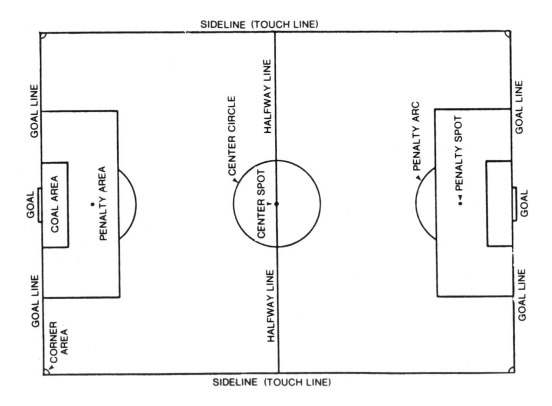

FIFA: The Fédération Internationale de Football Association, the international organization that governs world soccer. Formed in 1904, it now has a membership of over 140 countries. Its functions include ruling on differences among member nations over interpretation of the rules, and organizing the World Cup.

50-50 BALL: A loose ball that both teams have an equal chance of controlling.

FINISHING: The final touch to an attacking move. It includes any type shot on goal. Good finishing means accurate shooting.

FIRST-TIME: To play a ball—to pass or to shoot—immediately after it arrives without attempting to bring it under control.

FLANK(S): The side areas of the playing field.

FLAT POSITIONS: Players alongside each other, forming a line across the field, are in flat, or square, positions.

FLICK PASS: A short pass, made on the run with the outside of the foot.

FOOTBALL: Soccer is a game played with the feet and with a ball. Its natural name is football. And this is the word that is used in one form or another, in most of the world to describe the sport. In the British Isles it's football, in France it's *le football*, in Spain and most of South America *el futbol*, in Brazil *o futebol*, in Germany it's *fussball*. In fact, most of the world finds it rather hard to understand how Americans can use the word "football" for a game in which the foot is much less important than the hand.

FOUL(S): There are two types of fouls in soccer. The more serious ones are: dangerous charging, charging from behind, holding, striking, pushing, tripping or kicking an opponent, jumping at an opponent, and handling the ball. These offenses will result in a direct free kick being given against the guilty team, or a penalty kick if the foul occurred in its penalty area. The less serious fouls include obstruction, ungentlemanly conduct, and the taking of more than four steps by a goalkeeper while holding the ball. For these an indirect free kick is given.

FOUL THROW: *See* Throw-in.

FREEBACK: *See* Sweeper.

FULLBACK: *See* Tactics.

FUNNELING: A defensive tactic. When a team that is attacking loses possession of the ball, its players immediately retreat toward their own goal and concentrate in the center of the field toward their penalty area.

GOAL: What is at each end of the field, consisting of two goalposts (or uprights) and a crossbar, backed with a cage of netting. The goals are eight feet high and eight yards wide. Also, what counts in soccer; the method of deciding who wins. Each time the ball, *all* of it, goes over the goal line, between the posts and beneath the crossbar, a goal has been scored.

GOAL AREA: A rectangular area, marked by a line, in front of each goal. It is 20 yards wide and 6 yards deep. Inside this area the goalkeeper cannot be charged unless he has possession of the ball—although the modern trend is to bar *all* charges on the goalkeeper.

GOAL AVERAGE: A figure obtained by dividing the number of goals a team scores by the number scored against them. A team scoring 100 goals and giving up 50 has a goal advantage of 2.00, while a team that scores only 50 but gives up 100 has a goal average of 0.50. In some countries the goal average is used to determine league placings among teams that have the same number of points. Another method is by goal difference, in which goals against are subtracted from goals for. Thus, a team that scores 100 goals and allows 50 has a goal difference of 50. *See also* Standings.

GOALKEEPER or **GOALIE:** The player who defends the goal. It is a little difficult to think of him as a soccer player because his functions are so different from those of the other ten members of the team. His main weapons are his hands, not his feet. He may handle the ball anywhere within his own penalty area. Should he venture beyond this, he becomes just another player, and if he then handles the ball, a foul will be called against him. When he has possession of the ball, he can take only four steps before he must get rid of it. The goalie is required to wear different colors from the rest of the team.

GOAL KICK: When the attacking team plays the ball over the opponent's goal line (other than into the goal), play is restarted by the defending team taking a goal kick. The ball is placed at the edge of the goal area and kicked upfield by the goalkeeper or a defender.

GROUNDER: A shot on goal in which the ball is kept low, in contact with the ground.

HACKING: Kicking at an opponent's legs. It is, of course, banned, but when the first soccer rules were published in 1863, many clubs protested vigorously that it was an important and legitimate part of the game.

HALFTIME: The interval between the halves. Under international rules it should not exceed five minutes, but this is a rule that is rarely observed. Ten minutes is the average.

HALF-VOLLEY: To kick the ball immediately after it has bounced, when it is only a fraction of an inch off the ground. The dropkick, sometimes used by goalies to clear the ball, is a form of half-volley.

HALFWAY LINE: The line marked across the width

of the field, dividing it into two halves. Players must be in their own half of the field at kickoffs, and they cannot be off side in their own half. *See also* Offside.

HANDS: The only soccer player allowed to use his hands is the goalkeeper, and then only inside his own penalty area. Any other player who handles the ball will be penalized by a direct free kick against his team, or—if he is within his own penalty area—a penalty kick. But the handling must be intentional. If the referee judges it to be accidental, he will let play go on. In soccer, "hand" means any part of the arm below the armpit.

HAT TRICK: Three goals by one player in one game. The term is borrowed from cricket where it used to be the custom for the club to present a new hat to any bowler (the equivalent of a pitcher) who dismissed three batsmen with three successive balls.

HEADING: Playing the ball with the head, a very important basic soccer skill. The ball is met with the middle of the forehead; the skull is at its hardest and thickest at this point, and great power can be put into head shots.

HISTORY: Kicking something around seems to have been one of man's favorite pastimes for four thousand years, probably much longer. Around 2000 B.C. the Chinese played a sort of kicking game using a ball, and the Greeks and the Romans also had a sport of this type. Probably the Romans took their version of it to England. It took the English some time to catch on, but by the thirteenth century a wild game, using an inflated bladder as a ball, was being played all over the country. Villagers were rushing madly about, trying to kick the bladder all the way to the next village, while their neighbors tried to stop them. As these villagers often went rushing through churchyards, the sport of *futballe* was declared "unseemly" by the church, and Englishmen were told to stop playing it.

In 1349 King Edward III was greatly upset by the thought of his subjects fooling around playing football when they should have been practicing their archery. He banned the sport. But it made no difference; the people continued to play, and gradually the game became less of a melee and more recognizable as a sport. It achieved respectability when it was taken up by the exclusive private schools in the eighteenth century. The game was also being played by the new working classes in the industrial cities of northern England. The trouble was that there were no common rules for the sport, and each group played more or less as it liked—until 1863 when a meeting of the London Football Association drew up the first widely accepted set of rules for the sport.

By 1885 professionalism had been legalized, and

soccer began its expansion, carried all over the world by traveling Britons. The sport was firmly established in Europe and South America in the early years of this century. In fact, North America was one of the very few areas where it was not an immediate success.

HOLDING: Grabbing hold of an opponent or his uniform. It's illegal.

HOSPITAL BALL: A badly directed pass that is a little nearer to an opponent than the teammate it was intended for. Both players will run for the ball and the unfortunate teammate, who will arrive second, stands a fair chance of being injured.

INDIRECT FREE KICK: A kick awarded against a team that has committed one of the less serious offenses. A goal cannot be scored direct from the kick, the ball must first be played by a player other than the kicker. All opposing players must be at least ten yards from the ball. *See also* Fouls.

INJURIES: Surveys have shown that the knee is the part of the body most frequently injured in soccer, and that the goalkeeper is the player most often hurt.

INJURY TIME: Time added on by the referee (who is the official timekeeper) at the end of each half to make up for any time lost when play was stopped for treatment to an injured player.

INSTEP: The hard, bony part of the top of the foot. It is the surface that makes contact with the ball in the normal soccer kick.

INSWINGER: A type of corner kick or center that curls in the air toward the goal.

JOCKEYING: When a player in possession of the ball faces a defender, each will be trying to jockey the other into an unfavorable position. A defender who feels that he is stronger on his left side (i.e., off his right foot) may allow an attacker more room on that side, almost inviting him to run that way.

KEEP BALL: Soccer's version of freezing the ball, involving a succession of short, safe ground passes to teammates. There is no attempt to advance the ball, which often travels backward and ends up being passed back to the goalkeeper.

KICK AND RUN: A crude type of soccer, without any plan or system and with very little skill. The ball is kicked in the air, as hard as possible, toward the opponent's goal, and the forwards run downfield after it, hoping for the best.

KICKER: A rough player, one who is always fouling opponents. It's another word that, like "booter," is sometimes used incorrectly to denote a soccer player.

KICKOFF: The start of the game. The ball is placed on the center spot and is kicked forward. It is not in play, and the game has not started, until it has rolled the distance of its circumference, about 27 inches. The kickoff is also used to restart play after a goal has been scored, the team that gave up the goal taking the kick.

LINESMAN: A subordinate official who assists the referee. There is one on each side of the field. His job is to run up and down the touchline and to signal with his flag when the ball goes out of play, indicating which team is to get the throw-in. When he spots players off side, or other infringements, he also raises his flag. This is only a signal to the referee; if the referee disagrees with the linesman's judgment, he will simply ignore the signal.

LINKMAN: *See* Tactics.

LOOSE BALL: A ball that is not controlled by either team and is up for grabs.

MARK: In man-to-man coverage the defender is said to mark the attacker. The closer he plays to him, the tighter the marking; the further away, the looser the marking.

MIDFIELD: An ill-defined area, but corresponding roughly to the middle third of the field. It is the area in which attacking moves are built up but from which there is no direct threat to the goal. Goals are rarely scored from the midfield area, and unless penetrating attacking moves can be started, control of midfield is valuable only as a defensive measure.

MIDFIELDER: *See* Tactics.

MISKICK: The player's nightmare. There are as many ways of miskicking a soccer ball as there are of mishitting a golf ball. It can be sliced, pulled, topped, ballooned, or—horror of horrors—missed altogether.

NARROWING THE ANGLE: This is what the goalie and, to a lesser extent, the other defensive players seek to do. It means reducing the area of the goal that an attacker can shoot at, and it is a matter of simple geometry. With the goalie standing in the middle of his goal line, a forward 12 yards out should be able to score easily with any fairly hard shot wide of the goalie's reach—which gives him quite a large area of the goal to aim at. If the goalie advances six yards, however, the ball will have to be kicked at a much sharper angle, and much more accurately, to get it past him and into the goal. The angles available for scoring shots have been considerably reduced. Flying leaps and diving saves have their place, but a goalie who is forever flinging himself spectacularly all over the place is usually one whose positional play is at fault.

NASL: The North American Soccer League. The NASL began its operation in 1967, but two years later it suffered almost total collapse when it was suddenly reduced from seventeen to five clubs. Since that low point it has slowly rebuilt its strength and is today a coast-to-coast league of twenty teams:

Northern Division
Boston Minutemen
Hartford Bicentennials
New York Cosmos
Rochester Lancers
Toronto Metros
Central Divison
Chicago Sting
Dallas Tornado
Denver Dynamoes
St. Louis Stars
San Antonio Thunder
Eastern Division
Miami Toros
Philadelphia Atoms
Tampa Bay Rowdies
Washington Diplomats
Western Division
Los Angeles Aztecs
Portland Timbers
San Diego Jaws
San Jose Earthquakes
Seattle Sounders
Vancouver Whitecaps

Past Winners
of the NASL Championship

1967	Oakland Clippers
1968	Atlanta Chiefs
1969	Kansas City Spurs
1970	Rochester Lancers
1971	Dallas Tornado
1972	New York Cosmos
1973	Philadelphia Atoms
1974	Los Angeles Aztecs
1975	Tampa Bay Rowdies

NATIONAL TEAM: An All-Star team composed of the eleven best players in the nation. FIFA has issued regulations outlining who may play for which country. Generally it is a question of where a player was born rather than where he plays. Naturalized citizens may play for their adopted country, provided they have not already played on another national team. Competitions for national teams include the Olympics (for amateurs) and the World Cup (for professionals).

NUMBERING: It has always been the custom in soccer to number positions rather than players. The traditional numbering was 1—goalkeeper, 2—right fullback, 3—left fullback, 4—right halfback, 5—center halfback, 6—left halfback, 7—outside right, 8—inside right, 9—center forward, 10—inside left, and 11—outside left. Whoever played center forward wore number 9. If, in his next game, the same player was switched to outside right, he changed his number to 7. The above system was based on the so-called pyramid formation, but the coming of modern tactical formations has outdated this system, and the numbers no longer have much positional meaning. In the NASL the American—and more sensible—system of assigning a different number to each player, which they wear whatever position they play, has been adopted. *See also* Tactics.

OBSTRUCTION: When a player who is not attempting to play the ball uses his body to prevent an opponent from getting to it. The referee will give an indirect free kick against the guilty team.

OFFSIDE: The offside rule requires that an attacker must have at least two opponents between him and the opposing goal line when the ball is passed to him. Under normal circumstances one of these two players will be the goalkeeper. A player cannot be offside in his own half of the field; he cannot be offside if he receives the ball directly from a corner kick, a goal kick, or a throw-in or if he receives it from an opponent, and he cannot be offside if he is behind the ball—i.e., if he is running toward the opposing goal and the ball is in front of him. It is not the player's position when he receives the ball that matters. It is where he was when the pass to him was made that counts.

The NASL, with permission from FIFA, has modified this rule by limiting its application to a 35-yard zone at each end of the field.

OLYMPICS: Soccer has been an official Olympic sport since 1908. Ostensibly a competition for national amateur teams, Olympic soccer has, since World War II, been dominated by Eastern European countries.

OLYMPIC SOCCER CHAMPIONS

1908	Great Britain	1944	No competition
1912	Great Britain	1948	Sweden
1916	No competition	1952	Hungary
1920	Belgium	1956	USSR
1924	Uruguay	1960	Yugoslavia
1928	Uruguay	1964	Hungary
1932	No competition	1968	Hungary
1936	Italy	1972	Poland
1940	No competition	1976	East Germany

ONE-FOOTED: Something no soccer player can afford to be. He must be able to kick and control the ball equally well with either foot.

OUTSIDE LEFT: *See* Tactics.

OUTSIDE RIGHT: *See* Tactics.

OUTSWINGER: A type of corner kick or center that curls in the air, swinging away from the goal.

OVERHEAD KICK: A spectacular kick useful when a player finds himself facing the wrong way with no time to turn around, or as a surprise move. The player literally up-ends himself, throwing his feet up and his torso downward. When contact is made with the ball the body is parallel to the ground and some three or four feet above it. The pumping action of the legs just before the ball is kicked resembles the motion of pedaling a bicycle. Also called a somersault kick or bicycle kick.

OVERLAP: An attacking move in which a defender—usually a fullback—comes forward to join in the attack, taking up a position out on the wing.

OVER THE TOP: A dangerous play in which a player tackling another for possession of the ball comes in with his foot high so that he goes over the top of the ball, making life very unpleasant for the legs and feet of the man in possession. It is, of course, illegal.

OWN GOAL: If a player miskicks or misheads and the ball goes into his own goal, it counts—for the other team. The player's name will appear among the list of his opponent's scorers with the letters *o.g.* (for own goal) after it.

PELÉ: Edson Arantes do Nascimento, a Brazilian soccer star who uses the name Pelé. Born in 1940 in Tres Coracoes, a small town in the state of São Paulo in Brazil. Pelé was too poor as a boy to afford a soccer ball, and he often practiced with a stocking stuffed with rags. Spotted by a club scout at the age of eleven, Pelé was playing for the Santos' first team by the age of fifteen. A year later, in 1957, he became the youngest player ever to play on the Brazilian national team. He has scored over 1,200 goals in first-class soccer, averaging over 70 per season. During his years with the Brazilian national team, Brazil won the World Cup three times.

Pelé, 5′9″ and 160 pounds, was declared a national asset by the Brazilian government so that he could not be bought by a foreign club. He spent his entire career with one club, Santos, until October 1974 when he announced his retirement. His soccer skills had made him one of the richest athletes in the world. In June 1975 Pelé amazed the soccer world when he agreed to play again and signed a three-year contract worth $4.5 million with the New York Cosmos of the NASL.

PENALTY: A penalty kick. The term should not be applied indiscriminately to any offense.

PENALTY KICK: When the defending team commits one of the nine serious offenses (*see* Fouls) inside its own penalty area, the attacking team is awarded a penalty kick. The ball is placed on the penalty spot, 12 yards from the goal, and the player taking the kick has only the goalkeeper to beat. All the other players of both teams must be outside the penalty area. The goalie must stand on his goal line and is not allowed to move his feet until the ball is kicked. The chances of the goalkeeper saving the shot are not high—most penalty kicks result in goals.

PITCH: A British term for the playing field.

PLACE-KICK: Any free kick, direct or indirect.

PLAYERS' POSITIONS: *See* Tactics.

POSTS: The two eight-foot-high uprights that support the crossbar and together with it make up the goal.

READING THE GAME: To size up accurately and quickly the opposing team's strengths and weaknesses; being quick to anticipate its moves during the game.

RED CARD: When the referee ejects a player from the game, he will call the player to him, enter his name in his notebook, then wave a red card in the air, indicating to everyone that the player is being sent off the field. The player's name is sent on to the appropriate disciplinary authorities. *See also* Yellow Card.

REFEREE: The man in charge. His word on the field is law, and his decisions are final. He starts the game, and because he is also the official timekeeper, he alone says when it is over. No player can enter or leave the field without his consent. He calls the fouls and has the power to caution or eject players. He is also responsible for seeing that the ball and the players' equipment conform to the rules. Under American college and high school rules, two referees are used, and timekeeping is performed by an official timekeeper. *See also* Rules.

RULES: The official rules of soccer are issued by FIFA and are known as the international rules. Minor variations are permitted, but most countries adhere closely to these international rules. In the United States there are three separate sets of rules—the NASL (professional), college, and high school—each of which differs from the international rules. The more significant of these differences are shown below:

NASL rules allow four (instead of two) substitutes per game and limit the application of the offside rule to a 35-yard zone at each end of the field.

College rules allow five substitutes per game, who can be resubstituted without limitation. Two referees are used but no linesmen (instead of one referee and two linesmen). A player who has been ejected from a game may be replaced by another player (under international rules his team must play a man short).

High school rules allow unlimited substitution. The two-referee system is used.

SCHEMER: The brains of the team, the player who schemes out attacking moves, usually from a midfield, or link position.

SCREENING: The way in which a player in possession uses his body to shield the ball from an opponent. By putting himself between the opponent and the ball, he can make tackling extremely difficult. This is not the same thing as obstruction, in which a player *not* in possession of the ball attempts to block an opponent.

SHOOT: To make a scoring attempt on the goal, especially by kicking the ball hard. Head shots are also referred to as headers.

SIDELINE: *See* Touchlines.

SLIDE TACKLE: An effective method of taking the ball away from an opponent but one that is usually used only as a last resort. It is employed by a defender who has been beaten; running alongside or slightly behind the man who has beaten him, he gains the extra yard by lunging at full stretch with one leg to poke the ball away. In performing the slide tackle, the tackler ends up on his back and thus puts himself out of the game for a brief moment.

SOMERSAULT KICK: *See* Overhead Kick.

SPOT-KICK: A penalty kick, so called because the ball is placed on the penalty spot, a round mark 12 yards in front of the goal.

STANDINGS: The method most commonly used in soccer to determine places in league standings is a point system allowing two for a win, one for a tie, and none for a loss. The NASL uses a system awarding six points for a win, three for a tie, and none for a loss, plus bonus points for each goal scored (by both winning and losing team) up to a maximum of three. In a game ending with a 4-2 scoreline, for example, the winning team would get six points for the win plus the maximum number of bonus points, three, a total of nine points. The losing team would get two points for its two goals. In giving scorelines, it is the worldwide soccer custom to give the home team first: Cosmos 1 Celtics 2 means that the Cosmos were beaten 2-1 on their own ground.

STOPPER: Originally applied to the center half of the old pyramid system when he was moved back to become a third fullback with the role of tightly marking the opposing center forward. It is still used to denote a defender who has the job of tightly marking a striker. *See also* Tactics.

STRIKER: Any of the central attacking players in the 4-2-4, 4-3-3, and 4-4-2 formations. *See also* Tactics.

SUBSTITUTION: The use of substitutes—even to replace an injured player—was for years forbidden by the soccer authorities. In the 1960s the international rules were at last relaxed to allow a maximum of two substitutes for each team. There is no free substitution; once a player has been taken out of a game, he cannot reenter it. In America the NASL permits four substitutes per team per game, the colleges allow five, with resubstitution permitted, and the high schools allow free substitution.

SWEEPER: A fullback who plays an ultradefensive role in the *catenaccio* formation. Also called a *libero*, or freeback. *See also* Tactics.

TACKLE: An attempt to take the ball away from an opponent. It is the feet that do the tackling, though the shoulder may also be used to charge a player off the ball.

TACTICS: For over fifty years, until 1925, soccer was dominated by the pyramid formation:

Goalkeeper
x

Right fullback   Left fullback
x   x

Right halfback   Center halfback   Left halfback
x   x   x

Outside   Inside   Center   Inside   Outside
right   right   forward   left   left
x   x   x   x   x

A goalkeeper, two fullbacks, three halfbacks, and five forwards—also referred to as a 2-3-5 formation. Tactics were straightforward: the goalkeeper and the fullbacks played defense, the forwards played offense, while the halfbacks played both. Despite the heavy emphasis on attack, it was felt that defenders were favored by the old offside rule, which required an attacker to have *three* opponents in front of him. In 1925 the rule was changed and the number reduced to two. The result was a great jump in the number of goals scored, and defensive play had to be reorganized to cope with the new situation. The center half, who up until then had primarily been an attacking player, was withdrawn into an entirely defensive role, playing as a third fullback between the other two. He became known as the stopper. This gave a 3-2-5 formation, which, it was soon realized, was weak in midfield. The answer was to withdraw first one, later both, of the inside forwards to midfield giving a 3-4-3 formation, also known as the W-M. This was the common formation throughout the 1930s and 1940s. In the 1950s the accent in soccer became heavily defensive, and the 4-3-3 was developed, with a line of four fullbacks. The Italians perfected an even more defensive system, the *catenaccio*, with a single fullback playing behind the other four, a 1-4-2-3. A less defensive modern system is the 4-2-4, developed by the Brazilians.

The coming of new systems has meant that the old player position names, based on the pyramid, have become outdated. New names are now used and are shown below as applied to the 4-2-4 formation:

Goalkeeper
x

Right   Right   Left   Left
fullback   centerback   centerback   fullback
x   x   x   x

Midfielders (or Linkmen)
x   x

Outside right   Striker   Striker   Outside left
x   x   x   x

It should be remembered, however, that soccer is an extremely fluid game and that during a game a team may be constantly changing its formations—playing 4-3-3 one minute, switching to 4-2-4 the next.

TARGETMAN: A tall, strong forward who plays a rather lonely role as the spearhead of the attack in certain modern formations. The ball is fed to him—usually a long pass out of defense, in the air—and his task is to control it or to head it down to his teammates running up to support him.

THROW-IN: When the ball goes over the touchline, it is put back into play by means of a throw-in taken by the team that did not kick the ball out. There are rules defining the exact way in which the ball must be thrown. Both feet must be on the ground, outside the field of play or on the touchline; the ball must be thrown over the head, using both hands equally. The thrower may not play the ball a second time until another player has played it. If the throw is taken improperly, the ball is given to the opposing team to throw in.

TIME: Under international rules a soccer game consists of two 45-minute halves, with a 5-minute interval. The referee is the official timekeeper. There are no time-outs called by players or coaches. Apart from small variations, e.g., 35-minute halves for schoolboy games, these are the rules that are followed throughout the world. The one exception is American high schools, where the rules recommend that the game be played in four quarters of 18 minutes with a halftime interval of 10 minutes. In college and high school games an official timekeeper, and not the referee, keeps the time.

TIME-OUT: Time-outs cannot be called by players or coaches in soccer. The referee is the only one who can stop the clock, which he will do as little as possible—usually to allow an injured player to be treated or if he feels that a team is deliberately wasting time.

TOE-END: To kick the ball with the front of the toe. Such kicks are rarely used because little real power or accuracy can be obtained by toe-ending the ball.

TOUCHLINE: The line at each side of the field. A ball going over the touchline is said to have gone into touch. Also called sideline.

TRANSFER(S): The buying and selling of players by clubs is known as the transfer market. Unlike baseball, football, and basketball, where player-for-player swaps are the rule, soccer transfers are usually straight cash purchases. In England, and particularly in Italy and Spain, enormous sums of money are involved. The first four-figure transfer fee came in England in 1905 when a player was bought for £1,000 (worth $5,000 in those days). In 1963 a Rome team paid $580,000 for a player, a world record that stood until 1968 when Juventus of Turin bought Pietro Anastasi for just over $1 million. The current record is $2.2 million paid by Barcelona to the Dutch club Ajax for their star forward Johann Cruyff. During the 1970s, professional soccer players' organizations in many countries started to press for "freedom of contract," under which a player, once his contract had expired, would be free to negotiate with any club he pleased. If freedom of contract is widely accepted, then clubs would no longer have to pay a player's former club, and the days of huge transfer fees would be over.

TRAP: To bring the ball under control. Since the ball is likely to arrive at any angle, at any height, and at any speed, there are many different ways of trapping it—with the sole, the inside or the outside of the foot, the thigh, or the chest.

TRIPPING: Any sort of tripping—or attempt to trip—is illegal in soccer. The offender will have a direct free kick given against his team.

UNGENTLEMANLY CONDUCT: Soccer's version of unsportsmanlike conduct. Examples are swearing, waving the arms about to interfere with opponents, and dancing about and gesticulating "in a way calculated to distract opponents." The referee will caution the ungentlemanly player and give an indirect free kick against his team.

UP-AND-UNDER: An example of primitive soccer. A long, high pass designed to come down in the opposing goalmouth as forwards rush in underneath it.

UPRIGHTS: The goalposts.

USA: Soccer's history here goes back to the last century. The game, in its crude early form, was played at Harvard and Yale. It was also the game that Rutgers and Princeton played in their historic 1869 encounter. A handling game, based on rugby, was preferred however, and this quickly developed into football. Within the colleges soccer became a minor sport; outside it was primarily a game played by immigrants who were keeping alive a sport they had learned in the old country. Until quite recently this was still the position. A look at the names of many of the teams shows their ethnic origin only too clearly: Los Angeles Scots, Philadelphia Ukrainians, New York Greek-Americans, New York German-Hungarians.

Professional soccer arrived in 1916 when Bethlehem Steel and a number of other companies imported foreign—mostly Scottish—professionals. The American Soccer League was formed in 1933, but its activities were limited to the Northeast. Soccer remained a minor sport until the 1960s when a new pro league, the North

American Soccer League, was started, and a great surge of interest in the sport began at the high school and college levels. For the first time in its long history in the U.S. soccer has a nationwide professional league and is becoming an American sport played by Americans.

USSF: The United States Soccer Federation, the governing body of soccer within the USA. Formed in 1913, USSF is a member of FIFA. USSF's functions include making sure that the various levels of soccer played in this country conform to the required international regulations. In theory USSF has powers to discipline organizations that disobey it, but in practice these powers have proved somewhat weak. To start with, USSF was for years run by immigrants and devoted its attentions almost exclusively to soccer played by immigrant groups. The high schools and colleges were virtually ignored, with the result that they went their own way, developing their own versions of the rules. Then, USSF has always had considerable trouble trying to impose its will on pro leagues and clubs.

But the soccer explosion of the 1960s saw the beginning of a new attitude at USSF, and the emphasis was at last placed on the development of the game at the youth level.

UTILITY PLAYER: A player with all-around ability who can be used in attacking, midfield, or defensive roles.

VOLLEY: To kick the ball on the fly before it hits the ground.

WALL: A maneuver for defending against free kicks within scoring range. A number of defenders, usually from three to six, will stand close together forming a wall ten yards from the ball. The idea is to block as much of the kicker's view of the goal as possible. The kicker is thus left with a much smaller area to shoot at, and the goalkeeper's task is made correspondingly simpler.

WALL PASS: The give-and-go, so called because in soccer games played by boys in the streets the ball is bounced off a wall instead of being played to a teammate.

WOODWORK: The wooden structure that makes up the goal, the two goalposts and the crossbar.

WORLD CUP: The greatest of the international soccer competitions and, in terms of worldwide interest, the greatest of all sports events. Its official title is the Jules Rimet Cup, named after the Frenchman who founded it. It is open to any country that is affiliated with FIFA, and the finals are played every four years, between the Olympic Games' years. It is a competition for national teams, either amateur or professional, but inevitably it is dominated by the pros.

The first tournament, played in 1930, attracted only 13 countries, but interest grew rapidly after World War II. For the 1978 tournament the number of entries is 102 countries. By a series of regional play-offs, these will be reduced to 14 teams, which along with the defending champions and the host country make up the final 16. These teams gather in the host country for the final rounds that are played over a period of about three weeks.

WORLD CUP WINNERS

1930	Uruguay
1934	Italy
1938	Italy
1950	Uruguay
1954	West Germany
1958	Brazil
1962	Brazil
1966	England
1970	Brazil
1974	West Germany

The United States has reached the final rounds of the World Cup on three occasions—in 1930, 1934, and 1950. In 1930 the Americans got as far as the semifinals, but perhaps a greater moment of glory came in 1950, during the competition in Brazil. After losing their first game, 1-3, to Spain, the Americans beat co-favorite England, 1-0. The American players were carried off the field by ecstatic Brazilian fans.

YELLOW CARD: To administer an official caution to a player, the referee enters his name in his notebook, then holds a yellow card in the air as an indication that the player has been cautioned. The player's name is sent on to the appropriate disciplinary authorities. Under international rules a player cannot receive two yellow cards in one game. The second time he must be shown the red card and ejected from the game. *See also* Red Card.

Jimmy Connors, the Brash Basher of Belleville, Ill., *at twenty became the youngest winner of the U.S. Pro championship.*

ACE: A perfect serve, either hit so hard or placed so accurately that the receiver has no chance of returning the ball, which sails past him untouched or barely touched.

ADVANTAGE: The point following deuce. The umpire generally calls the name of the player holding advantage (e.g., "Advantage Ashe") whether he is server or receiver. Also called ad in informal play; ad-in is the score called when the server has the advantage; ad-out refers to the advantage being held by the receiver; ad-court refers to the left court, from which the advantage is always played.

AGE-GROUP TENNIS: Diaper-to-doomsday competition is available in the U.S., where sectional and national championships are determined for males and females of practically every age. It starts with the 12s (for those twelve years old and under) and continues through the 14s, 16s, 18s, 21s. After that come the usual adult tournaments. Then, for men and women, the 35s, 40s (for women only), 45s, 50s, 55s, 60s, 65s, and 70s. And on all four surfaces: grass, clay, indoor, and hard court. Maybe there'll be a 100s division one day.

ALLEY: An addition to the singles court on both sides in order to provide space for doubles-court play. The alley is formed by the additional four and a half feet on both sides. This area, totaling nine feet, is in use during play following the serve.

AMATEUR: One who plays the game with no monetary reward involved, although some living expenses may be reimbursed. Prior to the advent of open tennis and the prize-money boom in 1968, the word was much abused. Amateurs at top tournaments were frequently referred to as "shamateurs": players who accepted compensation under the well-known table and did not take checks or report their earnings as income. Alleged amateurs at the top earned more than the few outright touring professionals.

"Pro" was considered a dirty word in most tennis circles until open tennis and a flood of prize money made the profession respectable. There is still a semantic problem with "amateur" in the Communist countries, which continue to term their foremost players "amateurs," even though they are clearly professional and accept prize money. An absurdly titled event is the European Amateur championships, annually won by men and women from Communist countries whose annual incomes compare favorably to those of American professional basketball players.

AMERICAN FORMATION: *See* I Formation.

AMERICAN TWIST: A top-spinning serve that takes a high bounce and can present difficulties for the receiver, particularly on grass where the bounce is tricky. It was originated by Holcombe Ward, a Harvard man, and developed by him with his college friend Dwight Davis around the turn of the century. Their use of the stroke during the first Davis Cup match in 1900 was a revelation to their English opponents, whom they baffled and beat.

AROUND THE POST: A stroke hit by a player drawn so wide that it goes into the opposing court

Arthur Ashe, a product of Richmond, Va., has won numerous titles around the world, including Wimbledon, World Championship Tennis, the National Amateur and the U.S. Open.

without clearing the net. In this rare case the shot is within the rules even if the flight of the ball is not higher than the net.

ASHE: Born in 1943 in Richmond, Va., Arthur Ashe is the first black male of prominence in tennis. He won the National Intercollegiate title for UCLA in 1965 and has played Davis Cup since that year. In 1968 he scored a first that may never be duplicated, winning the National Amateur and the U.S. Open in the same year. His finest year, however, was 1975 when he attained the world's number-one ranking by winning WCT (World Championship Tennis), Wimbledon, and making the semifinals of the Masters.

ATP: The Association of Tennis Pros, an organization of male touring pros comparable to a union, embracing most of the leading pros. Founded in 1972, it has been influential in governing tournament conditions, conduct, prize-money amounts, and structure.

ATP COMPUTER RANKINGS: A rating system including every male playing pro in the world, whether or not affiliated with ATP. The ratings are issued three times a year, based on performance over the previous twelve months, and are used by most tournament committees to determine seedings and which players should be admitted to the draw should there be more entries than positions.

AUSTIN: Henry ("Bunny") Austin, a leading English player of the 1930s, who deserves a salute for liberating the male leg. In 1931 he created the first tennis shorts by taking a scissors to his long white flannels, the traditional trousers worn by all tournament players up until that time, even in the tropics.

AUSTRALIAN FORMATION: *See* I Formation.

BACKHAND: The stroke hit from the side of the body opposite the hand holding the racket—from the left for a right-hander and from the right for a left-hander.

BAGEL JOB: A shutout set, 6-0. The loser's score looks like a bagel. A double bagel or triple bagel could be a shutout match. Also used as a verb: to bagel, or shut out. The term was coined by Eddie Dibbs, a leading American player, in 1973.

BALL: The bouncing object hit back and forth over the net by the players. It is two and a half inches in diameter and two ounces in weight. Balls are pressurized, with the pressure varying slightly according to national origin. The American ball is high pressure, thus livelier and more in use for the power game popular in the United States. The European ball is lower pressure, easier to control yet harder to hit for an outright winning point. The nap of the ball also varies, depending on the surface on which it is played. It is

thick for abrasive surfaces such as concrete and asphalt, medium for clay, and light for grass.

BALL BOY: A much sought-after assignment at the big tournaments, especially the U.S. Open at Forest Hills, N.Y. The ball boy (or ball girl) must be as invisible as possible and cannot distract or keep the players waiting for the ball. At Forest Hills there are tryouts (minimum age fourteen), with candidates tested for throwing arm, speed, agility, and knowledge of tennis. They are paid the prevailing minimum wage, receive free uniforms, and get a chance to see the matches free.

BASE LINE: The court's back line, joining the sidelines, from which the serve is delivered.

BASELINER: A player who hangs back at the rear of the court, generally quite steady, keeping the ball in play with ground strokes.

BATTLE OF THE SEXES: In 1973, fifty-six-year-old Bobby Riggs, Wimbledon champion of 1939, derided women's pro tennis, boasting that he could beat the best of the lot. Margaret Court, number one in the world for many years, took the challenge in an alleged winner-take-all match for $10,000 at Ramona, Calif. Riggs psyched her out and won, 6-2, 6-1. He then was challenged by Billie Jean King, who has also held the number-one ranking many times. This time a widely ballyhooed and televised match for a $100,000 prize on September 20 at the Astrodome in Houston, Tex., caught the public fancy, and a record tennis crowd of 30,472 appeared, paying as much as $100 apiece for closeup seats. King proved to be tougher mentally and physically, winning, 6-4, 6-3, 6-3, and taking the lioness' share of perhaps $300,000 divided among the two and their agents.

BELL CUP: An annual team competition between American and Australian women, launched in 1971 by the American cosmetics manufacturer Jesse Bell. Australia won three of the first four matches.

BIG FOUR: The championships of Australia, France, England (Wimbledon), and the U.S. These nations have been the leaders in tennis and were considered the Big Four in Davis Cup because they were the only ones to win that trophy until South Africa, and then Sweden, joined the club by winning in 1974 and 1975 respectively. Victory in all Big Four events in one year constitutes a Grand Slam.

BIG W: Wimbledon, England; the site of the British national championships.

BILLIE JEAN: Billie Jean King, born in 1943 at Long Beach, Calif., perhaps the greatest female champion produced in the U.S. Certainly she has been more influential in promoting the game than anyone else in her articulate and outspoken advocacy of women's

Billie Jean King subdued Bobby Riggs in their ballyhooed $100,000 Battle of the Sexes at Houston's Astrodome.

tennis and professional tennis in general. She won the Wimbledon singles 6 times (1966, '67, '68, '72, '73, and '75) and also took 13 doubles and mixed doubles titles at the Big W, tying the all-time record. She ranked number one in the U.S. a record 7 times before retiring from singles in 1975.

As a leader in founding the women's pro tour in 1971, she was that year the first female to make over $100,000 in prize money and the first American, male or female, to do so. Her 1973 triumph over His Piggishness, Bobby Riggs, made women everywhere rejoice. In 1974 she became the first woman to boss male pro athletes as player-coach of the Philadelphia Freedoms in World Team Tennis, a league she and her husband, Larry King, helped found. They also founded a magazine, *womenSports*, and were involved in numerous enterprises both related and unrelated to tennis.

Billie Jean's militant stance in pushing for equal prize money for women at major tournaments (achieved in 1974 at Forest Hills) and championing of women's-liberation causes earned her an alcove in the feminists' pantheon. *See also* Battle of the Sexes.

BRASH BASHER OF BELLEVILLE: Jimmy Connors, who emerged from Belleville, Ill., in 1973 at twenty to become the youngest winner of the U.S. Pro championship and head toward the top of the game. A tremendously hard left-handed hitter with a two-fisted backhand, he experienced the finest international season in 1974 of any American since Don Budge's Grand Slam campaign of 1938, winning Australia, Wimbledon, the U.S. Open, and the U.S. Indoor and Clay Court titles to become number one in the world.

His court manner was frequently abrasive and rude. He was a maverick, refusing to join the ATP or play Davis Cup. In fact, he was involved in a number of lawsuits against the ATP and its president in 1974-75, Arthur Ashe. Connors showed signs of maturing toward the end of 1975 when he dropped the suits and made his Davis Cup debut.

BREAK: A service break or loss of a service game. If the server loses the game, he is broken, sometimes in spirit as well as fact.

BREAK POINT: Potentially the last point of a game being won by the receiver. If the receiver wins it, he breaks. If the server wins it, he prolongs the game and may eventually pull it out. Obviously a critical point. The following are break points (with the server's score first): 0-40, 15-40, 30-40 advantage receiver.

BROTHERS: Several pairs of brothers have been prominent in the game, most conspicuously Englishmen—the Renshaw twins, the Baddeley twins, and the Dohertys. Willie Renshaw (1861-1904) won the Wimbledon singles event seven times (six straight between 1881 and 1886) and the doubles seven times with Ernest Renshaw (1881-1899). Ernest won the singles once. Reggie Doherty (1874-1910) won the Wimbledon singles four straight years, 1897-1900. Laurie Doherty (1876-1919) won five straight years, 1902-06, and together they won the doubles a record eight times. The Dohertys won four straight Davis Cups for Britain, 1903-06; Laurie never lost a match in that competition.

Wilfred Baddeley (1872-1929) was the youngest Wimbledon singles champion at nineteen in 1891 and added two other singles titles in 1892-95. With his brother, Herbert Baddeley (1872-1931), he won the Wimbledon doubles four times between 1891 and 1896. Among other prominent brothers have been the American Wrenns (Bob and George), the Kinseys (Howard and Bob), the Larneds (Bill and Edward), and the Wrights (Beals and Irving). Bob Wrenn won the U.S. singles four times 1893-94 and 1896-97 and ranked number one in those years, while George Wrenn also ranked in the First Ten. They played on the U.S. Davis Cup team together in 1903. The Kinseys won the U.S. doubles championship together in 1924, and Howard was one of the original touring pros (*See also* Pyle), losing the first U.S. Pro final to Vincent Richards in 1927.

Bill Larned (*See also* First Tens) held high ranking more than any other American, standing in the First Ten 19 times between 1892 and 1911 (number one 8 times), winning the U.S. singles 7 times between 1901 and 1911, and playing on 6 Davis Cup teams (helping win the Cup in 1902). His younger brother, Edward Larned, ranked in the First Ten with him thrice, number six in 1903. Beals Wright was in the First Ten 11 times between 1899 and 1910—number one in 1905 when he won the U.S. singles—and played on 4 Davis Cup teams. His brother, Irving Wright, was in the First Ten with him twice, number nine in 1907. In 1921 Fred Anderson beat Frank Anderson in the title round of the U.S. Indoor championship, the only time brothers have met in a major American final. In 1942 Bob and Tom Falkenburg of Fairfax High in Los Angeles won the National Interscholastic doubles title, and Bob went on to capture the Wimbledon singles six years later. The three Amritraj brothers—Anand, Vijay, and Ashok—have been outstanding players from India (*See also* Madras Monsoons).

BUCHAREST BACKFIRE: A flamboyant stroke associated with Ilie Nastase—a blind flick over the left shoulder made with the back to the net after catching up with a lob over the head. Maria Bueno, a champion of the early 1960s, perfected a similar shot, but the wide TV exposure of Nastase has made him seem the originator. (Actually, he learned it from his early doubles partner and mentor, Ion Tiriac.)

BUCHAREST BUFFOON: Ilie Nastase, born in 1946 in Bucharest, Romania, is an erratic sporting genius whose talent and speed has made little Romania a factor in the world picture. He carried his country to three Davis Cups finals (1969, '71, and '72), which were lost to the U.S. In 1972 he was the first Eastern European to win the U.S. title at Forest Hills, and he has won the climactic event of the year, the Masters, a record four times (1971, '72, '73, and '75). An individualist who says, "I am a little crazy," Ilie is both engaging and enraging with his on-court burlesques, his mimicking and baiting of foes, his unpredictable rages and walkouts. He is the most fined player ever. In 1975 he was disqualified in three matches for misbehavior, and he reaped the highest fine, $8,000, for failing to try in the Canadian Open final against Manuel Orantes.

BUDGE: Many feel that Donald Budge of Oakland, Calif., was the greatest player of all time, and most experts rank him no less than number two behind the great Bill Tilden. Budge took the Grand Slam in 1938 when he was twenty-two, won the U.S. and Wimbledon singles in 1937-38, and helped the U.S. win the Davis Cup those years as well. Noted for his powerful backhand, Budge won the U.S. Pro title in 1942.

CALIFORNIA COMET: That's what they called Maurice McLoughlin (1890-1957) when he came out of San Francisco in 1909 to shake up the game with a markedly different crash-bang offensive style. With little more than a rocketing serve backed by stiff volleys he won the national singles in 1912-13.

CANNONBALL: An extraordinarily swift serve. Maurice McLoughlin was the first of the big servers. At one time Pancho Gonzalez's serve was said to be the fastest; his blasts were timed at 117 miles per hour. Later, Mike Sangster's serve was clocked in special tests at 154 miles per hour.

CAPTAIN FRASER'S ANTIQUE SHOW: With all professionals eligible for Davis Cup for the first time in 1973, Capt. Neale Fraser of Australia brought back some of his country's all-time heroes to form the oldest—and probably the best—team to grace the Cup event: Ken Rosewall, thirty-nine, Mal Anderson, thirty-eight, Rod Laver, thirty-five, and John Newcombe, twenty-nine. With Laver and Newcombe playing both singles and joining in the doubles, the Aussies blitzed the Cup-holding U.S., 5-0, in the final.

CARRY: *See* Double Hit.

CENTRE COURT: This is the cathedral of tennis, a covered stadium surrounding the principal court at Wimbledon, a structure much like an Elizabethan theatre. On this grass court the championship finals are played along with the most important matches of the Wimbledon fortnight. It was built in 1922 and holds 14,000 spectators, 1,500 of them on each side in the open standing-room areas. Also, center court can mean the main court in any arena.

CHALLENGE ROUND: A type of final once common to tennis, particularly the Davis Cup, and now out of use, whereby the champion was privileged to stand aside the following year, waiting for a challenger to be determined by an elimination tournament. Then the challenger would face the reigning champion for the title. This format was discarded by the U.S. championship in 1912, by Wimbledon in 1921, and by the Davis Cup in 1972. That year the Cup-holding U.S. played through the tournament along with the other nations entered, reached the final against Romania, and retained the title.

CHANGE GAME: At the completion of each odd game of a match, beginning with the first game, the players change sides in order to equalize playing conditions—sun, wind, court surface, etc.

CHOKING: What a player is doing who can't perform to his normal ability when the going gets rough and the pressure is on. Most players recognize that it can happen to the best of them, and they are not ashamed to admit it.

CHOP: A short, slicing stroke that puts the ball in an underspin that causes it to bounce very low in an unexpected direction.

CLAY: The most popular surface for the game. Clay courts are found throughout the world. The ball bounces high and slow on clay, giving players more time to make a stroke and thereby producing longer rallies. The French championship in Paris is considered the world-title clay-court event. A National Clay Court championship is held annually in the United States.

¹COURT: The area on which the game is played. A tennis court can be surfaced with anything from anthills (in Australia) to cow dung (in India) to wood, clay, grass, linoleum, AstroTurf, or other synthetics. The dimensions are always the same: 78 feet long and 27 feet wide (35 feet wide for doubles). The game began on grass courts in England, but that is an uncommon surface now, although the biggest tournament of all, Wimbledon, is still a grass event.

²COURT: Margaret Smith (later Mrs. Barry Court). She came out of Albury, Australia, where she was born in 1942, to establish herself as the most prolific champion in history. At the conclusion of 1975 she had amassed 59 Big Four (Australian, French, Wimbledon, U.S.) championships in singles (24), doubles (18), and mixed doubles (17), and she was the only woman to win any of these singles titles after giving birth to a child. After having two children she was still playing. Remarkably strong and well conditioned, she has an awesome reach and is frequently called The Arm by opponents. She made the second female Grand Slam in singles, winning all the Big Four titles in 1970. She and Ken Fletcher made a mixed-doubles Slam in 1963. Margaret is considered by many to be the greatest of all women players.

CROSS-COURT: A diagonal shot across the court from the left or the right.

DAVIS CUP: A competition (limited to males) open to teams representing nations throughout the world. It was originated by Dwight Filley Davis, who was a student at Harvard and played on the first team, competing against the top players from Great Britain. The Americans won in the inaugural year. *See also* Big Four.

DEUCE: A game or set score meaning the opponents are even. The deuce factor provides that games and sets can go on and on. In a game the score is deuce at 40 all or three points each. To win, a player must take two straight points from deuce. The first point after deuce is advantage, and the score keeps reverting to deuce unless one player wins the two straight points. A set becomes deuce when the score becomes five games apiece. To win the set, a player must be two games ahead, thus winning two straight games from 5 all, 6 all, 7 all, etc. The longest deuce set ever played was 49-47 during the longest match ever played. Dick Leach and Dick Dell beat Tom Mozur and Len Schloss, 3-6, 49-47, 22-20, in the 1967 Newport (R.I.) Invitation.

DONKEYS: Consistent losers on the pro circuit.

DOUBLE FAULT: When the server misses with both serves, thus losing the point.

DOUBLE HIT: Striking the ball twice during the same stroke, a misfortune that means automatic loss of the point. Also called a carry.

DOUBLES: A team game with two players on each side of the net.

DOWN-THE-LINE: A shot along either sideline.

DOWN UNDER-TAKER(S): Any of the prominent Australian players. Since World War II, the men from down under have dominated the game, winning 12 of 24 Wimbledon singles, 15 of 24 U.S. singles, and holding the Davis Cup 15 of 24 years.

DRAW: The lineup for a customary elimination tournament. Names of the players are drawn blindly, usually from a cup, and placed in the order drawn on a bracketed draw sheet that indicates who opposes whom.

DROP SHOT: A softly hit shot, intentionally aimed to barely clear the net in order to win a point outright, or to pull the opponent in close.

DWIGHT: Dr. James Dwight (1852-1917), a Boston physician who spent considerably more time practicing tennis than medicine, is considered father of the American game. He won the first tournament ever played in the U.S., a sociable round robin at Nahant, Mass., in 1875, was a founder of the USTA (then the U.S. National Lawn Tennis Association) in 1881, and served as its president a total of twenty years. He also was national doubles champion five times with Dick Sears between 1882 and 1887.

ELBOW: Getting the elbow is choking or tightening up at a critical point, a bad reaction to pressure. However, tennis elbow is an actual physical affliction, a painful malfunctioning of the elbow that strikes not only tennis players. Physicians have not found a sure cure.

EMMO: Roy Emerson. Although Emmo stands well behind countrywoman Margaret Court in number of major titles won, he is still first among men, with a total of 28 Big Four (Australian, French, Wimbledon, U.S.) championships in singles (12) and doubles (16). Born in the Australian bush town of Black Butt in 1936, he is a superb athlete who became an inspirational team man, taking part in a record eight Davis Cup triumphs for Australia between 1959 and 1967. His Wimbledon singles titles were in 1964 and 1965.

ERROR: A mistake that loses a point during a rally, such as hitting the ball out or into the net.

FAULT: Failing to put the ball into play with the serve, either by serving into the net or beyond the confines of the service court. It is also a fault to step on the base line while serving or to swing and miss the ball altogether. One fault isn't disastrous, but two lose the point.

FEDERATION CUP: An annual worldwide women's team competition among nations, which was begun in 1963. The format is best-of-three matches (two singles and a doubles) during an elimination tournament.

FIRST TENS: Two select groups set forth annually by the USTA, one of men and one of women who rank number one through number ten in singles. The First Ten selections are based on tournament results of the previous season. This began in 1885 for men, when Dick Sears was number one, and 1913 for women, when Mary K. Browne was number one. The most frequent selections for First Tens have been Bill Larned, 19 years between 1892 and 1911 (he was number one 8 times), and Louise Brough, 16 years between 1941 and 1957 (number one once). The rankings continue beyond the First Ten.

FOOT FAULT: An infraction by the server when he steps on the base line or serves from the wrong side of the center line. On a first serve it is not serious. On the second he loses the point.

FOREHAND: The stroke hit from the same side of the body as the hand holding the racket—from the right for a right-hander, from the left for a left-hander.

FOREST HILLS: The scene of America's most important tournament, the U.S. Open, which offers more than $200,000 in prize money. The host for the tournament is the West Side Tennis Club in the Forest Hills section of New York's borough of Queens. The tournament and section are generally referred to simply as Forest Hills. The West Side Tennis Club dates back to 1892, when it was located on Central Park West (between Eighty-eighth and Eighty-ninth streets) in the borough of Manhattan. Forest Hills is the club's fourth home and the site of the national championships since 1915. The tournament was played on grass until 1975, when that surface was replaced by clay.

FORO ITALICO: The scene of the Italian championships in Rome. A bastion of marble and pines alongside the Tiber, it is the world's most handsome setting for a major event. It was built as Foro Mussolini during the dictator's reign.

FOUR MUSKETEERS: Henri Cochet, René Lacoste, Jean Borotra, and Jacques Brugon. During a brief, bright period (1927-32) France dominated the tennis world and held the Davis Cup because the Four Musketeers bloomed together.

GAME: The contest within a set and a match. One player serves throughout a game. To win a game, the player must win four points, unless the score is three points apiece, known as deuce. Then the player must get two straight points to win the game. The points in a game are called 15, 30, 40, and game—in that order. To win a set, the player must win six games, unless the score is five games apiece. Then it is a deuce set, and the player must take two straight games from deuce to win.

GEM AND PERERA: Although Walter Wingfield patented lawn tennis in 1874, Englishmen Maj. Harry Gem and J. B. Perera preceded him by some time in playing outdoors on grass at Edgbaston as early as 1858.

GIBSON: Althea Gibson (now Mrs. William Darben), born in 1927 at Silver, S.C. She made a social and racial breakthrough as the first black to be accepted in major tennis and to win the significant championships at Forest Hills and Wimbledon in 1957 and 1958. She was also the first black to play tennis for her country in the Wightman Cup in 1957. She turned professional in 1959 and earned more than $100,000 from gate receipts playing exhibitions against Karol Fageros on a tour with the Harlem Globetrotters. That was the extent of her pro playing career, since the prize-money days for women were still nearly a decade ahead. She is now a teaching pro, having also had a brief fling at the women's pro golf tour.

GOOLAGONG: That lovely Aboriginal name ("tall trees by still waters") belongs to Evonne Goolagong Cawley, 1971 Wimbledon champ, one of the most graceful and good-natured players in history. Born in 1951 at Barellan, Australia, she is the first of the original Aussies, the Aborigines, to make a mark in tennis, and the first nonwhite to win a title of South Africa, the singles in 1972. Though married to Roger Cawley, Goolagong plays under her maiden name.

GORE: Spencer Gore (1850-1906), who won the opening Wimbledon of 1877 and became the first tennis champion. He later deprecated his feat, noting that tennis wasn't much of a game.

GRAND MASTERS: A prize-money tournament circuit inaugurated in 1973 for the cream of the crocks—ex-champs over forty-five—by Cincinnati businessman Al Bunis. Dealing in nostalgia and featuring such yet imposing players as Pancho Gonzalez, Frank Sedgman, and Torben Ulrich, it was a financial success. In 1975 Sedgman earned more than $60,000 in prize money, his second best financial year since he turned pro in 1953.

GRAND PRIX: A series of men's tournaments, including all the major championships across the world between May and December (plus the Australian Open in January), in which bonus points are awarded for each victory. At the close of the year the leaders in points collect bonuses, ranging in 1975 from $100,000 for first place (Guillermo Vilas) to $6,500 for thirty-sixth (Corrado Barazzutti). Moreover, the top eight qualify for a $100,000 December play-off called the Masters, won in 1975 by Ilie Nastase (for $40,000) in Stockholm. Jack Kramer, outstanding player, promoter, and administrator, originated the idea in 1970 to give cohesion to the pro season. Sponsorship, first undertaken by Pepsico that year, passed to Commercial Union Assurance Company in 1972.

GRAND SLAM: The rare feat of winning the four major singles championships (Australian, French, Wimbledon, U.S.) all in the same year. Don Budge did it in 1938, Maureen Connolly in 1953, Rod Laver in 1962 and 1969, and Margaret Court in 1970.

GRASS COURT: Tennis began on English lawns, and grass has been the traditional surface in Britain, Australia, and the United States. It is fading in America as maintenance costs mount and more suitable all-weather courts are developed. In the U.S. only a handful of exclusive clubs in the Northeast keep up grass courts. For play the grass is cut short, lower than two inches, and has the appearance of a golf green, although a grass court must be much sturdier to resist running and sliding. Because the bounce is low and the ball skids and skips, the grass-court game is extremely fast, favoring an attacking player with strong serve and volley who gets to the net quickly. This contrasts widely with the clay-court game and its premium on base-line play. Although Forest Hills has grass for its members, the U.S. Open, at that site, switched to clay courts in 1975.

GRIP: The method of holding the racket. Basic grips are the Eastern, Western, and Continental, but there are also numerous (but slight) variations adapted by individual players. Many players, notably Pancho Segura, Chris Evert, and Jimmy Connors, have done well with the unusual baseball grip—using both hands—but most common is the one-handed grip. Also, the leather wrapping around the handle of the racket, frequently changed by the top players to adjust to feel and wear. The diameter of the handle varies slightly and is a measurement that is marked for purposes of purchasing a racket. A player chooses one with a grip that is most comfortable for him.

GROUNDIE: *See* Ground stroke.

GROUND STROKE: A stroke hit from the back-court area after the ball bounces. The return of serve is a ground stroke.

HACKER: An ordinary player—a term applying to most of us—the tennis equivalent of the golfing duffer. Also used in good-natured ribbing by the pros. It came into vogue in 1966, when Aussie Fred Stolle, Wimbledon runner-up and German champion, came to Forest Hills to find himself surprisingly unseeded. "I guess they think I'm just an old hacker," he said. After he won the title, Fred said, "There's still some life in the old hacker." He was twenty-seven and has been the Old Hacker since.

HADOW: The resourceful Englishman, P. F. Hadow, the Wimbledon champ of 1878, who is credited with raising our sights by first stroking the lob during that tournament. He must have been ashamed of himself, because he never played again.

HALF VOLLEY: The stroke by which the ball is blocked as soon as it hits the ground. Like trapping a baseball.

HALL OF FAME: Like several other sports, tennis has enshrined its all-time heroes and heroines, mounting plaques in their honor in a combined Hall of Fame and tennis museum at Newport, R.I., site of the first American championship in 1881. Since its founding in the Newport Casino in 1954, the Hall has inducted 52 male and 25 female players, as well as 4 administrators and 1 journalist of prominence.

HANDSOME EIGHT: Eight players who were dubbed and signed by Dave Dixon as the personnel for the newly organized World Championship Tennis (WCT) late in 1967. They were John Newcombe, Tony Roche, Roger Taylor, Nikola Pilic, Cliff Drysdale, all of whom were recruited from the amateur game; and Pierre Barthes, Butch Buchholz, and Dennis Ralston, who had been touring as pros. This raid of the amateur ranks by Dixon hastened the acceptance of open tennis by the ILTF a few months later.

HARD COURT: This can be confusing because in the U.S. "hard court" means cement, asphalt, or similar paving, while in Europe, Australia, and most other countries the term applies to clay courts. The U.S. annually held a National Hard Court championship on cement until 1972.

HATCHETWOMAN: Chrissie Evert, who burst upon America's consciousness in 1971 as a sixteen-year-old schoolgirl zooming through the U.S. Open in a series of upsets to become the youngest Forest Hills semifinalist. Since then, nothing she has won has been regarded as an upset, including Wimbledon in 1974, the French and Italian titles in 1974 and 1975, and the U.S. Open in 1975. Seldom has she lost. Called Machinetta ("The Little Machine") in Italy, she is a grim reaper with her two-handed backhand but a pleasant young woman away from business. She was a world's Top Ten player while still in high school in Ft. Lauderdale, Fla., and was ranked number one in 1974-75. In 1975 she set a seasonal prize-money record for all players, male or female, of $360,227. Her sister, Jeanne, younger by three years, is also a pro and one of the better American players.

HEAVYWEIGHT CHAMPIONSHIP: Jimmy Connors was billed as the heavyweight champion of tennis by his shrewd manager, Bill Riordan, as part of the buildup for a televised match between then Wimbledon-U.S. Open champ Connors and ex-dominant champion Rod Laver at Las Vegas early in 1975. Connors won and also beat the next challenger for the heavyweight title, John Newcombe, and the Columbia Broadcasting System adopted the title for promotional use in future such challenges.

HOP: Harry Hopman, an Australian born in 1906, the most successful Davis Cup captain and coach. He was instrumental in developing the Aussie dynasty in tennis that lasted for a quarter century, beginning with Frank Sedgman in 1950. Hopman captained the team to a 1939 victory, returned to the nonplaying position in 1950, and continued through 1969, during which time he won 15 more Cups with such standouts as Lew Hoad, Ken Rosewall, Rod Laver, Neale Fraser, Ashley Cooper, Mal Anderson, Roy Emerson, Fred Stolle, Tony Roche, and John Newcombe. He emigrated to the U.S. to continue his coaching career.

I FORMATION: An unorthodox doubles alignment with the netman standing directly ahead of his partner, the server, instead of in the adjoining court. The

Chris Evert, like Jimmy Connors, does well with a baseball grip—using both hands.

purpose is to confuse the receiver. Also called the tandem formation, as well as the Australian formation (in the U.S.) and the American formation (in Australia).

ILTF: The International Lawn Tennis Federation. Since 1913 it has been the world governing body of tennis, embracing the amateur bodies of nearly one-hundred countries. The ILTF has little control over professional tennis other than the power to approve or disapprove open tournaments, and it seats delegates on the Men's International Professional Tennis Council.

IN THE ZONE: A state of great confidence when one is playing sensationally, even above expected ability. "I'm sure in the zone today." From "The Twilight Zone," a TV program about otherworldly behavior and situations.

IPA: Independent Players Association, an organization founded in opposition to the ATP by Bill Riordan, tournament promoter, and then manager of Jimmy Connors. Connors appeared to be the only member of his private union. There may have been others, but their names weren't revealed.

JAG: A verb coined by Aussies meaning "to hit the ball unstylishly but somehow getting it over the net," as in Rod Laver remarking, "I just made up my mind to jag a few, keep it in play, until I found my timing."

JOHNSTON AWARD: An award for outstanding sportsmanship presented annually to an American male by the U.S. Lawn Tennis Association. It was named for a tiny but indomitable competitor, the late Billy Johnston (1894-1946), who was national champion 1915-19.

KANGAROO KIDS: In 1953 Australian nineteen-year-olds Lew Hoad and Ken Rosewall bounced into the world picture by successfully holding the Davis Cup for their homeland. They were the youngest players to win the Cup, and in 1975 Ken Rosewall was still among the Top Ten players.

KICKER: An American twist serve taking a high bounce.

KING'S CUP: An indoor team competition for European nations, along the lines of the Davis Cup. It was named for the donor, King Gustave V of Sweden, the tennis fanatic who played into his nineties.

KOOYONG: A stadium in Melbourne, Australia, where the third largest crowd in tennis history, 22,000, gathered for the Australian-U.S. Davis Cup finale in 1957. An Aboriginal name, "kooyong" means haunt of the wild fowl.

LANGRISHE: May Langrishe, the first female champion. She carried the day at Dublin in 1879, when the Irish championships was the first tournament to include women.

LEAMINGTON: The Leamington Lawn Tennis Club, the first club founded for the distinct purpose of tennis. It was established in 1872 at Leamington in Warwickshire, England. Maj. Harry Gem served as the first president. The club no longer exists. *See also* Gem and Perera.

LET: The signal for a replay. If a serve hits the top of the net and proceeds into the proper service court, the serve is replayed. If a point is interrupted or interfered with in any way (such as a ball from a nearby court rolling through), let is called, and the point is replayed.

LINER: A shot landing on or touching a line. It is a good shot.

LINESMAN: An official who judges whether a shot is out or good. A full squad of linesmen for a match is ten. Add the umpire, net judge, and foot-fault judge, and you have quite a crowd presiding over one match. The players feel outnumbered on court.

LINGERING DEATH: A tie breaker based on Jimmy Van Alen's original theme, but adhering to the deuce principle of winning only if ahead by two or more points. The goal is to reach seven points, but the winner must be two points ahead, thus at 6-6 the tie breaker could continue indefinitely. This form is usually called the 12-point tie breaker, a misnomer since it may stretch well beyond 12. *See also* Tie Breaker.

LITTLE MISS POKER FACE: Helen Wills Moody from Berkeley, Calif. On court she never smiled, although she had plenty of reason to do so. She won the U.S. singles title in 1923, '24, '25, '27, '28, '29, and '31 and the Wimbledon in 1927, '28, '29, '30, '32, '33, '35, and '38—a record collection of the two most prominent prizes. She was born in 1905.

LITTLE MO: Maureen Connolly (1934-56) of San Diego, Calif. As much for her thundering ground strokes as for her size, this 63-inch woman was compared to the battleship *Missouri* (Big Mo). When she was nineteen (1953), she became the first woman to score a Grand Slam in singles. She won the U.S. singles in 1951, '52, and '53 and Wimbledon in 1952, '53, and '54.

LOB: A high arching stroke meant either as a defensive shot (enabling the hitter to regain position) or to go over the head of an opponent at net. *See also* Hadow.

LONGWOOD: Longwood Cricket Club in Boston, the oldest tennis club of significance in the United States. Founded in 1877, it was the scene of the first Davis Cup match in 1900. Site of many national championships, Longwood has held the U.S. Pro championship since 1964. Among its members have been Dick Sears, first U.S. national champ; Dwight Davis, donor of the Davis Cup; and Hazel Wightman, donor of the Wightman Cup. Slightly older is the New Orleans Lawn Tennis Club, organized in 1876.

LOVE: A zero score. A love game is a blitz, with the winner taking four straight points. A love set is six games to nothing. Probably derived from the French word "l'oeuf," meaning egg—and implying the old goose egg.

MADRAS MONSOONS: The Amritrajs, the most remarkable brothers to emerge from Asia, an assault-minded trio of Indians out of Madras—Anand, born in 1952; Vijay, in 1953; and Ashok, in 1957. Each winning three times, they held the Indian junior championship nine successive years among them. Anand and Vijay carried India to the 1974 Davis Cup final, which was forfeited to South Africa as a protest by the Indian government against apartheid. Vijay was a Wimbledon quarterfinalist in 1973.

MASTERS: The climax of the tennis year is the eight-man Masters play-off among the top finishers in the Grand Prix. Begun in 1970 at Tokyo, where Stan Smith won, the Masters is staged in a different city each year. Ilie Nastase has been extremely masterly, winning in 1971, '72, '73, and '75, taking $40,000 first prize in the $100,000 event the last year.

MATCH: A contest between players or between teams, e.g., a Davis Cup match.

MATCH POINT: The point prior to completion of a match. The player in the lead needs only one more point to win. This can be a very dramatic spot, and sometimes the player behind in the score saves numerous match points and goes on to victory.

MILLIONAIRE(S): Rod Laver was the first tennis player to earn more than a million in prize money, crossing that barrier in 1971. Ken Rosewall followed in 1972. Then Arthur Ashe had a record male season of $325,550 in 1975. At the close of 1975 the three stood this way: Laver ($1,499,870), Rosewall ($1,252,198), Ashe ($1,039,415).

MIPTC: Men's International Professional Tennis Council, a board of control for the pro tournament game. Formed in 1974, it seeks to regulate schedules and conditions of play and conduct for the pro game. It is made up of representatives from the ILTF, ATP, and various tournaments.

MIXED DOUBLES: Doubles with one male and one female on each side.

MOONBALL: A high, floating ground stroke used in base-line rallying to slow down the pace. It's not as high as a lob and is usually hit with top spin. It is most associated with a leading American, Harold Solomon, who can hit them forever and who coined the term in 1972 when his moonballing epic, a marathon victory over Guillermo Vilas during the French Open, consumed more than five hours.

NET: The webbed barrier dividing the court at middle and over which the ball is to be hit. At the center point it is three feet high and at either end three and a half feet.

NET CORD: A shot that hits the top of the net and drops into the opposite court. Also, the cord or wire cable that supports a net.

NET JUDGE: An official seated at one end of the net below the umpire's chair to detect lets on serve. During the serve he rests his hand on top of the net to feel whether the ball hits the top of the net. If it does, he calls "Net!" and the serve is replayed as a let if the ball lands in the proper court.

NET RUSHER: An attacking player who follows his serve to the net and continually seeks the closeup position to make winning volleys.

NEWK: John Newcombe, a power hitter, the last champion in the Australian dynasty that began in 1950 with Frank Sedgman and lasted roughly a quarter of a century. Born in 1944, Newk won the Wimbledon singles in 1967, '70, and '71, joining Rod Laver as the only two men to win more than twice in the post-World War II era. He won the U.S. title in singles in 1967 and 1973 and the Wimbledon doubles six times (five with Tony Roche) as well as playing a strong role in four Australian victories in the Davis Cup and five in the World Cup.

NEWPORT BOLSHEVIK: Jimmy Van Alen, the scoring radical who revolutionized the game by conceiving tie breakers, No-Ad, and VASSS. A man of wealth and social position with a Newport (R.I.) estate, Van Alen, born in 1902, didn't seem the type to espouse radicalism in an essentially conservative game. Only through great persistence did he push his ideas to acceptance.

NO-AD: A form of scoring originated by Jimmy Van Alen that eliminates deuce and replaces 15-30-40 with 1-2-3. The maximum points for a game are seven. At 3-3 (normally deuce) the next point is game point for both sides, with the receiver to elect choice of courts. No-Ad has been adopted by World Team Tennis and the National Collegiate Athletic Association annual tournament. *See also* VASSS.

NOT UP: The call when a player hits the ball just as it has bounced the second time on a close play. Usually the net judge makes the ruling, but if there are no officials, it is up to the offending player to call it against himself and accept loss of the point.

NTL: The National Tennis League, an organization formed by George MacCall in 1967 to promote professional tournaments. Under contract were Rod Laver, Ken Rosewall, Pancho Gonzalez, Andres Gimeno, Fred Stolle, Roy Emerson, Billie Jean King, Rosie Casals, Ann Jones, and Francoise Durr. By 1970 NTL had been put out of business and absorbed by rival WCT.

OPEN: A tournament that may be entered by both amateurs and professionals, generally offering prize money. Not until 1968 did the ILTF permit opens. The first, the British Hard Court championship, was won by pro Ken Rosewall. Now all the leading national title events are open.

OVERHEAD: A stroke, usually a smash, executed like a serve by raising the racket above the head and swinging down hard.

PANCHO: Two great pros, Richard Gonzalez and Francisco Segura, both of Los Angeles, carry the nickname. Gonzalez won the U.S. singles in 1948 and 1949 and the U.S. Pro title eight times. Segura, distinctive because of his brilliant two-fisted fore-hand, won the U.S. Pro championship three times. Remarkably, both were still active and playing tournaments in 1970 when Gonzalez was forty-two and Segura forty-nine, and Gonzalez ranked number nine in the U.S. in 1972.

PASSING SHOT: A ball hit past the opposing netman on either side beyond his reach.

PLACEMENT: A shot aimed at a particular sector and hit so well that the opponent can't touch it.

POACH: In doubles, when a player, hoping to make a winning volley, crosses in front of his partner.

POINT: The smallest unit of scoring. A game is won by a player winning four points except in the case of deuce. The first point of a game is called 15, the second 30, the third 40, and the fourth is game. At 40-all the score is deuce. Each point is begun with the serve, and one player serves an entire game. In keeping score, the server's score is called first, e.g., in 15-40, 15 is the server, and 40 is the receiver.

PROFESSIONAL: A player who plays prize-money events for money or a teacher who gives tennis lessons for money.

PUSHER: A player who hopes to wear down his opponent by maddeningly returning everything with soft looping strokes. A pusher hangs back at the base line, a good retriever, patiently waiting for a big hitter to blow his cool and the match. Also known as a pooper, puddler, or puffball artist.

PYLE: C. C. ("Cash and Carry") Pyle, a flamboyant sports promoter of the 1920s, launched professional tennis in 1926 when he signed the legendary French-woman Suzanne Lenglen to make a tour of one-night stands against a topflight opponent, a format that was the essence of the pro game until open tennis came about in 1968. As Lenglen's foe, Pyle signed a leading American, Mary K. Browne. He completed his barnstorming troupe by signing Vincent Richards, Howard Kinsey, Harvey Snodgrass, and Paul Feret—the first group to play openly for money.

RACKET: The implement used in hitting the ball; an oval frame attached to a long, straight handle. The frame is crossed horizontally and vertically with strings.

The best strings are made of lamb intestine, which is known as gut. Nylon is also widely used. A racket may be of any size or material. Although wood frames predominate, metal, namely steel and aluminum, has become extremely popular. Fiber-glass and graphite rackets are also produced.

RALLY: An exchange of shots during a point.

RANKING: A player's standing in regard to other players. National rankings lists are made up annually for tournament players by the governing associations in almost every country. Sectional rankings, too, are made within the U.S. Tennis Association. An annual world ranking is also selected by a group of sportswriters. In the U.S. the finest record was made by Bill Larned (1872-1926), who was placed in the First Ten 19 times between 1892 and 1911 and was number one eight times. Rankings are based on tournament performance.

REFEREE: The official in charge of a tournament.

RICHEYS: Texans Nancy Richey Gunter, born in 1942, and Cliff Richey, born in 1946, the only brother-sister act to achieve ranking in America's First Ten, having done so together eight times between 1965 and 1973. Nancy was number one in 1964, '65, '68, and '69, and Cliff was number one in 1970. Both played for the U.S., Cliff in Davis and World Cup and Nancy in Wightman and Federation Cup.

RIORDAN CIRCUIT: The first viable indoor circuit for men in the U.S., organized by Bill Riordan, dynamic promoter from Salisbury, Md., and then manager of Jimmy Connors. He started in earnest in 1964 by transferring the nearly defunct U.S. Indoor champion-ship from New York to Salisbury, where it became a thriving event. He expanded to eight tournaments by 1975. A combative type, Riordan fought the growth of WCT and the ATP; founded his own player organiza-tion, called the IPA (Independent Players Association); and kept his series of winter tournaments going as a one-man operation that he called the Independent Circuit but that was generally known as the Riordan Circuit. *See also* IPA.

ROCKET: Nickname for Rodney Laver, an Austra-lian who won his second Grand Slam at age thirty-one as a pro in 1969, having won his first as an amateur in 1962. He is considered the best player of the post-World War II era, having taken Wimbledon in 1961, '62, '68, and '69. He also won the U.S. Pro title in 1964, '66, '67, '68, and '69.

ROLAND GARROS: The stadium in Paris where the French championship has been played yearly since 1928. It was named for a heroic French aviator of World War I.

RUBBER: An individual singles or doubles match in a team competition such as Davis or Wightman Cup. The usage is British and European.

SCRAMBLER: A player who hustles for every point and manages to get the ball back somehow, though probably not very stylishly. A dogged retriever.

SEARS: Richard (Dick) Sears (1861-1943), who won the first U.S. championship in 1881 at Newport, R.I., while a student at Harvard. After winning the first seven titles he retired unbeaten in 1887.

SEEDING: The deliberate, instead of chance, placing of certain strong players so that they will not meet in the earlier rounds of an elimination tournament. It was introduced to major tennis at Wimbledon in 1924 and soon became standard procedure. Seeded players (those judged by a tournament committee to be the leaders on the basis of performance and ability) are listed in numbered order prior to the draw. Then the seeds are separated by being planted in positions specified by tournament regulations. Thus the top two players, numbers one and two, are located at opposite ends of the draw, and if the seeding runs true, they will meet in the final.

SERVICE or SERVE: The act of putting the ball into play and beginning a point by hitting the ball from the base line diagonally over the net and into the opponent's service court. Any motion (underhand, sidearm, or whatever) is permissible. However, the overhead stroke is nearly universal.

SERVICE COURT(S): There are two, since the server alternates from the right to the left side of the court with each point. The service courts are bounded by the sidelines, the net, and the service line, which is 21 feet from the net; they are divided from one another by the center line. Each court is 13½ feet wide by 21 feet deep.

SERVICE WINNER: An unreturned serve, though not an ace.

SET: The second highest unit of scoring. The winner of six games takes the set, except when the score is 5 all in games. Then it is a deuce set, and the winner must win by two games, unless tie breakers are used, usually at 6-all games. In that case one tie-breaker game decides the outcome of the set, whose score would be 7-6.

SET POINT: The point prior to the completion of a set. The player ahead needs only one more point to win the set. But the player behind may still save the set point and go on to win the set himself, thanks to the deuce factor.

SITTER: An easy opportunity; a ball softly hit close to the net and well within reach, which can be smashed away for a point.

SLICE: Hitting under the ball, which produces underspin and a low bounce.

SLIMS CIRCUIT: The first notable attempt to bring women into the prize-money era of tennis was made successfully by Gladys Heldman, publisher of *World Tennis* magazine, who in 1970 began forming a circuit for the women separate from that of the men and sponsored by Virginia Slims cigarettes. With Mrs. Heldman as the organizational wizard and Billie Jean King as spokeswoman and all-conquering champion, the women's game took off in 1971. By going it alone, the women no longer had to play second racket to the men in cash or publicity, and their prize money rose dramatically to nearly $1 million in 1975 for ten tournaments in the U.S. For women the Virginia Slims championship—a play-off among the top eight women at the conclusion of the circuit in the spring—is, along with Wimbledon and the U.S. Open, one of the three most important events. It was won by Chris Evert in 1972, '73, and '75 and by Evonne Goolagong in 1974.

SMASH: An overhead stroke brought down hard like a serve.

SPIKES: Spiked shoes with ⅜-inch metal spikes that are sometimes worn on wet grass courts to help a player's footing.

SUDDEN DEATH: A tie breaker of definite length, either 9-point or 13-point, settled by a sudden death point when the score is 4-4 or 6-6. It was conceived by Jimmy Van Alen. *See also* Tie Breaker.

SUPREME COURT: The trade name for a synthetic carpet court favored for a majority of major indoor tournaments.

SUTTON SISTERS: May, Violet, Florence, and Ethel Sutton of Pasadena, Calif., the most accomplished sisters in the game's history. May (1887-1975), who became Mrs. Tom Bundy, was the best, the first American to win Wimbledon (1905); she was also the mother of Dorothy Bundy Cheney, who ranked in the American First Ten during the 1940s. In 1913 Ethel Sutton Bruce at number two and Florence Sutton at number three were the first sisters to be ranked together in the First Ten, a feat emulated by Chris and Jeanne Evert in 1974.

TANDEM FORMATION: *See* I Formation.

TAPSCOTT: Baring not all, but enough to shock Britain, Billie Tapscott, a South African, helped emancipate the female leg by appearing at Wimbledon uncovered by the traditional long white stockings in 1929. Naked calves were altogether new and sensational at the Big W and became the fashion in time.

TEAM TENNIS: *See* WTT.

TEEN ANGEL: Beneath flowing golden locks ran the most extraordinary teen-ager to play tennis— Sweden's Bjorn Borg, a factor internationally from age fifteen, when he became the second youngest Davis Cupper. He won the French Open and U.S. Pro championships in 1974 and 1975, the youngest to seize both, well before his twentieth birthday, which occurred June 6, 1976. At the close of 1975 he led Sweden to its first Davis Cup, 3-2 over Czechoslovakia, by winning both singles and (with Ove Bengston) the doubles. Borg did this without the loss of a set, joining Norman Brookes (Australia, 1909) and Jack Kramer (U.S., 1946) as the only men in the history of the competition to win nine of nine sets in the finals. Moreover, his achievement of 19 straight singles victories over 1973, '74, and '75 was a Davis Cup record.

TENNIS: The name of the game, generally speaking, although the proper name is lawn tennis. This distinction was made soon after an Englishman, Maj. Walter Wingfield, patented the game in 1874. He called his game Sphairistike. That was awkward and was usually shortened to "sticky," so he changed the patent to "lawn tennis." Mary Ewing Outerbridge, a society belle from Staten Island, N.Y., is credited with introducing the game to the United States in 1874. She came back from a trip to Bermuda with some tennis balls and rackets, items so baffling at the time that customs officials held on to them for a week trying to figure out how much duty to charge. They settled it by charging no duty at all. By 1881 the first national championship for men was played, and in 1887 a similar tourney was held for women.

TIE: A team match between countries, such as Davis or Federation Cup. It is an old expression, used mainly in Britain and Europe, seldom in the U.S. In the Davis Cup a tie is composed of five rubbers. *See also* Rubber.

TIE BREAKER: A means of ending a tied set in one game, rather than continuing in a theoretically endless deuce set in which one side must be two games ahead to win after 5-5 in games. It's another scoring innovation from the fertile mind of Jimmy Van Alen. Usually the tiebreaker is invoked at 6-6 in games, although Wimbledon and a few other tournaments prefer to wait until 8-8. Serve alternates during the tie breaker, which is won by the first side to reach a specified number, depending on the form of tie breaker. The most comprehensible is Van Alen's Sudden Death 9-point maximum, won by the first to reach five points. There is also a Sudden Death 13-point maximum, won by the first to reach seven, which is used by WCT. A variation on Van Alen's theme is the Lingering Death, won by the first to reach 7 points provided there is a 2-point margin. Otherwise it continues until one side is ahead by 2 and could theoretically last indefinitely, although the longest recorded was 19-17 at Wimbledon in 1974, Bjorn Borg over Premjit Lall. Tie breakers came into noticeable use in 1970, when Sudden Death was adopted by the U.S. Pro championships and the U.S. Open.

TILDEN: Big Bill Tilden (1893-1953) from Philadelphia, considered the greatest player of all time. He won the U.S. singles seven times, 1920 through 1925 and in 1930, and Wimbledon three times, 1920, '21, and '30. He played in more Davis Cup final rounds (11) than any other man and helped the U.S. win the Cup seven straight years between 1920 and 1926. He won the U.S. Pro title 1931-35.

TOP SPIN: Spin produced by hitting over the ball to create a high bounce. It also helps control a hard-hit ball, preventing it from traveling too far.

TOURNAMENT: The basic form of competition. The most common is a single-elimination tournament with a minimum of eight entries. Departure of losers cuts the field in half at each round as a tournament narrows to two entries in the final. The world's three premier tournaments—Wimbledon, the U.S. Open, and the French championships—normally have draws of 128 men and 64 women, with seven and six rounds of play respectively.

UMPIRE: The official in charge of a match, keeping and calling score, usually from a high chair at one end of the net.

U.S. PRO CHAMPIONSHIP(S): The first tournament for professionals was the U.S. Pro, won in 1927 by Vincent Richards at the long-since-vanished Notlek Tennis Club in Manhattan. Total prize money was $5,000. The largely unnoticed and unsuccessful event was played all over the country until moving to its present site, the Longwood Cricket Club in Boston, in 1964, where it prospered and was the fountainhead for the solid growth of the pro game, with prize money rising to $100,000 by 1975. The most frequent winners were Pancho Gonzalez, eight times, and Rod Laver, five.

USTA: The United States Tennis Association (formerly U.S. Lawn Tennis Association), the governing organization of amateur tennis in the United States. It also operates the U.S. Open. Founded in 1881, it embraces seventeen sectional associations from New England to southern California. In 1975 the L for "Lawn" was dropped from the association abbreviation as dated, since so little tennis is now played on grass.

VASSS: The Van Alen Streamlined Scoring System. Devised by James Van Alen, who was anxious to make the game more readily understood by the general public and to eliminate long drawn-out matches. VASSS replaced love-15-30-40 with zero-1-2-3 and eliminated deuce altogether. He devised the tie breaker to avoid deuce sets. In VASSS No-Ad the first player to win four points wins the game. In VASSS Single Point the scoring is changed altogether. The first player to reach 31 points wins the set, with the tie breaker to be used if the score reaches 30-30. Few tournaments have adopted Van Alen's system, although World Tennis and the National Collegiate Athletic Association use No-Ad.

To many, "Big Bill" Tilden *is regarded as the greatest player of them all.*

Tie breakers, either Sudden or Lingering Death, are established.

VOLLEY: To hit the ball during the play before it touches the ground, usually at the net.

WCT: World Championship Tennis. This most ambitious and successful organization to promote professional tennis was formed in late 1967 by Dave Dixon of New Orleans in partnership with Dallas sportsman-oil millionaire Lamar Hunt. Dixon signed eight players (*see also* Handsome Eight), and the firm was in business, though shakily, and Hunt and his nephew, Al Hill, Jr., bought out Dixon after a few months operation and huge losses. Gradually, under director Mike Davis, the concept of the World Championship of Tennis developed—a series of tournaments throughout the world involving most of the leading men and pointing to play-offs in May among the top eight finishers in singles and doubles.

Ken Rosewall won the first WCT play-off over Rod Laver in Dallas in 1971 and collected a $50,000 first prize. Rosewall repeated in 1972 and was then succeeded by Stan Smith, John Newcombe, and Arthur Ashe. Smith and Bob Lutz won the first WCT doubles in 1973, and they were followed by Bob Hewitt-Fred McMillan and Raul Ramirez-Brian Gottfried. WCT broadened its operations by constructing tennis resorts (Lakeway World of Tennis outside Austin, Tex., and Peachtree World of Tennis in Atlanta), marketing tennis clothing, and opening tennis academies. Prize money for thirty WCT events in 1975 amounted to more than $2 million.

WHITE CITY: A stadium in Sydney, Australia, where the second largest crowd in tennis history, 25,578, attended for the Australia-U.S. Davis Cup finale in 1954.

WIGHTMAN CUP: The annual women's team competition between Great Britain and the U.S., begun in 1923. The format is best-of-seven matches—five singles and two doubles. The cup was donated by Mrs. Hazel Wightman of Boston (1886-1974), winner of a record 45 U.S. titles in singles and doubles. She played in the first Cup match, won by the United States, 7-0. The United States led in the series through 1975.

WIMBLEDON: The game's leading tournament, considered the world championship. Played on the grounds of the All England Lawn Tennis & Croquet Club in the London suburb of Wimbledon, the English title event is known formally as The Lawn Tennis Championships and called, universally, Wimbledon. Launched in 1877, it has always been played on grass and has been an open since 1968. Championships are decided in men's and women's singles and doubles, mixed doubles, junior boys and girls singles, and veterans (over age forty-five) doubles. Always a sellout, the tourney draws about 300,000 spectators over twelve days; a record attendance of 337,598 was set in 1975.

WINGFIELD: Maj. Walter Wingfield, an Englishman, patented the game in 1874, an adaptation of court tennis that he eventually called lawn tennis.

WINNER: A shot hit for an outright point. Also called a placement.

WORLD CUP: An annual team competition between Australian and U.S. male pros, begun in 1970. The event has been played at Hartford, Conn., since 1972, and Australia led 5-1 following a 4-3 victory in 1972.

WTA: The Women's Tennis Association, an organization of the leading female pros, similar to a union and comparable to the ATP. Billie Jean King was the guiding light in the 1974 founding, and she was the first president.

WTT: World Team Tennis. City franchises, the foundation of major pro sports in the U.S., came to tennis in 1974 with the establishment of World Team Tennis, a league with sixteen teams from Boston to Honolulu. Founded by Dennis Murphy, Jordan Kaiser, and Larry King (husband of Billie Jean), WTT was a radical undertaking, involving tennis players and equipment and some of the basics but actually creating a new game: team tennis. Women and men were on pro teams together for the first time, sharing the load; a match consisted of five sets (men's and women's singles, men's and women's doubles, and mixed doubles) with victory going to the team that scored the most points cumulatively, using No-Ad scoring. Large salaries for top players lured from the traditional tournament game during WTT's May-September season, and low attendance, resulted in huge financial losses, failure of several franchises, and realignment of WTT for 1975 with twelve teams. Losses remained heavy, but plans were made to operate in 1976.

Denver won the title in 1974 and promptly folded. Pittsburgh, led by Evonne Goolagong, won in 1975. The founding of WTT precipitated a war with the ILTF that was settled after numerous lawsuits. Most of the leading female players—including King, Virginia Wade, Goolagong, Rosie Casals, Francoise Durr, Betty Stove, Kerry Melville Reid, and Margaret Court—signed on, as well as such men as John Newcombe, Tom Okker, Marty Riessen, Vijay Amritraj, and Fred Stolle. WTT encouraged a complete break with tennis customs, urging the customers to cheer and boo.

WATER SPORTS

Mark Spitz is doing the butterfly enroute to one of the seven gold medals he won in the 1972 Olympic Games at Munich, Germany.

WATER SPORTS

BOATING

ABAFT: Toward the stern; behind.

ABEAM: At right angles to the keel.

ABLE: Seamanlike; a worthy sailor.

ABOARD: In or on a boat; on board.

ABOUT: To go on the opposite tack. Thus the expression "ready to come about."

ADRIFT: Not made fast; lying loose on the water.

AFLOAT: On the water.

AFT: At the rear of the boat; at or near the stern.

AMERICA'S CUP: A silver trophy symbolic of international yacht-racing supremacy. The Cup was named for the U.S. schooner *America*, which won the 100-Guinea Cup against England's best at the Isle of Wight in 1851. The trophy was deeded as the America's Cup by the owners to the New York Yacht Club in 1857 as a perpetual challenge cup. To date twenty-two successful defenses of the Cup have been made by Americans. The most famous challenger was Sir Thomas Lipton, who spent millions in racing *Shamrock* (five of them, 1899-1930). Competition was held in 130-foot J boats in Lipton's day, and it was revived after a twenty-one year lapse in 1958 in 12-meter sloops. The races, which take place off Newport, R.I., have featured in the 12-meter era such notables as Bus Mosbacher, the winning skipper in two defenses; designer Olin Stephens, four of whose 12-meter yachts have defended the Cup; and Ted Hood, sailmaker, skipper, and designer, who was at the helm of *Courageous* in the 1974 defense against Australia's *Southern Cross*.

AMIDSHIPS: Halfway between bow and stern; in the middle; lengthwise.

ANCHOR: The heavy object used with a line or cable to hold the boat in a desired position when on the water.

ANCHORAGE: A sheltered place where boats can anchor without interfering with harbor traffic.

ASTERN: Behind the boat.

AWEIGH: Clear of the bottom, as in "anchor's aweigh."

AYE: Yes in nautical jargon. "Aye, aye, sir."

BACKSTAY: A wire or heavy rope cable fastened at the stern to support the mast.

BACKWINDING: When one sail throws wind onto leeside of another sail on the same boat.

BAIL: To remove water from the boat with a pump, pail, bucket, sponge, or any like object.

BALLAST: Any heavy material placed in the bottom of the boat for stability; the weight in the boat, people or objects.

BARNACLE: A saltwater shellfish that attaches itself to rocks, ship bottoms, etc. Enough of them will markedly reduce a ship's speed.

BATTEN: A thin strip of wood or other stiff material slipped into prepared pockets to help hold the sail's shape. As a verb, to fasten with strips that help hold hatches tightly closed. "Batten down the hatches."

U.S. skippers, crews and ships have been invincible in the more than 100-year history of the America's Cup, having withstood 22 challenges, including this one in 1962 when Weatherly (foreground) defeated Australia's Gretel.

BEAM: The widest part of the boat. A boat is said to have an eight-foot beam when it measures eight feet at its widest point.

BEAM SEA: When the sea is running at right angles to the boat's course, it is a beam sea.

BEAR AWAY or **BEAR OFF:** To sail away from the wind.

BEARING: The direction, or point of compass, in which an object lies in relation to the boat.

BEATING: Sailing as close into the wind as possible. Also known as sailing on the wind.

BEFORE THE WIND: When the wind comes from aft.

BELAY: A command to stop. Also, when a line is made fast, it is belayed.

BELAYING PIN: A wooden or metal pin fitted into the boat's rail for the securing of lines.

BELOW: Under the deck, or in the cabin.

BEND: To fasten or attach. A sailor doesn't tie two lines together, he bends them; likewise, he bends the sails onto their spars.

BIGHT: Usually, a loop in a rope but actually, any part of the rope except the ends.

BILGE: The space under the cabin floor; the curved or angular part of the hull where bottom and sides meet.

BINNACLE: The protective casing for the compass. Also, in some quarters, a binnacle is a female barnacle.

BITTER END: The last links in an anchor chain or the end of a rope.

BLANKET: When windward boat takes wind from leeward boat's sails.

BLOCK(S): Pulleys.

BOARDBOAT: A sailing surfboard.

BOLLARD: A low, heavy post on a pier used for holding the boat fast to the dock.

BOOM: The spar (pole) to which the foot (lower edge) of a sail is bent (attached).

BOOM CRUTCH: A notched, upright holder of metal or wood on which the boom rests when the sails are furled.

BOOT TOP: A narrow painted stripe at the waterline that accents the division of topsides and bottom.

BOW: The front end of the boat; forward.

BOW CHOCKS: Metal fittings on the bow through which dock and anchor lines are

BREAK OUT: To open up, as in break beans. Also, to unfurl, as in break out fittings or the

BRIGHTWORK: The polished shiny varnished surfaces.

BULKHEAD: A wall; a vertical partition.

BUNK: A sailor's bed usually anchored to the

BUOY: A floating buoys to keep sailors away from bottom. There a

hazards, there are mooring buoys (to mark moorings), net buoys (to mark fishermen's nets), racing buoys (to mark changes in course), etc.

CABLE LENGTH: A measure of 100 fathoms, or 600 feet.

CAN BUOY: A cylindrical buoy usually painted black and marked with an odd number. It indicates the port side of a channel when entering.

CARVEL: A method of construction in which the outside planks of a boat are flush; the edges of the planks meet evenly. Thus a boat is carvel-planked or carvel-built.

CAT: Catamaran, a twin-hulled boat.

CATBOAT: A sailboat with one sail.

CAULKING: The fibrous material used to fill the seams between planks on a wooden boat to make it watertight. To apply this material is to caulk.

CENTERBOARD: A movable plate or board held in a slot in the center well of a sailboat that can be raised or lowered into the water. It is used to keep the boat from sliding sideways. Similar plates or boards held by bolts to the sides or slipped in slots at the gunwales are known as leeboards or daggerboards. Their purpose is the same as the centerboard.

CHAFING GEAR: A canvas or rope wrapped around the spars or rigging to prevent wear due to rubbing.

CHART: Marine map of the waterways with symbols showing aids to navigation, shoals, water depths, hazards, etc.

CLEAT: A fitting of wood or metal to which lines are fastened.

CLEW: The lower corner of a sail.

CLINKER: A method of construction in which each outside plank of a boat overlaps the plank beneath it. Also known as lapstrake.

CLOSE-HAULED: Sailing or pointing as close to the wind as possible.

CLOVE HITCH: A useful knot for making a line fast.

COAMING: The protective sides around the cockpit above the waterline to keep the water out.

COCKPIT: The area of the boat where passengers may sit but more particularly where the helmsman operates.

COIL: To arrange a line in circular turns.

COME ABOUT: To change the course of a boat going to windward by heading up into the wind and sailing away on a new tack. Also known as to tack.

CRINGLE: A ring sewn into the sail so that a line can be passed through it. Clew cringle, tack cringle, and reefing cringle all refer to the position of the cringle on the sail.

CUDDY: A small, protected space forward. It can be used for storage or as a cabin, which is known as a cuddy cabin.

DAGGERBOARDS: *See* Centerboard.

DAVIT: A curved metal spar projecting over the side or stern used for lifting and lowering small boats. It can also be used forward on large boats to manipulate the anchors.

DEADLIGHT: A heavy, circular glass set flush into the deck or bulkhead for the passage of light into the space below.

DINGHY: A small rowboat, sometimes fitted with a removable mast and sail.

DITTY BAG: A small, usually draw-stringed bag for carrying small articles.

DOUSE: To lower a sail.

DOWNHAUL: A tackle or single line by which the tack of a sail is hauled down.

DRAFT: The depth of a boat from the waterline to the bottom of the keel.

DRY ROT: Decay in wood usually due to dampness coupled with poor ventilation.

EARING: The line that makes the cringle fast to the boom.

EASE: To slacken or loosen up on a sheet; to pay it out. In steering, to let the helm come back slightly after having put it over to its limit.

EMBARK: To go on board; to start on a voyage.

EVEN KEEL: The position of the boat when it rests evenly on the water.

EYE SPLICE: A loop spliced in the end of a line.

FAKING DOWN or **FLAKING DOWN:** A way of coiling a line so that each turn (known as a fake or a flake) overlaps the preceding one enabling the line to run out rapidly without tangling. Also, to secure a sail by putting one fold to starboard and the next to port, alternately.

FALL OFF: Turning off to leeward, or away from the wind.

FATHOM: A measure of six feet.

FEATHER: To turn the blade of an oar to a horizontal position when it is out of the water. This a wind resistance.

FENDERS: Objects placed alongside a boat to protect the hull from chafing.

FLAW: A gust of wind heavier than the prevailing breeze.

FLOTSAM: Floating debris, such as trees, brush, driftwood, and the like.

FLUKES: The flattened pieces of iron at the ends of anchor arms.

FLY: A small pennant at the masthead.

FOOT: The lower edge of a sail. To foot is to travel forward through the water.

FORE AND AFT: In a line with the keel.

FORWARD: The area considered the front part of a boat; toward the bow. Also known as fore.

FOUL: The opposite of clear; jammed or tangled. An anchor is foul if its line is turned about fluke. A line is foul if it can't run freely. The tide is foul if it is setting in the opposite direction to a boat's course. A boat fouls another if she touches her.

FRAME: The ribs of the hull.

FREE: Whenever a boat is not close-hauled.

FREEBOARD: The vertical measurement from the main deck or rail to the waterline; the part of the boat out of the water.

FURL: To roll up and secure sails.

GAFF: A spar along the top edge of a four-sided fore-and-aft sail.

GALLEY: A boat's kitchen.

GEAR: A collection of items such as canvas, ropes, spars, belongings, etc.

GENOA JIB: A sail set before the mast that overlaps the mainsail.

GO ABOUT: To tack. Also known as to come about.

GOOSENECK: A fitting that secures the boom to the mast.

GOOSE-WING JIBE: A jibe in which the boom jibes but the upper part of the sail does not.

GRANNY: An incorrectly tied square knot.

GROMMET: A metal ring sewed into a sail or a hammock. Also, a ring of rope made from a single strand tied up on itself.

GUNWALE: The boat's rail or the upper edge of its side. Pronounced "gun'l."

GUY: A line that steadies a spar.

HALYARD: The line used for hoisting the sail.

HATCH: A small opening through a boat's deck or cabin top into the area below.

HEAD: The top area of a triangular sail. Also, the compartment with the ship's toilet. Also, to head up is to steer up into the wind; to head off is to steer away from it.

HEADBOARD: The fitting sewed into the head of a sail with one or more holes to receive the shackle of the halyard.

HEAVE: a line is to throw, as in heaving a line. To heave on is to throw one's weight into pulling the line. Also, to heave to is to steer the boat into the wind with the helm leeward and sails trimmed so that the boat will come up and fall off alternately. Also, the rise and fall of a vessel in the water.

HEEL: To lean over. Also known as to list.

HELM: The device with which one steers the boat, e.g., the wheel, the tiller, a paddle, etc. When using a tiller to control the rudder, the sailor puts the helm up to move it to windward; down, to leeward.

HELMSMAN: The person who steers the boat.

HIKE OUT: To sit up on the rail of a small sailboat and hang out over the water to bear one's total weight in the opposite direction of the boat's list.

HULL: The main body of a boat, excluding deckhouses, flying bridges, and other superstructures.

IN IRONS: A boat that is unable to go off on either tack, since the wind is dead on. Also called in stays.

IN STAYS: *See* In Irons.

IRISH PENNANT: An untidy loose end of rope.

JETSAM: Objects that sink when thrown overboard, as opposed to flotsam, which floats.

JIB: A triangular sail set forward of the mast, or of the foremast in a schooner.

JIBE: To change tack by letting the wind cross over the stern of the boat. Since the boom can swing violently from one side to the other in this maneuver, care must be taken to trim the sails effectively.

JIBSHEET: The line that controls the trim of the jib.

JURY RIG: A makeshift boat

KEEL: The backbone of a boat; the main structural timber extending from stem to sternpost.

KETCH: A two-masted sailboat with smaller mast aft but forward of the rudderpost.

KING SPOKE: The upper spoke of a steering wheel when the rudder is amidships. It is usually marked in some fashion.

KNOCKDOWN: To get a knockdown is to be heeled over by a sudden flaw or squall.

KNOCK OFF: To steer a course farther from the wind. Also known as to fall off.

KNOT: A unit of speed that equals one nautical mile (6,080 feet) per hour. Also, to bend a line.

LANDFALL: The first sighting of land when coming in from the sea.

LANDLUBBER: A person who is more comfortable on land than at sea. It comes from land lover.

LANYARD: A small line used to make anything fast: a cord or braid made fast to an object for ease of handling or hanging, such as a knife lanyard, a whistle lanyard, a bucket lanyard, etc.

LAPSTRAKE: *See* Clinker.

LASH: To secure by binding with rope or small lines.

LAY: The twisting of a rope's strands. Also, to lay to is to halt the boat. "Lay aft" is a command to go aft. "Lay on your oars" is a command to stop pulling.

LAZARETTE: A storage space below deck aft on some boats.

LEE: Away from the direction of the wind. To lee bow the tide is to have the current setting against the lee bow.

LEEBOARDS: *See* Centerboard.

LEECH: The after edge of a sail.

LEEWARD: Toward the direction or side opposite to that from which the wind is blowing. Pronounced "loo'ard."

LEEWAY: Drift to leeward, or in the direction toward which the wind is blowing.

LIMBER HOLES: The holes in the floorboards that allow bilge water to drain into the lowest part of the hull.

LINE: Ropes.

LIST: The inclination of a boat to one side; leaning, heeling.

LOCKER: A closet or built-in drawer for storage. A footlocker is a small trunk.

LOG: A diary or record book of a boat's activities. Also, an instrument for measuring the distance sailed.

LUFF: The forward edge of a sail. Also, to luff up is to sail into the wind in order to reduce the boat's speed. Luffing occurs when the sails are improperly trimmed or when the boat is steered directly into the wind, causing a fluttering of the sail and a cessation of forward motion.

MAINSAIL: The boat's principal sail, set on and abaft the mainmast. It is set aft of the mast on a sloop and aft of the mainmast on a schooner.

MAINSHEET: The line that controls the trim of the mainsail.

MARCONI RIG: A rig having a high mast and a triangular mainsail. Also called a Bermuda rig.

MARLINE: A two-stranded, tarred, small-size line, laid up left-handed. Pronounced "marl'n."

MAST: A vertical pole supporting a sail.

MIZZENMAST: The after and shorter of two masts on yawls and ketches. The sail on this mast is known as a mizzen sail.

MOORING: A heavy anchor or weight permanently in position. One end of the mooring line is made to float by a mooring buoy.

NUN BUOY: A cylindrical buoy painted red and marked with an even number. It indicates the starboard side of a channel when entering.

OAKUM: A caulking material made of tarred rope fibers.

OARLOCK: A device with jaws to hold the oar while pulling. Also called a rowlock.

OFFSHORE WIND: A wind blowing off the land.

ONE-DESIGN CLASS: A class of sailboats that have all been constructed to the same set of specifications and measurements. Thus racing within the class will be on an even basis, no handicap required, as each boat is as similar to its sister ship in sailing characteristics as possible. Under these conditions, success in racing depends upon the skill of the skipper and his crew.

OUTBOARD: Toward the sides of a vessel, or outside of it. An outboard-motor boat is one where the motor is attached outside the boat.

OUTHAUL: A device or rope used to haul out the aft corner of a sail toward the end of the boom.

OVERALL: The length or fore-and-aft measurement of a boat.

OVERHANG: The projection of the bow and stern of a boat.

OVERHAUL: To go over a line or sail hand over hand to see that all is clear and not twisted. Also, to haul the parts of a tackle so as to separate the blocks. Also, to overtake a vessel. Also, to renovate or refit a vessel.

PAINTER: The line in the bow of a boat used to tow it or to make it fast.

PALM: A sailor's leather thimble that fits over the palm of the hand.

PAY OUT: To slack, let out, or ease off a line or chain.

PEAK: The upper and after corner of a gaff-headed sail.

"PIPE DOWN": An order to be quiet.

PITCH: The fore-and-aft movements of a boat as its bow and stern rise and fall with the action of the waves.

POINT: To head into the wind. A boat is said to point well if she sails close to the wind. Also, a division of the compass: 1/32 of the circle, or 11¼ degrees.

PORT: The left side of a vessel when facing the bow. Also, an opening in the side of a vessel.

PORT TACK: Sailing with the wind coming over the port side.

POWER BOAT RACING: Competition in various classes of motor-driven craft.

QUARTER: The part of a vessel between the beam and the stern. The terms "port quarter" and "starboard quarter" refer to the left and right sides, respectively. "Broad on the quarter" is in a direction 45 degrees, or four points, from astern.

REACH: A course with the wind abeam or near the beam. On a close reach the boat is somewhat freer than close-hauled but forward of the beam. On a broad reach the wind is somewhat abaft the beam.

REEF: A ridge of rock or coral or sand at or near the surface of the water. Also, a part of a sail that can be folded and tied down to reduce the area exposed to the wind. To reef is to reduce the said area by partially lowering the sail and fastening it to the boom.

REEVE: To pass a line through a block or a hole.

RIGGING: All the stays and ropes of a boat. The stays supporting the mast are called standing rigging. Ropes used in setting and trimming sails are called running rigging.

ROADSTEAD: A more or less open anchorage.

RODE: The line attached to the anchor of a small boat.

ROLL: The sideward, rocking motion of a boat caused by the wind and waves.

ROLLING HITCH: A knot useful in bending one rope to a standing part of another or to a spar.

ROTTEN STOPS: The light lashing used to furl a sail when it is sent aloft in stops.

RUDDER: The steering device attached to the stern and activated by the tiller.

RUN: To sail before the wind, i.e., with the wind behind the boat. Also known as running before.

SCHOONER: A fore-and-aft rigged vessel with two or more masts.

SCOPE: The length of anchor chain or line out when a boat is at anchor. To give more scope is to pay out on the anchor line.

SHACKLE: A U-shaped piece of metal with a pin across the open ends. Some pins screw in; some snap in; some have a cotter pin.

SHANK: The principal part of an anchor connecting flukes and stock.

SHEER: The sweep of a boat's deck.

SHEET: Any line that is used to trim a sail.

SHOAL: An area of shallow water.

SHROUD(S): Stays that run from the head of the mast to the sides of the boat to help support the mast.

SLACK: The opposite of taut. To slack away or to slack off is to pay out. Also, the period in the tide between flood and ebb or between ebb and flood.

SLAT ABOUT: To flap, as said of sails.

SLOOP: A one-masted vessel with two or more sails.

SPAR(S): The masts, gaffs, booms, etc.; any supporting pole on a ship.

SPINNAKER: A large, light, triangular sail set on the side of the mast opposite the main boom.

SPLICE: To join rope by tucking the strands together, weaving without knotting.

SQUALL: A sudden and violent burst of wind.

STANDING PART: The fixed part of a rope; the part made fast.

STARBOARD: The right side of a boat when facing the bow.

STARBOARD TACK: Sailing with the wind coming over the starboard.

STAY: A piece of rigging (usually wire) used to support a spar. The heading runs from the masthead to the stem. The jib is set on a stay.

STEM: The vertical timber.

STEP: To set in position, as the bow of a boat.

STERN: The after or back end of a boat.

Don Aronow roars to victory in his single-engine inboard in a Long Beach-San Diego Hennessy Cup power boat race.

STOCK: The crosspiece of an anchor.
STOP: A narrow band of canvas or piece of small line used in furling a sail.
STOW: To put away, as to stow gear.
SUPERSTRUCTURE: The housing above a deck; cabins; wheelhouse, flying bridge, etc.
SWAB: Mop. A seaman "swabs down"; he does not "mop up." In the navy the mop men are called swabbies.
TACK: Any of two or more consecutive straight runs making up the zigzag course of sailing vessel when going to windward. *See* Port Tack and Starboard Tack.

Also, the lower forward corner of a fore-and-aft sail. When used as a verb, to tack is to come about.
TACKLE: A system of blocks and lines arranged to add power in hauling.
TELLTALE: A short piece of yarn or ribbon tied to a shroud to indicate the direction of the wind.
THROAT: The part of the gaff near the mast. The throat halyard is the rope by which the forward end of the gaff is hoisted.
THWART: A set or bar set crosswise in a small boat.
THWARTSHIPS: At right angles to the fore-and-aft line. Also known as athwartships.

TILLER: A bar connected with the rudder. By this bar the rudder is moved as desired.

TOPPING LIFT: A line by which the outer end of a boom or pole is supported.

TOPSIDES: Sides of the hull between the waterline and the rail or gunwale of a boat.

TRANSOM: Transverse planking that forms the after end of a square-sterned boat. In outboard boats it is that part of the boat from which the motor is suspended.

TRICK: A period of duty at the helm.

TRIM: To trim the sails is to put them in correct relation to the wind by means of pulling in or easing on the sheets. Also describes the way in which a boat floats. If she is too heavily loaded forward and the bow is depressed, she is trimmed by the head. If she is depressed aft, she is trimmed by the stern.

TRUNK: The vertical shaft in which the centerboard lifts and lowers. Also known as well.

TURNBUCKLE: A metal device consisting of a thread and screw capable of being tightened and slackened. It is used in obtaining the correct tension in the standing rigging.

TWO-BLOCKED: All the way up. Literally, it is when two blocks of a tackle have come together.

UNDERWAY: When a boat is moving through the water. Variations on this: She makes headway when going forward, sternway when going backward, and leeway when being set sideways by the wind.

UNSHIP: To take anything out of its place. Also, to take a boat apart.

VEER: To slack off and allow to run out; thus, "veering more anchor line." Also, a change in wind direction.

WAKE: The track or path a moving boat leaves behind as it travels through the water.

WATERLINE: The line to which the surface of the water comes on the sides of a vessel. This water level can vary with conditions such as wind, waves, boat load, etc.

WAY ON: The movement of a boat through the water.

WEATHER SIDE: The windward side, or the side toward the wind.

WHIP: To bind the strands of a rope's end with thread or cord.

WHISKER POLE: A light pole used to prop out the jib on the opposite side from the mainsail when running before the wind.

WINDWARD: Toward the wind; the direction from which the wind is blowing.

YACHT: A boat used for pleasure.

YAW: To swing from side to side. A ship yaws when she steers badly in running before the wind in a seaway, usually in heavy seas.

YAWL: A two-masted boat with mainmast forward and mizzenmast aft of the rudderpost.

SURFING

ANGLE: To ride a surfboard along the face or front wall of a wave, to right or left. Angling nearly parallel with the face of the wave gives you a much longer ride than coming straight in toward the beach.

BACK-OFF: An offshore wave that breaks and continues as unbroken green water.

BACK OUT: To drop off the back of the wave instead of riding it. If the wave is too big or too small, everybody's got a right to change his mind.

BACK PADDLE: When a surfer decides not to ride a wave, he back paddles or backstrokes off the top of it.

BACKPEDAL: Walking backward to the rear of the board.

BAGGIES: Long shorts, often blue jeans chopped at the knee.

BAIL OUT: A term borrowed from aviation, bailing out means a fast goodbye to the surfboard—by diving or jumping—in order to avoid a rough situation.

BARGE: A big, heavy, awkward surfboard.

BEACH BUNNY: A girl more noted for hanging around surfers than for her ability on a surfboard.

BELLY: The bottom of a surfboard.

BELLY BOARD: A small board, usually less than three feet long.

BIG GUN: A surfboard used in heavy surf, like that in Hawaii, where the long, open stretches of the Pacific permit the buildup of waves 15 or more feet in height. Also known as an elephant gun.

BLASTER: A very hard breaking wave. Also known as bomber.

BLOWN OUT: A surf made choppy by high winds and therefore difficult for surfing.

BODY SURFER: A wave rider who uses only his body for surfing.

BOMBER: *See* Blaster.

BOMBOARA: The term used by Australian surfers for a big wave that breaks outside or seaward of the normal line of surf.

BOTTOM TURN: A swing of the surfboard to left or right at the base of a wave after sliding down its face to gain momentum.

BREAK: The point at which a wave curls over and begins to spill water down its front wall. This occurs when a wave runs into shallow water (shore break) or into man-made obstructions such as piers or piling (pier break).

BUN HUGGERS: Surfing trunks.

CARVE AND DESTROY: An Australian way of describing the bloodthirsty practice of riding a surfboard carelessly through a surf crowded with other surfers and swimmers. Also known as carving up the mob.

CATCH A RAIL: In sideslipping a surfboard, the leading edge or rail may get too low in the water and dig in—thus throwing the surfer.

CHANNEL: Deep water where surf doesn't usually form.

CHEATER FIVE: Riding the front of the board with the five toes of either foot hanging over the nose is advanced surfing. But, if your weight is mainly back on your rear or trail foot, that's a cheater five because you're not really up there.

CHOKE: Afraid of riding high waves. Also known as hairing out.

CLEANUP or CLEAN-UP SET: A big wave or a set of big waves will sometimes develop outside the normal line of breakers, catching waiting surfers "inside" at the mercy of a crashing wall of water. That's a clean-up, so to speak.

CLIMBING: A maneuver in which the surfer puts his weight on the inside rail, causing the board to climb back to the top of the wave.

CLOSED DOOR: Surfers try for a wave that peaks at a certain point, with the breaking crest traveling out left or right from that peak so that they can ride along just ahead of it. On even beaches, the whole line of the wave may break at once, thus closing the door on the surfer.

CLOSEOUT: A surfing area where waves cannot be ridden or simply conditions that do not permit surfing.

"COWABUNGA": An ancient but honorable surfing cry that can be loosely translated as "Wow!"

CREST: The top of a wave. Just in front of the crest (and paddling hard to match its speed) is where you ought to be if you want that long ride to the beach.

CRITICAL: The state of a steep wave as it is about to break.

CURL: As the crest of a wave pours over forward, it forms a curl much like a rug being rolled up at one edge. The surfer ideally rides just in front of the traveling curl, hoping to keep up with the open end of it and avoid being totally wrapped in water. Also known as tunnel, tube, or hook.

CUSTOM BOARD: A surfboard tailor-made for an individual surfer, as opposed to regular stock models. The custom boards, which are naturally more expensive, can be designed according to the surfer's weight, height, style of riding, and type of surf he expects to tackle.

CUTBACK: A surfer riding ahead of the curl may get too far in front of it and so lose speed. A cutback, or turn toward the curl, will get him back where the action is, but then he must turn again to be going in the same direction as the curl.

CUTOUT: The abortion of a ride by dropping over the back of a wave and letting it pass through. Also called a pullout.

DIG: To paddle hard. Also known as to scratch.

DING: Any dent, nick, or break in a surfboard—usually a result of the surfer's not hanging onto his board and losing it to a bunch of rocks waiting onshore.

DRIVING: An all-out effort to position the board for maximum speed.

DROP IN: To slide from the top to the bottom of a wave, usually to gain speed for a bottom turn in the direction of the curl.

DROPPER: A very steep, fast-riding wave.

ELEPHANT GUN: *See* Big Gun.

FACE: The front or shoreward wall of a wave, rising from the trough to the crest.

FEATHER: The wind-blown fringe of foam on the crest of a wave.

FIN: The vertical stabilizer extending down from near the stern of a surfboard as an aid to control. Also, swimfins, the foot flippers used by body surfers and scuba divers for greater speed. Also called skeg.

FIVE TOE: Curling five toes over the front of the board.

FOAM: A sometime word for surfboard, because most boards today are made of polyurethane foam (a plastic) covered with a fiberglass skin.

FREE FALL: Falling from the top of a wave.

GETTING BOMBED: Getting hit by a wave.

GOOFY-FOOT: One who surfs with his right foot forward on the surfboard. (Most surfers put their left foot forward.) If you tend to put your right foot forward when sliding on the ice or a waxed floor, you may be a natural goofy-foot. But it's no worse than being left-handed.

GRAB THE RAIL: To pull out by grasping the edge of the surfboard away from the face of the wave and pulling the board in through the wave to save you from a bad ride.

GREMLIN or GREMMIE: A beginner in surfing, or sometimes a fairly good one who happens to be a pain in the neck.

GUN: A surfboard.

HAIRING OUT: *See* Choke.

HAIRY: Very difficult, dangerous surf.

HAMBURGER: A violent collision with rocks, jetty, or pier.

HANG FIVE: A ride on the surfboard's nose with the toes of one foot right up on the leading edge.

HANG TEN: Hanging ten toes over the front of the board, one of the ultimate accomplishments in surfing. It requires not only skill but special conditions: a fast-moving curl, plenty of speed and planning action to get upward pressure on the board's nose, and—ideally—positioning of the board on the wave so that the breaking curl provides downward pressure on the rear deck as the board travels across the face of the wave.

HAOLE: Hawaiian for newcomer or visiting surfer.

HEAD DIP: When, in a sporting gesture to the wave, the surfer traveling laterally along its face dunks his head into that green wall.

HODAD or HODADDY: A beach bum with a loud mouth but little or no surfing ability.

HOLDING THE RAIL: Holding the edge of the board to avoid falling off.

HOOK: *See* Curl.

HOTDOG or **HOTDOGGER:** A fancy surfer who goes for the trickier stunts on the board. The term may be applied to show-offs but also to expert surfers who have a bit of the acrobat in them.

HUEY: An Australian surf god, as legend has it.

INSIDE: Between the breaking point of the waves and the shore.

ISLAND PULLOUT: A way of cutting short a ride by walking to the nose of the board and turning it back into the face of the wave. Also called a nose pullout.

KAMIKAZE: Surfing with arms stretched out wide.

KICK OUT: To shift the weight rapidly to the back of the board so that the nose rises and the board can be pivoted on its tail to aim it back over the crest of the wave and so end an unpromising ride.

KICK TURN: An abrupt change in direction accomplished by stomping heavily on the right or left side of the board's tail to increase turning action.

KILLER SURF: Surf with 15-foot or higher waves.

KNOTS or **KNOBS:** Calcium deposits that form bumps below the knee and on the bridges of the feet—a result of irritation caused by knee-paddling.

KOOK: A clowning novice.

LAND CRABS: Pretend surfers who never get wet.

LATE TAKEOFF: Taking off after the wave has already broken.

LINE: A type of wave that gives a very fast ride because of its long, steep wall.

LOCKED IN: Positioned just right in the curl of the wave and traveling right or left toward its shoulder, a bit ahead of the break.

LOG JAM: Too many surfboards in the same place.

NOSE: The front of the surfboard.

NOSE PULLOUT: *See* Island Pullout.

OFFSHORE: Wind that is coming from the shore toward the sea.

OPEN DOOR: The ideal wave breaks at a certain peak, with the break curling along the line of surf, giving the surfer an "open door" to ride continuously out of the moving curl onto the unbroken shoulder of the wave.

OUTSIDE: Seaward side of the surf line. Also, a call to other surfers to heed the approach of promising new waves.

OUT THE BACK: Australian for outside.

OVER THE FALLS: An out-of-control plunge down the face of a wave into the trough below.

PAIPO BOARD: Hawaiian for short surfboard.

PALMING THE WALL: To dip a hand into the front wall of a wave while angling along its face in order to aid balance or slow down a bit.

PARAFFIN: A wax applied to a surfboard's upper deck to improve footing.

PEAK: A wave with its highest point at the center, and tapering off at the sides.

PEARLING: Dropping down the face of a wave with the weight too far forward, so that the board's nose digs in and the whole rig goes "pearl diving" toward the bottom.

PIER: *See* Rock Roulette.

POLY: The Australian nickname for a surfboard made of polyurethane foam (as most of them are).

POP-OUT: A mass-produced surfboard.

PRONING OUT: Going belly down and flat out on a board, often to avoid pearling or wiping out.

PULLOUT: Stopping a ride by turning back seaward, either through the wave or over its top. Also known as a cutout.

QUEEN MARY: A surfboard that is much too large for its rider.

RAILS: The sides of a surfboard.

ROCK DANCE: Walking over rocks to retrieve a surfboard.

ROCKER: The convex belly of a surfboard as seen in profile.

ROCK ROULETTE: Surfing among boardwalk pilings or rocks. Also known as pier.

ROLLER COASTER: A ride along the face of a wave, alternately moving from the crest to the trough and back up again.

ROLL-OVER: A defensive maneuver by surfers threatened with collapsing walls of water, other surfboards, or debris. The action is to grab one rail of the board and roll it over so that the surfer is underneath with the board as protective roof.

ROTO-MOTO: *See* Spinner.

SCOOP or **SPOON:** The slight upward curvature at the nose of a surfboard.

SCRATCH: *See* Dig.

SECTIONING: What a wave does when it breaks unevenly or in several places at once, making things difficult for the surfer.

SET: A group of waves.

SHOULDER: The unbroken part of the wave just to left or right of the breaking crest.

SKEG: *See* Fin.

SLIDE: To ride left or right along the face of a wave; same as angle.

SOUP: Foam, white water, or swash that a broken wave throws up on the beach.

SPILLER: A wave, produced by a gently sloping bottom, that does not truly break but rather spills water down its face.

SPINNER: A 360-degree turn by the surfer (not the board) in mid-ride; when repeated again and again, it's called a roto-moto.

SQUATTING THROUGH: Bending low on the board to avoid being hit by the crest of the wave.

STALL: To put the brakes on, usually by shifting the weight backward, when the board begins to outrun the wave; to stall out is to stop the slide altogether.

STOKED: Turned on, excited, plugged, pumped, wired in.

STRINGERS: Hardwood strips set lengthwise into the surfboard for added strength.

SURFBOARD: What the surfer rides on. Boards have evolved from the big solid planks of early Hawaii, through hollow models and balsa wood, to the fiber-glassed polyurethane foam of today. While masters of the really big surf may favor the long, narrow, fairly heavy "guns" ranging up to 11 feet, some variation of the basic Malibu design is more maneuverable and more popular. The Malibus have a slightly convex or saucer-shaped bottom, which allows for easier turning, and a tipped-up nose to help eliminate submarining. Boards come in all sizes, weights, and shapes to accommodate the individual surfer. The price of a good one will be more than $150, but many shops carry second-hand boards for much less.

SURF-IN: A planned festival of surfers and non-surfers.

"SURF'S UP": Rallying cry when the waves begin to build to good surfing conditions. Opposite of "surf's down."

SWASH: *See* Soup.

SWELL: An unbroken wave.

TAKEOFF: The first part of catching a wave.

TAKE THE DROP: Riding the wave down.

TANDEM: Two people riding on one board.

TEN TOES: Curling all ten toes over the front of the board.

TOES OVER: Curling toes over front of the board.

TRAIL FOOT: The foot nearest the tail of the board.

TRAIN: Lines of waves in series. Also called a set or session.

TRIM: To maneuver and balance the board so as to make the most of the wave.

TUBE: *See* Curl.

TUNNEL: *See* Curl.

TURNOFF: A good ride by a surfer.

WAHINIE: Hawaiian for female surfer.

WALK THE BOARD: To control the speed of the board by walking back and forth.

WALK THE NOSE: To walk toward the front of the board.

WALL: The steep shoreward face of a wave about to break.

WALLED OUT: A sea too violent for sane surfing.

WAVE(S): These swells in the ocean's surface are caused by wind, which lifts particles of water into ripples. As the ripples rise and fall, they offer more surface to the wind and grow into a chop, ultimately becoming a swell. Waves from distant storms, once started, will travel long distances on their own momentum. There is no actual forward movement of water in a wave; the swell travels through the water like a hump in a shaken blanket, but the water stands still except when the crest spills forward in a breaking wave. Waves normally break when they encounter shallow water of a depth of 1.3 times their height.

WEDGE: Where two waves angling in from different directions come together. Also, a wedge-shaped piece of polyurethane foam used to repair a surfboard.

WET SUIT: A synthetic rubber suit used for surfing in cold weather.

WHIP TURN: Repositioning the board quickly after taking off on a wave.

WIPE-OUT: Total end of a ride by falling or being knocked off the surfboard.

WOODIE or **WOODIE-WAGON:** An old-time station wagon with wood exterior paneling, favored for hauling surfboards to the beach but now very scarce.

SWIMMING

ACROSS-THE-BOARD JUDGES: Two judges who are stationed on each side of the finish line to record the order of finish by lane.

AGE-GROUP SWIMMING: A nationwide program sponsored by the Amateur Athletic Union during the 1950s in an answer to the Australians' domination of international competition. With the guidance of Beth Kaufman, the "mother of age-group swimming," and Dr. Sammy Lee, two-time Olympic gold medalist in diving, swimming and diving competitions were reorganized into new age categories.

Concentrating on starting youngsters into competition early, and holding frequent meets at many accessible locations all over the country, competitors were divided into groupings of ten-year-olds and younger, eleven- and twelve-year-olds, thirteen- and fourteen-year-olds, and fifteen- to eighteen-year-olds.

When age-group swimming started, there were only

a handful of competitors. Now there are about five-hundred thousand competitive swimmers throughout the United States. From this program have emerged many young champions who reach international championship status while still in their teens. *See* Water Babies.

AQUACADE: A swim show using exhibition-caliber skills in swimming and diving. The stars, performing singly or in groups, are enhanced by the use of theatrical techniques. One of the most famous aqua-cades was held during the New York World's Fair in 1939. The producer of the show, Billy Rose, starred his wife, Eleanor Holm, 1932 Olympic gold-medal back-stroker. The sexy Eleanor had been suspended from the 1936 Olympic team by the U.S. Olympic Committee, which charged her with breaking training by drinking champagne, smoking, and partying too much.

ARTIFICIAL RESPIRATION: The method used for restoring breathing to a nearly drowned person.

AUSTRALIAN CRAWL: A two-beat crawl. *See also* Beat, Cavill, Freestyle, and Crawl.

BACKSTROKE or **BACK CRAWL:** A rhythmical and graceful stroke, which became popular after the 1912 Olympic Games, that can readily be taught to beginners, as breathing is so easy. The stroke has many similarities to the front crawl, except that it is done on the back. The leg movements are almost identical to the timing and action of the flutter kick.

The swimmer who is given the most credit for developing the present backstroke is Adolph Kiefer, who was nine times national champion in eleven years and holder, at one time or another, of every world backstroke record, in addition to being an Olympic gold medalist in 1936.

In competitive swimming, the swimmer is only required to push off on his back and continue swimming on his back throughout the race. The backstroke is used in the first quarter of the medley relay and the second quarter of the individual medley.

BACKSTROKE START: In racing, this is the only stroke that starts without a dive. The swimmer, already in the water, faces the starting end, with both hands resting either on the end or rail of the pool or on any part of the starting platform or block. The start is accomplished when the swimmer pushes backward, throwing his arms back over his head into the water.

BACKSTROKE TURN: Although the rules for backstroke competition indicate that the swimmer must be on his back during the whole of the race, he may come out of this position to achieve the turn.

BALLET SWIMMING: *See* Synchronized Swimming.

BEAT: The regular leg thrash of the flutter kick used in the crawl and backstroke. The number of beats in the

kick is measured by the total number of downward thrusts of both legs in relation to a complete cycle of both arm strokes. Thus a six-beat crawl is one with six leg beats to one cycle, or three beats per arm stroke. *See also* Flutter Kick.

BELLY WHOPPER or **BELLY FLOP:** A dive in which the diver lands flat on the water surface, with his belly taking the impact of the entry. It is neither graceful nor skillful in appearance, and it usually hurts.

BOBBING: Alternately going below the water surface and above it in a vertical position with the head up. It is a combination of leg and arm movements plus the natural buoyancy of the body that brings the swimmer up.

BREASTSTROKE: The first stroke to be used for recreation and competition. Perhaps this is because it is swum with the face out of the water, and thus the swimmers are able to see and breathe more easily. It is still one of the most popular strokes for distance, survival swimming, and lifesaving. The tradition of breaststroke swimming was firmly established after the first successful English Channel swim by Capt. Matthew Webb in 1875. He used the breaststroke.

In competition the body must be kept always on the breast, with both shoulders in line with the water surface. All arm movements are simultaneous, in the same horizontal plane, with the hands pushed forward simultaneously from the breast. Up-and-down leg movements are prohibited, and thus the frog or whip kick is used. The breaststroke is used in the second quarter of the medley-relay course and in the third quarter of the individual medley.

BREASTSTROKE START: A start that is usually a little deeper than the entry used for the freestyle, as the swimmer is permitted one arm pull and one leg kick before the head surfaces. It is a forward start.

BREASTSTROKE TURN: The swimmer must touch the end of the pool or course with both hands simultaneously at the same level before pivoting around to change direction.

BREATHING: The manner of taking a breath while swimming. In the breaststroke and backstroke the swimmer can breathe without turning the head from side to side. In the crawl or freestyle the swimmer can take a breath from the same side all the time or from alternate sides. He inhales through the mouth and exhales under water through the nose or through the mouth and nose.

BREATHING ARM: The arm on the side of the body on which the crawl swimmer takes a breath. The arm is on the recovery when inhaling and is pulling when the swimmer is exhaling.

BUDDY SYSTEM: A safety system used at summer camps and school pools for watching groups of swimmers in the water. When the signal is sounded (usually a whistle), the buddies, or previously designated partners, raise hands out of the water together so the counselor or swim instructor can count the swimmers.

BUOYANT: A swimmer who has the ability or tendency to float is said to be buoyant.

BUTTERFLY START: A forward start similar to the entry used for the breaststroke.

BUTTERFLY STROKE: A variation of the breaststroke developed in 1935 by coach Dave Armbruster of the University of Iowa and first demonstrated by Jack Sieg, one of his swimmers. In 1954 the International Swimming Federation came out with a new set of rules separating the breaststroke from the butterfly, thus increasing the number of competitive strokes to four.

The stroke permits a dolphin kick, which is an up-and-down simultaneous movement of the legs and feet, instead of the side-to-side motion used in the breaststroke. The arm stroke is an overarm, executed by both arms reaching simultaneously, overhead and out of the water, before pulling down below the surface. This stroke is used in the first quarter of the individual medley and the third quarter of the medley relay.

BUTTERFLY TURN: The same as for the breaststroke. *See* Breaststroke Turn.

CANNONBALL: An entry an individual makes into the water when he leaps from the diving board or other high place into the air, tucking and clasping his legs tightly under him in the tuck position before hitting the water with the force of a cannonball.

CAVILL: Frederick Cavill, an English-born swimmer who emigrated to Australia in 1878. He built and operated that country's first swim tanks (pools), where he taught swimming to his six sons as well as to the general public. On a trip to the South Seas the Cavill boys took note of the way the natives swam—using an overarm stroke and a kick that splashed above the water. Back home in Australia the boys, notably Percy and Sydney, began using their "splash" stroke in competition and discovered it was the fastest way to "crawl" through the water. Before long the record-making stroke became known as the Australian crawl.

CHANNEL SWIM: Swimming across the English Channel. Capt. Matthew Webb was the first to swim the 20-mile span from Dover, England, to Cape Gris Nez, France, on August 25, 1875. The first woman to conquer the Channel was nineteen-year-old Gertrude Ederle, an American, who swam from France to England on August 6, 1926.

COURSE: The designated distance over which a competition is conducted. *See also* Long Course and Short Course.

CRAWL: The fastest known stroke, used almost universally in modern freestyle racing and thus now known as the freestyle. In recreational swimming, as in the racing form, variations occur in the number of leg beats taken to each arm cycle as well as in the way the swimmer breathes. However, the stroke is always done with an overarm movement, face down in the water; the swimmer breathes by turning his head to the side, and he uses a flutter kick. Credit is given to Australia and its swim enthusiast, Frederick Cavill, for the development of this overarm stroke. *See also* Freestyle, Cavill, and Beat.

DEAD MAN'S FLOAT: *See* Float.

DIP: A quick swim. When done without a bathing suit, the swim becomes a skinny dip; when in the moonlight, a moonlight dip; etc.

DIVE: The way in which a swimmer enters the water or goes below the water's surface. *See also* Belly Whopper, Fancy Dive, Backstroke Start, Breaststroke Start, Freestyle Start, Surface Dive.

DIVING WELL: A pool, separate and apart from the competitive swimming pool, that is used for competitive diving.

DOG PADDLE: The unschooled way a human propels himself through the water. Children's paddling is often more chaotic, with the arms alternately clawing at the water to move forward; breathing is irregular, legs thrashing and inconsistent. A more mature dog paddle can be rhythmic and steady, but the arms never go out of the water and the head is never submerged. Thus the stroke closely resembles a dog moving through the water.

DOLPHIN KICK: The up-and-down leg movement used in the butterfly stroke. There is a slight bending of the torso and considerable bending of the knees in order to get the needed amount of thrust. The legs are close but not intensely pressed together, with the kick no more than a flexible flick, which is similar to a dolphin's tail movement. There are usually two kicks for each arm stroke, with the second kick being stronger. Also known as a fishtail kick.

FALSE START: When a swimmer in competition takes off before the starter's signal.

FANCY DIVE: Entry into the water with acrobatic skill and grace. It can be headfirst or feetfirst. In competition the dive is executed from a springboard (diving board) or a platform. The platform or tower is the highest above the water. In Olympic competition the two springboards are 1 and 3 meters above the level of the water; the platform is 10 meters (approximately 33 feet).

There are three basic diving positions the body may assume in the air before entering the water: straight (layout), pike, and tuck. In a straight dive the body is

Fancy diver *Pat McCormick is the only two-time winner of both the springboard and platform events at two consecutive Olympic Games.*

extended with arms stretched out in front; the legs are on the same level, straight out in back with toes pointed. In the pike the body is bent at the hips, the legs straight at the knees, the arms reaching to touch the toes, which are pointed. The tuck position is where the body is rolled up like a ball, knees together with hands clasped around them.

The variations on these forms are many and can involve some fancy acrobatics from a forward or backward or armstand takeoff, to a head-first or feet-first entry into the water.

One of America's greatest divers was Patricia McCormick, a double gold medalist in the springboard and platform dives in the 1952 and 1956 Olympics. This record has never been duplicated by man or woman. Some of the most daring and spectacular noncompetitive high diving can be seen in Acapulco, Mexico, where natives plunge from the cliffs 130 feet above the water (about the height of the Brooklyn Bridge).

FINA: The International Amateur Swimming Federation, the ruling body for international swimming, including the Olympic Games.

FINISH MARK: The end wall of the pool if the race finishes there. It can also be a vertical plane whose upper boundary is a rope at least three feet above the water from which hangs a slightly weighted string of pennants or flags to designate the end of a race in the middle of a lane.

FINNING: A noncompetitive way of moving through the water on the back. The hands and forearms rotate slowly under the water near the hips, with the palms catching the water and pushing it toward the feet. For those who have difficulty keeping the feet and legs up, a slight but easy flutter kick will help keep them up and the body horizontal. *See also* Sculling.

FISHTAIL KICK: *See* Dolphin Kick.

FLOAT: A buoyant raft. It may be anchored offshore to serve as a swimming and diving raft or be placed adjacent to a permanent dock. Also, a verb, when the body rests easily on the surface of the water with virtually no motion. Almost anybody can learn to float. In fact, only about two percent of the population are regarded as sinkers; they will sink to the bottom with air in their lungs, unless they move their arms and legs.

Floating is a must for all swimmers because it is one of the easiest techniques to learn and can be used for survival in an emergency situation. People can float for many hours, since very little energy is expended. There are several different floating positions:

1. The tuck float, commonly called the jelly fish, turtle, or animal float;
2. The horizontal float on the stomach, commonly called the dead man's float or the prone float;
3. The horizontal float on the back, called the back float;
4. The vertical float, standing up without touching bottom.

FLUTTER KICK: A fast, vertical kicking of the legs, alternately and rhythmically. The fairly straight legs thrash up and down mostly under water, the hips serve as the fulcrum for the movement. The power comes more from the feet, however, and thus the ankle is fully relaxed and flexible. The knee is slightly bent on the recovery, or upbeat, of the leg movement. This kick is used in the freestyle (crawl) and the backstroke, the number of beats per arm stroke varying to suit the swimmer.

FLY: A shortened form of butterfly and used freely as a synonym.

FREESTYLE: According to the official AAU rules, an event designated freestyle may be swum in any style other than butterfly, breaststroke, or backstroke. However, since the crawl is the fastest stroke for the majority of swimmers, it is the stroke most commonly chosen in freestyle races. Freestyle also is used synonymously with crawl. *See also* Crawl.

FREESTYLE START: In this racing dive, the swimmer's toes grip the far side of the mark. From a somewhat crouched position, and using all possible leg spring, the swimmer plunges into the water, back straight, arms straight ahead, to about 8 inches below the surface.

FROG KICK: The leg action used in the breaststroke. As required in breaststroke competition, the motion is parallel to the surface of the water with no vertical movement at all. The knees are drawn forward and outward with the heels fairly close together in froglike fashion. The legs are then pressed backward and outward as the feet travel around in an arc. The movement gets faster as the legs are brought together and then straighten out. This creates a kind of whip action, and thus is also known as the whip kick. Onetime national champion Chet Jastremski is credited with developing this kick under his coach James ("Doc") Counsilman of Indiana University.

GAINER: A fancy dive in which the diver faces the water but rotates backward instead of forward as is done in a front dive.

HEAT: A preliminary race that determines who will qualify for the finals. This is necessitated by the fact that there are many more entrants than lanes in the pool.

HIGH BOARD: This usually applies to the three-meter springboard.

HURDLE: In diving the jump taken at the end of the diving board following the last step and preceding the plunge off the board. Both feet must touch the board

Greased and ready for her Channel swim, Gertrude Ederle became the first woman to conquer the 26-mile body of water between France and England.

simultaneously at the end of the hurdle, which is judged as part of the dive.

INDIVIDUAL MEDLEY: An individual competitive event in which the swimmer swims one-fourth of the course in the butterfly, one-fourth in backstroke, one-fourth in breaststroke, and the last in freestyle (or any stroke other than the first three)—in that order.

INTERNATIONAL SWIMMING HALL OF FAME: Since its founding in 1965 in Fort Lauderdale, Fla., more than 150 outstanding contributors to the sport have been chosen by a poll of coaches. Included are swimmers, divers, water poloists, synchronized swimmers and coaches. Such immortals as Johnny Weissmuller, Gertrude Ederle, Buster Crabbe, Esther Williams, Don Schollander, Adolph Kiefer, Chris Von Saltza, Pat McCormick, and Mark Spitz fill the alcoves of this repository of swimming lore and memorabilia.

INVERTED CRAWL: Another name for the backstroke.

JACKKNIFE: A dive done in the pike position, with the arms extended toward the insteps.

JUDGE(S): The officials in a swim competition. There can be lane, stroke, turn, place, and takeoff judges, depending on the scope of the meet and the officials available. Their purpose is to establish the finishing order of a race as well as the acceptability of starts and turns. In fancy diving from three to nine judges can be available to evaluate each dive.

JUNIOR OLYMPICS or JO PROGRAM: A program inaugurated in 1949 by the Amateur Athletic Union through permission of the United States Olympic Committee. It sponsors competitions all over the country for boys and girls from six to eighteen years of age in seventeen sports, including swimming.

KELLERMAN: Annette Kellerman, an Australian long-distance swimmer credited with having liberated women's swimwear in the bloomer period. She was arrested for indecent exposure while wearing a clinging, one-piece suit on a Boston beach in 1907. Fortunately, a tolerant farsighted judge dismissed the case. In addition to her contribution to women's swim fashions, she starred in silent films and toured the world as a vaudeville headliner and physical-fitness lecturer. Hollywood swim star Esther Williams portrayed her in 1952 in the movie *Million Dollar Mermaid.*

KICK: The manner in which the legs move for propulsion through the water. *See also* Flutter Kick, Dolphin Kick, Frog Kick, and Scissors Kick.

KICKBOARD: A buoyant board about 1½ inches thick, 18 inches wide, and 30 inches long. It is grasped by the swimmer in a prone position and used to practice and develop kicking technique. Also known as a flutter board.

LANE: The specific area in which the swimmer is assigned to swim—e.g., lane 1, lane 2, etc. The preferred width is seven feet, with the lanes separated by ten-inch wide painted lines of contrasting colors on the bottom of the pool and floating lane markers on the surface of the water. A competitor can be disqualified for swimming out of the proper lane and interfering with another swimmer.

LAYOUT: A straight dive. *See also* Fancy Dive.

LEG: The part of a relay event that is swum by a single team member.

LIFESAVING: The techniques used to assist those in danger of drowning. In addition to swimming skills, the lifesaver must have a knowledge of holds and carries, how to break holds, and of artificial respiration. The American Red Cross has a series of standardized tests that train swimmers in these techniques.

LONG COURSE: The designated distance of 50 or 55 yards (50 meters) over which a competition is held. A world record can only be made in a long-course pool of 50 meters or more. *See also* Short Course.

MARATHON SWIM: A swim outside a pool usually covering the distance of a natural body of water, such as a strait, a channel, a river, or a bay. In such attempts, the swimmer is challenged to overcome all sorts of natural hazards—tides, winds, debris, cold, heat, and even creatures of the sea.

One of the most unique achievements in long-distance swimming was made by Mihir Sen of Calcutta, India. In the year 1966 he swam the Palk Strait from India to Ceylon (25 hours 36 minutes), the Strait of Gibraltar from Europe to Africa (8 hours 1 minute), the Dardanelles from Europe to Asia Minor (13 hours 55 minutes), and the length of the Panama Canal (34 hours 15 minutes).

In 1975 Diana Nyad, one of the best of the female marathon swimmers, swam the 28 miles around Manhattan Island in the record time of 7 hours 57 minutes. Also known as endurance swim. *See also* Channel Swim.

MASTERS SWIMMING: Masters competition is open to all AAU registered athletes twenty-five years of age and older who are no longer engaged in amateur competition. Once an athlete registers as a Masters swimmer and competes in a Masters swimming event, he is restricted to competing in Masters events only and is no longer eligible for Senior AAU competition. A Masters swimmer, however, may compete in non-AAU aquatic events, but the times recorded in these events will not be used for official purposes, district rankings, or in qualifying for other Masters AAU competitions.

MEDLEY: *See* Individual Medley.

MEDLEY RELAY: An event among teams of four swimmers each in which each team member swims one-quarter of the total distance for the team. The first swimmer uses the backstroke, the second the breaststroke, the third the butterfly, and the fourth the freestyle (or any other stroke other than the first three).

MERMAID: An imaginary sea creature with the head and upper body of a woman and the tail of a fish. Our real-life mermaids are swimmers with the skill of a fish and the body of a beautiful woman. Esther Williams was one of America's most popular mermaids, appearing in a score of MGM movies as the swim star of the decade (1950-1960). The male counterpart is known as a merman.

OLYMPIC SWIMMING: Swimming became a recognized amateur sport in many countries in the late nineteenth century. Swimming events for men were held in the first modern Olympic Games in Athens in 1896. Not until 1912 were events for women added to the Olympic schedule. In 1976 the Olympic events for men and women included the 100, 200, 400, and 1500 meter freestyle; 100- and 200-meters in the backstroke, breaststroke, and butterfly; 200- and 400-meter individual medleys; 400-meter medley relay; and 800-meter freestyle relay (400-meter for the women).

OPTIONAL DIVE: In competitive diving, a dive selected by the competitor that is a recognized dive but not a repetition of a required dive.

OVERARM: An arm movement in which one or both arms come out of the water on recovery.

PACE: When a competitor paces himself, he is regulating his speed to conserve energy for the final sprint.

PACING CLOCK: This is a large clock on a wall of the pool enclosure that is big enough for a swimmer to see while swimming. It can also be mounted on wheels and kept out of doors at the edge of the pool in plain view. The clock is divided into 60 seconds instead of 12 hours, and the passage of one minute of time is marked by a sweeping second hand.

PEAK: That point at which a swimmer gives his best performance.

PIKE: A dive in which the body is bent at the hips, the legs straight at the knees, the toes pointed. Also, the position of the body in a pike.

PLATFORM DIVE: *See* Fancy Dive.

POOL: In competitive swimming the pool may be indoors or outdoors and should be heated to a temperature of 78 to 80 degrees. The minimum specifications are that it be at least 75 feet long, 45 feet wide, and 4 feet deep.

RECOVERY: That part of a stroke where the arm or arms extend forward before the pull through the water. The recovery is largely in the air in the freestyle (crawl), backstroke, and butterfly and in the water in the breaststroke, sidestroke, and dog paddle.

RELAY: A race between four-member teams. Each swimmer on a team must complete an alloted one-quarter of the total course whose distance can vary. Each swimmer after the first must wait until his previous team member has completed his leg of the race. If a swimmer starts before his teammate has touched the wall, the whole team is disqualified.

RESUSCITATION: *See* Artificial Respiration.

REVERSE SCISSORS KICK: A kick in which the under leg reaches forward, the top leg back. *See* Scissors Kick.

SAILOR'S DIVE: A headfirst entry into the water with the arms held straight at the sides. This is not recommended in a shallow pool.

SCISSORS KICK: A kick done while the swimmer is lying on one side. The knees are drawn up together until they are on a level with the hips. The top leg is then thrust forward from the body while the bottom leg moves back. The legs are then pulled together, simulating a scissors motion.

SCULLING: A motion similar to finning except that the hands move in and out of the water. *See also* Finning.

SEEDING: The deliberate (rather than chance) placing of swimmers in specified heats. Placement is based on the best competitive times submitted by all entries.

SHORT COURSE: A competitive course not less than 25 yards but less than 50 yards. The pool must be at least this long for accredited American records.

SIDESTROKE: A non-competitive stroke, restful and slow, often favored by children and elderly swimmers. It is done with the body on the side. The topside arm reaches forward under the water and pulls downward until it is resting straight at the side with fingers pointing toward the feet. The lower arm, on which the body rests, pulls upward until it is resting straight up and forward, with the head resting on it. This stroke uses a scissors kick. *See also* Scissors Kick.

SPEARHEAD PRINCIPLE: A placement order in a final championship race held in a standard eight-lane pool. The swimmer with the fastest heat time is placed in lane 4, the next fastest in lane 5, and then, in the same lower-time order, lanes 3, 6, 2, 7, 1, and 8. This order gives the better swimmers the chance to see each other while they're racing and also helps the officials determine the correct order of finish. If any qualifying swimmers have the same heat times, their respective lanes are determined by a draw.

SPITZ: Mark Spitz, an American swimmer who won an unprecedented seven gold medals in the 1972 Olympics in Munich, Germany. The twenty-two-year-old Californian set four individual world marks and was an integral member of three relay quartets also setting world marks. In 1975 Spitz (which means "peak" in German) still held world and American records in the 100- and 200-meter butterfly.

STARTING PLATFORM or **STARTING BLOCK:** An individual block for each lane at the starting end of the pool used for a competitor's entry into the water. The surface of the block must not be less than 20 inches square and the front edge not exceed 30 inches above the water's surface.

STROKE: The way a human makes progress through the water. The major racing strokes are freestyle (crawl), breaststroke, butterfly, and backstroke. There are other strokes used in recreational swimming, such as sidestroke, dog paddle, and finning. Also, the component parts of these strokes. For example, a swimmer completes one stroke in the freestyle when he has completed a cycle of one pull with each arm.

SURFACE DIVE: The method used to get down under the water, which can be either feetfirst or headfirst. The headfirst dive is done by jackknifing the body at the waist, lowering the head below the surface and raising the legs straight up and out of the water. The hands are kept in front, over the head, for protection. In the feetfirst dive, the swimmer takes a good breath and then submerges by pulling the palms of the hands through the water and up from the hips. The stronger the upward pull, the quicker the descent.

SYNCHRONIZED SWIMMING: Aquatic techniques or movements done in an organized and planned pattern and performed by groups of swimmers swimming in harmony to selected backgrounds, usually musical. The origin of the term is credited to Norman Ross, who used it during the 1934 Chicago World's Fair. It includes such aquatic activities as water ballets, aquacades, and water pageants. All of the standard swimming strokes can be adapted for synchronized swimming. The strokes are best executed with the face above the water and the feet or the kick modified so that no splash is made unless specifically desired. Stunts may be performed from the three basic body positions—layout, tuck, and pike.

TANDEM SWIMMING: Two swimmers swimming in unison while linked together. The front swimmer, who strokes the arms, links feet around the waist of the rear swimmer, whose kicking legs add to the forward movement of the twosome. The same principle can be used by more than two swimmers.

TANK: A swimming pool. Also, the tank of water into which exhibition diving stars plunge in a circus or aquacade or other such entertainment.

TARGET: A marking, like an *X*, that is painted in a contrasting color on the end wall of the pool in the center of each lane to provide a visual target for the swimmers. The target lines should be at least ten inches wide and extend at least four feet below the surface of the water.

TARZAN: The hero of a series of motion pictures about a superathletic jungle man, produced in the 1930s and starring at different times swim champions Johnny Weissmuller and Clarence "Buster" Crabbe as Tarzan. Weissmuller was the winner of three Olympic gold medals and twenty national individual indoor and outdoor titles starting in 1922. Buster Crabbe was a gold medalist in the 1932 Olympics and a national titleholder eight times.

THRASH: The leg motion in the flutter kick.

TOUCH: A competitive swimmer completes the course by touching the finish mark. The winning swimmer beats others to the touch.

TREAD WATER: A swimmer treads water in order to stay afloat in a vertical position in deep water in the same spot. This is largely done by the legs simulating a slow scissors kick or a rotary bicycle movement. The arms can be used too, in a sculling or finning manner.

TRUDGEN: A stroke that was the forerunner of the crawl; developed in late 1800s by J. Arthur Trudgen, an English competitor and swim teacher. Since the breaststroke was the first stroke used in competition, Trudgeon combined the scissorslike kick of the old English stroke with the overarm movements he observed swimmers using during a trip he made to South America. The new stroke, which is still used today for recreational swimming, was an overarm sidestroke done on both sides—one arm pull and one scissors kick done on each side. The head is held above the water, and thus the stroke is often used by beginning swimmers and in synchronized water ballets.

TUCK: A position of the body in which the knees are drawn up together toward the chest in a compact ball.

WALKING: An illegal action consisting of walking along the shallow end of the pool, which results in disqualification. Standing for a rest is permissible, but walking or jumping from the bottom is not.

WATER BABIES: As a direct result of the age-group swimming program, many preteen and teen girls rose to international stature. These youngsters were known as the water babies. For example, in the 1960 Olympics the women's swimming team consisted of fourteen swimmers and three divers whose ages averaged only sixteen and a half, with the youngest, Donna de Varona, only thirteen. Led by "sweet sixteen" Chris von Saltza, winner of three gold medals and a silver, these talented teen-agers took five of the possible nine titles and three second places.

WSI: Water Safety Instructor, a swim teacher who has passed a prescribed course given by the American

Red Cross at an official aquatic school. The instructor learns to teach swimming by means of a standardized series of progress tests, which qualify the students as beginners, intermediates, and advanced swimmers. A WSI can be a swim counselor at a summer camp for children or an instructor at a private or public swim club.

WATER SKIING

AMERICAN WATER SKI ASSOCIATION: A governing body organized in 1939 by Dan Hains and Bruce Parker that sanctions annual national and regional tournaments. The first Nationals was held at Jones Beach State Park, N.Y., that year and was won by Parker.

AQUABAT: An extremely versatile skier, usually a trick performer or clown at exhibition meets.

AQUABATICS: Antics on water skis requiring skill and daring.

AQUABELLE: Woman skier, usually a performer.

AQUAMETER: This word, now used generically, was the trade name for a device used to measure boat speed.

AQUAPLANE: Forerunner of the water ski; a flat board, usually five to six feet in length, towed behind a boat, with a rider holding on in standing position to the loose end of the towline.

BACK BINDING: A second binding placed on a single ski behind the main one, for supporting one foot behind the other.

BALLS: The floating markers around which a competitor must ski on a slalom course. *See also* Buoy.

BANANA or BANANA PEEL: A slalom or trick ski with tapered ends and rounded tips, which resembles a banana.

BAREFOOTING: Skiing on bare feet.

BARREL ROLL: Spiral tumble after falling on the jumping ramp.

BINDER or BINDING: The usually adjustable toepiece and/or heelpiece attached to the ski, into which the foot fits.

BOAT GATE: Marker buoys placed three yards apart indicating the path of the towboat on a slalom course.

BOBBLE: To lose balance but make a quick recovery; a near slip.

BRIDLE: The portion of the ski towline that leads from the ends of the handle to the single main towline.

BRUMMEL HOOK: A patented metal device that permits quick change of handle attachments without tying or splicing to ski towlines.

BUOY: A floating marker for courses in competitive skiing. There are slalom buoys, gate buoys, guide buoys, etc. The buoy, 9 to 12 inches in diameter, is usually made of rubber or plastic and is anchored into position. Makeshift buoys can be empty plastic bottles or inner tubing.

COMBO: A pair of conventional skis, one of which has an extra binder for use as a single slalom ski.

COURSE: The measured water layout, marked by buoys, for water-ski competition.

CYPRESS GARDENS: Located in Florida, the major site for exhibition water-ski shows, which began in the early 1940s. These spectacular demonstrations have played an important part in the growing popularity of the sport.

DEEP-WATER START: A start made by skier in water deep enough so that the skis don't touch bottom.

DOCK START: A start made from a dock, as opposed to the water. It can be from a sitting-down or a standing-up position.

DOUBLE CUT: A maneuver where the ski jumper acquires speed greater than the towboat by cutting sharply across the boat's wake when approaching the jump ramp.

DOUBLE HANDLES: A pair of handles, one for each hand, primarily used in slalom.

DOUBLES: A team of two skiing behind a single boat. Mixed doubles refers to the couple being of opposite sexes.

EDGE: To bank or cut skis sharply into the water.

FIN: A metal or wooden vertical attachment at the bottom of the ski to increase stability and keep the ski from skidding sideways. Also known as a keel or runner.

FOULED LINE: A tangled line; a snafu.

FREEBOARD: The distance from the waterline to the top of the deck of the towboat. Better water-ski towboats have low freeboard for less wind resistance in keeping a straight course as well as for greater ease in boarding from the water. Also, a board pulled behind a towboat or a ski without a binding.

GATE: The entrance to a slalom course, consisting of two buoys spaced about 12 feet apart, through which the boat and skier pass on the start of the run.

HANDLE: The bar on a ski towline, usually made of

wood or metal and covered with rubber or similar material for better gripping and hand comfort.

HELICOPTER TURN: Full 360-degree turn in the air made after a jump from a ramp or over the wake of a towboat. In motion the skis resemble the blades of a helicopter in flight.

HITCH: The device on a towboat to which the towline is attached.

"HIT IT": A call from the skier to the towboat driver to increase engine speed.

HOOK: An abrupt, poor turn by a slalom skier around a buoy. A hook is often the prelude to a fall or the missing of the next buoy.

HOT DOG: A fancy, hot-shot skier. Also known as a ski cat.

"IN GEAR": A call from the skier to the towboat driver to shift the engine from neutral to idling speed. This call precedes "hit it."

JUMP: The inclined ramp cleared by the ski jumper. Also, as a verb, to spring into the air either over the wake of the towboat or over the ramp.

JUMP JACKET: A flotation device secured around the skier's body for protection and to keep him afloat.

JUMP START: A stand-up start from a dock requiring the skier to spring up from the dock at the exact moment that the towline becomes taut.

KEEL: *See* Fin.

KITE: A batlike wing held by a skier for certain maneuvers.

KITING: Taking off from the water to a slightly

airborne position by means of increased speed and the use of a kite.

LANDING: To come to the shore after making a run. Also, to hit the water after making a jump. Also, the dock from which the boat operates.

LEE SHORE: That section of a body of water that is closest to the shore, offering the greatest protection from the wind. This is important in considering the setting out of a water-ski course, since the smoothest skiing water is by the lee shore.

LINEOFF: The shortening of the towline after one or more slalom competitors have negotiated the course successfully at the maximum prescribed boat speed.

OBSERVER: The occupant of a water-ski towboat who must be present in addition to the driver. The observer sits facing the skier and relays the wishes of the skier to the driver.

180: A half turn of 180 degrees, which a skier makes either clockwise or counterclockwise.

PASS: The straight run, in one direction, that the skier makes over a trick, jump, or slalom course.

PICKUP BOAT: The two-manned powerboat stationed alongside a water-ski competition in order to pick up downed skiers.

PLANE: The action of skis in riding on the surface of the water, as opposed to when water is being displaced. Also, the action of the boat as it rides cleanly on the surface of the water.

PLATES: The metal pieces used for fastening bindings to skis.

POP: To spring up in jumping-jack fashion when leaving a ramp or going over the boat's wake.

PYLON: A ski tow hitch, usually nearer to the boat's center of gravity than a transom hitch. The American Water Ski Association specifies that the top of the pylon be three to five feet above the surface of the water.

RAMP: An inclined plane mounted on a float out in the water used for jumping. Official specifications call for it to be 21 to 22 feet long and 12 to 14 feet wide, having a 2-foot depth under water and a height at the takeoff edge of 5 feet for all except men skiers (6 feet). Also, on shore, a ramp is a launching facility inclining into the water.

RIDE OUT: To ski from one area to another in a tournament or to leave the course entirely.

RUN: A two-way pass by a skier over a designated course, as in the slalom event.

RUNNER: *See* Fin.

SAFETY SIDES: The inclined additions set at an angle to the jump ramp to help prevent injury to a jumper who may have fallen or misjudged his approach to the ramp. In sanctioned water-ski competition these sides are mandatory.

SAMUELSON: Ralph Samuelson, who introduced water skiing to America in 1922 at Lake City, Minn. The early skis were eight feet long and nine inches wide (similar to snow skis) with simple leather straps to hold them on. By 1925 Samuelson was jumping 60 feet over five-foot high, lard-greased floats.

SAUCER: A disc attached to the towline that can be ridden by a skier who tucks it between his legs.

SIDE SLIDE: A basic maneuver on trick skis in which the skier turns his ski or skis at right angles from the direction of the towline.

SKEG: A runner or keel placed on bottom rear portion of skis for maneuvering purposes.

SKI CAT: *See* Hot Dog.

SKIER'S SALUTE: A maneuver in which the skier lifts one of his skis high out of the water and almost parallel to it, pointing in the direction of his forward motion. This is the way a skier salutes.

SLALOM: Skiing in zigzag fashion either on one or two skis. This can be done in and out of a prescribed course of buoys or back and forth through the wake of a towboat.

SPLICE: The joining of two pieces of rope by interweaving.

SPRING: A quick body thrust at the top of the ramp, which helps the skier attain height and distance in making a jump.

STEPOVER: A maneuver in trick skiing in which the skier turns and lifts one of his skis, or his off-ski foot, and crosses it over the towline to touch the water on the other side.

SWAN: A graceful maneuver achieved on a single ski by leaning forward, arching the back and stretching the free leg backward and slightly upward.

THREE-SIXTY: A full 360-degree turn made by a skier within his own circumference, clockwise or counterclockwise, while he is being towed in a forward direction.

TOE TURN: A swivel turn done on trick skis while holding the towline with toe or toes.

TOWLINE: The tow rope used in water skiing, which is usually about 75 feet long and made of quarter-inch plastic, Manila, or linen fiber.

TRICK HANDLE: A handle made from a special design with the flexibility to be adapted for trick maneuvers.

TRICKING: Aquabatics on water skis. Trick skis are usually shorter and lighter than conventional skis and have no runners or keels, thus permitting turnarounds. Also known as trick riding.

TURNAROUND: Whirling around in the circumference enscribed by the length of the skis; may be clockwise or counterclockwise.

TURN CIRCLE: A loosely defined area at either end of a water-ski course used as the turnaround point for the towboat and skier.

WAKE: The turbulent trail left at the rear of the towboat as it moves through the water.

WHIP OFF: To leave the end of a towline while still moving at skiing speed before coasting in for a landing.

WORTHINGTON: Willa Worthington, the most celebrated woman skier of all time. Young Willa learned to ski on Lake Oswego, N.Y., in 1943. She won her first Nationals in 1946 at Holland, Mich., which was followed by seven more national championships and three world crowns.

WRAP: The action of a trick skier in adjusting the handle so he can do a 360 in the air off the ramp or wake.